Advance l

This engaging story, presented with such clarity of vision, reflects Kathryn's brilliance, wit, and empathy. I couldn't put it down. Kathryn is one of those rare, other-centered individuals, and the insights she provides are a gift.

— Eileen Cooper, Health Care Administrator

Kathryn's courage, honesty, vulnerability, and discipline, along with her unwavering commitment to her inner life, provide companionship, guidance, and empathy for seekers everywhere.

— Karen Arkin, Psychotherapist (Retired)

Passing her own rigorous, sentence-by-sentence raw truth test, Kathryn has gifted us with a memoir that generously and courageously reveals her practice life from the heart to the bone. Journaling privately to ourselves, cringing at times at what we place on the page, prepares us to one day write an account of our way of being. If only I had the courage and grace that Kathryn Kaplan exhibits here.

— David S. Fearon, Ph.D. Co-author with Peter B. Vaill of Practice as a Way of Being, Professor of Management Emeritus, Central Connecticut State University

An epic poem of self-reflection to be savored page by page, chapter by chapter. It's like a dense piece of chocolate—best enjoyed in nibbles.

— Stephen Stept, *WordsWorthWriting*

This book comes at a time when all people, especially women, need to find wholeness within themselves. Kathryn's search for her own acceptance of her many talents—intellectual, emotional, creative—serves as a model. Her approach is well organized, practical, and poetic.

— Sandy Prins, MS – ECSE, Grief Counselor

Kathryn Kaplan offers the reader a fascinating and practical path to greater self-knowledge and growth. Laying bare her own experience, she writes with candor, humor, and insight, offering the reader a highly useable approach toward leading a fuller life. Instructive, without being instructional. A compelling read.

— Nancy B, consultant to organizations

Authentic, beautifully written and unique, *Becoming Visible to Myself* is a masterpiece forged through the determination it takes to be true to oneself. Through this memoir, you will experience the difference between change and transformation.

— Carol Gorelick MBA, Ed.D

This multi-talented author skillfully weaves together accounts of how she came to grow from, rather than resist, her own vulnerabilities. Any professional who has labored to better understand herself will find confirmation and consolation here. Kathryn's memoir will inspire you—with its examples of courage, healing, and grace.

— Janet Bickel MA, Leadership and Career Development Coach,
and author of *Equip Your Inner Coach*

It takes a generous spirit to reveal one's own deepest insecurities to map the path from suffering to triumph. Dr Kaplan's generosity is bountiful. Her quest to become visible to herself is an extraordinary feat of tenacity and psychic exploration. Move over Drs. Freud, Jung, and Erikson—Dr. Kaplan surpasses you all.

— NBD, Psychotherapist

I found my joy again after reading Kathryn's emotionally honest and inspiring journey of healing. She's a brilliant, creative, and highly impactful writer who reminded me I wasn't alone.

— Karen S, Corporate Receptionist (Retired)

Kaplan's engaging and vivid memoir takes readers on her extraordinary journey of finding her true self ("IT"). She is both expert storyteller—delivering a brave, soulful, authentic, and reflective account of her life—and master practitioner—offering many practical tools and resources through her personal and professional learning and growth. This creative treasure is meticulously structured and formatted with Kaplan's original illustrations, poems, photographs, and journal entries interwoven throughout. A powerful and captivating must read!"

— Nancy Xenakis, DSW, LCSW, MS; Adjunct Faculty, Silver School of Social Work, New York University; Guest Support Coordinator, Toni's Kitchen

Becoming Visible to Myself

An Unexpected Memoir

by

Kathryn L Kaplan, PhD

Published by Christmas Lake Press 2023

www.christmaslakecreative.com

ISBN: 978-1-7377000-6-7

Interior layout by Daiana Marchesi

Dedicated to

Peter B. Vaill, DBA
November 5, 1936–March 24, 2020

"Geometry Lesson"
As you are forever process,
forever on some leading edge
or other:
Honesty, for a leading edge,
is to be forever before some abyss
or other.

Peter wrote this poem about me in 1988, reframing my angst before a major presentation. We were in touch throughout my career and I wouldn't have been as successful as a consultant, educator, and published author without him.

Table of Contents

Foreword

Congratulations on discovering this book and welcome to a most profound healing journey!

Chances are you're one of the legions of us who were born to caregivers who, by dint of their own early childhood damage, were ill-equipped and unable to welcome us with unconditional love and benevolent regard. Our perplexed little souls—that came in anticipating being lovingly tended and cherished—began, early on, adapting ourselves to what little might be available. We quickly learned to be "good little babies" who waited quietly in cold and wet diapers until our caregivers finally came, not in response to our crying in complaint, but for reasons of their own.

As we of this tribe grow in our consciousness, we continually seek to discover how we might become more worthy of love—the love that should have been there just for our being. We diligently search to uncover what might be wrong with or missing in us and how to fix that. Never, for a moment, do we understand that the love is absent not because we are in any way deficient but, in fact, because our caregivers do not have it to give.

When Kathryn first contacted me about working together (in 1995) she had recently completed a unique and extraordinary dissertation for her PhD in organization development. Weaving together her in-depth interviews with thirty-two pioneering women leaders in the field, she'd created a collection of Poem Portraits and collages that spoke powerfully to the challenges faced and mastered by these women moving in that formerly white male bastion. It was an amazing project, synthesizing (and revealing to me) her intellectual brilliance and astonishing creativity.

Yet, as impressive as were her talents and gifts so, too, was the compelling intensity of the emotional torture with which she'd been living all of her life. Nothing she ever did seemed worth anything to her. She was filled with self-recriminations for not being enough, not being self-confident, not being in control of her weight, not trusting herself, not having successful intimate relationships, and on and on. Yet, through it all, shone Kathryn's fierce commitment to uncovering her true self and, as she puts it, "living my life with me in it." No amount of being dismissed, criticized, misunderstood, or judged could deter her from her passionate, determined quest.

In this, Kathryn was not alone. She fit the distinct pattern of the tribe of women I regularly work with. We come to spend large portions of our lives trying to fix in ourselves what was never actually broken. But nothing we do with or in ourselves can ever fix the damage in our caregivers. Whatever we may achieve or accomplish, no matter how brilliantly, never has any impact on their lack of capacity. In the face of such repeated failures in this endless quest to prove ourselves worthy and loveable, virulent inner critical voices develop in us, pouring vitriolic scorn on and devaluing whatever we may be doing. We perpetually feel not enough.

Like Kathryn, we develop a heightened sensitivity to other people's behavior towards us—even (and especially) their subtle, covert, and unowned less-than-conscious responses. All of this leaves us feeling exhausted, incredibly vulnerable, and out of sync with those around us. We already live in a feelings-phobic world, one that views vulnerability and emotional responsivity as embarrassing, humiliating weaknesses that should, at all costs, be well-hidden. The photoshopped images and perfectionistic descriptions of curated lives presented on various social media platforms add to the shame we feel for needing to process feelings stirred by encounters that, while inconsequential for the other(s) involved, are emotionally triggering for us.

A vast number of self-help books offer guides for helping us resolve our insecurities. Quite often, these turn out to be recipes of the one-size-fits-all variety. Over almost sixty years as a psychologist/therapist working most often with women who suffered emotional neglect as children, it has become clear to me that what most helps us heal are not so much the recipes and guides but, rather, the wisdom revealed in the uncensored tales from real-life journeys. As we read these unvarnished, emotionally authentic, warts-and-all stories, we can identify with the journeyer, trying things on and feeling our way into what resonates for us in our own unfolding.

In our four years of actively working together, Kathryn made significant headway in understanding the source of her relentless self-criticism. But it was through her relentless, energetic, and thorough reexamination of the examined life she cataloged in her journals, that she finally silenced the self-doubting voice. Reading this memoir, I was reminded that Kathryn's magic is always finding the right next therapist, book, insight, quote, and opportunity to synthesize into her ever-growing sense of self. Her considerable skills as a qualitative research scholar enabled her to mine gems of extraordinary wisdom from her twenty-five years of journals and employ the process of review to birth this powerful and empowering book. It is so heartening to see her fully claim her own voice and come home to her deepest, richest self, all while giving herself permission to go only as fast as her slowest part felt safe to go.

I've felt deeply honored by Kathryn's request that I write the foreword for this extraordinary book and, in this way, help midwife its journey into the hands of those who will find solace, support, and recognition in its tales.

What you hold in your hand is a remarkable gift: the story of Kathryn's illuminating journey. May journeying with her help to move you forward on your own journey to wholeness!

Warmest blessings,

Robyn L. Posin, PhD
Ojai, California
October 2022

Preface

Have you ever felt unloved, and therefore, unlovable? Deeply unworthy at the core no matter what you do, achieve, explore, or intend? These feelings have consequences. They influence the choices we make and the paths we take. As an emotionally neglected child, it was my job to grow myself up and be a good little girl. In my teens, that looked like being a leader in various clubs and making sure I got into college with a practical major. In my professional life, I tried to heal myself through accomplishment. At the same time, I tried to find and fix what was missing by working with many therapists. I was addicted to self-help books, sure that someone else had the answer—if only I could find it. Eventually I took myself seriously enough to change careers and get a PhD. I then worked as a leader in medical centers and taught at universities for twenty-five years. But none of it was enough.

That is the essence of my story, but until recently, I didn't really know it. When my husband and I decided to scale back our business and move to another country, I finally had the time and inclination to review the thirty-two journals I kept during those same twenty-five years. Yes, thirty-two journals. I wrote a lot. Journaling, which also included drawing, collage, note-taking, and quote-taking, was a tool that helped me stay grounded, curious, and creative. Reviewing what I called "My Wise and Wonderful Black Book Series" in a structured way gave me not only the insights but also the integration I had been seeking.

Read this book if you find that relating to other people's stories about their personal and professional challenges is a salve for your own struggles. While I had the unusual experience of finding a methodology (qualitative research) that was helpful to me during my academic studies, and then applying it to my quest to find myself, you don't need to be an academic to understand or use my approach. My intended audience is women who are striving to find their voice and become whole. My story is for people who may be in therapy, recovering from codependency or addiction, or just feeling they are not where they want to be. If you are a student, however, or you work in the helping professions, you may find that my case study augments your research, insights, or interactions with clients and patients. My underlying message is that it is OK to discover who you really are, and after doing so, to be that person and a leader in the world.

Obviously, this process of becoming visible to yourself is not an overnight occurrence. It takes a great deal of exploration to find clues to unanswered and frequently suppressed questions. And it takes a great deal of emotional honesty and courage to feel safe enough to know what you didn't know, especially if you are highly sensitive, have experienced years of self-doubt, and never felt like you fit in. There is also time spent grieving what wasn't and how long it has taken to accept that reality.

My pivotal discovery was realizing I grew up in a narcissistic family. But narcissism is more than a diagnosis. Learning about its dynamics in an emotional rather than clinical way was difficult. I often wasn't aware of how—or why—I got triggered at work when there were similar dynamics of repressed anger, cold dismissiveness, self-absorption, or betrayal. I just knew I seemed to suffer in a way most of my colleagues didn't. Then there was the fact that no amount of praise for me was ever enough; whatever flowed in flowed right out through the leaky vessel of my undefined and therefore unworthy self. I even had trouble praising myself for jobs well done because I never felt I had found my purpose.

If these themes sound similar and intriguing to you, keep reading. You will see a version of yourself in these pages. If you have trouble accessing your inner self, give journaling a try and see where it leads you.

If you already keep a journal, my examples can help you go deeper. And if you have a journal collection, consider the approach I will delineate here to identify your own themes, patterns, and insights. You may find, as I did, that there is freedom in structure. If you practice exploring without expectations, you can unhook from perfectionistic tendencies that keep you stuck and rob you of joy.

What to Expect

The following is a brief overview of the book's structure. It begins with my struggles, revealed through reflections based on my experience in life. Key to my foundation is my endless searching, intense creativity, and passion for research, all of which played into my quest. Eventually, I began to answer my own questions as I learned more and more about the patterns of narcissistic families. You will learn about my two careers: psychiatric occupational therapy (OT) and organization development (OD) in health care. You will see the weaving of the personal—feelings, therapy, friends, and family—with the professional. You will also be invited to read my actual journal entries, poetry, and art—the primary source material for this book and of my life. You will be amazed at my many attempts to understand myself and the variety of approaches I have studied and implemented. My range of efforts to discover myself should give you permission to experiment in your own life journey.

The core of the book takes you on an in-depth journey through my collection of journals, organized by the themes that my exploration revealed to me. Beginning with "Visibility," and ending with "My Life with Me in It," you will follow my ongoing journey of self-discovery and integration. I include many of the steps I took along the way to understand and embrace the psychological concepts relevant to my childhood, my varied responses to personal and professional challenges, and my growing self-awareness. My intent is to invite you to learn along with me. The path is a winding road, so you will revisit some of the same issues in various places, and always from a different vantage point. As in therapy, some repetition is unavoidable and necessary.

Each section starts with a quote I found in my journals that relates to what I am exploring. The sections are organized into chapters by the underlying motivations common to each. Chapters Three through Eight flow from "Achieving" to "Letting Go," "Feeling" to "Accepting," and finally, "Awakening" to "Living Fully." When you encounter examples from my journals, I cite them in parentheses by journal and page number. Even though you won't be able to refer to my original journals, the citations help me to know where I located the entries and to show you a convention common to qualitative research, which you may choose to adopt should you do your own extensive journal review. After my review, I include an epilogue that addresses what happened next, which only makes sense in the context of all that came before.

Part One of the book is the *what* of becoming visible to myself. Part Two is the *how,* offering practical application for the reader. In Chapter Nine, "How to Begin Journaling," you will find a list of the benefits of keeping a journal and examples of what to put in one. Included throughout both the memoir and practical application portions of the book are actual entries from my journals, which give you a real sense of the variety, purpose, and joy inherent in my approach. Chapter Ten, "Advanced Journal Review," provides additional information for those who might want to take on a journal review of their own collection. This can be a springboard for making your own journal insights come to life. The point is to find what helps you become more visible to yourself.

Finally, an appendix, "Tools and Resources," offers books and strategies that have helped me over the years. Since I don't advocate one self-help model or set of techniques, you are encouraged to explore what might be useful for yourself or to recommend to others.

Who Am I?

I'm a woman who has used my qualitative research skills to write a "dissertation on myself." That means I synthesized information, captured the essence amidst complexity, and strove to present it with simple elegance. By diving into my journals by topic rather than time, I tell my story through themes rather than chronology. I have made transparent over one hundred actual journal entries, messy and imperfect and real. As one of my mentors said in 1998, "You are like a holographic microscope. You look at the whole picture with microscopic attention." This is not to scare you, but rather to say I am a bit unusual in my capacity to see the big picture as well as granular details. I'm the person you might have worked with who not only likes to start projects but also to carry them through from the initial vision to the very end.

My husband Patrick always respected my privacy even though all my journals were in full view on my shelf. Then, when I began my journal review, I asked him to read through a couple and tell me what he thought. He said he was amazed and had no idea how creative, diverse, and intense they were: "They are a masterpiece of a mind locked away for twenty-five years, an encyclopedia of your development with breadth and depth." Even knowing me for almost thirty years, he said he "learned how many ways your brain works and requires expression. How your journals function as a steam release valve, so you don't explode or get buried alive. How their purpose is to give you permission to be your full self and be heard."

Who Are My Readers?

As an in-depth exploration of my journey to wholeness, my story is clearly not for everyone. In fact, I divide my potential readers into three categories: those who really get me, those who don't and never will, and those who need my story to help them discover their own truths. Those who really get me include my life partner, my two sisters, a handful of close friends and family, several therapists, and a number of treasured colleagues. They have read this book in its development, providing valuable feedback and encouragement. To them I am most grateful for their support, intelligence, and love. To those who haven't read the early manuscript, I still say you don't need this book. You already know me, and you don't have the same issues. I'd hate for you to feel I shared TMI ("too much information," as they say). Just keep loving me as you know me and following your own path.

Then there are the acquaintances and colleagues who are no longer in my life. These are people from whom I may have learned a few things, and they from me, but in general we did not click. We may have had political agendas that kept us from having trust, different styles that rubbed us the wrong way, and other reasons never discussed but which often left me feeling challenged, alone, and betrayed.

My cousin suggested an alternate title for this book, based on all the reasons I didn't want to bring the manuscript to publication: *Don't Read This Book If You Know Me!* We laughed uproariously at how on-target that was, but of course a title like that would have the opposite effect. Imagining the worst-case scenario, people who know me (but are no longer acquaintances or colleagues) might grab this book for their own justification and satisfaction. Licking their lips after eating me alive, they would blame me for having offered my most tasty vulnerable parts on a silver platter. To these people I say, save yourself the trouble and do me a favor—don't read this book!

Who then are my core readers? Those of you who don't know me but are seeking what I have to offer, to find in yourself a version of what I found in me. The heart of intimacy is mutuality, and this book is an intimate sharing of my experiences of pain and processes for alleviating it. My ultimate readers are those who are suffering, struggling, and searching.

They would relish hearing someone talk about her inner life with candor and intelligence. They wouldn't need the content to be the same as theirs, because they would understand that the point of my examples is to give permission to excavate their own thoughts, feelings, and circumstances.

What finally pushed me to publish this book was my empathy for those of you who need it. I have been an accomplished achiever since I was a child, during school and graduate degrees, and throughout my career. I learned the rules so I could later break them, adapt them, and transform them. At the same I was anxious, afraid of my emotions, and had difficulty feeling certain about making decisions. Lacking confidence, but ever resourceful, I became addicted to searching for explanations for my pain and methods to alleviate it. Sensing it was not appropriate to share these concerns at work—although sometimes I did, and it hurt me—I found a private place to explore my discoveries: my journal.

It is my hope that you can learn from my experience, benefit from my insights, and shorten your time to discovering your own missing pieces. May you find the wholeness you seek and the companionship you need to face your darkness with courage and compassion. With these tools and inspiration, you, too, can become visible to yourself. As the young poet Anne Reeve wrote in a letter to Emily Dickinson, "I believe it is only through the gates of suffering, either mental or physical, that we can pass into that tender sympathy with the griefs of all of mankind which it ought to be the ideal of every soul to attain."

Acknowledgments

When I completed my dissertation in 1994, I couldn't wait to write the acknowledgments. In four pages I thanked everyone from the women in the study to my computer for not crashing. My appreciation was heartfelt and true. When I read books, I love to read the acknowledgments to find out how much help the author had and how long it took from idea to implementation.

This book evolved through many stages. I am truly grateful to the family, friends, and colleagues who reviewed the manuscript and supported me along the way. And I wouldn't be who I am without the therapists, mentors, healers, and coaches who have patiently listened and given me tools and insights to further my development. Yet, when I published *Directive Group Therapy* in 1988, my biggest accomplishment in OT, I reflected that in the end, the only person's opinion that mattered was the publisher's.

The same holds true for this volume. My manuscript would never have turned into a book had it not been for the exquisite partnering of Tom Fiffer, book coach and publisher of Christmas Lake Press. Tom would argue that bringing books to fruition is his job and he needs no acknowledgment. But I know how I work best and he was the perfect counterpart for me.

Interestingly, finding him began a period of "Grace" that had long eluded me. When he said he'd read the manuscript and would get back to me in two weeks, he did—to the day. He said, "I love your wonderful book and want to publish it." We immediately began rereading and revising together. He would send his comments chapter by chapter for me to edit on Tuesdays and I'd send them back in time for our weekly Thursday conversations to talk through changes and suggestions. In four months of shared diligence and openness to the process, we polished, sharpened, occasionally sawed, and also fashioned uniquely shaped parts to fit gaps where the reader was sure to want more. Suddenly, the work was ready to be submitted for copyediting and the remaining steps for turning a manuscript into a book. Again, Tom put together a terrific team, including copyeditor Erika Rundle and designer Daiana Marchesi, whose expertise, care, and attention to detail made what you are holding in your hands (in paperback or on your tablet) this beautiful finished product.

Not only punctual and reliable, Tom also had a knack for sensing when there was more to an anecdote than I had written. His comments stimulated me to dig deeper to fill in the missing pieces and find a relevant illustrative entry from my journals. A storyteller extraordinaire, he encouraged me to move beyond my tendency toward academic writing and reveal my emotional reactions to what I had learned.

Himself an author of books based on troubled relationships, he knew the terrain of which I traveled and spoke. He prodded me to add dialogue and description to make my experience more vivid and compelling for the reader. Returning to and recounting my more painful memories was challenging, but I was always excited to see how these additions enriched the narrative. I was happy Tom found the arc of my story compelling and that my original structure was sound. But since I'd presented my story through successive themes rather sticking to chronology, he injected logic and prompted me to add dates and context where needed.

While some reviewers thought I had two books—a memoir and a sort of workbook, Tom saw the unity in the "what" of my memoir and the "how" of my journal process. And while many early readers enjoyed seeing a dozen or so examples of my journal pages (intended to give them permission to be more creative and expressive), Tom envisioned my journal entries not as examples but essential and informative illustrations, resulting in one hundred or more carefully chosen passages woven throughout the whole book, exposing the reader to many different styles of thinking for facilitating self-awareness.

Since I came from a narcissistic family, his nonjudgmental and generous feedback was crucial for me to feel safe enough to reveal my truth. Our relationship paved the way for me to revise with care and clarity. So dear readers, you are now the recipient of the benefits of Tom's kindness and expertise, which truly brought out the best in me. I can only wish you "would-be writers" the type of partnering that will bring out the best in telling your story the way it is meant to be written and shared.

INTRODUCTION

Ever the Seeker

It is only with the heart that one can see rightly;
what is essential is invisible to the eye.
—Antoine de Saint-Exupéry, *The Little Prince*

The first thing to know about me is I have always been a seeker—someone looking not just for answers but also "the" answer—"IT." What was this "IT" that was always eluding me? You know it well, whether you have it or whether you're still looking: that effortless sense of confidence, self-esteem, something solid inside you can trust, that feeling everyone craves and so many of us believe only others enjoy, the basic knowledge that we're really OK. But I didn't have it. My experience of myself was that something essential was missing. I felt I had no direct access to my core—and that filled me with shame. It didn't matter how much I excelled as an achiever, how many professional accolades I accumulated, how many happy moments I managed to experience. None of these brought "IT" any closer. I remained stuck in what I called "My Sad, Sad Story," my explanation and rationale for feeling disconnected from my soul's longing. Sadness was my default, looming large as my ultimate and inescapable truth, no matter how much evidence to the contrary stared me in the face. My quest to find me *defined* me, so when I looked in the mirror, I didn't see a successful professional, a caring wife, or even a woman struggling to find herself. I saw no one, and I grieved my absence, because without "IT" I was nobody. I was empty inside. *Invisible*. Only now do I understand that the "IT" I was seeking was *me*—the me who could accept me and even love myself.

My seeking always followed the same cycle. Even though I was repeatedly told it's an inside job and journey, I didn't know what that meant or how to go about it. What I could do was read yet another self-help book, take yet another workshop, and place yet another new mentor on a pedestal thinking (hoping, praying) he or she would give me what I needed. I became a self-taught expert on self-help literature, to the point where my husband, Patrick, used to tell me, "The next book you write should be titled, *The Last Self-Help Book*." In it would be my thoroughly annotated review of the best books for bettering yourself. Organized by categories, it would include losing weight, fulfilling relationships, achieving dreams, dissecting family dynamics, and unearthing past traumas. Eventually, I would find my voice and write, but in the meantime, I kept seeking. Diving in with great enthusiasm and energy, I convinced myself the *next* book, course, or guru would be "IT," the newest font of wisdom I had found would unravel my mystery and put my misery behind me. Sadly, inevitably I would perceive first a quiet disappointment, followed by the empty realization that the answer wasn't there. Still, I would persist, because you never know, maybe "IT" will be in the next chapter or presentation or therapy session. As I completed each engagement, I'd appreciate what I 'd received but remain even hungrier for what I hadn't—the answer. This only made me more addicted to the search, and being resourceful, I had no difficulty finding my next fix.

As an adult, this endless seeking seemed rational. The answer wasn't yet visible to me, but it was clearly just around the corner, or the next corner after that. If I could just try a little harder, go a little farther . . .

At the same time, my difficulty finding "IT" didn't surprise me. In fact, it made perfect sense. As a child, I had always felt there was something wrong with me, something essential missing, something I feared I would never find. Knowing this made me unbearably sad, and even sadder was the knowledge that I had to keep this to myself. You see, we never talked about feelings in my family; they simply weren't acceptable, and I didn't want to upset my parents, who never acknowledged—or allowed their children to acknowledge—the emotional climate beneath the surface in our home. Any feelings that did manage to come out were immediately cut down with a look of annoyance (Mom) and a silent dismissal (Dad), but my inner sadness showed on my face when I didn't think anyone was looking, like the picture of me on the back cover at around six years old.

Like most children, I idolized my parents. My perfect mother had short dyed-red spiky hair, unique clothes, and a no-nonsense attitude. She was so talented, self-confident, and well put together; by comparison, I always felt "fat, ugly, and stupid." And in contrast to her sophisticated look, I had no idea what my style should be. So it kind of made sense that she was always dissatisfied with me, though I was never clear about what I did to warrant her frequent irritation. My perfect father was like a metronome, even and quiet, never skipping a beat, and never challenging my aggressive mother when she gave me "the look"—or anyone else. To be their perfect child, I became so good at sacrificing my needs, so as not to trigger my mother's reactivity, that I don't think anyone in the family realized I even had needs, felt sad, or felt much of anything. I reflexively pasted on a perpetual smile and tried to be a good girl in all things, but the real me was invisible, even to myself. I was sure it was my fault my mom wasn't interested in who I really was, and my dad ignored my nonverbal pleas for his approval. As a young child I once asked a teacher about how the world came to be and why we were here. I was sharply told not to take myself so seriously. What might have been a budding philosophical propensity was quickly squashed. Likewise, when I pondered "how do you spell 'spell,'" I was dismissed, rather than having my inquisitive mind engaged. Self-deprecating to a fault, everyone outside my family told me I was too hard on myself and shouldn't beat myself up. I had no idea the critical voice in my head wasn't how the whole world judged me. But since the most important people in my life *did* judge me, I beat them to the punch and judged myself first. If my mother didn't seem to love me, I must have been unlovable. If my father didn't pay attention to me, I must not have been very interesting. My friends in high school always said, "Your mom just isn't the motherly type." It wasn't until graduate school when my parents visited me and we sat on my little couch that I noticed she was so thin; Mom actually had no lap. No wonder she wasn't affectionate when I was young! I don't ever remember her sitting down with me to read or snuggle as a child.

Knowing I was missing something, and convinced it was a part that more confident people had, I felt defective and utterly alone in my sadness. I rarely expressed anger toward either of my perfect parents, only turning it on myself. Anger turned inward feels like depression; sadness was much more comfortable for me than anger. Besides, what right did I have to be angry? I was grateful, even guilty, for all the material comforts we did have, and I knew to keep private any complaints about what I can now identify as emotional deprivation. I also wasn't marginalized by society's prejudice, so I kept the truth about not feeling loved, seen, and accepted by my parents from others, and in many ways, from myself. How, then, was I to see myself, much less find my voice or claim my story, under these circumstances? How was I to find my calling in the world when my little world was fake and fragile? Who was I to even have a calling, to deserve a happy and fulfilling life? Perhaps the most memorable moment of receiving love as a child was when my cousin's maid once sat on their lawn with me and showed me how to make my first collage by tearing colored paper. This woman I barely knew gave me quality time and her love, which I never forgot and, gratefully, was able to take in.

My 1000-Piece Jigsaw Puzzle Life

Don't waste energy trying to be something you're not. Being true to yourself is the essence of finding your voice—lead by letting it ring true.

—Sally Helgesen, *The Female Advantage: Women's Ways of Leadership*

As I grew up and eventually left home, bits of insight began to contribute to my growing self-knowledge and emotional stability. Being a synthesizer, I liked to weave together quotes from books, insights from therapists, and any other clues that tugged at my consciousness. These resembled the dots of a pointillistic painting or many pieces of mosaic tile art; alone they didn't make sense or create a discernable pattern. Decade by decade, however, the jigsaw puzzle picture became clearer as I learned to look at my early years from a different, emotionally educated perspective and with knowledge of terms and concepts that helped me see my experiences in a new light. Gradually I assembled a sort of patchwork quilt, a symbolic fabric to add to my self-awareness collection and put into my journals for safekeeping.

All along, I knew something was interfering with achieving my full potential, and I was determined to figure out what it was. When I say determined, I mean it. Every night in bed I barraged myself with questions: How do I fulfill my potential? Will I ever fulfill my potential? Why don't I? Why can't I? Why do I keep trying? At age sixty-two I wanted to give up. I'd ask myself, what if I died tomorrow? What difference would it make? What wouldn't get accomplished if I continued to live? Fortunately, now I know: my significant research contribution to organization development (OD) in 2015, my research on my journal collection in 2020, and of course, this book! Thank goodness my determination won out. Here's a brief and broad-based timeline of what my initial review of my life history and turning points revealed.

I was born guilty. First off, my birth was caesarean, so I didn't have to struggle to get free of the womb; I was lifted out. Weeks later Mom got sick and left me with my grandmother in Chicago while she and Dad took a monthlong break from bonding with me in California. Feeling the aloneness, I sought to comfort myself by vigorously rocking back and forth on my hands and knees in the crib, even moving the crib, I was told. That started the pattern of my dad saying, "Isn't she cute?" and my mom being annoyed. I took to compulsive thumb sucking for comfort, developing a corn on my thumb that I liked to rub. In exasperation, my mom took me to a German dentist at age six who yelled at me to stop and then get out of his office because of my nonstop crying. Afraid of both his anger and his accent, I quit that very day.

But my secret rebellion as a child was to pick the scabs when I had chicken pox, because I was told they would leave scars and I desperately wanted an outward sign of my suffering. Luckily, although I imagined etching long vertical lines down my face, and was willing to take that risk, I ended up with only a few small divots near my eyebrow and cheek. The truth is, I really wanted to be a good girl so I would get love and attention. I frequently went to my mom's side of the bed in the morning and earnestly asked, "Am I mature today?" An odd question for a young child, but I felt so inadequate, and that made me sad. I did whatever I could to become accomplished and make my parents proud of me. But they didn't seem to notice when I was sad or needed help.

If I longed to be mature, my bas mitzvah decreed me so. At thirteen, I was the only one in our Reform Jewish family to go through this ritual. Family and friends were invited, and I recited a prayer while up on the pulpit. When my dad came up to bless me, all the hard work memorizing Hebrew and carrying an ugly, embarrassing, two-ton briefcase of Hebrew books to school for over a year was worth it. This achievement was my first real accomplishment and it set the stage for how to get recognition in my family. I did feel proud, but I felt anything but mature. My mom didn't want me to pick out my dress, my hair was too short, I didn't have breasts worth mentioning, and I wouldn't get my first period until high school. Who was I to enjoy myself, or anything? The party that night with a deejay had all the boys on one side and all the girls on the other, a stark division much like the gap between me and my as-yet-undiscovered self. I felt shy, awkward, and inadequate compared to the more developed, outgoing, and popular girls.

In my twenties, I went to an occupational therapy (OT) conference on psychiatric patients and their psychological needs. Needs? I never even considered I might have needs, too. At one session, the facilitators spoke about emotions, like anger. I reflected on the denial of anger in my family and wondered, *why is there a word for anger if it wasn't supposed to exist in my life?*

In my thirties, I heard at a conference on healing and recovery that there is something called "A Looking Good Family," where appearances, not substance, are most important. These families commit subtle hurts—invisible to outsiders and unmentioned at home—that constitute serious impediments to healthy development and self-esteem. I then remembered how before we left the house to go out to dinner, my dad would have us all stand in front of the long closet mirror to make sure we all "looked good." Suddenly, I could see why people would gravitate to my parents and then wonder why their three daughters often didn't seem as happy, charming, or talented. Living under the pressure of maintaining our perfect family image, I would never criticize my parents, not even in therapy.

Fortunately, in my forties, I discovered that when I could go no further, something often showed up, which I called "Grace." Grace could not be orchestrated, manipulated, or demanded. It just appeared. Grace arrived when a colleague volunteered to organize my report without my asking, or the perfect article to help me with my work was left out on a mentor's desk, or an email invitation to the exact workshop I needed slid into my inbox. Then, at the workshop, I heard an idea and saw a book that was surely meant for me. When I finally was able to end my twenty-year marriage, I left with courage and dignity, enabling me to meet Patrick Knowlton and start a thirty-year relationship that slowly evolved from boyfriend to ultimate partner and husband. Grace is about synchronicity, moments of magic, and taking a leap of faith.

In my fifties, on the way to a celebration of Patrick's and my marriage (a private spiritual commitment ceremony blessed by his priest and a rabbi) with dear friends, I was hit by something I never saw coming—a car struck me while crossing the street to go home. As part of my recovery, I read—a lot. One line in an article by Calvin Trillin offered me a new understanding of my childhood. In a tribute to his wife Alice after she died of cancer, he mentioned their priorities for raising their daughters, noting they had agreed on a simple notion: "Your children are either the center of your life or they're not, and the rest is commentary." So clear and straightforward. There was no question where my parents stood on this divide—and where that left their daughters. It also helped me reflect on the "accident." The day before it happened, I had been sitting in the CEO's office talking about strategy, but the subtext I heard, even if not explicitly said, was about how my life was too easy and I wasn't suffering enough. The CEO was recovering from a disastrous car accident and my subconscious internalized her criticism. I had already spent my childhood sacrificing myself to authority figures—my parents—so, my unconscious reasoned, why not continue the pattern with the CEO and find a way to have plenty to suffer over and therefore win her approval?

It turns out this pattern was embedded deep in my psyche. My mother was no stranger to suffering. Her mother's first husband had died young of tuberculosis, and her second husband (my mother's father) died shortly after my mother was born. At sixteen, my mother had been hit by a car and spent months in a full body cast. To pass the time, she read the dictionary cover to cover, an experience that made her critical of the way her children spoke. I am sure she didn't truly want me to suffer, but she was stuck on the idea that I couldn't relate to her (nor her to me) because I hadn't truly suffered. So unbeknownst to me, my boss was echoing my mother. You can't make this stuff up! This unconscious material is so sneaky, particular, and private.

Finally, in my sixties, I made a discovery that filled in the missing pieces. In *Will I Ever Be Good Enough? Healing the Daughters of Narcissistic Mothers*, by Karyl McBride, I saw myself in descriptions of the author's experiences: feeling oversensitive, indecisive, self-conscious, and lacking self-trust and confidence, regardless of accomplishments. She, too, wondered what she had to complain about since she had a roof over her head, clothes to wear, and food to eat. But as a psychotherapist, she decided to push past her self-protective denial and find out why she—and many of her clients—never felt good enough. Taking seriously the longing so many shared for nurturing and empathic love, she studied maternal narcissism and the impact it has on daughters. She didn't blame the mothers, because they had their own barriers to giving love and a history of not receiving it themselves. Instead, based on her research, she established a three-part strategy: understanding narcissism, realizing its consequences, and taking responsibility for healing.

Finally, I was not alone in feeling something was missing and not understanding why.

Finally, I felt validated that not having essential emotional needs met mattered.

Finally, I understood that even without neglect and abuse, subtle cases like mine lead to denial, worry, and fear of being selfish.

Finally, I understood that when a daughter takes on the role of meeting her mother's needs, feelings, and desires, that daughter feels guilty for wanting her needs met at the same time.

Finally, I was meeting "IT" where it lived.

How did I become aware of all this? When did I experience the "Aha!" moment that enabled me to finally stop seeking? As my mother wrote in an essay on aging, "It is a slow process that happens overnight." The slow part of the process is that I have been keeping journals for the last twenty-five years, creating "My Wise and Wonderful Black Book

Series." Journaling has been my lifeline and helped me navigate my way through work, relationships, family, and therapy. It has been like a best friend, my comfort clothes, and sacred space. The intimacy I developed through journaling has helped me know and accept my struggles. As I read through my journals, a picture of who I really was began to form. I saw not only my struggles but also how I had managed to work through them. I saw not only my failures but also my successes. I saw not only my missteps but also my inspired leaps. I finally saw myself in the mirror of my own writing. That vision became the genesis of this book, and I decided to share my process of discovery with others in the hope it would help them find "IT" faster than I did.

PART ONE

My Journey Through Journaling

CHAPTER ONE

Finding My Voice

"I can tell you that what you're looking for is already inside you."

— Anne Lamott

Before I immersed myself in the pages of my journals, I had denied myself permission to write my story for a well-rehearsed series of reasons. But I was aching to find my voice and write my truth, and I could feel my strong women writer role models, whom I quoted liberally in my black books, urging me on:

Brené Brown has said, "Owning our story and loving ourselves through that process is the bravest thing that we will ever do."

Oprah says, "Turn your wounds into wisdom," and through her book club, endorses the brave souls who do just that.

A piece of wall art by Kelly Rae Roberts in front of my computer for many years read, "Your beautifully messy complicated story matters (tell it)."

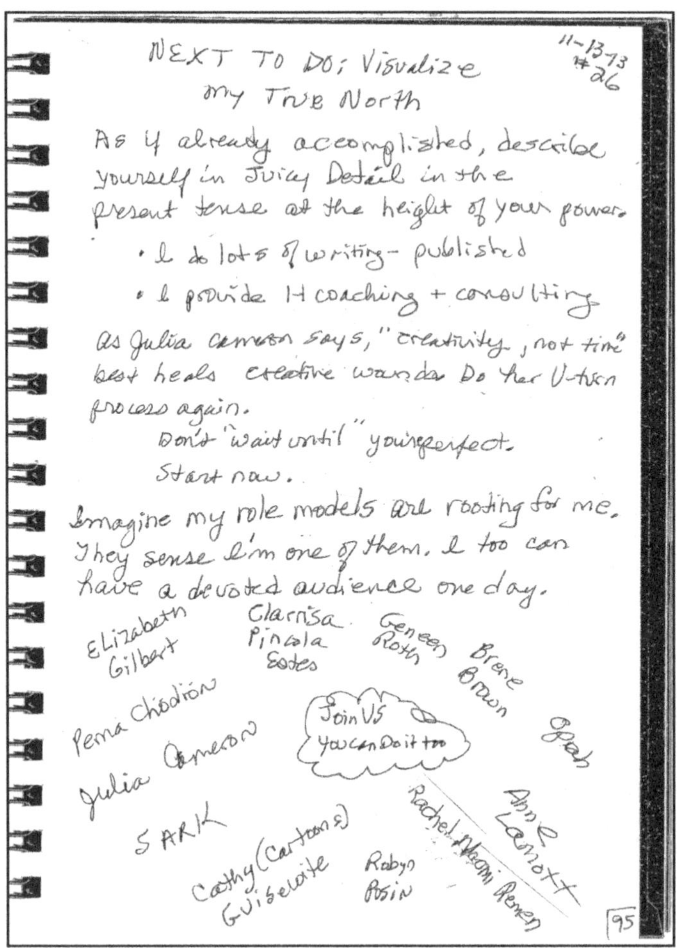

Image 1: Role models rooting me on to write my story.

So, when I found myself out of work and searching for what to do next (beside writing in my journals), I finally gave myself permission to write every day—for six months—without beating myself up. This may seem like a small thing, but for me it was a huge breakthrough. I started in December of 2013, doing all the exercises from three of Julia Cameron's books I hadn't previously read. Having devoured almost all of her other writing, her wisdom and encouragement flowed through my veins. I wrote with as much aliveness as I could, setting aside my academic training and drawing on what I had learned decades before from Natalie Goldberg's *Writing Down the Bones: Freeing the Writer Within.* I claimed successes, explored grief, and allowed myself to be freer than I had ever been.

But wouldn't you know it, my pesky inner seeker, always looking for external guidance and validation, wasn't quite done with me yet. For the last chapter of the manuscript, I kept trying to write my story using someone else's framework. I started by analyzing *The Hero's Journey* by Joseph Campbell, and then, I began looking at my life from a feminine perspective, as described by Kim Hudson in *The Virgin's Promise* and in Lissa Rankin's blog on the divine feminine. Next, I applied Maureen Murdock's *The Heroine's Journey* to my development and challenges. I even wrote my story as an obituary for never having fulfilled my potential. Finally, I tried to write my story as if it were a television series.

Ugh. I realized I was stuck and had the good sense to stop.

Eventually, I told my seeker to take a break and asked myself, "What can I learn from *me*?"

To find out, I employed the coaching process I'd used with countless clients to see if I could get over the hurdle of "Who am I to tell my story?" I wanted to see if I could form a narrative and honor, as the poet Mary Oliver wrote, my "one wild and precious life."

Coach Kathryn: So, tell me a little about what you are trying to do.

Client Kathryn: Well, I'm trying to own my experience and write my story. But it's not working. I feel stuck and unworthy. I've tried so many times, and I see others do it, but for me, I just feel like I can't or don't deserve to do it.

Coach Kathryn: I can appreciate how hard this is for you. I have compassion for the bind you put yourself in, and I see how feeling as you do stops you from starting. I also think I can help. Would you be willing to explore why each of your reasons for not telling your story makes sense to you?

Client Kathryn: Well, sure, if you think it will help. I certainly know my negative reasons well. First of all, my early wounds were subtle, so

I imagine others who have suffered real hardship will criticize me for discussing my challenges. I mean, what right do I have to complain? Growing up in a lovely suburb of Chicago, my two younger sisters and I had financial security from our doctor father and creative stimulation from our artistic mother. My grade school was almost entirely white and Jewish, and while I studied Jewish persecution in Sunday school, and Jewish history is part of my cultural identity, I didn't experience daily prejudice or microaggressions. I didn't even learn about white privilege until I conducted research with a diverse group of women who had done inner work on racism and were helping clients deal with oppression. Second, having been raised to keep family matters private, I assume others will feel that revealing our family dysfunction is inappropriate and self-indulgent. Third, I stop myself from writing my story because I can't guarantee a successful outcome and reception. What if no one is impacted by or even interested in what I have to say? There are wars, climate crises, and systemic racism in the outer world. Who cares about the inner world? And how would those who might be interested find this needle in the haystack of so many other publications? Besides, we all die in the end, so what difference could my efforts make? Finally, on a practical level, while my journals provide an intimate and in-depth look into *my* life, they are comprised of notes, quotes, fragments, sketches, scribbles, etcetera. With so much inner anxiety, it's hard for me to think straight about my life, much less create a narrative out of all the creative chaos.

Coach Kathryn: Thank you so much for sharing your reasons for not writing. Yet, I know you really want to tell your story. Would you be willing now to think of a response should each one of your objections be true? Imagine you are supporting a friend who is similarly troubled. For example, "Yes, my wounds were subtle, and others may not think them significant or worthy. So what? This was *my* experience. Maybe I can shed light on this type of history for others who don't have my insights."

Client Kathryn: Now that you put it that way, yes, perhaps people who didn't live my experience could learn from me, just as I learn from reading about people who went through things I didn't.

Coach Kathryn: Great, keep going!

Client Kathryn: Well, I suppose I could be mindful of the reader and still authentically expose my core issues—that wouldn't be self-indulgent. Sure, I had white privilege, but it's important not to let guilt or criticism stifle owning all aspects of the life I was given. I could even be honest about wanting a guarantee and being afraid of taking risks by writing. I certainly wouldn't be the first. As we know from social media, online bullying, and the op-ed pages, no one is beyond criticism. Everyone can be thrown under the bus, or as it is now referred to, "cancelled." Given that, I guess I have to challenge myself to say what is most true and important for me to express.

Coach Kathryn: Nice breakthrough. Now, relating to what you said about dying, how can you find meaning in the time remaining, however long that is, which none of us knows?

Client Kathryn: I think the key will be to set priorities based on my desires and not my fears. I don't want to give up prematurely and limp without aliveness until the end. Not when I have the power to change that vision.

Coach Kathryn: Yes, you do have that power. And I think you have already begun.

Client Kathryn: Thank you. It's funny how talking to myself with the compassion, tough love, and intelligent advice I could always offer others never seemed possible until now. Instead, I would bury myself in work, trying to meet the expectations of other leaders. When I came up for air, I'd have that nagging feeling of betraying myself. Others clearly valued me, or they wouldn't have kept relying on me for the contributions I made. So it finally dawned on me that what I had been doing at work was actually significant. This gave me the courage to dig deeper and listen to my inner voice, which was telling me what I really wanted—and deserved—from my job. I think I'm ready to try this same approach in writing my story.

I guess how I feel now is that I am reminded of the process I often resist but eventually works for me. I have lots of pieces to consider, like the many tiles my mother used to make a mosaic table in my childhood. My concerns pull me one way or another, but together they create a pattern. When I think about my most relevant value in this process, it's what will give my life meaning: I will die satisfied knowing I finally owned and told my story. There are real costs of criticism and public humiliation for my sensitive self. But on balance, the possible benefit to others who may identify and be helped by my experience outweighs the risks.

Image 2: A photo my mother took of one of her many mosaic projects, 1958.

Seeking a Legacy

As I released old thinking and behaviors that interfered with creating a memorable future, it became clear there was something else I wanted, something I hadn't realized I'd been seeking—a legacy. How did I want people to feel about me? What did I want my contribution to be? How did I want to be remembered?

In college, I'd idolized Carl Jung and Margaret Mead, aspired to emulate their traditions of research, and dreamed I might initiate paradigm shifts like the ones stimulated by their publications. I wondered how I could go beyond my individual circumstances and leave such a lasting and impressive legacy. This was one of the reasons I decided to never have children; I wanted to put most of my energy into learning and work. But having studied the myth of the hero, I knew we can't make a contribution in this complex world alone. I was a natural team player, and I learned through academics to build on the foundation laid by others. I soon put that desire for greatness aside, and instead, invested my time and energy into a practical work life: first, as a psychiatric occupational therapist and then, as an OD consultant. I would do what I could with what I had, to leave the world (or at least the individuals and organizations I encountered) a better place than I found it.

As an internal OD consultant in healthcare, my last position at a medical center was a large role with broad scope: my mission was to help create organizational change. I worked with leaders at every level to engage and implement their visions. Rather than have my own stake in the ground about what the organization's culture should look like, my role was to uncover what the leaders and staff thought, what the industry needed, and what were plausible solutions. It was the perfect job for me to stay effectively invisible, while committing myself to excruciatingly hard work. My focus was on creating innovative programs, an exacting and time-consuming process. My efforts included creating a physician leadership program, building a foundation of mutual respect, developing management, and facilitating an institution-wide program called the Schwartz Center Rounds, designed to give voice to vulnerability and emotions within the hierarchical and decisive medical culture. These contributions were compelling for me because I'm a project person. As an entry in one of my journals makes clear, "I do in-depth, multimedia, meaningful, collaborative projects." However, over time, this work never seemed to feed my soul. Working through conflicts and identifying strategies with clients was stimulating, challenging, and meaningful. But it just wasn't enough. There were outside forces preventing the organization from ever reaching a sustainably thriving trajectory. And personally, I hadn't experienced "Grace" in decades.

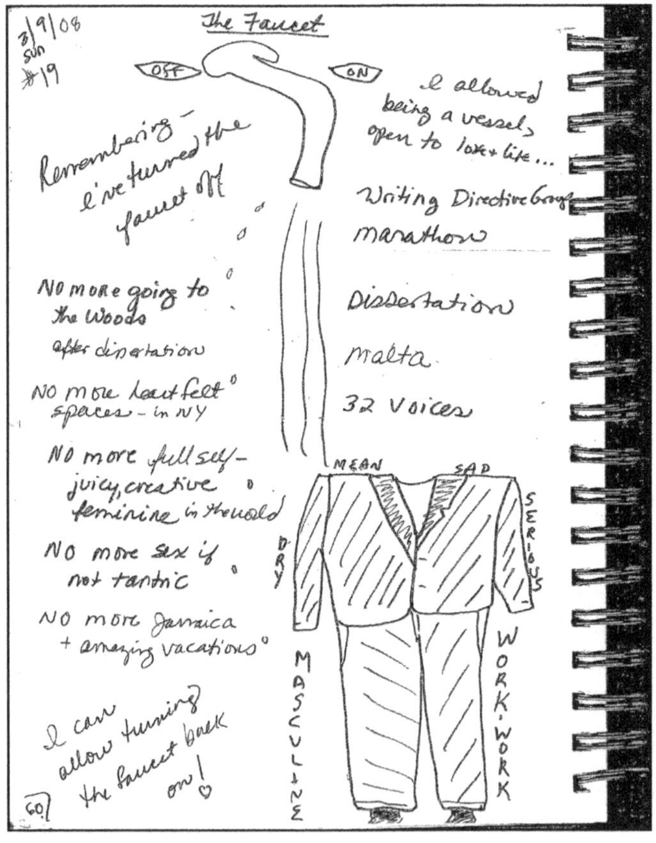

Image 3: Turning off the faucet of my natural flow.

Or was it enough? During six months of gently coaching myself and writing in a "no beating myself up zone," I realized I had not only betrayed myself, but also betrayed others by failing to recognize—and celebrate—my greatest accomplishment: the in-depth qualitative research study I conducted for fulfillment of my PhD in organization behavior and management. Through interviewing thirty-two successful women pioneers in the male-dominated field of OD, I not only learned about their challenges and contributions but also developed deep and lasting connections with them as they shared their stories. While I had published the research, I always had a deep desire to write a mainstream book about these women for a broader audience of professional women and men. I had learned from friends and colleagues familiar with my work that there was much applicability of their generational work experience and personal journeys beyond OD. But I never did, and it was one of my greatest regrets. While the old me started to beat myself up over this perceived failure, the newer me compassionately reminded myself it wasn't too late.

I acknowledged the impact of the work I *had* done to reveal the struggles and oppression of women consultants, who had valuable lessons for working in patriarchal organizations.

I acknowledged the gift I had given many women leaders by helping them succeed through my consulting work and coaching practice.

I acknowledged that the expertise I thought I'd lacked to write a book was there, all along, in my publications on women's leadership.

I asked myself, "What *could* I do?" To finally satisfy my desire to honor the women who had made a significant contribution to me and to the field, I conducted and published a follow-up study twenty years after my original dissertation research. This work was healing to me and a critical part of leaving a legacy that both the field and I valued.

Feeling better about my professional legacy, I considered my personal one. Naturally, my thoughts turned to my parents, who were always larger than life to me. They'd accomplished so much. How did I compare, or more accurately, how could I compare? I felt so much in their shadow growing up that I gave them nicknames to reinforce their exalted status. I watched as "Meemo" and "Big D" hosted sophisticated parties and invited people over to admire their extensive art collection—which included art and sculpture they had created. They were always active and pursing their interests. My dad, Harold, was a physician in private practice as well as a sculptor and writer of short stories. He played golf, bridge, and was in a writers' guild with my mother. He had a kind face, reminding me in his later years of Tony Bennett, and a subtle humor his friends appreciated. My mom, Francine, was always doing art in some form—welding, jewelry, photography, and painting—and later writing essays and a fictionalized memoir. They were runners, always well-dressed, eager to attend the latest movies, and ready to discuss theatre and local cultural events. I also thought they alone had found the secret to love and marriage—and kept it a secret. They touched many lives and created many objects of beauty. Then, I sat at my parents' sides and watched them die, one after the other. Though we had an ambivalent connection, I loved them so much and was honored to give each of them what they needed at the end of their lives. Helping them in this way gave me a new sense of permission and perspective.

Still, the vacuum they left was astounding. I knew how to be in their orbit, but I had no idea how to be in my own. I had once again betrayed myself, through a lifetime of elevating their needs above mine. After they were both gone, I distilled another legacy by observing how they lived and what I was now able to notice and put into words. *Enjoy your life while you can with what gives you joy and meaning. Fame fades and lasting contributions are for the most talented few. Life goes on, and even someone who was incredibly well-known and prolific will be judged in the context of a changing political and social landscape.* At the end I realized what my parents left was not just their creative output, but the moments they created, the life they enjoyed together. That legacy wasn't necessarily about greatness but simply about the impact people have while they're still here. And when I acknowledged my work and my life had already had that impact on so many, I felt released from the quest. I could leave my legacy to the hearts and minds of people I may have inspired and influenced.

Yet, with the question of my legacy settled, other critical questions remained.

Addressing My Core Questions

Live the questions now. Perhaps you will then gradually,
without noticing it, live along some distant day into the answer.
—Rainer Maria Rilke, *Letters to a Young Poet*

As a young woman, I was expected at school and with friends to express ideas, desires, and preferences, just like everyone else. But I always panicked. I didn't know what the "right" answer was. I gravitated toward people who had certainty, yet I often sensed they were perplexed, and sometimes irritated, by my usual hesitancy. I couldn't explain it or change it. All I knew for sure was I was doing everything I could to find "IT."

Conducting the in-depth review of my journals to finally either find "IT" or put it to rest, I discovered a few other questions that arose organically and were important to me. They are:

Why has it taken me so long to write my life story?

What do I mean by "integration"?

What do I mean by "resonance"?

To answer the first question, the reason it has taken me so long to write my life story is because *it takes as long as it takes*. I remember Toni Morrison saying in an interview that novels have their own time. That revelation was such a comfort. I have always been driven to be efficient and get results as fast as possible without sacrificing quality. I excelled at doing that for work projects, but I now realize the journey to self-discovery has its own rhythm and pace. There are things we aren't aware of that need to be felt, lived through, and accomplished before more clarity, healing, and integration can occur. We must give ourselves permission to go at our own speed. As my husband Patrick always cautioned, "Slow down!"

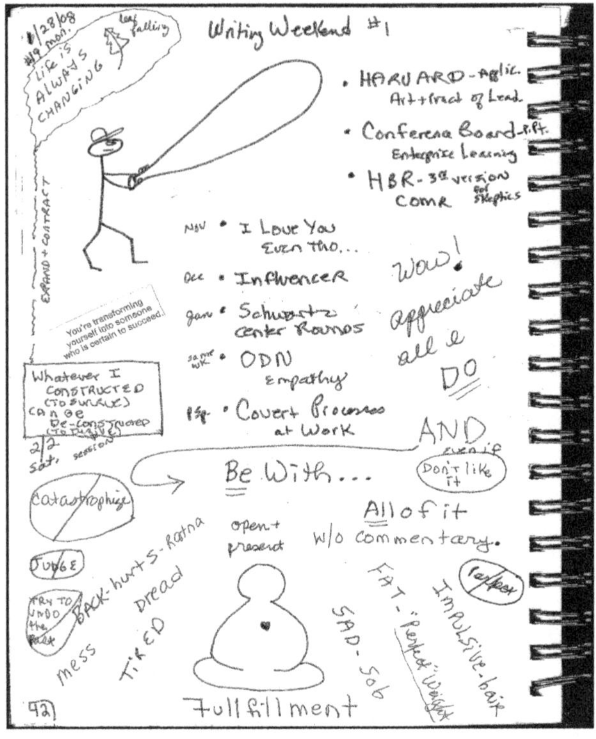

Image 4: Hitting the ball (of all my work accomplishments) out of the park.

Integration is a complex word. Is it self-acceptance, being centered, in harmony with what I call my Deepest Wisest Self? I have decided that for me, integration involves knowing my many parts inside and having them exist in a dynamic wholeness. Not a unified single voice, but more like an orchestra or chorus. My most mature part is the conductor who makes time to hear and develop each of the instruments playing the music of my soul. Sometimes the sound is discordant and out of balance. It takes lots of listening and practice, knowing finally, there is no fixed destination—what I call my "THERE."

I also think of integration as the art of collage. My final entry in my very first journal was a collage image. I had glued shiny gold and red paper into a large circle signifying yin and yang. It symbolized what I wanted for myself: the wholeness I saw in the women I studied. Above the circle I had written the intention for 1994 to be "The Year of My Self-Authorization." I can tell you that wishing did not make it so. I used to sing the song from *Pinocchio* to myself, beginning with "When you wish upon a star, makes no difference who you are. Anything your heart desires, will come to you," and ending with, "When you wish upon a star, your dreams come true." These promises neglected to include that, while I may get what my heart desires, for me the process is always complicated by *how long it takes and how hard I make it.*

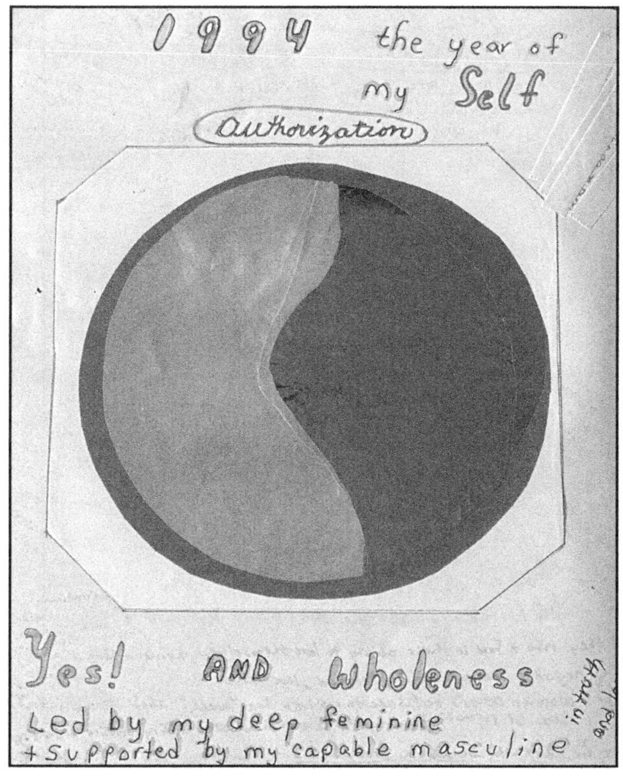

Image 5: Yin and yang, symbols of wholeness for the year 1994.

The third question requires an understanding of resonance. According to its dictionary definition and use in daily life, resonance is a common vibration where two things move in unison. So, when something resonates with me, I understand and can sense it without explanation or problems, like an inner Geiger counter. In relationships, resonance means you understand someone on a deep emotional level. A poem, piece of music, movie, or news event can move you without your knowing why. When hearing someone's experience of loss, you may resonate with it because you feel the same way, or perhaps, because you fear such a loss. When we identify with someone else's story, it is because there is some truth that gives us clues to our own story and soul.

Image 6: Resonating and gently moving forward with inner trust.

I now understand that as a child, my deep emotions were systematically shut down. I couldn't resonate, because I was forbidden to trust or even acknowledge my experience, thoughts, and feelings. You see, when I was little, I never knew my strengths or weaknesses, only that I had better accomplish a lot and be perfect so my perfect parents would be proud of me and not disappointed. I desperately needed to be perfect "Little Kathy," and that meant striving for approval in any situation. But getting approval didn't make me feel real or seen, so I started the endless searching for who I was, looking for clues so I could eventually connect the dots. Whenever I found a clue that resonated, I collected it, hoping one day everything would make sense and my search would have been worth it. Naturally I became a book hoarder. But really, I wished someone else could just tell me. Give me the answer and get on with it!

Over a lifetime of workshops and conferences, I learned a few key things that resonated with me. One was that the way we learn our strengths and weaknesses is through getting mirrored by our parents. In a healthy environment we get feedback on what we did well and what we needed to do to be stronger in other areas. Absent that, children look for mirrors outside themselves and their family. Sometimes even adults can't find what they are looking for, like the woman on the cover of this book, who appears to be looking outside herself to find what can only be found inside herself. Another thing I learned from these venues is that our wounds become our greatest gifts. My lack of self-knowledge somehow made me naturally good at mirroring others. I could compassionately and easily reflect back to others what strengths I saw in them, often writing for them a uniquely created "poem portrait" and matching collage image. With these insights on time, integration, and resonating, I was ready to better understand my family.

Who Are These Women?

Women of a generation
fueled with passion
for values and social causes
happened upon a field
that spoke their language
that promised an avenue
for expressing deep commitments
and bold parts of the self

These are the women
with the diversity lens
who swim with the sharks
who think outside of the box
beyond white patriarchy
who deconstruct OD
and reconceptualize
in their own tradition

Women who are rewriting
the way business is done
the way cultures change
the way paradigms are framed
the way relationships are tended
finally getting recognition and satisfaction
distinguishing themselves
with success and visibility

These are the women
defining themselves differently
knowing what they offer
willing to take on the fights
grieving the unfulfilled potential
the pain of racism and injustice
they see what's hidden and speak out
empowered without collusion

These are the women
who are living their best years fully
whose life and work are one
angry, sad, strategically authentic
doing the work with humor
and wisdom, good will and truth
with diverse, creative solutions
influencing our ever changing world

Image 7: Group Poem Portrait, "Who Are These Women?"

Image 8: My photo of the group collage of all the women in my study.

Understanding My Family

It was the best of times, it was the worst of times . . .

—Charles Dickens, *A Tale of Two Cities*

My earliest childhood memories of each parent begin when I was three. Karen had just been born, and we lived in Rock Island, Illinois, where my dad was a medical captain in the army. One morning Mom was brewing coffee and, as usual, adding a little salt to make the grounds less bitter. I perked up, "That's sugar, Mommy, not salt." She snapped back, "You're wrong, it's salt." My thought had been to help her, and I naively asked, "Why are you mad?" She said she wasn't, and then it turned out I was right about her wrong ingredient. This emotional encounter, with her denial of her feelings and withholding of an apology, was enough to make me stop trusting my senses. By the time I was four, the damage was done. My mother was active in the Officers' Wives' Club, which hosted a fashion show to benefit two Army relief groups. I still have the newspaper photo of me with one of the wives checking my "full-skirted blue nylon dress." You don't need to look closely to see me wishing I didn't have to participate and feeling so inadequate compared with my beautiful and poised mother, who was always right, even when she was wrong.

I really missed my dad when he was away, preparing to be a physician in the Korean War, which thankfully ended before he was scheduled to leave for active duty. Mom said I developed a tic where my shoulders would tense up toward my ears, which I find an endearing memory. When Dad returned, I spent as much time in his arms and company as possible. He sculpted a clay bust of me, immortalizing his love of me as a cute little girl. While sitting there, I'd ask him questions. We practiced counting and I said, "Count to infinity." I didn't understand why he said he couldn't. He was patient enough to have me step on a stool while he taught me to make scrambled eggs. He brought us a little dachshund, whom I loved, but Pinky bit the postman and had to be given away. I would dance silly dances with Dad in the basement, wearing the Annie Oakley-style Western skirt and vest he'd brought back for me from the Army base in Texas. In contrast to the fashion show dress, which was definitely not me, I loved this outfit.

Image 9: Photos of two outfits as a child.

Growing up my life wasn't all bad, and that's why I found it hard to face what was going on below the surface. Better to just leave it there. A collage of confusing memories; a catalog of contradictions: Mom, as a working artist, taught me about creativity. When I was in grade school, she was putting mosaic tiles on any surface—tabletops, an outdoor pillar—even letting me help her. Later, she had an art studio built in the back room, and though she spent hours there by herself, she didn't mind me popping in momentarily to watch her create jewelry, balance metal sculptures, or work on her accessory fashion designs. She never watched TV with Dad and us kids, and while I missed her and a sense of belonging, she was setting an example of doing what she found valuable. When Mom was a docent at art museums, she exposed me to modern art. But she sometimes deserted me in the galleries, walking away with her nose in the air, taking her knowledge with her. On the other hand, there were times we would fall on the floor laughing together. Like the time we were at a health resort. It was unusual for Mom to take all three of her daughters somewhere, but Grandma had left her money, and she, for once, included all of us. She came up behind me during a hike and teased me, because she knew I had sneaked a chocolate chip cookie and she wanted to know when I ate it! Mom preferred her time alone, but she always cooked dinner for the family and was never late to pick me up at school. She set a gorgeous table for family celebrations and was good at delegating when she needed help. Other times, I felt set up and abandoned, like when Mom said she wanted to buy me a piece of jewelry for my sixteenth birthday. Once in the store, I was overwhelmed and had no idea what to choose. When I asked for her guidance, she grew irritated and walked out, leaving me to follow, eyes downcast, without getting anything. Of course, it was my fault. If I had only known what I wanted, I would have gotten it. Instead, I exhausted her limit of patience and enthusiasm, so I deserved to get nothing, except her annoyance.

Dad always wanted us to be "happy" and superficial, but when he took me to my Saturday guitar lessons, he let me talk about what I saw in the clouds as I looked out the car window. The day I was diagnosed with mononucleosis in high school, my father the doctor refused to let me lead the pep rally the following day, a first foray into leadership (and extroversion) about which I had been enormously excited. He made me stay in bed for six weeks, while I felt punished, depressed, and resentful. Mom stayed in the kitchen or went out and ignored me, rarely asking how I was feeling. The maid brought me soup when I was hungry. My illness seemed to be an inconvenience to them. The only benefit for me was growing my bangs out—and realizing who my real friends were by who visited and who stayed away. Maybe being neglected was better for me than being smothered with negative attention, but still, I felt quite alone. Dad was quick to express anger with my middle sister, Karen, who was three years younger, but not toward me except by being critical and disapproving. Lisa, who was eleven years younger than me (and later in life changed her name to Robin) would vigorously disagree with his allopathic medical approach, as he would with her beliefs in alternative medicine. As the oldest, I secretly wished he had encouraged me to follow in his footsteps as a doctor. But that never happened. He just wanted me to stay his "cute little girl" and marry someone with "financial potential," which I eventually did.

In college during the seventies I loved being a hippie, participating in marches, and becoming politicized about feminism and racism. During that time I met a boy, not Jewish, two years older, with an inviting smile and a cool leather bomber jacket, yet also aspirations to go to law school—a kind of safe bad boy. When we started living together, my parents weren't too happy. In fact, said they'd give us money for our rent *if* we got married, which we did. As my parents got to know him and us as a couple over the years, our looking-good relationship fit perfectly with what Mom and Dad had and valued. But years later, as I began to listen to my inner voice, I realized he wasn't the right choice for me and I would need to leave the marriage. My mom didn't understand why, if I was the one to take the initiative, I didn't just go off into the sunset happily free, instead of suffering through the emotional roller coaster ride I signed up for. My father never fully accepted my decision, and to show his disapproval, he repeatedly sang the virtues of my first husband in front of Patrick to humiliate him and aggravate me. But I knew my heart, and this time I followed it.

Even though some of my high school friends' mothers were nurturing and emotionally available, it was only when I met my best friend, Nancy, when we were working with psychiatric patients after college, that I became aware of what loving mothering could actually be. Our upbringing and mothers were similar, but she somehow was able to transcend her mother's limitations. When Nancy had children, she made sure she gave them what she had never received. After working in her psychotherapy practice all day, she would come home and play with her two daughters on the floor, have healthy snacks waiting for them, and stay up in the middle of the night when one had a bad dream or was sick. At my PhD graduation party, which my dad offered and generously paid for, my mother looked to Nancy to give me the praise and hugs that she couldn't—or wouldn't. "You tell her," she said.

One day many years later, a piece of the puzzle of my mother's constant irritation with me became clear. My parents were visiting me, and we were out for a walk before they left. I screwed up my courage and asked Mom why she was walking behind us and seemed so annoyed. Having stepped on the land mine, I waited for the explosion. Instead, I got a flash of honesty. Finally, she confessed that she was always jealous of my connection with Dad. She wanted him all to herself. A rare moment of understanding passed between us.

Looking back, I remember how excited I was to spend time with my father. When I was a child, he and I had fun watching TV together and doing calisthenics on the floor with my belly on his outstretched arms and legs. It had never occurred to me that when he came home every night for dinner at six, Mom hated the way I'd race to the door yelling, "Daddy's home!" Despite my joy at his arrival, I didn't feel a reciprocated enthusiastic embrace. Instead, he walked down the hall to his bedroom to take off his tie before meeting us at the dinner table, where he sat straight-backed at the head while Mom served the meal with the grace of a hostess, and the daughters dutifully sat in our assigned chairs, waiting for a nibble of genuine attention.

I didn't realize how emotionally limited my parents were until I read about narcissism. That was a defining moment for me. I finally understood why I didn't get, from either of them, the kind of love I needed as a child or the support I craved in terms of my career or relationship advice. My needs were inconvenient, because their wants, needs, and desires were their primary focus and would always come first. With Mom being all about herself, there was no mirroring to help me develop my sense of who I was and what I could do or be. I ended up feeling either not enough or too much, because in any situation I was supposed to fit in and meet other people's needs.

It is therefore unsurprising that, not ever wanting to make my child feel as miserable as I felt, I decided never to be a mother myself.

What really stuck with me from *Will I Ever Be Good Enough?* was McBride's diagram of narcissistic families. I used to characterize our family to myself, just as she did, as spokes on a wheel with Mom as the hub. We all vied for her attention. My sisters and I mostly spent one-on-one time with my parents to decrease competition and conflict among us. When our parents were being unfair to one of the sisters, it never occurred to us to join forces and stand up for each other. Especially when Mom was being dismissive and aggressive, I would look at my father and wonder why he didn't protect us. I somehow knew it was his job to do that, but he never did. He only had eyes for Mom. She ruled and he enabled her self-absorption, trying to meet her endless need for attention and justifying her entitlement.

The family unspoken rule was "it's all about Mom." Her face set the tone and I checked it first to find out how a dinner, car ride, or any activity was going to go. If she was absorbed with her morning bagel, careful not to smear her lipstick, I knew to leave for the school bus without saying anything. If she was in the front seat while Dad drove us to a restaurant, I could tell from her tight shoulders and stare straight ahead to keep quiet. If I came home and she turned around with a smile while cooking, I could relax my guard and give her a kiss hello. I'd be embarrassed when I was with her while she was having one of her rude moments: when impatient in a public setting, expecting to have her needs met immediately and not wait her turn, or when at a doctor's appointment and given advice she didn't want to hear or follow, not respecting the expertise she had sought.

The sisters' role was never to rock the boat and always to mask our real feelings. Our job was to maintain our image as the perfect family and pretend everything was OK, which McBride says is a survival mechanism. Given this early lack of emotional safety and trust, it is the hallmark of daughters of narcissistic families to lack confidence in their own decision-making. They also lack boundaries in relationships because they were taught to repress their feelings and needs so as not to interfere with what the mother wants. This was certainly the case with me.

I learned later from a therapist that setting boundaries was for yourself, no matter what the other person felt about it. She said you didn't need to be rigid or cruel, but you did need to be firm. This took years for me even to be willing to try. The imprint of narcissistic parents was so strong I resisted ever putting my needs above, or even with, someone else's. Because my parents never hit me, locked me in the basement, or gave away all my toys, I didn't understand how insidious and damaging subtle emotional neglect and abuse could be.

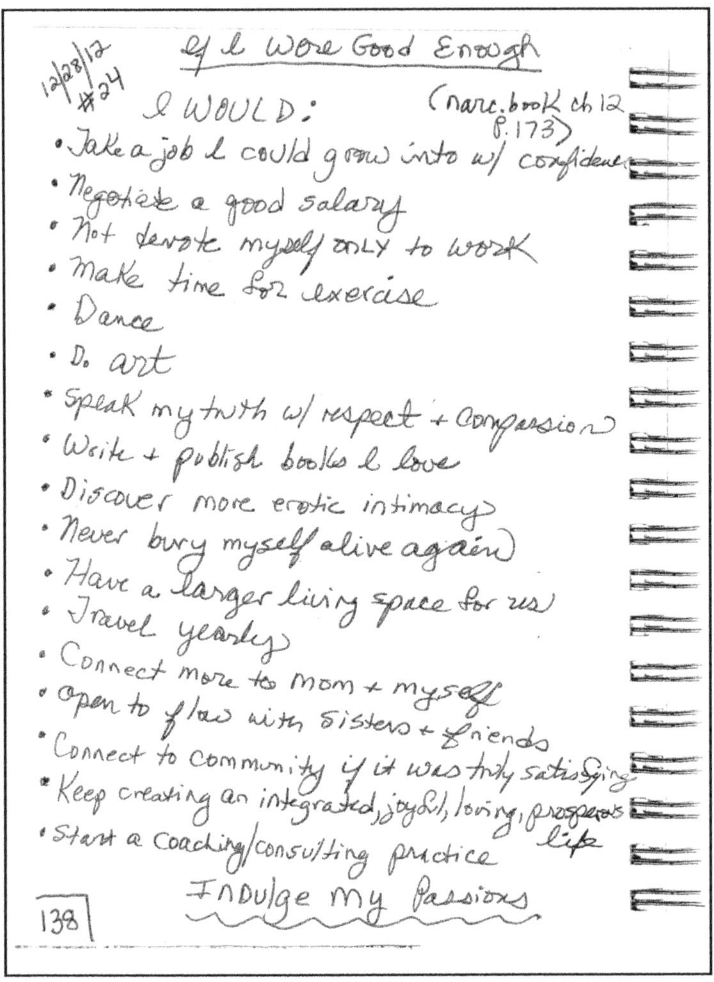

If I Were Good Enough

12/28/12
#24

I WOULD: (narc. book ch 12 p. 173)

- Take a job I could grow into w/ confidence
- Negotiate a good salary
- Not devote myself ONLY to work
- Make time for exercise
- Dance
- Do art
- Speak my truth w/ respect + compassion
- Write + publish books I love
- Discover more erotic intimacy
- Never bury myself alive again
- Have a larger living space for us
- Travel yearly
- Connect more to mom + myself
- Open to flow with sisters + friends
- Connect to community if it was truly satisfying
- Keep creating an integrated, joyful, loving, prosperous life
- Start a coaching/consulting practice

INDULGE MY PASSIONS

138

Image 10: "If I were good enough," an exercise from McBride's book.

With my private battle finally making sense, I continued to try to heal through implementing the recommendations in McBride's book. At work I tried to stop focusing on never disappointing others. No wonder I never achieved the legacy I wanted. I now feel compassion for my suffering, and amazement that I've done as well as I have. It has taken me years of various types of therapy to believe what so many others take for granted: that I have a right to my perceptions and can trust my instincts. Despite the empathic therapist who tried to teach me what a loving internalized maternal voice would sound like, it's only in the last few years that I have been able to talk to myself with care and concern.

Neither my challenges with my parents growing up nor my awareness of their issues as an adult ever changed my enduring love for them. When it was time for each of my parents to pass on, first Dad and three years later, Mom, I called my sisters and told them I felt moved to go across the country and be with them during their final days. They supported the idea. I could do this because I finally had compassion for myself and for them. I believe in their final months my parents finally saw a glimpse of who I really was and appreciated me giving from my heart what they each needed at their poignant moment. I will never regret taking the high road and staying focused on all the good things they gave me.

While I experienced immense healing from helping my parents' transition, my internalized patterns didn't simultaneously disappear for me in the workplace. I reported to, and was triggered by, a CEO who was a woman, and a VP who was a man. Each was the embodiment of what I grew up with, from "the look" of dismissiveness from my mom to the patriarchal arrogance of my dad. I worked hard to manage their challenging personalities and difficult dynamics, as did many other leaders during my eight years at the organization. But apparently, these issues, which many of my colleagues seemed to take in stride, had a greater emotional charge for me.

Now, I'm in a different place, and I often ask myself the following questions:

How is it that today, when I feel stuck and down, I can tolerate the extremely uncomfortable feelings and surrender, adjusting my plans for the day?

How is it that I now know a negative situation will somehow move me toward a solution that I couldn't get to without it?

How is it that I also know the positive feelings of achievement and happiness don't last either?

And how is it that, finally, I am not fighting the fact that there is no permanent destination of peace and perfection?

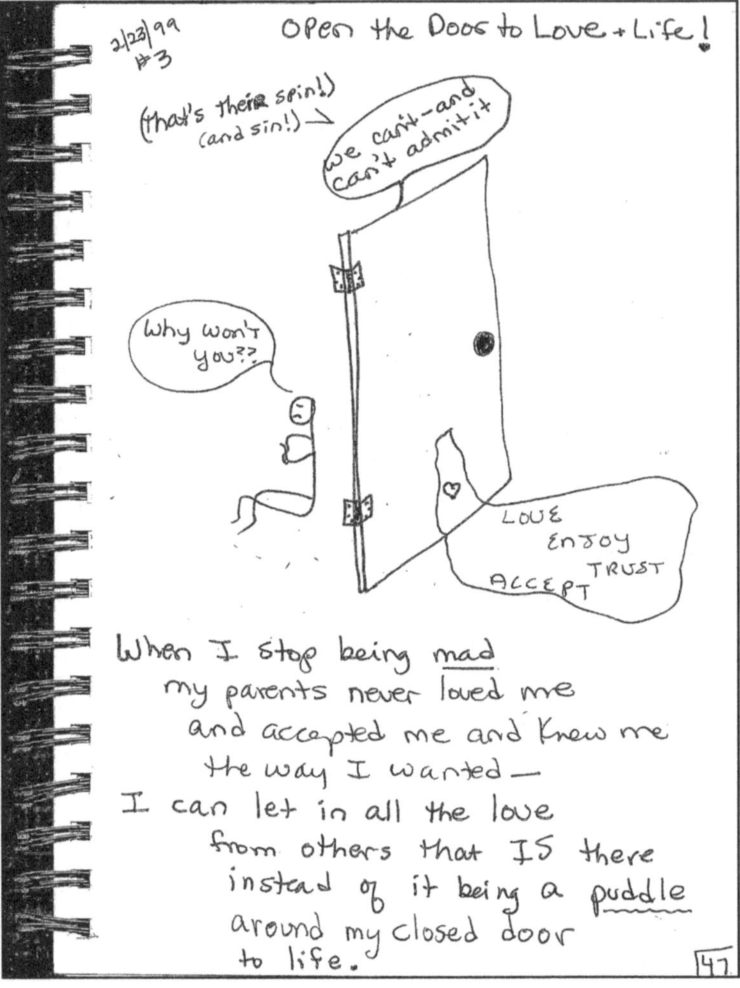

Image 11: Finally able to open the door to love.

I can tell you it is not from meditating, a spiritual bypass, willpower, affirmations, or sheer determination. I think the answer is actually rooted in all my searching and finally finding what I needed: a self. I started listening to my soul's longing and daring to give myself the love and attention I sought elsewhere. Of course, my approach has been convoluted, extensive, and intense. Many would not have the tolerance for such a nonlinear and energy-expending effort. But for me, I was in so much emotional pain I had to find relief. You might not have seen it from the outside (when I was introduced at the psychiatric unit my friend Nancy thought my last name was Captain and she was intimidated!) but I know how long I suffered on the inside. I am talking over six decades of not trusting myself or accepting myself—practically my whole life. That is why I'm finally sharing my experience: to offer support, healing, and hope to others who suffer in a similar way.

Both writing and revisiting my journals has been the saving grace, a vehicle to help me process and deal with my awkward moments, disappointments, missteps, and grief. They also helped me face the truth: that I may have sold myself short because I couldn't move beyond my early programming. When I caught myself fearing both success and failure, I looked to the two silver bookmarks on my meditation altar for inspiration. One features a quote by George Eliot, "It is never too late to be what you might have been." Those words always motived me to keep striving for clarity. But what if at some point it was too late? The other contains a quote by Edith Wharton, encouraging self-acceptance and surrender: "There are two ways of spreading light: to be the candle or the mirror that reflects it." I have been afraid to be the candle, even though I thought I should be, often tried to be, and habitually have beaten myself up for falling short. Yet, I am an excellent mirror for others, and that fills me with genuine satisfaction. In writing about what I learned from my journals, I am hoping to help others see their true reflections. The book is not a call to "look at me;" it's a call to look *with* me as you look inside yourself to find your own voice, light, and truth.

I'll always be a seeker, but I've happily given up searching for "IT." Why look when I can finally see in the mirror that "IT" is right in front of me and feel in my body that "IT" is right inside me? Again, the answer is on my altar table. I have a large green malachite rock with shiny bumps and deep crevices. Clearly imperfect, yet I consider it perfect as is—all part of what it is meant to be. Now, I can't be bothered keeping up on the endless stream of self-help literature. Even when I receive notice from an author I have followed for years, I don't get past reading the sample I requested on Kindle. Why? Because at long last I know I am the authority on my life. Which means I no longer have to turn elsewhere to find myself or figure myself out. As imperfect as I am, the reality of aging is more immediate. I am daily aware that I will one day die. I don't know when or how, but I know the facts. Do I really want to waste more time on the treadmill of reading someone else's version of what is wrong with me and how to fix it? Do I really want to keep chasing my own outdated and unproductive notion of perfection? Do you?

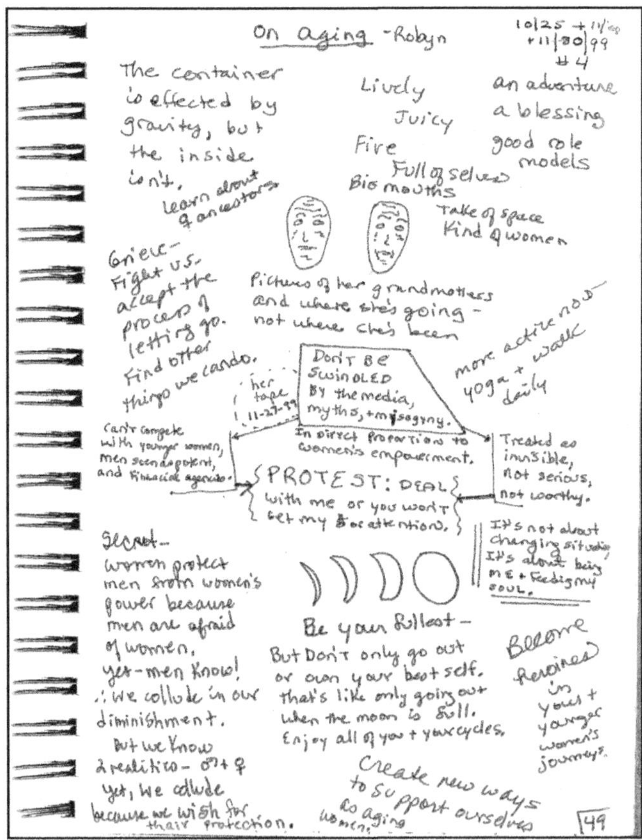

Image 12: The reality and possibilities of aging.

CHAPTER TWO

Me and My Journals

If you could say it in words,
there would be no reason to paint.

—Edward Hopper

Even before I began keeping journals, I was inspired to do small drawings of what I called "Heartfelt Spaces." I would be walking along in Washington, D.C., and an interesting streetlamp and bench would call to me. I'd immediately sit down, take out my black pen, and start drawing what captured my attention. I'd be captivated by certain houses, including the White House, and I'd draw them. (I even framed the White House drawing and sent it to the President as an inauguration gift!) Eventually, I would get commissions from friends to render my version of an apartment or room of a house that was special to them or represented a new phase of their life. Never erasing a line as I was drawing, I felt if I just kept going, it would all come together. If I picked apart each item to perfect it, it would never match the vision in my head, and I knew I'd just stop in frustration. Once completed, in my unique, almost naïve perspective, I would add color, usually with watercolor paints. Oddly, I never used shadows. I even entered an art show with a piece called "No Shadows," which could have been the title of my whole collection.

I had no formal art education. I did this art for my soul. It was satisfying. I had no thought of selling or appealing to an audience. If people were interested, that was a bonus. For instance, once my childlike drawings were used to illustrate a tour business brochure in Washington, D.C. The owners said my charming style matched the feeling of the students and schools who were their clients.

Image 13: My first commissioned "Heartfelt Spaces" drawing.

After receiving my PhD, I moved to New York City for my new career, and even though every neighborhood offered an abundance of potential Heartfelt Spaces, I never received that tug to continue the drawings. But my creativity did not die; it just found other avenues of expression.

My journals became a new venue for Heartfelt Spaces, a term that had expanded to include activities that brought me joy, connection, and deep satisfaction. A Heartfelt Space could be visiting friends and family, going on vacation, collecting art images, or even adding entries in my journal. What goes in my journals *resonates* with me; there is no need to analyze or debate. It's a pull from something during my day that catches my attention and begs to be included. For me, the act of journaling is an act of self-love. I create these Heartfelt Spaces purely for myself. I'm happy if others appreciate something from my journals, but I don't need their contentment to be able to feel my own.

The idea to start a journal didn't actually come from me, but from the facilitator of a storytelling group a friend from my doctoral program encouraged me to join. There were six other women, and we seven sisters called ourselves The Pleiades, after the constellation. Together, we went beyond ourselves as individuals to become a cluster of stars. While I worried it would be a distraction from my dissertation, it ended up redefining my work with those thirty-two women in OD. I wasn't just researching them. I was distilling their stories.

The facilitator told us to write notes, draw ideas, collect pictures that evoked feelings, and gather any other items that sparked our interest. In the group, we would share our insights as stories, letting each other's journeys ignite our own. Soon poems, prayers, and patterns would emerge. Not only did this very first journal lead to completing my study with creativity and inspiration, but it also started me on a path to continue keeping a journal once the group ended and we moved on.

I had an unusual and positive experience with my PhD program at George Washington University (GWU) School of Business and Public Management. Part of what made it special was the intensive encouragement and expert guidance of my committee chair, Peter B. Vaill, who was the director of the PhD program, and to whom this book is dedicated. Peter's perspective and wisdom opened the door for me to interview thirty-two successful women in OD who had their own consulting firms, at a time when most consultants were men. The generosity of what these women shared and the lessons I learned from distilling meaning from their stories, using qualitative research, was the most satisfying experience of my life. Not only did I complete a 424-page dissertation, but I also included art and poetry to capture the essence of the women in my in-depth study.

Peter also validated my need for a sacred space to create and do research. He said for introverts, having a private room is more important than anything else. Being extremely extroverted, my new boyfriend Patrick didn't understand this need. One night, we were supposed to meet to go to an outdoor food fair, and he never showed up. Instead of stewing like a victim, I used the time to sit on my bed and create a Heartfelt Space of my studio apartment. It felt great to honor the container that was supporting me in doing my dissertation and living as a newly divorced woman.

Image 14: My drawing of my first studio apartment.

Mastering the multiple steps of qualitative research brought me my mantra for not getting overwhelmed or ahead of myself: *Know where you are and be where you are*. Later, when working full-time in my new career, I added: *Know who you are and be who you are*. Keeping a journal has helped me in two ways: to value being introspective and also to provide a container for my agony. I once had a boss who said not to let my emotions leak in public, so the journal let me be my whole self in private without getting shamed. It didn't matter if I was working around the clock, there was always time to write in my journal.

What to Do with My Journals

Faith is taking the first step even when you don't see the whole staircase.

—Martin Luther King, Jr.

Years later, Patrick (the aforementioned boyfriend who became my second husband) and I were planning a move abroad, though he called it an "extended travel adventure," and we had to limit what we took with us. I pared down my possessions to the smallest amount possible but found myself buying a large plastic container for all thirty-two volumes of my journals. As a collection, the seven-by-ten-inch hardbound spiral sketchbooks were heavy and took up significant space, yet without having spoken to anyone about them, I had an intuitive sense that they were valuable to me. Even though I couldn't assert why they were important, I honored the gut feeling that my subconscious was preparing me for something not yet clear. Still, I asked myself, *Why do you want to drag your past with you, if you are creating a new future?* My answer was visceral: the journals *wanted* to come with me. It was as if they spoke to me, demanding to be with me. I couldn't ignore them, couldn't risk not discovering what they clamored to offer. With that, my journals and I joined forces for whatever was to happen next.

Image 15: A photo I took of my journal collection.

I used to think that when I died, I would leave the journals to my two sisters to sort out. I felt they would value having something I considered the "most me." Both sisters are artistic and writers, and I hoped that if they saw a purpose in them, they would somehow figure out how to share my journals with the world. But once I trudged through the process of letting go before our major move, I realized a major truth—*nobody wants your stuff!* We had sculptures and books and jewelry and so many things we treasured, but no one desired these things or saw the value in them that we once did. We soon found ourselves living at the neighborhood Goodwill and a local thrift shop, as well as the shredding service at FedEx—all eager and willing to accept our donations. With all the decisions made about our stuff, I realized it would be up to me to discover the meaning of my journals either sooner or later.

Sooner arrived with startling synchronicity when I shared my process of journaling with two new friends in our new home—Mexico. Ana was a local entrepreneur with a master's degree in anthropology and fluent in both Spanish and English. She told me she wanted to keep a journal but didn't know how. I showed her my collection occupying the shelves and she said, as if conveying a message, "There are treasures in there, go find them." That was all the inspiration I needed to start mining my journals for whatever nuggets I could find. After I shared some early writing about my journaling process with Ana, she told me to "Go deeper." And I did. Then, Madeleine, an artist from South Africa, expressed interest in reading about my journal process, even though she had no interest in keeping a journal herself. While I had begun by writing about the benefits of journal keeping, she encouraged me to write more about my life story, and I soon saw the connection. As she read the beginning of this book, she asked me to write more.

With similar feedback from two different friends, I changed course. Rereading my journals, I started extracting unexpected stories. It became clear that my journal review process was as important as the stories within the books, because my review was enabling me to engage in a kind of alchemy, transforming the raw material of my experiences into insights and turning note nuggets into narrative. I saw the *what* and the *how* as two parts of a whole, and I decided to include my process and resources at the end of the memoir.

My Journal Review Process

The final phase of healing is using what happens to you to help other people.

—Gloria Steinem

Diving into my journal series is like being captivated by all the colorful things one discovers when exploring a coral reef. It's a private world, holding the secrets of the past and future. I remembered, once I started my new career, that *writing* in my journals helped me excavate the unfinished business of my childhood that was affecting my ability to be the best consultant, intimate partner, and person I could be. Now, the promise of *reviewing* the journals would be to answer the question I had asked so many times: What would my life be like if I knew *my essence* and had, as I'd always dreamed, *my life with me in it*? I had written some answers in the journals: I would have deep satisfaction rather than extreme discontent. I would be unblocked, more grounded, radiant, balanced, and in love with my life. I'd let go of whatever didn't serve me. I could freely move on and feel and express myself. Then, I would be able to contribute and connect, fulfilling my purpose.

My journal keeping began in earnest after what I always refer to as the one-two punch: ending my first marriage and completing my doctorate. Then, it took a while until I landed a job in my new field and moved to a new city, both of which gave me some stability. With that, I found the right size journal to begin "My Wise and Wonderful Black Book Series." Rereading these volumes now, I find the perspective of literary critic David Lodge helpful: "The special thing about writing a journal is that the writer doesn't know where the story is going, he doesn't know how it ends; so it seems to exist in a kind of continuous present, even though the individual incidents may be described in the past tense." In retrospect, I notice my journals largely focus on the two main topics Sigmund Freud long ago held up as the key to adult maturity and satisfaction, "Love and work . . . work and love, that's all there is."

Socrates supposedly said, "The unexamined life is not worth living." This continuing review of all my journals is the act of examination that has made all the difference in my life. I now have the ability to hear my fears and concerns. I may wish they'd go away, but I don't ignore them or beat myself up for their presence. I now know "all-or-nothing thinking" dominated most of my life, so I practice pausing when I feel something unwanted and try to accept that bad *and* good can exist at the same time. I may feel cranky about it and need to fume or cry, but I literally welcome all my parts and ask each to tell me how they feel and what they want. If they don't know, that's OK, too. I am more patient with my readiness taking as long as it takes.

I analyzed my thirty-two journals using the same methodology I used to understand the thirty-two interviews I conducted with the women in OD. (The synchronicity of these numbers was not planned, though it is curious.) When I started this review, I knew I needed to read the content with a focus, so I wouldn't spin my wheels. My fear was that I would reconnect with my angst from the past. I worried that connecting with some of the negativity and pain would jinx me now and ruin the peace and joy I feel most of the time. What actually happened was that I did connect with the emotional tenor of each journal, but in a mostly enlightening and rarely difficult way. The benefit of having journals is that they exist—so I didn't have to rely on memory and couldn't deny the truth of what I had written—in order to know myself more fully and deeply.

Not until Journal 14, in June of 2006, did I realize how much the journals might mean to someone else. I reflected on a note I had written on the inside cover:

> To: Whoever is reading this
>
> I have said to myself that these journals are the most important things I have. If I die before I am able to write a book from them, then know they are my truth. They are the best way I have to know, accept, and honor myself. They are sometimes creative, honest, and heartfelt. Other times they are messy, incomplete, self-indulgent, repetitive, too in my head, going around in circles and boring. So what? It's my life. And where I've been reluctant to speak my truth and stand my ground in the outer world, at least I've had a safe space for claiming myself in here. My pain, inadequacies, fears, joy, synchronicity, sacredness, desire, love, hate, confusion—it is all here. For this Grace I am grateful.

Completing my analysis of over five thousand pages, I realized there were certain entries of enduring value I could later refer to as my private references and personal self-help book: I called these "Keepers."

I gave each journal a title, wrote about themes by journal and page number, then looked for the themes and insights that were significant across the journal series. As I started writing the narrative, I decided to add actual entries when they demonstrated to the reader the various methods I used to capture ideas. As you will later learn, my inner Taskmaster is embarrassed they are so messy and wishes they could all be perfect, like a well-manicured English garden. My inner Poet, however, is delighted with each and every one, confident of the way they express their truth organically, like a sprawling yard of wildflowers.

Other times I noted the journal number and page when it made more sense simply to identify where I drew my conclusions and insights. Besides showing my rigorous methodology, this enabled me to easily find significant entries during revisions of the manuscript. Now I'm ready to share my synthesis of what I have learned, as I have become more and more visible to myself. I wasn't intending to write a memoir (hence the word "unexpected" in the subtitle), but my journey through journaling made it so. The entries called to me through the memories and the collages of my mind. You won't find as many descriptions of people, dialogue, plot, or action typical of most novels and some memoirs. But here you will discover my deeper story, told with emotional honesty and intensity, for you to resonate with, learn from, and hopefully, enjoy.

CHAPTER THREE

Achieving

Success is stumbling from failure to failure with no loss of enthusiasm.
—Winston Churchill

Visibility

One of the most baffling challenges in my adulthood and career was successfully ascending to leadership positions while preferring to stay unseen, behind the scenes. I loved being recognized and rewarded for my innovations and publications, but I couldn't stand the slings and arrows that came with the top job. I remember a new colleague learning about our team. I felt so appreciated when he said, "Every project I've observed has your name on it." Yet I also sensed that, at work, people didn't tell me what they really thought about me, and it made me feel paranoid. Perhaps I developed a persona of needing to be seen as perfect, as well as a fragility when my weaknesses were exposed. I had a drive to excel and help others do the same, but when it came to managing people, both above and below me in the hierarchy, I had difficulty standing my ground with bullies and allowing my full light to shine. I thrived when my work became the face of a project or program, but I wilted when I had to face criticism—or give it—preferring to hide behind my written words and avoid any type of confrontation. This pattern played out in a number of professional roles, including my positions at GWU Medical Center, Mount Sinai Medical Center and School of Medicine, New York University (NYU) Langone Medical Center, and Maimonides Medical Center. At a leadership workshop a year after I moved to New York, I wrote a poem (see Image 16) that details the journey I was on.

The Actors Institute
Leadership Workshop
October 3, 1997

CRANKY

What is it with this leadership?
Sometimes I hate it so
I end up like the "little engine that could"
"I think I can" is all I know.

I stay late after hours
Typing left-brained things like a machine
Then I end up so depleted
I have no energy or humor—I'm mean!

Some leaders, it seems, love to swoop in
(Acting like a bully or baby, bossy, too)
Creating chaos, context, and visibility
Stealing credit when really nothing did they do.

It's not that I want to be like that
But I compare myself, it's true
And take my frustrations out on me
Rather than confront and move on, I stew.

I know I excel at weaving together
Wonderful ideas and talents with care
Focusing on the successful outcome
And the satisfaction we will share.

So what am I really seeking
When my light shines like a star
Isn't it to make people's lives better
To be more of who they are?

Help me claim my quiet power
To know the leadership gifts I bring
So I can create, with love and truth,
And abundance for my purse string!

Image 16: My poem "CRANKY," about me and leadership.

In my first career as an occupational therapist, I initiated and developed the Department of Occupational Therapy and Related Services on the psychiatric unit of GWU Medical Center. Known for my program development and publications, I decided after six years to hire a highly competent occupational therapist to help our team expand our services. This should have been a good thing. But I quickly felt triggered when I began managing Beth because of how she responded—or rather didn't respond—to my guidance. With her dismissive attitude, she reminded me of my mother, right down to the distancing look on her face and the denial—now known as gaslighting—that it meant anything. At the same time, I felt a personal sense of compassion for her depressed mood and a desire to heal her.

Of course, I soon realized helping Beth on a personal level was impossible, never mind inappropriate. I had, unconsciously, hired a woman with parallels to my mother, and now having her in a subservient position, I would theoretically have the power to "cure" her. What a bind I put myself, and her, in. We could never have honest conversations about her needs and my expectations, because everything was filtered through my lens of fixing my mother and Beth's issues with authority.

So I punted, spending more and more time away, completing my master's degree, and retreating to being task-oriented instead of managerial. I remember Beth saying, "I disagree with how you use your time, and you don't do enough. You are more academic than clinical." I couldn't process her comment and I didn't know how to respond, other than defensively. As her manager, I was supposed to be focusing on her flaws, not the other way around. Beth's negative feedback deeply unnerved me, leaving me feeling fearful, vulnerable, incompetent, and most of all threatened. I can hardly express how overwhelming these emotions felt coursing through my body each day. Even now, my stomach turns as I remember. I had never felt like that before and I began searching everywhere for a consultant or therapist who could help me understand and navigate the situation, but no one seemed to be as alarmed—or interested—as I was.

Then the drama escalated. Beth was very social and aligned herself quickly with other staff on the unit, talking behind my back, eroding and eventually excluding me from the comfortable and productive collegial relationships I had previously enjoyed. She withheld information from me and was intrusive and dominating. I sensed she saw my blind spots and got others to focus on them, exposing a pathology of which I was not yet aware. I was terribly upset that she would never admit to her role in our dynamics, but then again, neither could I. For me, it was like wearing headphones with her hatred of me in one ear matching my self-hatred in the other; the noise was deafening and destructive. I didn't realize at the time that she was hitting my childhood humiliation wound; I still thought my parents were perfect and I had been the problem. I also didn't know the term "boundaries" at this time, and I certainly didn't know how to use them. When Beth said I was "not in touch with my anger," I was ready to explode, but because emotions had never been permissible for me, and were not appropriate as her manager, I said nothing. But as with my childhood sadness, my face showed it all.

Looking back at this difficult time, I'm reminded of the children's book by Michael Foreman, *Fortunately, Unfortunately,* which helps young people see situations in terms other than black-and-white, a perspective I would later call "both/and thinking." Unfortunately, I was in a situation that was causing me to have a meltdown. Fortunately, I found a way to escape, by deciding to leave the organization with as much dignity as I could muster, rather than fire my nemesis, as my boss advocated. Unfortunately, I left a position I loved and an organization where I had thrived and was disappointed in myself for letting Beth take away from my accomplishments there. Fortunately, I hadn't been a "bad" manager in trying to uphold standards for the department. Unfortunately, I had been a bad manager by not assuming responsibility for and taking action on her poor relationship with me, her boss. Fortunately, I vowed never to become a manager again. Unfortunately, I cut off my pathway to that type of career advancement. Fortunately, she didn't take away my reputation for innovative contributions, and I was soon asked to join the full-time faculty of Towson State University. That environment encouraged my creativity and allowed me to capitalize on my "bad" work experiences by using them as case studies in my teaching. After a while, my seeker kicked in and I saw my situation with a little more perspective. I identified with the reasons why 40 percent of leaders at many levels fail at managing others:

they are not willing to be unpopular when necessary
they lack confidence when making decisions
they do not hold employees accountable
they are perfectionistic, and
they avoid firing people.

Unfortunately, I remained anxious, even though teaching provided me a comfortable home at work with a peer group that was conceptual and academic, like me. Fortunately, this led to some synchronicity in which I heard about the field of organization behavior and management, which would turn out to engage me for the rest of my career. I have since learned that we never know at the time how events might ultimately turn out. As Kierkegaard said, "Life can only be understood backwards; but it must be lived forwards." In retrospect, I had to learn to forgive myself for being relatively young in my career and not yet being able to apply both/and thinking, accept and manage my emotions, and realize everyone has a "shadow." I even was able to recognize myself with humor when I saw one of Jim Unger's *Herman* cartoons. A wimpy person is just standing there as someone else observes and describes him, "It is a strange combination of guilt and paranoia . . . he thinks everyone is out to get him, but he also thinks he deserves it."

Fortunately, at a party someone told me about a professor and department I might resonate with. Jerry Harvey was teaching a class called "Behavioral Factors of Change" in the Department of Organization Behavior and Management at GWU. The readings and discussions were relevant to both OT and OD. I was encouraged to share stories of my prior work conflicts and take risks to understand the origins of my lack of confidence through poetry, essays, videos, and presentations. A poem I wrote, "Change-no change" (see Image 17), is relevant to how long it has taken me to change, write this book, and come to terms with myself and my life. I remember when I read it to the class, as we were all expected to do, they laughed in recognition of my growing self-honesty.

<u>Change-no change</u>

I say I want to change.
If only this or that,
then...
  I will be intimate
  then, I will have a baby
    then, I will lose weight
      then, I will clean the house

But did you ever notice
  how little
    I change?

Makes me suspicious about myself.

So what would I give up?
What makes change so hard?

First, my complaints--
I make everything a BIG PRODUCTION.
  If it isn't hard, I'm not interested.
  If I can't make it complicated, then forget it.

I can't keep a BALANCE.
I'm all or nothing.
Never have time, always behind.
Lots of ideas, too many to implement.

Then, I can't make DECISIONS...
or should I say, not without
great turmoil, fuss, ambivalence,
delay, frustration, and fatigue.

And finally, I always want to know
   WHY?
Why do I make everything a big production,
Why do I always need more time,
Why do I have trouble making decisions,
Why do I feel I have to understand myself
   BEFORE I can change?

Why SHOULD I change?

So what if I am a little compulsive,
  spinning my wheels,
    wanting everything all at once.

Who cares if I am a little messy,
  overweight and excessive in my desires,
    intense and extreme.

That's ME!

And I want to love me, faults and all.
And when I do, you know what I think?
I think I'll make some changes--or not!

Kathy Kaplan 3/5/85

Image 17: My poem, "Change-no change."

I might add here that my given name, Kathy Lou, always made me feel like a little girl. It wasn't until I completed my doctorate that I felt I'd earned the right to change my first and middle names legally. (I kept my last name, Kaplan, because it came from my father, whom I wanted to emulate.) As a nod to my little self, I spelled Kathryn with a "y" to acknowledge Kathy. I changed my middle name to just L, as a private joke that always made me smile. It has the sound of "el" as in Eloise, my favorite childhood role model, who, unlike Goody Two-shoes me, misbehaved and had fun adventures at the Plaza Hotel, in New York City, where I ended up for twenty years.

But at this time, I was still in Washington, D.C. After testing the waters, I signed up for the entire academic program, as it encouraged exactly the type of exploration for which I was hungry. The next course I took, one of my favorites, was called "Ethical, Moral and Spiritual Issues in Management." Professor Harvey used techniques such as writing letters to family members with whom we have conflicts to get deeper into the truth of our relationships and values and relate them to theory and practice. I wrote one to my mother and another to my father, both of which I've saved to this day. Here's a paragraph from a letter to my mother (from February 15, 1985) that shows my courage in speaking my truth, even though it never changed anything with her:

> *Sometimes with you I feel curious, suspicious, and almost paranoid about what you really think and feel about me. You have told me to take you as you are and don't read between the lines. But I have trouble doing that. Now, after all my therapy, I know better than to be expecting you to change for my sake. So what I am trying to figure out is what to do with the fact that I don't always believe you. I would guess you perceive that and imagine that THAT makes you angry at me. This is what I wish to hear from you. When I piss you off and why. When I have hurt you. What impact I have on you.*

She responded with her typical sardonic humor, abruptly ending our dialogue.

My dad didn't like the portrait I painted of him in a poem and basically told me he didn't want me to know him, his Myers-Briggs Type, or the effects of his own childhood. End of discussion. Oh well, you can't blame me for trying.

By the end of the first year in the doctoral program, we were required to create our own curriculum and get it approved by the board of the School of Business and Public Management. It was thrilling for me to go deep and wide in exploring my interests. For the first time in my professional life, I was taking myself seriously and the work was both joyful and stimulating. By following my intuition, I had arrived in a supportive academic environment, where I not only didn't have to be a manager, but I could also learn, from the safe distance of an organizational context, about the unconscious processes that defined my family.

After all my coursework was completed, I wrote my comprehensive exam reviewing literature as if it were a keynote address to students: "Don't Go to Graduate School to Become a Better Manager, Because It Doesn't Work." Slowly I was rebuilding my foundation from the inside out. I realized even though I was a good match for an academic career, I was being drawn to learning how to be an OD consultant. I didn't want to just teach it, I wanted to be a competent practitioner who could use conceptual skills and curiosity to bridge theory and practice.

One project in particular related to discovering the reasons for my profound dis-ease with my first job as a manager. For two years I perused the literature on unconscious processes that are revealed in organizations. What most resonated was the concept of "projective identification." Basically, this is a primitive defense mechanism in which someone deposits their unwanted feelings into someone else, who then takes them in as if they were their own. I decided that was what had happened between me and Beth, the occupational therapist I had hired. She split off ambivalently held parts of herself (such as her relationship with authority), and I accepted them. This process leaves the targeted person feeling depleted and fearful, and other colleagues feeling confused and manipulated. Beth's inability to take in feedback was projected onto me as criticism, and given my own issues, I swallowed it whole. It is also possible I projected unfinished issues with my mother onto her, but if I did, I was unaware of it, as I had not gotten clear on that piece yet.

Just as a diagnosis tends to alleviate the severity of symptoms even if feeling as unwell as before, I felt great relief understanding this complex intrapsychic and interpersonal mechanism. I went on to create a four-foot totem pole with masks and shields to represent the hierarchically arranged roles in organizations (the king, queen, star, and the masses), wrote a research paper describing my insights in depth, and exhibited my artwork (followed by a gallery discussion) entitled "Totem and Taboo Revisited," which built on Freud's *Totem and Taboo*. The theme included defensive maneuvers from parts of the self and from others. The masks symbolized the assumed role expectations and how each role was perceived. The shields were used to protect the self from others and as a personal defense against anxiety. I enjoyed being visible in this context, although my nervousness before the event is what prompted Peter to write the poem about me that appears on the dedication page. The 1988 art exhibition that was part of the Organization Behavior and Development Group Meeting was followed by another exhibit at The Actors Institute in New York City in 1997, which included my thirty-two Poem Portraits.

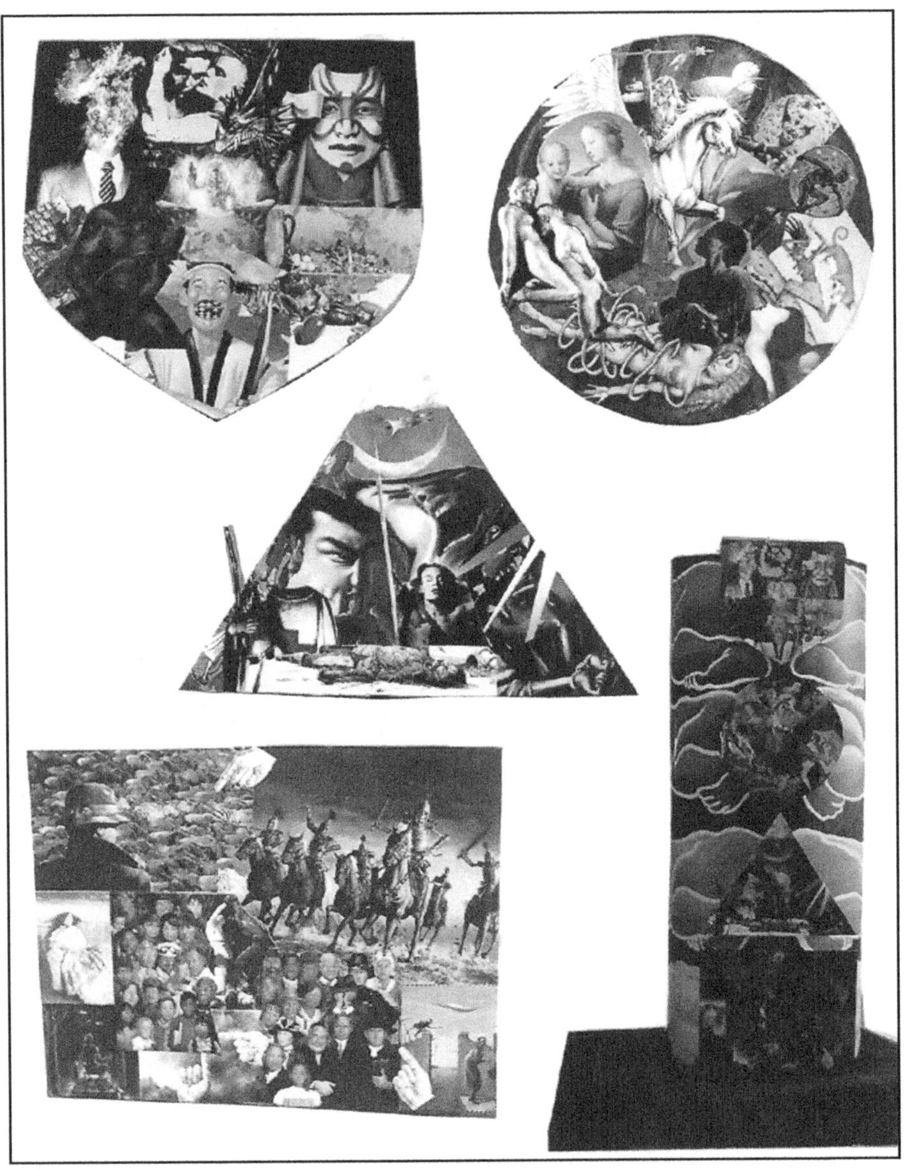

Image 18: Shields from my "Totem and Taboo Revisited" exhibit at GWU, 1988.

Image 19: A totem pole constructed with masks was part of my 32 Voices exhibit at The Actors Institute in New York, 1997.

Fast forward about eight years: After working at two other medical centers in OD, I was hired as the Chief Learning Officer at Maimonides and eventually promoted to Vice President of Organization Development.

I was gratified to be sitting around the boardroom table discussing strategy and direction with other executives. But even with an exalted title, I felt undeserving, as if I were riding their coattails. I practiced using humor, preparing contributions, and being in the moment, but none of this felt natural. I also took on leading a department, despite the misgivings based on my OT debacle, and not surprisingly, never felt as accomplished as my peers. I did enjoy the expanded responsibility, yet I didn't seem to flourish with heightened visibility. I didn't see a vice president when I looked in the mirror, only a little girl forced to hide her sadness and a flawed adult terrified of repeating the failure of her first job as a manager. I was also disappointed in myself that being anointed vice president didn't magically erase my fears and shame at feeling less than. I thought I had finally arrived, but apparently all parts of me weren't on board.

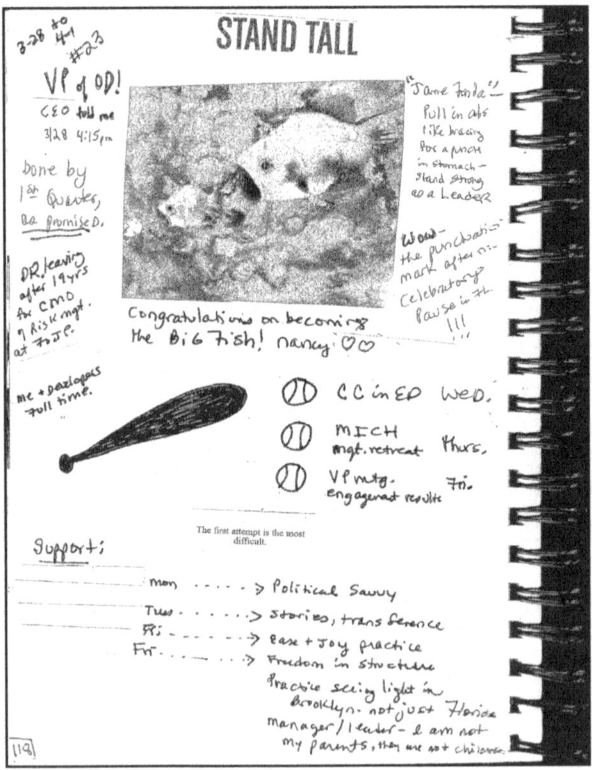

Image 20: "Stand Tall," my promotion to VP of OD.

If I'd had the confidence to express myself in person, people might have taken notice. Because I didn't want to disappoint people at work, I went from one therapist to another to get insight and support as I experienced intense anxiety in the face of my intense determination. I tried many approaches: spiritual, body work, inner child, psychodrama, grief counseling, short-term, long-term—all helped some, but none resolved my underlying pain from "IT." During a session with a somatic therapist I was seeing to help me acclimate to my new career, she told me, "Don't wait (weight) for the world to see you." She said I was gaining weight as protection to keep me grounded, but it kept me from fulfilling my potential. She cautioned that there will always be people who will treat me as if I'm not good enough. "Projection," she said, "is the search for recognition from others, which will always leave you feeling disconnected. Invisibility is pulling in energy, blending like a cake. Instead, you should talk to yourself the way you wished your dad had talked to you years ago." Encouraging me further, she improvised, "You're damn smart, Kathryn. Let's see how you engage this challenge. Stand up for yourself and what you know. Don't take personally how your mom withdrew and protected herself by doing art." The body worker motivated me to realize it's my turn to become the vibrant, successful person she saw (2; 29).

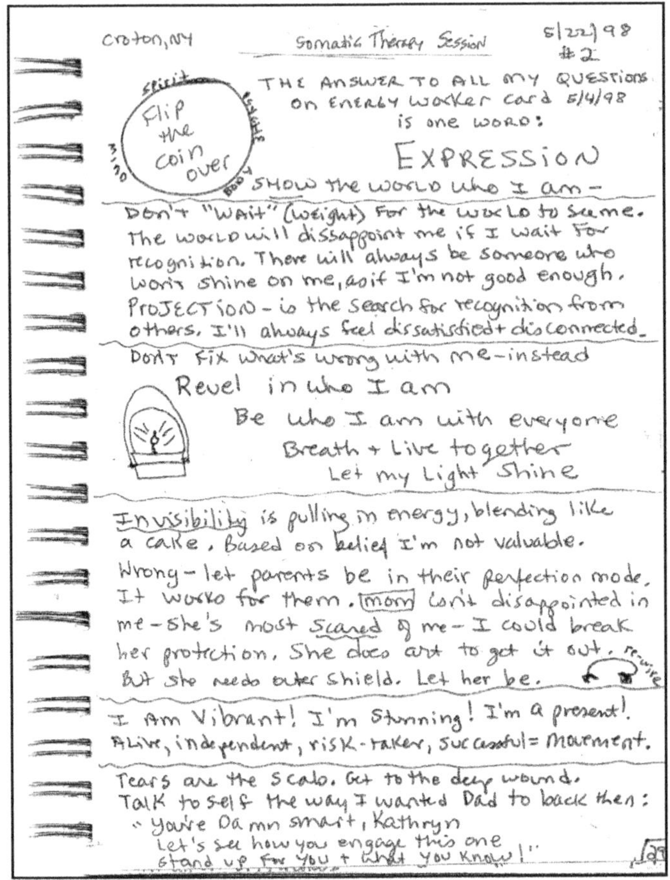

Croton, NY — Somatic Therapy Session — 5/22/98 #2

Flip the coin over
Spirit
Mind
Body

THE ANSWER TO ALL MY QUESTIONS on ENERGY WORKER card 5/4/98 is one WORD:

EXPRESSION

SHOW the WORLD who I am –

DON'T "WAIT" (weight) for the WORLD to see me. The WORLD will dissappoint me if I wait for recognition. There will always be someone who won't shine on me, as if I'm not good enough. PROJECTION – is the search for recognition from others. I'll always feel dissatisfied + disconnected.

DON'T FIX what's wrong with me – instead
Revel in who I am
Be who I am with everyone
Breath + Live together
Let my Light Shine

Invisibility is pulling in energy, blending like a cake. Based on belief I'm not valuable. Wrong – let parents be in their perfection mode. It works for them. Mom isn't disappointed in me – she's most scared of me – I could break her protection. She does art to get it out. But she needs outer shield. Let her be. re-wire

I Am Vibrant! I'm Stunning! I'm a present!
Alive, independent, risk-taker, successful = Movement.

Tears are the scabs. Get to the deep wound.
Talk to self the way I wanted Dad to back then:
"You're Damn smart, Kathryn
Let's see how you engage this one
stand up for you + what you know!"

29

Image 21: Advice and mirroring from my somatic therapy session.

Years later, when my beloved boss, mentor, and think partner at Maimonides received numerous awards, I lamented privately that I did not get the public recognition I yearned for. Once I was no longer working at this medical center, another therapist, a grief counselor, helped me see the futility of thinking I would get recognition when I was constantly hiding myself. She asked, "How could you be anything other than a seeker and achiever when you never conceived of another role for yourself?" This reminded me of the insightful—and painful—feedback I received once from a colleague at Mount Sinai early in my new career in

OD: "People are bewildered by your lack of confidence and ultimately let down by your lack of leadership" (8; 16).

Looking back farther for clues about invisibility, I found observations from my two sisters in my journals. Keep in mind, when I refer to them in this memoir, I am not speaking for them beyond what I've noted in my journals and what we have discussed. We grew up with the same parents, but everyone's lived experience is different. Robin wrote her own memoir and mentioned both Karen and me factually in a similar way. Their perspectives are, of course, important because they knew me when I was captain of the cheerleaders and president of Girls Club in high school. My sister Karen always felt my radiance attracted people to me and made me a natural leader. But even then, I felt uncomfortable with the inevitable conflicts when the teachers expected me, as captain, to remind my fellow classmates they shouldn't go out drinking and partying. Lisa once said, "You have clear heart vision, as if you have nerve endings exposed on your skin, the way you see what people feel, need, and want before they do" (2; 25). That helped me see my sensitivity in a positive light, and also, to see the need to develop healthy boundaries. In the process of having empathy for people who were in pain, and whose pain was projected to others as abuse, I would often lose myself. I had to develop the practice of staying grounded to observe the pain they were causing me and others.

During the year I was turning fifty and seeking to free myself (I called it "Kathryn's Jubilee") I was helped by a course and workbook, "Financial Freedom," from my sister Karen's spiritual community, which she shared with me and Lisa. I thought it would be fun for the three sisters, all in different states, to talk about it on a conference call. But Karen and Lisa said it made them anxious, so we spoke one-on-one, just as we'd interacted with our parents, which turned out to be a blessing. Each admitted to comparing themselves with me. Karen said she pulled back and felt "less than" when faced with my full-on enthusiasm. Lisa admitted that, at first, she judged herself for not going as quickly through the material. Then, she judged me for probably not doing it as deeply as she had. I got mad and said, "See, that quote from Nelson Mandela is a crock. As he said, 'As we let our own light shine, we unconsciously give other people permission to do the same.' But when I am my full self, it doesn't create permission in you, it creates envy and insecurity." Karen said if I could just come from love and forgive them for their feelings, she'd feel better. I loved them both and tried to process what they were saying, as my sisters and I know each other's truths intimately. But I concluded that I needed to separate more from family and protect myself. Otherwise, their feedback would reinforce my belief that I wasn't entitled to let my light shine (4; 133). Or to put it another way, I couldn't be fully visible if they didn't approve of me 100 percent.

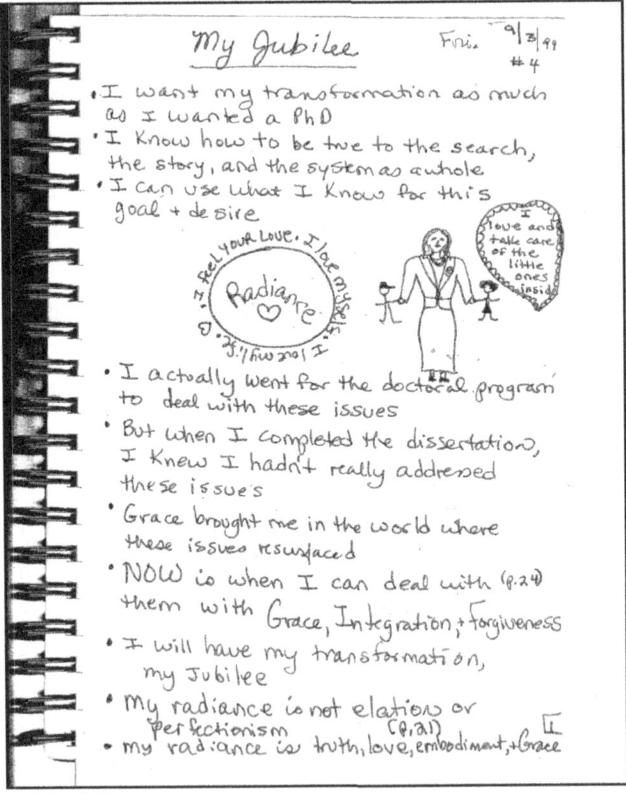

My Jubilee   Fri. 9/3/99 #4

• I want my transformation as much as I wanted a PhD
• I know how to be true to the search, the story, and the system as a whole
• I can use what I know for this goal + desire

• I actually went for the doctoral program to deal with these issues
• But when I completed the dissertation, I knew I hadn't really addressed these issues
• Grace brought me in the world where these issues resurfaced
• NOW is when I can deal with (p.24) them with Grace, Integration, + forgiveness
• I will have my transformation, my Jubilee
• My radiance is not elation or perfectionism (p.21)
• my radiance is truth, love, embodiment, + Grace

Image 22: "My Jubilee," turning fifty.

An early psychotherapist I saw for help when I was in transition from OT to OD said, "You should have been encouraged to be a child, when you were young." But then he saw how my caretaking in the family was both needed and denied. I strove to get past this tendency when it showed itself at work, not always successfully (2; 26). Also, I didn't want to be seen (as I saw my mom) as self-centered when I was visible, or to be visible for my flaws when I was inarticulate, overweight, less than graceful, or not acting skillfully. Learning about narcissism in families revealed the real origin of my predicament: the *double* double bind I found myself in while in grade school and high school. First, I wasn't to be better than my mom, but I wasn't to be deficient or needing anything, especially her help. Second, my dad just wanted me to make him look good but would never help me when I was struggling to be perfect, because he couldn't tolerate process. Note: I later went on to be an expert in process, learning from my mentor who wrote extensively about process wisdom. At this time, I recognized the extremely narrow range of acceptable behaviors I was allowed as a child, similar to what my studies later revealed about women in leadership in patriarchal organizations. Still, insight and awareness weren't sufficient to let me resolve my issues and move on, as it seemed my colleagues were able to do. However, I had times over the year of moving through achievements and terrors with action. Borrowing from the poem portrait "I Just Go and Do," I saw myself doing it too, in my way, in my journal.

I Just Go and Do

I don't think of my work as a practice
my practice is really me, I just go and do.
I'm about helping people and organizations
be who they can be, get to the essence of who they are
and carry that with them where ever they go—
that's when we'll have the most productive organizations.

Making a cultural shift is an ongoing opportunity.
I'm your partner, oppressed on two fronts—race and gender.
I just do me. Innately good. I resist the way we're taught.
Part of being a woman of color is how we pass on tradition
and look at patterns. I am willing to be outside of the box.
I feel our field grew up out of a white male model.

Part of who I am as a black person in this society
is that I never trusted my competence, my intelligence.
I've never written because I never wanted to be critiqued by white people.
But now I got a lot of things I want to say to young kids
about choices, about what taking responsibility for self is.

People who are change agents need to work our own stuff.
The diversity lens requires a fundamental commitment
to ongoing personal, not professional, development.
I was afraid of water, now I'm a scuba diver.
I was afraid of heights, I learned to ski.
There is no short cut to doing personal work.

I literally did not think I'd survive my 29th year
I was killing myself trying to be something I couldn't be—
I couldn't be white. I couldn't be a man.
I couldn't be a whole bunch of things
these organizations were requiring me to do.
I don't think we were put on this earth to do that.

There are like 50 million different things that guide me
somehow interwoven in a way that makes sense to me.
Personal change thinking and stuff that crosses boundaries
from individuals, groups, and systems. I trust my intuition
will never fail me to the degree I can't recover.

What's meaningful to me is when a year after a workshop
I hear somebody tell me all the different ways
they are seeing the world interacting differently.
I'm moving on to the wiser, more fully developed woman.
My success is the peace I feel inside and some significance about impact.

Image 23: Poem Portrait: "I Just Go and Do."

Image 24: Journal entry for "I Just Go and Do."

Losing Sight

Don't let what you can't do blind you to what you can.
—Helen Keller

As I progressed through my doctoral program, I started noticing flashing lights sometimes while I was reading and had difficulty seeing at night. A concerned eye doctor sent me to one of the foremost specialists in retinal disorders. He diagnosed me with Retinitis Pigmentosa, a progressive disease leading to blindness—with no treatment. Although usually inherited, no one in my family tested positive. Luckily, because I had late onset (most patients are completely blind by college age), the specialist predicted I wouldn't be totally blind for another thirty-five years, by which time I would be seventy. Though devastated, I also felt relieved, thinking at least I could finish my career.

Over the years, the disease seemed a metaphor for some of my issues: not keeping perspective, difficulty with seeing the truth in dark times, tunnel vision, and of course, visibility itself. It is true, I was eventually designated as legally blind because I had such a narrow field of vision. If I dropped something, I had to scan the floor systematically until the item came into view. Without peripheral vision, I frequently bumped into people because they seemed to arise out of nowhere, triggering my startle reflex. I also had night blindness and difficulty seeing in low-light situations. Limited depth perception made going down stairs treacherous. Once getting dressed in the early morning for an important presentation with high visibility, my coworker came up to me on stage afterward to say, "You were great, but did you know you had on two different color and style shoes?!" If I could think on my feet, I would have said, "I was hoping someone would notice," employing my dad's type of humor. But as I learned from a man whose son has a severe eye disorder, "Things may be difficult, but not impossible" (31; 138). That is now my mantra.

A close colleague used to reassure me that my growing insights about myself and others would compensate for my degrading outer vision. That may be true, but it's scary to wonder what I will do if and when the bottom drops out and I am totally in the dark. What really disturbs me about going completely blind is that others will be able to see me, but I won't be able to see them. It's like a cosmic joke that I'll be visible to others because of my disability and not for my talents and gifts (13; 63 and 26; 57). It's not that I won't learn to compensate; I have familiarized myself with mobility techniques and functional adaptations and have read many biographies of visually impaired people. It just seems like an ironic punishment for my ambivalence around visibility as a leader. People will know "that blind lady" on the bus, walking to the market, or on the arm of her husband at a restaurant. I'll be sure to look at their face when they talk even if I can't see them, hold out my hand in anticipation of shaking theirs, and try to show them I'm still a smart person. People have such fears of those who can't see. It's as if they have a cognitive disability as well and the disease is contagious. As I wrote about the totem pole, I will become taboo.

I am wholeheartedly grateful I have retained central vision, even at less than 5 percent. And just last year a new retinal researcher determined I may be able to continue to function for another ten years without being totally blind. Also, a new genetic test revealed the gene that has caused my disease (32; 57). Even though my parents didn't appear to have passed it on, and the parallels between my retinal symptoms and psychological issues are still apt, I am glad to know, as they say about the "Three Cs" of addiction recovery for families, "I didn't cause it, I can't control it, and I can't cure it." Still, I could cope even better if I knew there was some authority overseeing the universe and monitoring our afflictions with a checklist. They would look at my scorecard and say: "Yep, she's got blindness, is getting old, and has been miserable for most of her life. She's been hit by a car while walking twice. She still struggles with her weight and managing her environment. Check, check, check. No need to add cancer or heart disease. She'll just have to be careful not to have more accidents. That's it for her. Next!" (16; 42).

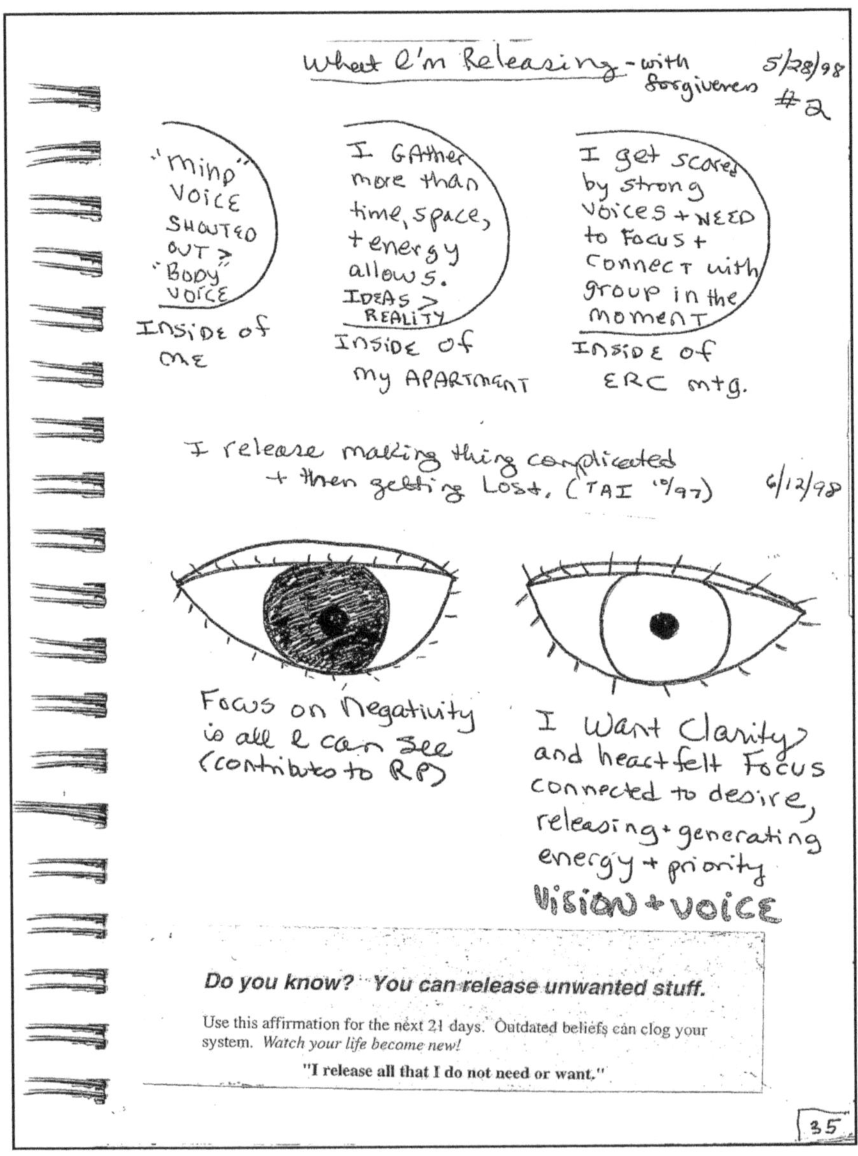

Image 25: Psychological issues reflected in my eye disease.

Organization Development

Why spend the majority of your professional life working on tolerable stuff for acceptable clients when . . . you can spend your days working on exciting things for interesting people?
—David Maister

What thrilled me about my second career as an OD consultant was that I discovered it based on my lived experience. In contrast, my first career I chose based on vocational tests. In high school I'd been a wreck not knowing what I should do, so at one point my mom took me to the Illinois Institute of Technology in Chicago for a battery of vocational tests to find the answer—as if the answer was to be found in an exhaustive set of multiple-choice test results and not through a gentle process of self-discovery. But after hearing the term "occupational therapy" for the first time, I found a mental hospital nearby and volunteered for the summer in their OT department. Besides helping sort tiles and do craft projects, I enjoyed and related easily to the patients. The first day, I got to sit in on a lecture on Erik Erickson's model of adult development—and I loved it. OT was a creative medical field—a sort of watered-down version of being a doctor and an artist. As such, it allowed me to emulate but not compete with my parents—a delicate balance that was always the key to surviving my childhood. Having a major in mind, I applied to the University of Wisconsin where I got to have a small home base in OT within the huge campus of forty-five thousand undergraduates.

It's not that OT was wrong for me, it's just that over time I became more interested helping leaders in healthcare than providing treatment to patients. OT is a creative health career that helps people of all ages and disabilities to function. It had a very structured approach for teaching it, and I felt well prepared to treat patients once I started working. Through my specialty in psychiatry, I answered a deep question I had, "*How sick is sick?*" The range from psychotic or suicidal to borderline personality disorder or mania became clear to me through the influx of patients to the hospital. In order to offer programs that met their needs, I created a group for the lowest functioning patients, called Directive Group Therapy, and then an interdisciplinary treatment program with the doctors, nurses, and social workers to address the whole unit's diverse needs. While writing a book explaining this new approach to mental health treatment, I finished my degree program to further my research, administrative, teaching, and clinical foundation. All these inputs made me a competent professional and innovative—if still invisible—leader.

What I didn't realize at the time was that much of what I was doing intuitively to create culture change was part and parcel of the field of organization behavior and management. People tend to be drawn to being a practitioner, as an OD consultant, because they understand in their bones that processes are needed to build teams, deal with conflict, and manage effectively. What really struck me and led to my new career was observing a nurse leader who everyone felt was toxic. When he finally left his position, nothing changed. I couldn't believe it. Why didn't it make a difference when the one person who seemed responsible for staff discontent was no longer there to cause problems? I later learned it was because an organization's culture is more of a determining factor than personality, strategy, or credentials. These are just the types of topics that are researched and studied intensely in my new field; I had signed up to be a lifelong learner of systems, change, and leadership.

Since my earlier interest was about dysfunction, my new question was: "*How do you influence and build healthy environments in which people can work?*" Instead of being the therapist treating patients, I wanted to stay in healthcare but become essentially the therapist to the staff who were treating patients, either directly or indirectly. That meant I designed interventions at the individual, team, department, and organizational level. Over the course of twenty-five years, I was a leader in four major medical centers, taught in five universities, published extensively, and became an expert in culture change, all before I fully understood the organizational culture of narcissism in my own family.

Of course, my journals reveal other aspects of the work that both challenged me and provided gratification. I felt doing OD was helping people and the organization, while at the same time healing myself. The work is about developing strengths in others consistent with their role, and to turn challenges, like my tentativeness, into a leadership strength. The OD practitioner's main tool is "use of self," and like other tools, it's important to keep it sharp and know how to use it. Because OD deals directly with conflicts, self-awareness as a leader, and becoming effective teams, it was in direct contrast to the norms of my family. My parents did not want feedback on their behavior, our family did not function as a team, and conflicts were avoided because expressing emotions were not allowed. Thus, when I encountered clients who were resistant and reminded me of my family, I lost confidence and a sense of certainty. But when I had clients who were eager to learn about themselves and be more effective, I was energized, resourceful, and engaged. I was like the woman I studied and called the "Cheshire Cat Consultant," who has boundless curiosity and "knows more than she shows."

The Cheshire Cat Consultant

The cat woman
can't contain her curiosity
moving inside and outside
every system and country she can find.

Pulled into new situations
by the dangling allure of
just wanting to know
what is it like?

What's a prison like?
Community mental health center?
A school? Steel mill? Airlines?
Computers? Schizophrenics? Entrepreneurs?

What's a start-up company like?
What's downsizing like?
What would it be like to help
a successful company become middle-aged?

Entering each organization
like a cat let out of a bag
racing around, loving the risks
high places and tangled yarns.

Preening with pride
as she turns tough issues around
with a delicate touch
for mutuality and major impact.

Playful in the sun light
savvy, competent, powerful
innovative, collaborative
passionate about all she's learned.

Writing now her many stories
styled and valued as a woman
grinning behind the Cheshire cat smile
that knows even more than she shows.

Image 26: Poem Portrait, "The Cheshire Cat Consultant."

During my first job as an internal OD consultant at Mount Sinai Medical Center, I felt like an apprentice because I was making my academic knowledge come alive with real departments and dilemmas. Our team was blessed with a core group of external consultants who were experienced and available to mentor us. Thus, I felt safe to learn and grow one case at a time, receiving valuable feedback just for me and my situations. For example, one consultant urged me not to identify with others who expressed my shadow. She observed in one group I was leading that some of the participants were unusually angry, and I let their expression go on too long, at the expense of the goals of the meeting. I didn't feel shamed or judged, but grateful to get nuanced feedback I could immediately put into practice (2; 27).

Another consultant responded to my fear of doing performance appraisals with the following advice: "You don't have to be perfect to evaluate others, but you do need to keep a boundary between your issues and theirs." At another time he said, "When you are uncomfortable, it is important for you not to show your insides to the group. Instead, focus on the needs of the people in the room. That is your job" (2; 27). Clearly, I had to learn to manage boundaries, which wasn't easy, but I could see the benefit in doing so. Because I so valued the exceptional work of these OD consultants, I was motivated to become as skilled and effective as possible. Coaching from one of the consultants validated that I had grown so much in three years and was valued for my artistic approach to consulting.

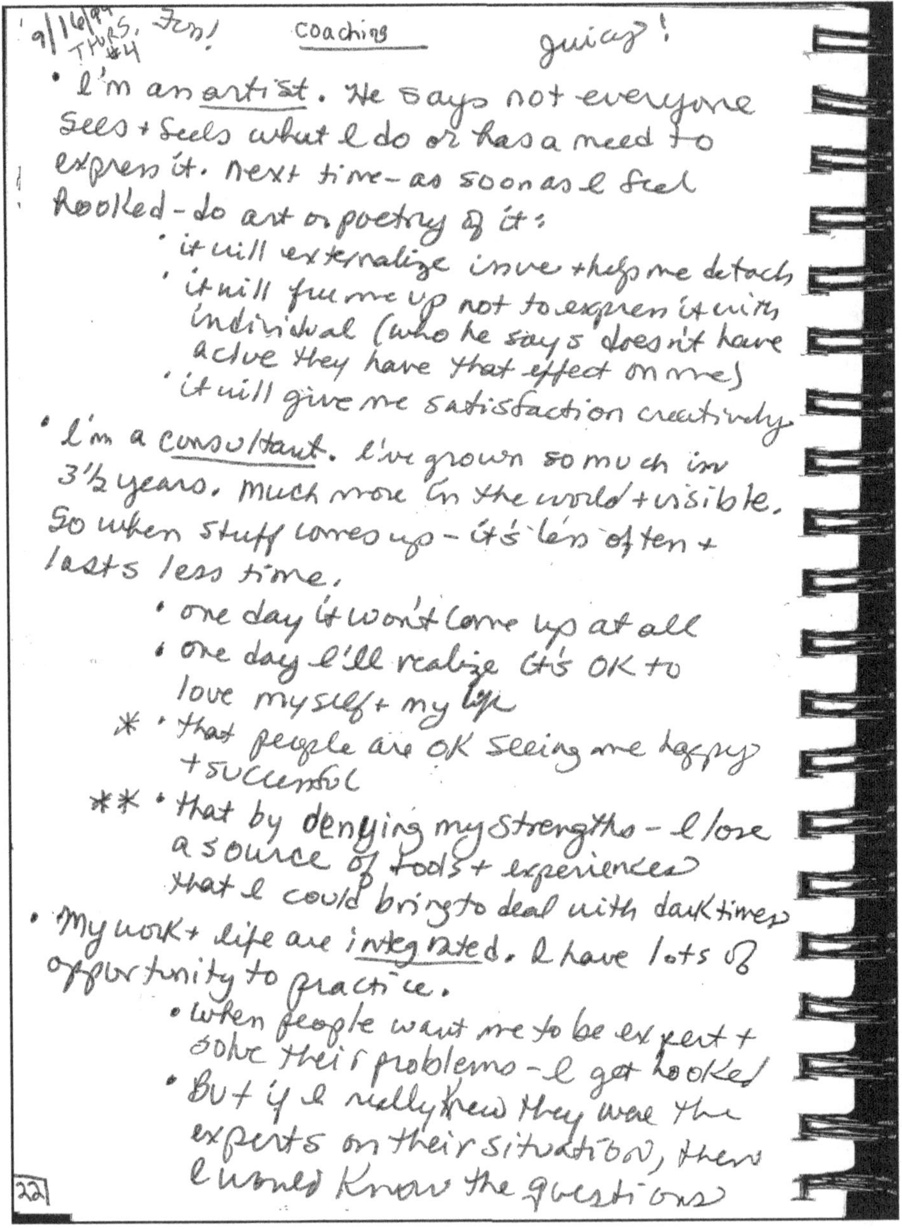

9/16/99 THURS. #4 Fun! coaching juicy!

- I'm an artist. He says not everyone sees + feels what I do or has a need to express it. Next time — as soon as I feel hooked — do art or poetry of it:
  - it will externalize issue + help me detach
  - it will free me up not to express it with individual (who he says doesn't have a clue they have that effect on me)
  - it will give me satisfaction creatively
- I'm a consultant. I've grown so much in 3½ years. Much more in the world + visible. So when stuff comes up — it's less often + lasts less time.
  - one day it won't come up at all
  - one day I'll realize it's OK to love myself + my life
  - * that people are OK seeing me happy + successful
  - ** that by denying my strengths — I lose a source of tools + experiences that I could bring to deal with dark times
- My work + life are integrated. I have lots of opportunity to practice.
  - when people want me to be expert + solve their problems — I get hooked
  - But if I really knew they were the experts on their situation, then I would know the questions

22

Image 27: Affirmation from an external consultant coaching session.

Although my introspective bent was appreciated, one consultant wanted me to focus less on learning about myself and focus more on taking action on behalf of clients. It turns out most of OD is more structured and superficial, by design, than the psychodynamic approach I absorbed both from therapy and from my previous work as an occupational therapist with psychiatric patients (7; 20). I was encouraged to "stay above the water line" and not always swim in the unconscious origins of behavior in my interventions. As I progressed in my career, I saw that the good thing about culture change was that it trumped individual psychodynamics, making me stimulated more by how to change the system and less by how to analyze myself (19; 35). My journal quoted my therapist telling me I was perfectly matched to learn and grow with the institution. I could be a teacher and mirror and finally realize I didn't have to know it all first—I could learn through experience and reflection. The clearer I was on the purpose and possibilities inherent in each meeting, the easier it was to keep my fears and tentativeness out of the way.

My Achilles' heel was telling colleagues I trusted about my anxieties when challenged by a power struggle, bully, or ambiguous situation. I was advised over and over not to reveal my weaknesses at work because they would be used against me (20; 16). And they were. The more I was stressed, the more I had difficulty containing myself, leaking my emotions. For example, if I shared with a coworker that I was worried our design might not be as effective as we wanted, even after it turned out well, the next thing I knew my reputation would be tarnished in that labor management group. My weakness would be noted more than the actual results. It was one thing to do that early in my career, but quite another when I was a senior leader. One thing I discovered on my own that helped me was realizing "I only have problems with problemed people" (20; 24). Therefore, on a good day, when I was struggling to figure out how to handle a complex situation, if I felt triggered, I learned to pause and reflect on the other person's dynamics and motives. It really wasn't all about me and my inadequacies. But at other times, when my unease showed on my face, I undermined my authority.

Still, I continued to improve and grow. I appreciated when a colleague felt I was worth his investment in pointing out ways I could be even more effective. For example, part of my role was to be a trainer, teaching skills and addressing issues in various venues. My default approach was to design beautiful workshops yet stay too wedded to my expectations on how they would play out, rather than being in the moment with the people and processes in the room. Over time, I mastered that tendency with two strategies. One was to always collaborate with a more extroverted partner who could be more spontaneous while I held the structure in mind (17; 66). The other was to learn what my training partners referred to as "the biscuit approach" or "force feeding" the information (18; 15 and 21; 79). This advice helped me break down the skills into component parts, rather than staying conceptual or vague, and let the learners take in the biscuit of information at their own level and pace. Since I was frequently on the faculty teaching graduate students, these strategies helped me even in an academic setting where the expectations for learning were higher. I was excited to realize people are people and the rules for engagement are similar in classrooms, programs, and interactive presentations.

Sometimes my trusted partners said I had two tendencies reversed and helped me to see what they were so I could shift my approach. It is typical in group dynamics to have those who try to dominate or distract. However, instead of keeping control as the leader, I too often would go with the flow. Then, when some people needed airtime to express a view or explore an issue, I could come across as judgmental instead of curious. My training partner said to think of training as a creative situation with many possibilities. My growing edge was to take more risks, think on my feet, and ask the group questions they could think through with their own answers. I needed to ground myself less on the details of the design and more on realizing no one knows what

I know or where I am going, and to learn to have confidence in that (17; 66).

The other reversal was when to be inside-out or outside-in. For instance, I was advised that when working with colleagues, say in a meeting, I could be direct rather than "perspective taking." In that situation I should own my expertise by saying what I think and know, going from inside myself to the outside group. Yet, when evaluating how well a retreat or meeting went, I could look at outcomes, behavior, and what others said. It was not the time to go into my "anxiety closet" of doubt and worry. Stay outside-in (8; 63).

So often at work I sabotaged myself by letting fear overtake desire, which led to dissatisfaction and concern I'd be punished for denial and avoidance. Instead, I wrote that my survival guide needed to include two strategies: First, to go through the middle of issues, not backtrack or go around them, and then speak my truth. By taking risks, I was more likely to get satisfaction and reward than from playing it safe. Second, I needed to hold myself with compassion each time I went back to fear, to think of meditation as a metaphor for what to do (8; 63). Meditating is not the absence of thoughts, but the opportunity to be gentle with yourself again and again, letting thoughts flow in and out. I needed to stay present to the reality of change and the magic of possibility (8; 25, 41).

I started seeing signs of this kind of inner shift in many ways. For the first time I could see my colleagues' flaws, which helped me accept my own. That made me realize how much I actually did have to offer as a leader. In another example, the therapist during my dissertation used to tell me that life gets simpler when you know yourself. Now I was seeing this was true because I did know what I wanted. I wanted a house in the woods to write and nourish my soul. I wanted prosperity so I could travel, have money for retirement, and not have to worry in emergencies. I reframed my issues as a spiritual journey and not things that needed therapy and fixing. I took the brakes off and showed my Signature Presence.

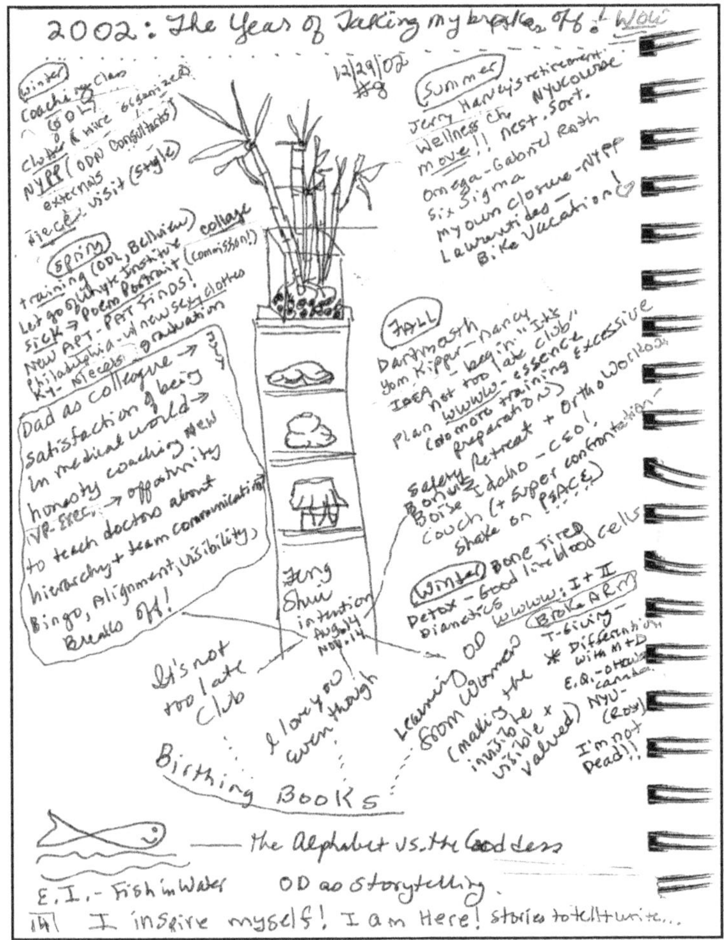

Image 28: "The Year of Taking My Brakes Off."

Procrastination

You cannot cross the sea merely by standing and staring at the water.

—Rabindranath Tagore

When I was in sixth grade, I couldn't write papers until my parents were asleep. I had so much anxiety deciding what to write, I'd wait until the night before the paper was due to get started. Then, with the rest of the house in total silence and darkness, I would sit at my dark wood desk with my little lamp shining on the white pad of lined paper and try to write neatly yet quickly before my hand cramped. Only then at the last minute could I battle my demons and eventually risk demonstrating my inadequacies. My need to please the teachers and not disappoint my parents could be relied on to override my thrashing around and belief I couldn't do the assignment. By morning, the paper would be done enough to turn it in. Sure, I was exhausted and didn't even know or care what I wrote. What was important was I made the deadline without getting executed for a no-show.

In high school I pretty much continued the pattern of procrastination, trying to turn in at the last minute the dreaded "junior theme." Mine was a research project on Walt Whitman. With so many expectations on how to proceed, I never really read his poetry and instead reviewed just enough of the criticism to construct a passable paper. I was glad to get it over with. Asking for help didn't seem to be an option. My parents, while expecting me to excel, never signed up to help with schoolwork.

When my mom took me for my driver's test, she was amazed to witness my lack of confidence and utter dread of not passing the first time. It was as if she was watching an intriguing animal at the zoo. Luckily, I passed, but Mom never concerned herself with my seemingly unnecessary emotional turmoil. Karen was seeing a psychiatrist at that time, so I secretly made an appointment to see him. I walked the six miles to his office in the next suburb, a distance normally only attempted by car or bus, but I persisted on foot. It was the farthest I had ever ventured alone, and without my parents' knowledge or permission. My determination reminded me of the first time I extended my limits by walking two miles home from first grade alone. I was only six and yet had this plan brewing for a while. I would watch carefully from the bus window and was pretty sure I could find my way and prove to myself I could be secretly independent. But this test of my character gave me more than I bargained for. Six blocks from home, by the big hill, a shady character in an unfamiliar car rolled down the window and asked, "Little girl, would you like a ride home?" I knew I had never seen him in our neighborhood and though he may have been harmless, I trusted my instincts——and my rapidly beating heart—to say no and keep walking.

Back to my secret therapy session: I was so nervous for being a bad girl by not admitting to my parents how upset their perfect daughter was, that I didn't really take in the drab waiting room or his relatively empty office. Once there, sitting in his beige jacket without a tie, slumped in his swivel chair, he seemed utterly bored by my perfectionism. With eyes closed, he finally said, "There is nothing wrong with you, you're fine. Go be a teenager." Feeling absolved for my actions up until that day, I asked earnestly, "But what about tomorrow?" He offered no solace and I left feeling alone and not understood.

Once in college, my fellow classmates would be perplexed during my presentations, when my usual pleasant demeanor devolved into hand wringing and isolation. They couldn't understand why I worked so hard when I seemed smart enough to exert less effort and enjoy their camaraderie more. My angst was visible and embarrassing, but it was only the tip of the iceberg. My terror of failure was more compelling and demanded my immediate attention. I had one OT professor who felt empathy for my predicament and, taking time to talk with me, helped me lower the temperature on my dread. Basically, she helped me see that I expected myself to be directive like my mom and authoritative like my dad. Yet, I had a naturally facilitative manner that I dismissed as weak and unacceptable. Although she assured me a different style could be just as effective, it would take decades of practice before I was able to own my facilitative style at work. By then, I also had to add "backbone" to my repertoire.

What finally cured me of procrastination was completing my dissertation, after all the coursework and comprehensive exams were done. The requirements for the program consisted of an extensive written proposal prior to conducting the research. The proposal was based on an exhaustive literature review and demonstrated mastery of the proposed methodology. With my research proposal accepted, I then had to implement the data collection, data analysis, and discussion of its significant contribution to the field. With this, I couldn't procrastinate: the work would take years to complete, obviously not something that could be done the night or week or even month before. In addition, every doctoral student had a faculty committee to monitor his or her progress on a regular basis. Finally, with people who cared about what I was doing, had a stake in me being successful, and had experience with helping students with the types of problems encountered by this rite of passage, I thrived, exceeding both their and my expectations. I am sure my high school teachers would never have believed, I became a researcher and overcame the last-minute antics of my youth. My parents never understood what I accomplished, so at last I freed myself up to just do what I set out to do.

At work in my second career as an OD professional in healthcare, I had trepidation when challenged by new types of assignments. While I knew I was strong academically, I was challenged to bridge knowledge from theory to practice. But I had strategies I'd developed that I could adapt to the healthcare environment. Setting my own deadlines gave me a sense of calm and control (16; 52). Then, I gave myself permission to ask for help, especially as soon as work was assigned or when I felt myself wanting to avoid any part of it because I lacked clarity (11; 89). I had enough self-knowledge about my approach that I no longer tried to write an outline first or have the main point clear before I began. If I just entered the void, eventually I would see connections and figure out how to proceed. Obvious to me was my growing confidence based on past success. I had comfort in having a team of colleagues and mentors who were a support, and I had lessened my perfectionistic strivings. I had actually worked through my earlier angst and could rely on myself to set meaningful goals and meet them. Now I could just dive in, and, like the subject of the Poem Portrait in Image 29, "swim with the sharks" (14; 103).

The Woman Who Swims with the Sharks

I just get out and do it.
I swim with the sharks.
If you want to catch me, come on
'Cause it's a business on the run.

Tracking energy, trusting the process
I provide a presence, a being self, a real self.
The artist doing oil paintings
Stepping back to see what is already there.

I dance the risky dance,
I know how to play with the guys in ties
Toe to toe with a hug and a slug
I'm the compassionate bitch they love.

Don't think I'd do this if I wasn't good.
I get respect, I know my stuff
But I focus on yours
Because I know what the work is about.

And I love it. It's so much fun,
I almost hate to charge you. I'm like a magician.
I pull a quarter from under your ear.
I hear the unspoken, and see the hidden.

Every time I show up
I put a slot in race and gender.
I know the games under my skin
But it still hurts, very sad.

So I move, I do what is needed
But sure would love a man
To share my work and roll over and say
"Honey, what about if we did this..?"

Instead, I'm like a dumb boxer,
A practitioner and that's all I want to do,
Not the hired help, surprise, surprise!
It's the African American woman ME.

At home now, in another country,
Moving in and out of systems,
Where they love that I'm one of them
And that I swim with the sharks.

Image 29: Poem Portrait, "The Woman Who Swims with the Sharks."

The only areas where I saw lingering procrastination were in my personal life. When I didn't feel fully motivated, for example, to exercise or deal with releasing my storage facility, I would delay and distract myself (21; 5). Once I felt frustrated enough with my lack of progress, I would either ask a friend to join me or figure out why I didn't want to do what I said I wanted to do. The other area was in waking up each morning. I am not a person who wakes up alert and eager to face the day. Every night I am immersed in vivid dreams and hate to leave that world abruptly. Even though I had early meetings and needed to be ready and on time, it was a struggle to switch gears. What I learned to do was wake up by using my writing process. I knew the fallacy of "marinating" when trying to write. Ideas did not get seasoned when "waiting until" they were ready. As I said, only diving in made a difference. Thus, I decided marinating in my dreams was counterproductive to my work goals and reputation. When necessary, I just told myself to dive into the day, and that worked (14; 103).

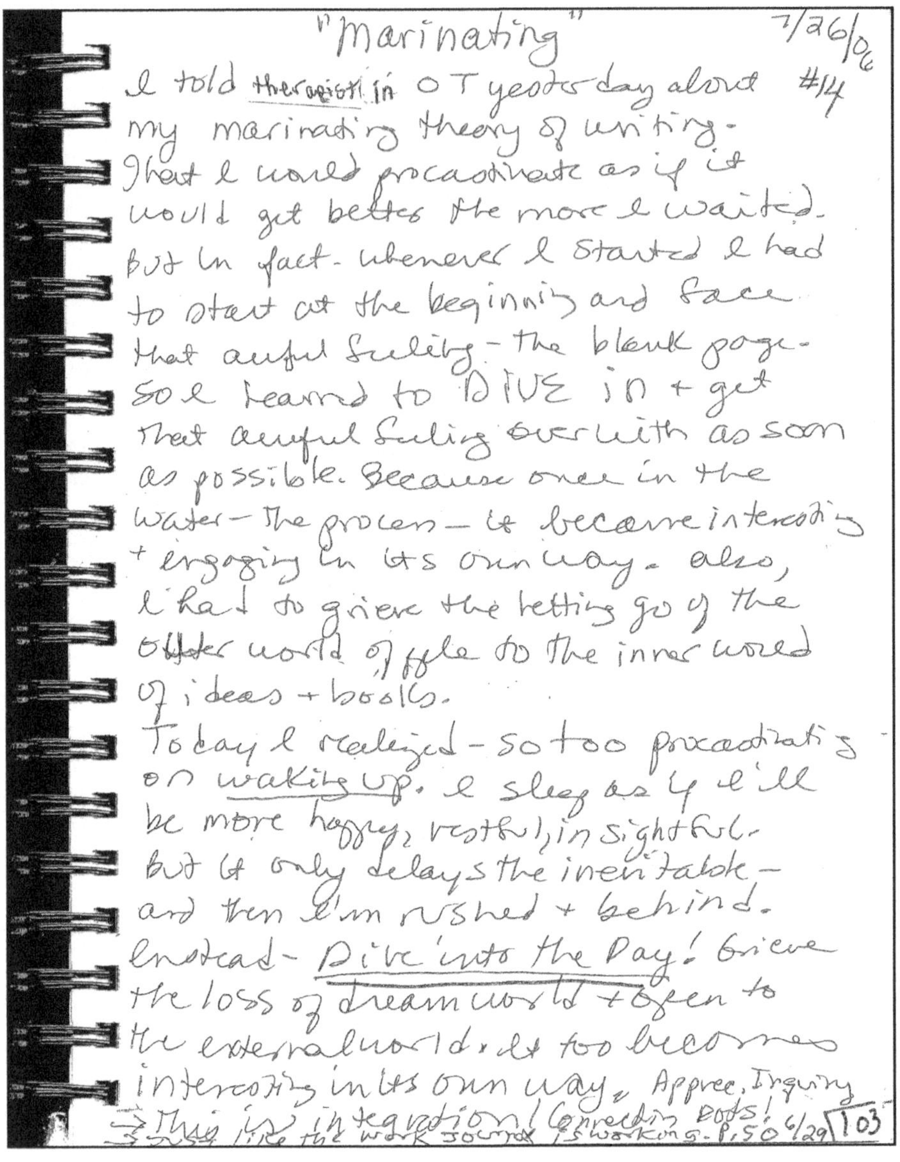

"Marinating" 7/26/06
#14
I told therapist in OT yesterday about
my marinating theory of writing.
That I would procrastinate as if it
would get better the more I waited.
But in fact - whenever I started I had
to start at the beginning and face
that awful feeling - the blank page.
So I learned to DIVE in + get
that awful feeling over with as soon
as possible. Because once in the
water - the process - it became interesting
+ engaging in its own way. also,
I had to grieve the letting go of the
outer world of pple to the inner world
of ideas + books.
Today I realized - so too procrastinating
on waking up. I sleep as if I'll
be more happy, restful, insightful.
But it only delays the inevitable -
and then I'm rushed + behind.
Instead - Dive into the Day! Grieve
the loss of dream world + open to
the external world. It too becomes
interesting in its own way. Apprec. Inquiry
→ This is integration! Connecting dots!
→ Just like the work journal is working. P.50 6/29 103

Image30: "Marinating," insights about procrastinating.

CHAPTER FOUR

Letting Go

Learn how to die and you will learn how to live.
—Mitch Albom, *Tuesdays with Morrie*

Ending Well

In late 1999 my therapist and I decided it was time to end, or at least pause. We had been working weekly (or as needed) since 1995. We started when I unraveled after completing my doctorate; somehow my topmost greatness was now my topmost grief, and it was bewildering to me why after such success I fell apart. I stopped my daily runs, put on weight (the same twenty pounds over and over, up and down the scale), and lived with an awful style for my hair. As planned, I had achieved my goals of taking myself seriously and being creative while meeting the academic requirements for my program. I had done it.

After such exquisite fullness and accomplishment, I should have expected—and accepted—a time to lie fallow in the void. Intellectually, I knew I was in a true transition, what William Bridges calls the "neutral zone" in between the ending of one phase and the beginning of the next. Being tired and lost made sense. I could have taken a vacation, volunteered in a garden, or attended a yoga retreat—any of these would have been a well-deserved reward. But I never voiced that desire because I imagined my father admonishing, "After all this work, you're going to do what?!" Just as I never voiced my desire to be a doctor when in college, I remained silent and lied to myself about what I really needed. Instead, I clung to the energy of completion throughout that year by pushing on and publishing an article on my work. Next, the OD Network asked me to design an all-day experiential workshop in the fall on my research about women in OD. This, too, was a success. I was riding high. One of the women in the study who attended wrote me a thank-you note. She said, "You are a woman in transition, tenuous, brave and strong. You delivered the workshop with gentleness, attentiveness, respect, and creativity." As with completing my doctorate, I felt seen for who I was, as well as grateful for the opportunity to offer my process and findings in a way that resonated with the women so deeply. They were clearly happy with me, my work, and the experience I provided them. But I couldn't stay happy with myself. Anyone else would be thrilled to have such a successful event and use it to further their career and next steps. However, I couldn't hold on to this positive feedback to help myself move forward. The nagging feeling that something was missing returned, as it always did. I found myself stuck and couldn't understand why.

Then, while walking down the street that summer, I couldn't stop hearing the voices of the women I had interviewed in my mind. For example, the woman who was "clear as a bell . . . knowing beginnings and endings are connected," and another who explained, "My life does not have meaning because of my work, but my work has meaning because my life has meaning. My own imminent approaching death . . . is always whispering, 'what has this day counted for?'" Inspired after seeing a one-woman show with my mother, I said to her spontaneously, "I would like to do that." She replied, uncharacteristically, that if I was serious, she would arrange an evening in her art studio in Chicago. I was shocked and excited. She invited her friends and clients. This was a big deal and it was really happening.

Never having been an actor, I hired a coach who helped me prepare and deliver my material. "The Poetry of Business" was a dream come true, with me reciting a half dozen vignettes, channeling the words and spirits of the women they represented. The words I wrote down from the enthusiastic audience included: shimmering, classy, eloquent, emotive, beautiful. Though I was determined to take in the praise, again, it was quickly forgotten because I couldn't believe words like these actually described me. I was a leaky vessel that couldn't hold a compliment. Each successive accomplishment filled me, only to quickly drain, reinforcing my crippling doubt that I deserved any of it or had actually achieved anything lasting at all.

The next day, more characteristically, my mom said, "What are you going to do next?" Of course, I was not allowed to bask in my glory; I had to top it. But I didn't know what was next, and I felt anxious and resentful, along with being paralyzed. Could I be both creative and practical in finding a way to support myself, like the dual focus I maintained for my course work? My rational mind said yes, but my psyche stopped me in my tracks. There was one thing I'd become an expert at—beating myself up. And though I knew it was neither creative nor practical, it was my go-to, my default, especially after I'd done something praiseworthy. I didn't have a next act, and I went home with my tail between my legs, discouraged and disappointed. The energy of the doctorate, the article, and the show was spent, because I couldn't hold onto any good feelings about myself. A concerned cousin, who was a psychotherapist herself, recommended I contact a therapist she knew in California who often worked with women over the phone. She thought we would connect due to our feminist, artistic, and psychological orientations—and we did.

I remember the therapist saying I was in "a tangle" and we would explore together how to "find the end of the yarn and weave a new fabric." The metaphor seemed apt, and we began the untangling with empathy and insights. Robyn Posin knew the knots I had tied myself in and how to loosen them. Meanwhile, Grace arrived—in the form of two calls out of the blue—to give me my next steps. First, one of the women in my study recommended me for a new program at Johns Hopkins University. With a team of three other women, we designed and delivered the first "Women, Leadership and Change" master's level certificate program. It was relevant to my background and interests, and the collaboration fit my interactive style. However, I couldn't live on the salary of a part-time faculty member. Once I acknowledged that fact out loud, I received a call from one of my doctoral committee mentors, recommending me for an OD consultant position at a large major medical center in New York City. I interviewed with the director of OD at Mount Sinai Medical Center, was offered the position, and negotiated a three-day workweek so I could finish teaching. Eventually, I went full-time and stayed there over eight years.

Having Robyn as a mirror helped me see my self-doubt for what it was—ungrounded in current reality and held over from my earliest parental programming. As the therapy helped me navigate these changes and address my issues as they arose, I became stronger and felt ready to fly solo. My confidence came from realizing I had internalized a major piece of work we did together. She helped me remember I had two parts that always needed to be heard and held: my big in-the-world self and my scared little ones inside who always say, "I can't." These were my light and my darkness, and they never go away, so they both needed tending (3; 80).

In preparation to end therapy, I drew in my journal a ripe fruit hanging from a tree, symbolizing the readiness of it to fall into my hand easily, not overripe and not needing to be pulled prematurely. The timing of our ending was, in my eyes, just right (3; 88). We reviewed milestones, reflected on sticky points, and anticipated future challenges. I would need to always protect the seedlings growing inside, keeping a "stay out" stance to prevent them from getting stepped on before they were strong enough to grow in their own soil. (See Image 31.) I expressed gratitude for Robyn's presence, steadfastness, and wisdom. She thanked me for my courage, dedication, and insights. Our parting was sorrowful, because she had helped me so much, but also sweet, because I was now strong enough to no longer need her weekly guidance. We were right for each other and would stay available in each other's lives, trusting the form and frequency as it evolved. As I wrote, "Robyn is a writer, an artist, a role model of integrity, a professional, a giver of permission, an outrageous aging woman, someone who lives to her edge and from her center, a giver of gifts, a gift to the world, the person who saved my life."

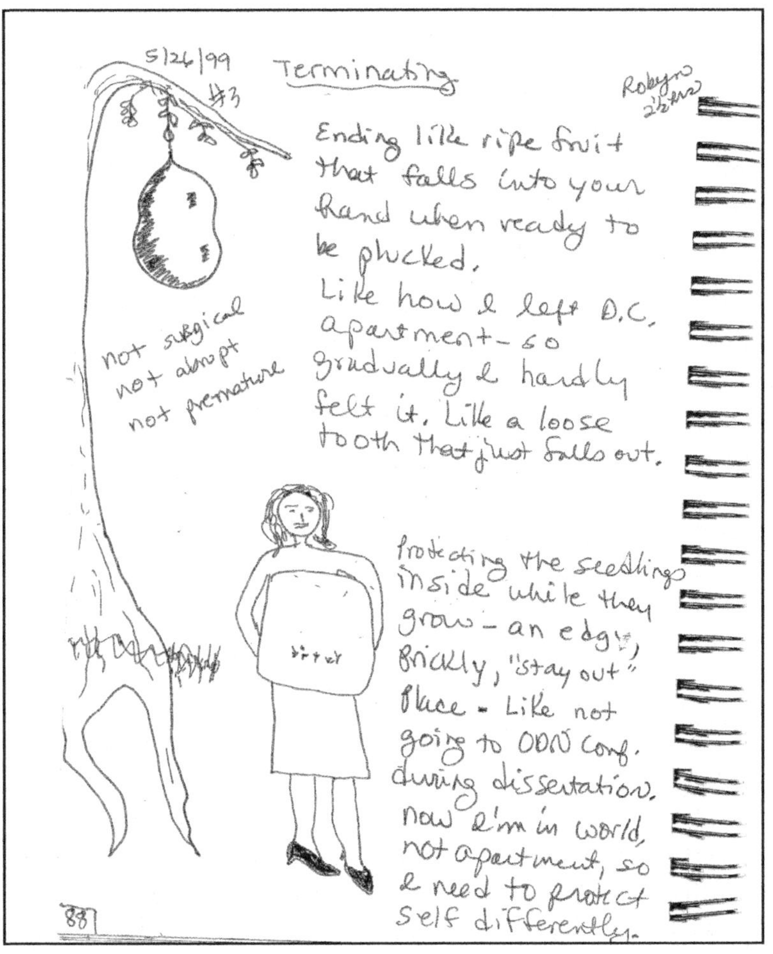

Image 31: Terminating therapy well.

It was perplexing to me why, with this exemplary experience of ending well, I ended each of my positions in medical centers so poorly. On reflection, it seems that in my eagerness to be healed, I had rushed off before mastering my training, much like the Karate Kid fighting bullies before he was ready.

Remember, in my first leadership position in OT, I left to get out of a bad situation, rather than stand my ground and manage effectively, as I had been counseled by my boss to do. Rather than firing a somewhat insubordinate subordinate, I had effectively fired myself. There was no party to honor me after eight years, but I still attempted to leave with dignity, saying my goodbyes gracefully, even as I handed over the management of the department to her. (Only years later did I receive validation that her leadership was destructive and I should have trusted myself more for the good of the unit.)

My next fateful ending came after the successful launch of an innovative and quite visible physician leadership program at NYU Medical Center. This too was a big deal. I did a stellar job designing, collaborating, and presenting, and the lead physician told me, “You were fantastic!” It was amazing how well I could be a clear vessel to create the type of programs desired by the institution, just as I had been that clear vessel in order to discern the depth of meaning and high-quality work of the women in my research study. To try to keep the vessel in the service of my inner self from leaking this time, I went on a long weekend retreat in solitude to reflect on the experience, hike in the woods, and take in the success. I took notes on the thirty-seven steps that led to the kickoff and reviewed the lessons I had learned: Let reality be my teacher. Trust I’m not alone. Have faith in myself and how I cope.

It was in this context, while still in the woods, that I auspiciously received another unsolicited call—this time from the CEO of a medical center in Brooklyn. She wanted to interview me for the position of chief learning officer, a first for them and for me. The timing was bad for NYU, as I had just given birth to the new program, but the opportunity to spread my wings in a new senior leadership position for culture change was compelling. Their offer was so exciting and enticing and full of the elusive recognition I had been seeking that I decided hastily and acted impulsively instead of slowing down to make sure all the parts of myself were on board or considering the strategic way to navigate the change (9; 81).

My journal is filled with over sixty pages of trying to process what happened before, during, and after. Even reading it now, my body remembers the intense anxiety from not leading with my Deepest Wisest Self. I was too upset to write dialogue, but I did describe how my boss was shocked and furious and claimed to feel betrayed. My nemesis on the physician leadership team, an aggressive woman who thrived in the medical center hierarchy, echoed the sentiments and began to bad-mouth me to the vice presidents, predicting I would fail in my role based on my display of such "poor judgment." I could see how they might have felt badly because they had invested in me and my leadership role. The woman leader had been concerned I'd get eaten alive if I didn't act strong. But I did step up and they saw that. It reflected poorly on them for me to leave. While I don't think they would ever own it, they actually betrayed me by overreacting and spreading rumors I didn't deserve. Any enjoyment of my substantial promotion quickly dissipated. Rather than feeling proud of having been sought out due to my accomplishments, I felt ashamed for abandoning my colleagues and reluctant to discuss my departure. Taking their cue from my embarrassment, they perceived me as I perceived myself. My tenure had been marked by exemplary programs and results, which was exactly why the new medical center wanted to hire me. Leaving a job at the top of my game was unexpected. Yet once again, I was leaving under a cloud.

Magically, at a friend's wedding, the bride and groom read a piece for their vows that resonated strongly with me (9; 82). Written by Canadian author Oriah Mountain Dreamer, the lines in their program jumped out at me and soothed my soul (9; 82): "It doesn't interest me if the story you are telling me is true. I want to know if you can disappoint another to be true to yourself; if you can bear the accusation of betrayal and not betray your own soul."

That message enabled me to turn things around. I found the strength to negotiate with my current boss to complete the first year of the physician leadership program by working there every Friday, an offer he gratefully accepted. On the other four days of the week, I began the fascinating and stimulating process of meeting the leaders at my new organization, Maimonides Medical Center. I analyzed their culture, strategic goals, and perceived new program options. As we formed a leadership task force, the group decided which endeavors were priorities and we got to work to develop them. After six months I received a raise and much praise for my leadership efforts and my fit with the institution. It is amazing how two random sentences of wisdom read at a wedding helped me achieve clarity, clean up the mess I made by leaving one job precipitously, and focus on bringing out the best in my new organization—and myself. Sometimes the universe simply sends you what you need.

Why did I have to leave like that? My husband Patrick had a theory: I just needed to accept that it worked for me and that it is how I leave (9; 81). His observation made me chuckle because I recognized it was true. But why? Why did leaving have to be painful? Because my childhood imprint made it excruciating for me to acknowledge my feelings and at the same time respect the feelings of those with whom I am in relationship? It never occurred to me that leaving could be mutually arranged, as it was with my therapist, without all the drama. When people, especially authority figures with big egos (reminiscent of my parents), are not available to me for a trusting relationship, I have protected them at my expense. In hindsight, if abandoning myself hadn't been an option, I believe I would have been able to feel my truth and find a way to express my need to depart with dignity and mutual respect. I hid the fact that my women mentors not only encouraged me to leave, to get out from under my boss who couldn't own his vulnerability and support me in the way I needed and deserved, but had also recommended me for my depth to the CEO. They were an "old girls' network" of which I wasn't aware. Their only advice was "be the diva you truly are, not the eternal ingenue."

Ironically, although I hated leaving abruptly, I later learned from the CEO that my old boss had applied for the same job, advocating to bring the whole team with him. They didn't want him or the team, but they decided they wanted to meet me. Therefore, the claim of feeling betrayed was disingenuous, and it was unlikely he would have let me go graciously. Instead, I believe he still would have made my move all about him and making him look bad. Thus, my instinct to make a clean break, even though disruptive, was correct.

Interestingly, I stayed at each medical center eight years, giving me time to get to know the culture, design programs to change it, and build sustainability before moving on to repeat the process somewhere else. At Maimonides I designed and developed many successful programs in collaboration with my work partners. Having learned the hard way about the limits of loyalty of a given institution, I decided to channel my dedication in the new job to a wider audience. I published articles on each innovative accomplishment, bringing national recognition to the organization and making it easier for other medical centers to build on our foundations, if appropriate. Sought out by the magazine *Chief Learning Officer*, I was photographed for the cover, with the interview placed as the key article in the October 2007 edition (18; 88). As I gained more stature externally, I gave numerous presentations at conferences, further extending our leadership visibility in the medical community. But the CEO was not pleased that I was getting recognition outside of her control, although it never occurred to her to *offer* me opportunities, for which I would have been grateful. In a leadership meeting, she made a belittling comment about the magazine that featured me. I felt diminished and fell back into hiding my light under a bushel. Then, as my mother used to do, she seduced me out, and I fell for it, again.

Deeper still, the dynamic I played out was rooted in my parents' perception of me. With my mother jealous of my relationship with my father, it seemed natural to me that the CEO would be jealous of my recognition and need to discredit me. And while I thought I was the only person there to be branded with a scarlet letter, I later learned of other colleagues who endured similar humiliations. Maybe it was the best I could do, all things considered. Eventually, I was able to use my wisdom in my role as a mentor to help others think through and act professionally when making job and career changes.

Of course, just as a leopard can't change its spots, I couldn't change my desperation to improve and my preference for mentors, gurus, and coaches to help me. A leadership coach I met at a conference was available to work with me, providing excellent strategies to get me to the next level. He sensed my commitment and saw how I created covenants, not contracts, for the highest good of all I served. My next level, he proposed, would be "allowing my aliveness and joyfulness to be expressed." It sounds touchy-feely, but it made perfect sense. He then provided a mirror, as Robyn had, for me to better see myself. In his view, my gifts were as "a connector who creates community, my clarity for capturing the essence of complexity, and as a creative and compassionate soul who gives voice to the human spirit" (18; 21). Because I felt safe and honored by him, I felt comfortable asking questions that had remained unanswered from past jobs and relationships.

Finally, I had answers and insights into what would have made ending the OT job better. My coach first showed me the options I could have exercised to address my troubling staff member's overreaction. One was humor: "Beth, if you really felt angry, why didn't you yell?!" Another was a mix of seriousness and sensitivity: "I only said one sentence to you, and you reacted way out of balance. What button just got pushed?" I could have then followed up with clear expectations: "Let's get to the bottom of this or there is no future for you here. Relationships are the foundation of our work" (18; 25). Then, my coach advised me not to give unsolicited feedback without setting clear expectations first. I owned that at the time, the staff member had asked for my expectations, but I didn't understand why or how to provide them (20; 90). Now I understood and was able to apply the lesson to the current team I managed. What a relief from something that had been needling me for decades. I hoped it would help me end my current job well when the time came in the future.

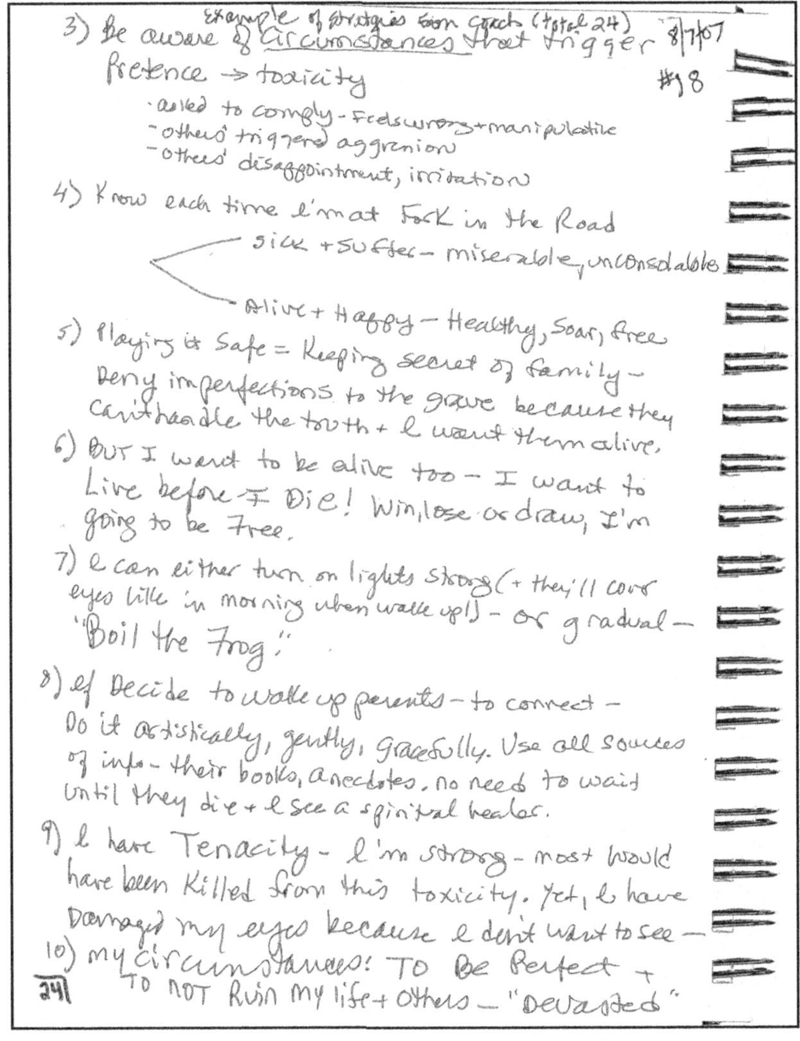
Example of strategies from coach (total 24)
3) Be aware of circumstances that trigger 8/7/07
Presence → toxicity #18
· asked to comply - Feels wrong + manipulative
- others' triggered aggression
- others' disappointment, irritation
4) Know each time I'm at Fork in the Road
sick + suffer - miserable, unconsolable
Alive + Happy - Healthy, Soar, Free
5) Playing it Safe = Keeping secret of family - Deny imperfections to the grave because they can't handle the truth + I want them alive.
6) But I want to be alive too - I want to Live before I Die! Win, lose or draw, I'm going to be Free.
7) I can either turn on lights strong (+ they'll cover eyes like in morning when wake up!) - or gradual - "Boil the Frog."
8) If Decide to wake up parents - to connect - Do it artistically, gently, gracefully. Use all sources of info - their books, anecdotes. no need to wait until they die + I see a spiritual healer.
9) I have Tenacity - I'm strong - most would have been Killed from this toxicity. Yet, I have Damaged my eyes because I don't want to see -
10) my circumstances! To Be Perfect + To NOT Ruin my life + Others - "Devastated"
24

Image 32: Effective and insightful work strategies from my leadership coach.

Fast forward five more years, to 2011. I lost weight (size-two skinny!), got promoted, felt joyful, and experienced greater integration. But then my father died. In terms of ending well, we did. In hospice, I helped him transition until the morning he moved on at age ninety-five. I stayed with my mom for one month to help her adjust to the end of their sixty-three years of marriage. When I returned to work, my face showed my sadness, and the CEO did not approve—just as my parents had disapproved of my exhibiting emotion, particularly sadness, at home. In addition to losing my father, I lost both my treasured work partner and beloved boss; he got a new job and she retired. And just like that, all the power dynamics in my life had shifted. In another failure of imagination on my part, it didn't occur to me to ask the CEO if we should establish a new leadership task force. The question in my mind was, who was I to suggest that? And at the root of that question was the missing "IT." Who was *I*, after all? With the benefit of hindsight, I now see that, as in other situations that didn't end well, I had options I didn't feel I could explore.

My journals show that my intuition knew more than I did consciously. I had inserted a quote by Pema Chödrön about "leaving the nest," suggesting sometimes we need to use courage to leave the familiar: "Do I prefer to grow up and relate to life directly, or do I choose to live and die in fear?" (24; 129). The very next day I was called into the COO's office with the VP of HR. They told me they were disbanding my department. I should return the next day to decide if there was another role I could propose in order to stay at the medical center. Shocked beyond belief, I declined. They said I hadn't done anything wrong; the decision was purely financial. But that didn't ring true. I was given six weeks to hand over my projects and leave with dignity, as well as a generous severance package, which made me feel a bit better. My process for leaving involved getting rid of all my books and files, writing my contributions and notes for others, the emotional part of letting go of this phase of my life, and the actual goodbyes (25; 96). Once again, there was no party. I did, however, have meaningful conversations with and receive gifts from selected colleagues and clients. Holding my composure, I emptied out my work apartment, office, responsibilities, and relationships.

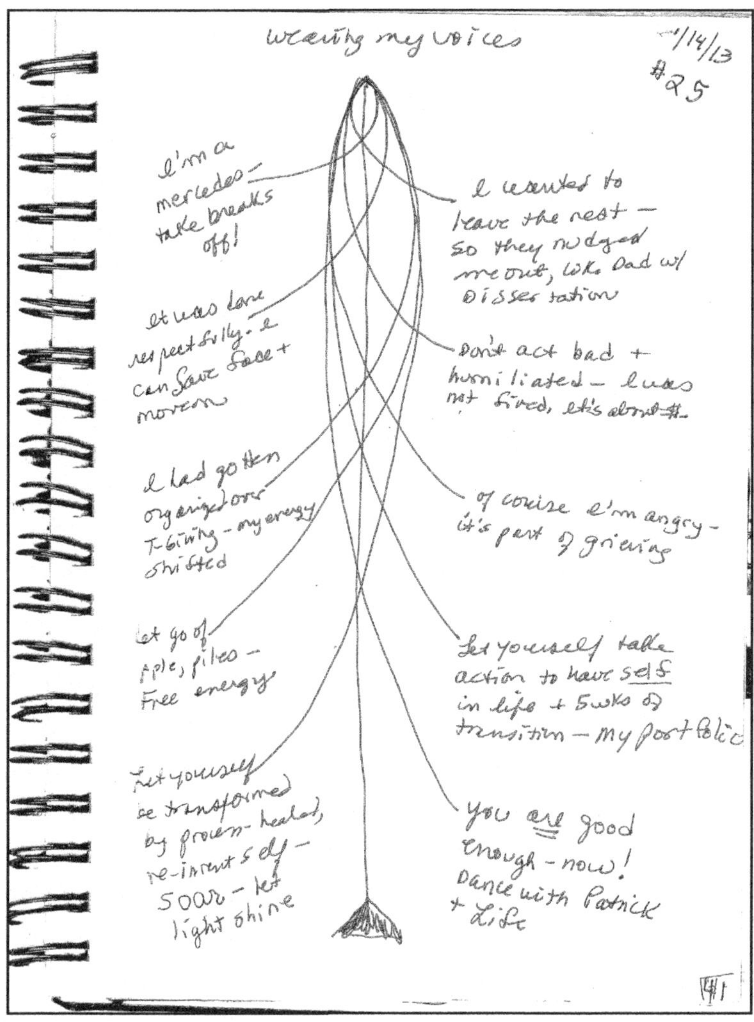

Image 33: "Weaving My Voices" in preparation for leaving my job.

This ending was graceful, but I would have preferred leaving on my own terms. Sensing diminishing fulfillment, I might have been proactive in looking for my next act. By now, moving up the ladder and increasing my visibility within organizations seemed like a curse. I didn't want another visible leadership position at a more prestigious medical center, inevitably leading to another abrupt and tumultuous ending. In fact, I didn't want to be part of an organization at all, because even though I had a talent for making organizations better, I seemed to end up worse with each successive position. I knew I worked hard and put my heart into my job, yet I eventually seemed to get caught in the political crosshairs.

Was it me? As Jerry B. Harvey's book title asks, *How Come Every Time I Get Stabbed in the Back My Fingerprints Are on the Knife?* I did see the familiar pattern of too much devotion to the work in spite of the decreased return on the emotional investment, but I didn't acknowledge that toward the end of my tenure with each organization, I was sensing a desire to leave. Not owning my restlessness, some nonverbal incongruity and withdrawal of energy was probably picked up on by those sensitive to such fluctuations. I remember feeling so relieved the day I moved all my files to our apartment and told Patrick, "I'm free!" That exuberance didn't last long though, because I was once again in transition and, as usual, not skillful at deciding what was next. I hate the void but once I leave the starting blocks, I am a long-distance runner and reliable finisher.

The partial answer came from my mother observing me with Patrick at the celebration of my dad's life several months after I left my last job. She had asked Patrick to facilitate the event and make it comfortable for each friend and family to share a story about Harold, and he executed this seamlessly. As the oldest daughter, my presence was also appreciated by my mother. She took me aside and said, "You and Patrick work so well together. Did you ever think about joining him in his consulting practice?" Never hearing such a positive suggestion from her, I jumped on the idea of becoming business partners and doing external consulting together. When we came home, Patrick was his usual supportive and practical self. Living in a typically small New York City apartment, he moved our bed forward and placed our IKEA bookshelves behind it so I could have a small office facing the wall. He moved his computer into the hall closet, accommodating his needs in order to keep the rest of the apartment aesthetically pleasing. He knew if it was left to me, all my books and files would make it look like a college dorm and overtake the art on the walls. So he made it work for both of us.

Patrick was open to the partnership but concerned when I didn't immediately bring in strategies for expanding our client base. Living together, he saw that I was still preoccupied by the loss of my internal OD career and the sting of public humiliation. My sadness leaked out as I reverted back to beating myself up and being stuck. When would I learn the lesson that starting fresh wouldn't feel right until I figured out how to end well? Yet again, I avoided what I now know I needed to do: the work of grieving to be able to move forward with more integration and sense of purpose.

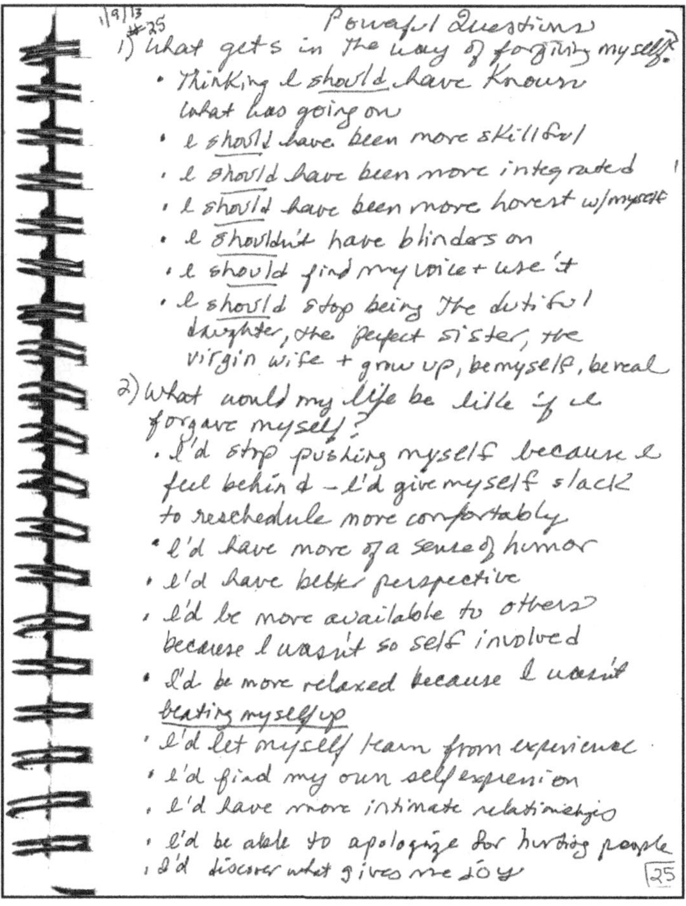

1/9/13 #25
Powerful Questions
1) What gets in the way of forgiving myself?
- Thinking I should have known what was going on
- I should have been more skillful
- I should have been more integrated
- I should have been more honest w/myself
- I shouldn't have blinders on
- I should find my voice + use it
- I should stop being the dutiful daughter, the perfect sister, the virgin wife + grow up, be myself, be real

2) What would my life be like if I forgave myself?
- I'd stop pushing myself because I feel behind – I'd give myself slack to reschedule more comfortably
- I'd have more of a sense of humor
- I'd have better perspective
- I'd be more available to others because I wasn't so self involved
- I'd be more relaxed because I wasn't beating myself up
- I'd let myself learn from experience
- I'd find my own self expression
- I'd have more intimate relationships
- I'd be able to apologize for hurting people
- I'd discover what gives me joy

25

Image 34: "Powerful Questions" to reflect on during the grieving process.

Grieve and Grow

Tidying sentimental items means putting the past in order.
—Marie Kondo

The past is just a story we tell ourselves.
—Samantha, the operating system from *HER*

Grieving is a process, not a onetime event in the face of suffering or sadness. Yet, I have avoided grief whenever possible and allowed it only for short periods when under duress. I have also eschewed the ritual of grieving with others, and in doing so ignored the advice of therapists, believing I needed to do everything independently. The hard-won truth is that just as a therapist holds up a mirror so we can see ourselves more clearly, another person is needed to hold space for our depth of feeling when we are grieving and witness our expression so it can later be transformed. I had unconsciously adopted my father's intolerance for process; my response to grief was to walk away. Reviewing my journals gave me the perspective I needed to revisit all my endings, such as job losses and the loss of my parents, through the lens of grief. This repetition and elaboration not only with professional but also personal situations is necessary to see the benefit of this added piece of internal work. I hope you can also see that grief shortchanged is a missed opportunity for solace, consolation, and ultimately wisdom.

When I was in the doctoral program, I felt a strong emotional connection to one of the students and it both excited and scared me. I didn't want to upset my first marriage, but it was so tempting to explore something new. Talking philosophy and understanding each other's projects was heady. Not accustomed to having so much energy, I began running long distances and eventually trained for and ran the Marine Corps Marathon. I felt so alive and wondered if this was the answer, the

"IT" I had been missing. Having doubts and not trusting my judgment, but not wanting to lie to myself, I went to a psychiatrist my friend Nancy recommended for a consultation, which turned into a year of therapy. I wished for an easy solution but didn't want to make a mess or hurt anyone. He listened, analyzed my dreams, and came to the conclusion that this fellow student was not right for me over the long haul. At that time, I didn't understand why the psychiatrist's assessment was that I was searching for the bonding I never had with my mother. He advised me to grieve the loss of something that can never be replaced. I guess he didn't know that I didn't know how. His certitude influenced me to let go, but looking back, I wonder why he didn't also teach me to grieve. Instead, I would take long walks with my unprocessed sadness, barely able to move forward, so bereft with loss upon loss. Believe it or not, this went on for years, with part of me holding on and wanting what I could not have, shutting down my aliveness long after I had let go of the relationship.

Serendipity led me to an intuitive, loving body therapist to finally work through my grief about the relationship with my fellow student, whom I still missed. She helped me see that I was missing myself, not him. She said, "If you had stayed with him, you would be like a tree that grew crooked. You need to see that everything you felt with him was already inside you" (6; 125). She went on to say, "Rather than cheat yourself by using his energy to complete you, you could find the wholeness in yourself over time" (7; 83). This was a revelation.

Grateful for her belief in me and a metaphorical explanation that made sense, I finally started to heal. I saw that each time I couldn't give myself permission to be curious or feel amazed, I needed to face reality, grieve, and grow to meet my real needs. Growing up as a child in a narcissistic family was like the tree growing crooked. It's difficult enough to leave a partner before the twist becomes too pronounced, but a child can't leave her parents. You can only twist yourself to adjust to them—something I called my "pretzel logic," a survival mechanism.

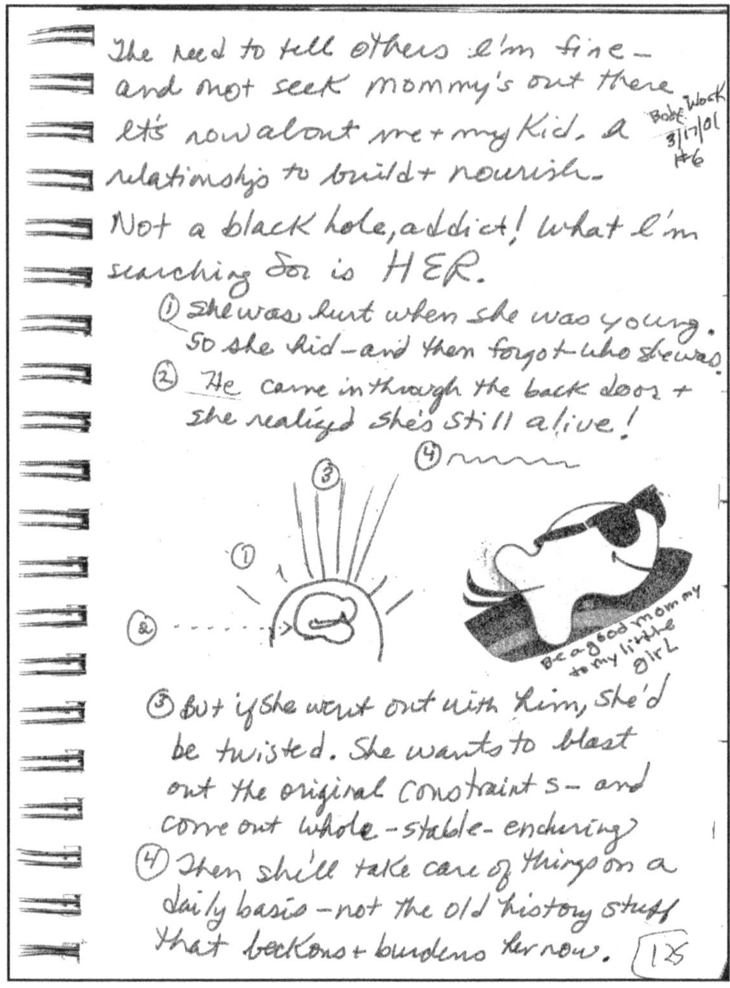

Image 35: Body worker insights for real self-growth.

In contrast, while it took me over ten years to decide what to do about my first marriage, it was only in working with a different therapist—one who was recommended to me because of our expressive art projects—that I fully felt my feelings. Her patient and insightful approach helped me clear the way to discern what I wanted to do. I couldn't come to a decision by myself because from the outside we looked so compatible. We had fun dinner parties, went on great vacations, gardened, and rarely fought. But because I was forbidden to express feelings in my childhood, when I did bring up a dissatisfaction or need, it created tremendous tension that neither of us knew how to address. Eventually, I realized I colluded with his criticisms of me and ended up abandoning myself. That's why it made sense that when he traveled for work, I felt guilty for sensing some relief and freedom. I wanted out from a dysfunctional dynamic where I was hypersensitive to his criticisms and couldn't filter or buffer them. Yet, songs would come to mind that made me worry if I left, I'd realize I made an irreparable mistake. Simultaneously, my fantasies were calling me to new adventures. Can you see how torn I was?

Reviewing my mixed emotions with this therapist, I remember our pivotal session vividly. Through sobs I said how much I *had* wanted the marriage to work out; recognizing that unfulfilled desire was the key turning point. I had tried everything I knew to save it, but nothing was working, and I finally acknowledged that I knew in my bones it could never work. Emotionally spent, I didn't need to wail anymore; she had witnessed my depth of feelings and I couldn't deny the truth of what they meant. With our couple's counselor, in the next session, I finally said the one sentence that changed it all, *"I want a soul connection and this isn't it."* My previous emotional release now allowed me to express my sad, true, and deeply uncomfortable feelings. We walked out and I immediately started looking for an apartment to move into near the university where I was a doctoral student. At this point I had to complete the comprehensive exams prior to doing a dissertation. My husband went back to work and stayed at a friend's house until I moved out about a week later to continue my studies.

This same therapist also helped me get unblocked in my doctoral program. I had written a dissertation proposal, but my heart wasn't in it. I was being a dutiful good girl, turning in something that was doable, but doable wasn't why I wanted a PhD. I signed on to take myself seriously, take risks, break new ground, and see what I was made of. I entered a new stage of grief as the therapist helped me see that I had gone through the paces academically but never really let myself learn. Now I had the opportunity to "take my little girl to school." I wrote to Peter Vaill, my committee chair, and he gave me enduring advice, "Don't write an apology, submit a real proposal." Relieved I wasn't thrown out of the program, I found what I really was curious to discover through research—women's voices in OD—and turned that in. It turned out that was a significant topic and step for me, but it wasn't a guarantee.

Once I completed the doctoral program and was working at Mount Sinai, I wanted as much support as possible to stay in reality and make a difference at the medical center. In what I refer to as my "full-court press," I actually met with three therapists over the course of two weeks. One kept me in the here and now with Gestalt approaches, one encouraged voice dialogue to hear all my parts, and the third integrated body work, insight, and grieving. Because of my history of emotional suppression from childhood, this third therapist looked at where I was stuck from the perspective of a normal action cycle—from gathering information, responding effectively, getting satisfaction, and resting after completion. She said my determination came from still trying to get what I didn't get from my parents: mirroring and nurturing. By staying loyal to them, I wasn't allowing in the support of my boss—or my boyfriend. She explained that since I had the awareness of my psychodynamics, I was at the "response barrier," unable or unwilling to respond effectively, and needed to really listen to what I wanted. Having been made to feel wrong for my actions as a child, I developed a pattern of either procrastinating and delaying action or acting hastily and impulsively. Satisfaction would only come after the release of the original construction of the dynamic set up in childhood (9; 15). Feeling disconnected and tired of working so hard, I was told that the sooner I felt the grief of not being taken care of emotionally, the sooner I'd experience my power. I couldn't control the outcome, but I could learn and grow from the experience of emotional neglect. For me, these were some major breakthroughs.

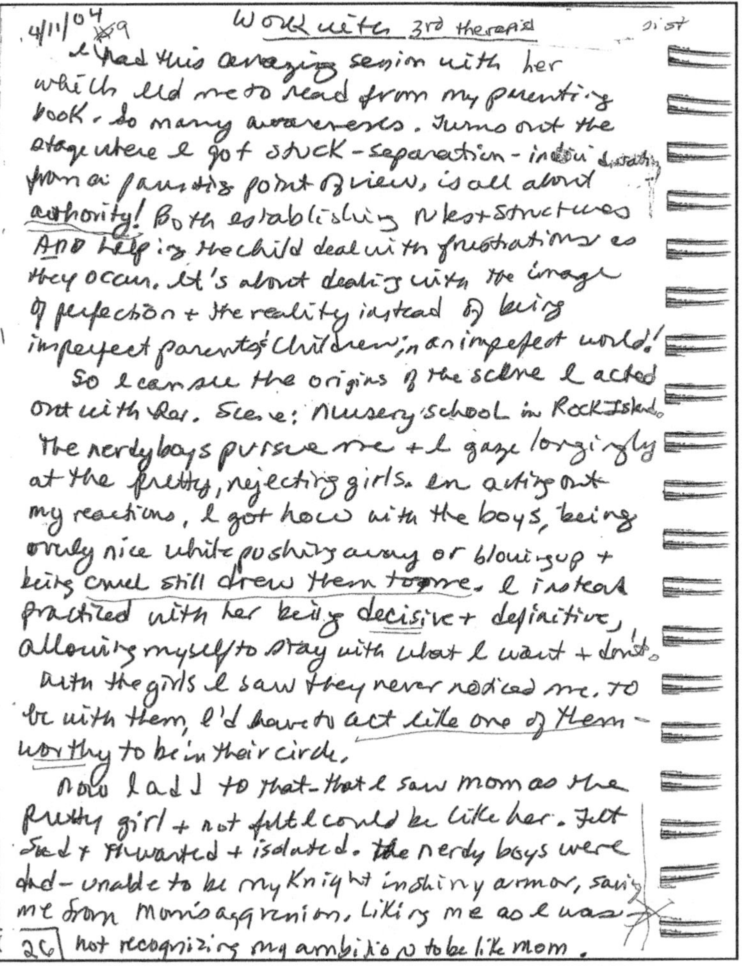
4/11/04 #9 Work with 3rd therapist

I had this amazing session with her which led me to read from my parenting book. So many awarenesses. Turns out the stage where I got stuck—separation-individuation from a parenting point of view, is all about authority! Both establishing rules + structures AND helping the child deal with frustrations as they occur. It's about dealing with the image of perfection + the reality instead of being imperfect parents & children in an imperfect world!

So I can see the origins of the scene I acted out with her. Scene: Nursery school in Rock Island. The nerdy boys pursue me + I gaze longingly at the pretty, rejecting girls. In acting out my reactions, I got how with the boys, being overly nice while pushing away or blowing up + being cruel still drew them to me. I instead practiced with her being decisive + definitive, allowing myself to stay with what I want + don't.

With the girls I saw they never noticed me. To be with them, I'd have to act like one of them—worthy to be in their circle.

Now I add to that—that I saw mom as the pretty girl + not felt I could be like her. Felt sad + thwarted + isolated. The nerdy boys were dad—unable to be my knight in shining armor, saving me from Mom's aggression, liking me as I was—not recognizing my ambition to be like mom.

26

Image 36: "Full-court press" therapy insights.

My growing insights and effective action—including the determination demonstrated by my full-court press—led to the universe providing the next leadership position at the next medical center. Reading about leadership I discovered that one of the jobs of leaders is to prepare people in the organization for loss (11; 89). Since I was finally practicing grieving small losses when needed, I upgraded my knowledge and skills to help leaders help their staff deal with the temporary losses inherent in making changes in their departments and teams. An intensive management retreat I was attending illuminated the difference between grieving and wallowing (12; 40). A book by a professor who has the same eye disease I do made the point in a different way. While grieving over the death of his brother, he realized there are worse things than being blind. That pain inspired him to create an identity not based on disability, but on inspiring others (19; 145). I too wanted to inspire others—by incorporating grief into the reality of treating patients, making medical errors, and facing death.

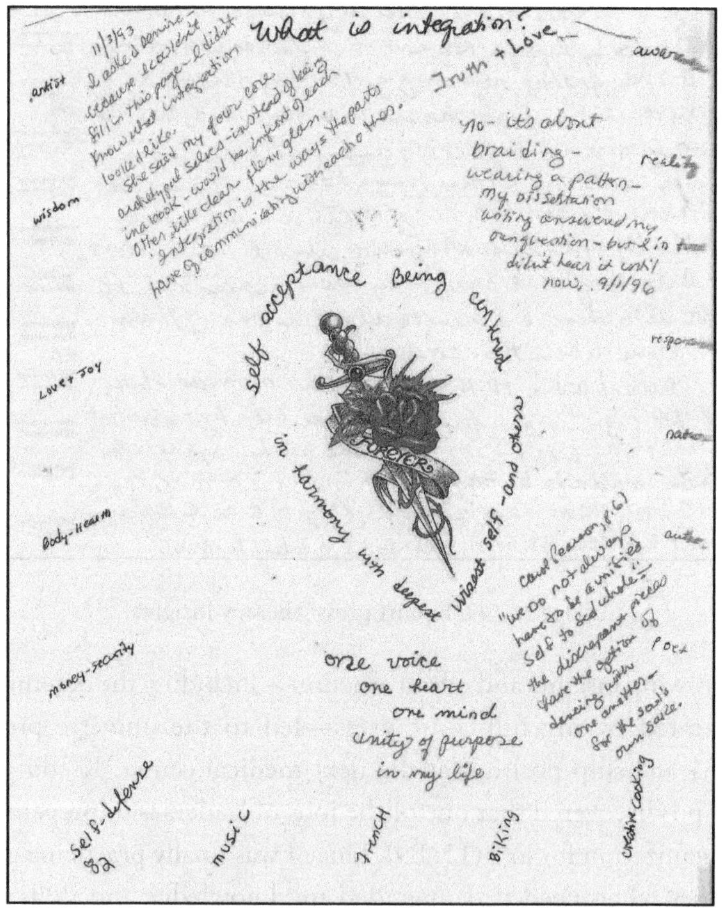

Image 37: My beginning exploration, "What is integration?"

Inspired to grow further, I returned to my first journal image for integration: the rose with both its thorns and flower. I pictured the vines wrapped around a sword, the sword being my unswerving commitment to heal and listen to the rose of my Deepest Wisest Self. Work provided my stake in the ground to be of service, and therapy was always the other strand wrapped around it to help me be my most accessible and self-accepting self.

At one point, I was so determined to change that I made a two-page chart of everything I currently did and how I wanted it to be different (13; 64–65). Calling it "flipping the switch," I was my most determined to finally make the change and wake up totally whole.

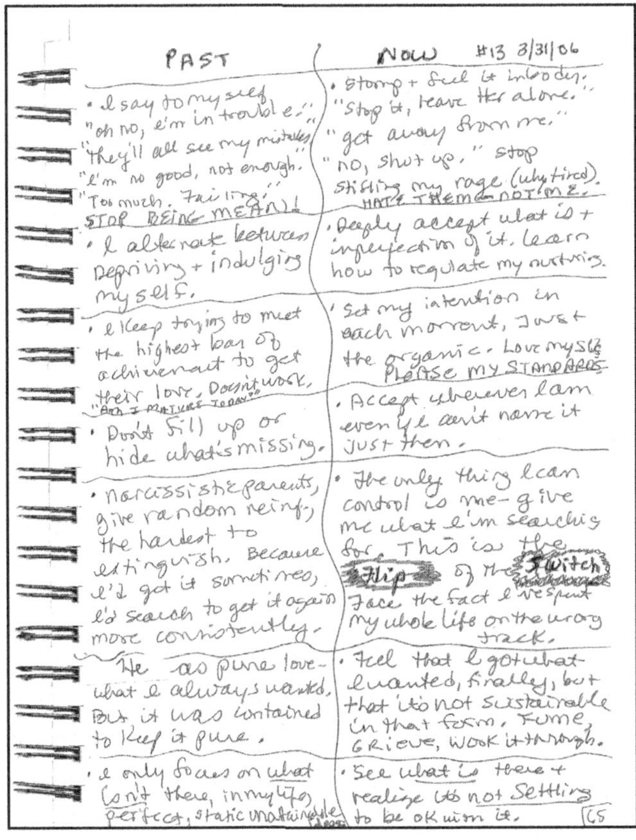

PAST	NOW #13 3/31/06
• I say to myself "oh no, I'm in trouble." "They'll all see my mistakes" "I'm no good, not enough." "Too much. Failing." STOP BEING MEAN!!	• Stomp + feel it in body. "Stop it, leave her alone." "get away from me." "no, shut up." stop stifling my rage (why tired). HATE THEM NOT ME.
• I alternate between depriving + indulging myself.	• Deeply accept what is + imperfection of it. Learn how to regulate my nurturing.
• I keep trying to meet the highest bar of achievement to get their love. Doesn't work. "Am I mature today?"	• Set my intention in each moment, just the organic. Love myself PLEASE MY STANDARDS
• Don't fill up or hide what's missing.	• Accept wherever I am even if I can't name it just then.
• narcissistic parents, give random reinf., the hardest to extinguish. Because I'd get it sometimes, I'd search to get it again more consistently.	• The only thing I can control is me - give me what I'm searching for. This is the Flip of the Switch. Face the fact I've spent my whole life on the wrong track.
[illegible] as pure love - what I always wanted. But it was contained to keep it pure.	• Feel that I got what I wanted, finally, but that it's not sustainable in that form. Fume, Grieve, work it through.
• I only focus on what isn't there, in my life, perfect, static unattainable [illegible]	• See what is there + realize it's not settling to be ok with it.

Image 38: "Flipping the switch" to get my life on the right track.

Finally, I felt I was firing on all cylinders, in the zone. But the universe had other plans for me. As I was crossing the street to our apartment at the end of the week to meet a couple who wanted to celebrate Patrick's and my commitment, I was amazed there were no cars during rush hour. All of a sudden, I was struck by a car making a sudden U-turn, neither of us seeing the other. Hurled into the air, I floated slowly to the ground, as if held on angel wings. Taken to the hospital by an ambulance, I was lucky only to have broken my shoulder and fractured my pelvis, neither requiring surgery, just rest.

I couldn't believe how I'd been blindsided by the accident. When I returned to work, the healer I was seeing said that instead of flipping a switch, I needed to stay in the dark, if you will, and let myself feel the depth of longing and loneliness I had avoided my whole life. I needed to grieve. She thought my life was on hold, as if I were waiting for the train of love I knew existed but never stopped for me. Meanwhile, all the trains of life were passing me by because I refused to get on (17; 36). My intention became to get rid of anything preventing me from being who I really was, my fully alive self, a self I simply had to allow to be and not keep trying to find. A heart-wrenching scene from *Doctor Zhivago* came to mind, unleashing my deep anguish: Yuri finally sees Lara, the love of his life, again, but can't call out to her. Letting myself feel more and more deeply, I strove to love myself while letting the unendurable past grief go.

Feeling that I was integrating, symbolically weaving the fabric of my life, I went with Patrick to a four-day intensive workshop called the Universal Experience (20; 49). It offered a profound sequence of activities to enact the ultimate letting go of life, to celebrate and grieve. As my spiritual therapist at the time echoed, "Everything has a shelf life, including life itself" (20; 112). This led me to read about the Buddhist path to growing up. Norman Fischer, an American Zen priest, offered two steps: First, forgive your parents with gratitude, making peace in your heart. Second, leave your parents behind, connecting to your own suffering and accepting it. By forgiving yourself, you strive to make your own suffering, and that in the world, better (20; 112).

If we just read other people's wisdom, and nod inside saying, "that makes sense," we avoid the hard work of relating it to our own experience. First, how could I forgive my parents if I hadn't seen them doing something wrong? Then, when I did realize how much they hurt me, why should I forgive them? Only when I could acknowledge and really feel the hurt and find the strength to forgive them, could I actually heal. Only then could I share my suffering as an offering to others who need that type of support and understanding. Quite a challenge.

At work, I continued to face the reality of clients' struggles, acknowledge what I could do to help, and accept when I wanted to be other than where I was. It was so much easier to work on the computer than feel the feelings that needed to be released. When I didn't express negativity in the privacy of my own journal, I became Velcro rather than Teflon at the office, attached to issues that didn't belong to me (21; 23). In addition to grieving, I analyzed beliefs getting in the way, such as my not being allowed to have negative feelings (21; 45). Then, I practiced letting go of the weight of the past by exercising and eating more nourishing food, allowing myself to rest, renew, and reward my body (21; 11). My husband Patrick shared how he had to grow himself up, but he forgave his mother and encouraged me to keep mourning and letting go (22; 31). But I couldn't. My wounds were still festering and not ready to heal.

You'll recall when my father died, I couldn't hide my sadness at work. This occurred about two years after I attended the Universal Experience workshop with Patrick. At the time, I decided to get bereavement counseling to process the loss of my father. Reading Sandi Caplan and Gordon Lang's *Grief's Courageous Journey*, I embraced their six recommendations for mourning: Accept the reality of death; let yourself feel the pain of the loss; remember the person who died; develop a new self-identity; search for meaning; and let others help you—now and always (24; 116). It took time, especially since my mother wasn't ready to honor her husband with family and friends until a year later. But losing Dad signaled the beginning of the end for me at the medical center.

After all the effort and results I put into work, the publications and innovations, it was terribly hurtful to be told it was time to go. Once gone from the institution, I realized I had time to prepare for eventual blindness. I learned mobility and technology adaptations from the Lighthouse Guild. They also assigned me a counselor to work through the grief and reality of my eye condition. Being an experienced social worker, she perceived the well of grief I had not only from my eyes and job loss, but unresolved issues from "being deprived of a childhood" (27; 37). She said it was time to feel the emotions of how horrible that was, how worthless I felt, and how I never saw my parents' responsibility.

She gave me an inventory to fill out with statements about what I felt, how I behaved, and what I believed about my relationship with my parents. Turned out I was still very enmeshed with my parents and my emotional world was still controlled by them. She said I needed to own my feelings, not make them dependent on my parents' understanding or agreement. I needed to face my needs and meet them myself, stop hiding from myself and basing my behavior on my parents' opinions. Then, she gave me five principles to help me be more realistic about life: Things do not always go according to plan; people are not loving and loyal all the time; pain is part of life; everything changes and ends; and life is not always fair.

I couldn't believe there was so much more to grieve. When people say self-development is like "peeling the onion" because there are so many layers, this must be what they mean. With her guidance I made my own space at home to encourage grieving and then shared with her what I was learning and feeling each week when we met. I found images of being persecuted and banished as a victim to a cellar, adapted a sad song by Linda Ronstadt to grieve with, and wrote the critical messages I had internalized in this scenario so many years ago. After putting it all in my journal for further reflection and grieving sessions (27; 37–38, 46), I let myself feel bereft and go to the truth of the pain, as the only way to finally move through it. Eyes closed, I would imagine taking in the pain of grief as if it were a sword puncturing my stomach; I had to take it in, finally, and let the pain spread to metabolize the sorrow. For comfort, I would hug my stuffed bear, Wart, and Bunny, my stuffed rabbit without a mouth. Obtained at a conference on grieving, they helped me feel loved while I cried. I had no idea at the time, but by taking the time to listen to my soul, not work, and grieve, I was "*creating my life with me in it.*" As I wrote, I could not have done this alone, because I couldn't:

Give myself empathy for my feelings

Give myself perspective on what I experienced

See a different way of viewing situations

Give myself permission to express myself without protection

Grieve without validation of my pain (27; 39)

The upside to not working at the medical center was that I had time to help take care of my mother and be there with her when she died. Even though I knew the last day was near, when she finally took her last breath I sobbed deep from my soul, just as I had the moment my dad died. It was so primal and real, necessary and cleansing. For all the therapy I spent trying to resolve feelings about my parents, I always deeply loved them. I treasured the time I had at the end of their lives just being together.

Two months after my mom died, I read an excerpt from *Beloved Dog* by Maira Kalman, about a dog named Pete, which described just how I felt:

> During our years together, I often asked Pete to say ONE word to me. Just one word. It is like asking to hear one word from a loved one who has died. Give me a sign you have not really left me. It is not going to happen. But it does not stop you from wishing and hoping for a miracle. So I would beg Pete to say one word. He never did. But of course, he spoke volumes. (29; 101)

I howled in grief. My parents deserved my loving pain. How I wished I could feel their presence and receive a sign they had not totally left me. After my dad died my sisters said that when they saw a feather on the ground it was from him. I told myself Mom left me pennies from heaven that I would spot when walking. Often now, I talk to them in my mind about my new life and how happy I am and how I wish I could share it with them. I love when they show up in my dreams. I love to review my journals about them and reread the virtual ceremony we wrote on the anniversary of their deaths, using anecdotes from family and friends.

On the day Mom would have been ninety, I reread the piece I wrote about her, "Meemo and Grace." I cringed at the agony I revealed about our relationship. I wept at the tenderness I felt about "my little mommy" at the end before she died (32; 90). One vignette stands out. Once when I visited Meemo and Big D, still in their house in the desert, I had decided to be brave. Sitting in the kitchen having a regular conversation, I asked if I could tell her something that was bothering me. She nodded and I said, "Mom, sometimes I feel like I'm walking on eggshells with you." She didn't ask why or encourage me to say more. Instead, she went to the refrigerator, got out two raw eggs, and had me stand next to her at the sink. She threw and broke them dramatically, saying, "No more walking on eggshells, ok?!" To me it was an example of her sardonic humor, and also her lack of empathy. My therapist was appalled, but I felt like it was progress for both of us, meager though it was.

Writing about our relationship led me to reflect more about my last job. I realized the pain of being let go was necessary for me to heal further. The recapitulation of the controlling masculine from my dad and the senior VP, and the wounded feminine from my mom and the CEO, were there for me to finally face. I wouldn't have left if the angry male senior leader hadn't wanted to take over my function. As a colleague affirmed after I left, he was intimidated by my collaborative approach and had to disparage it. It was uncanny how the CEO had the same dismissive look as my mother, shooting from her hip to change priorities at a moment's notice, and then expecting me to pick up the pieces. Both leaders were disrespectful of my talents and betrayed my trust. I had to go down the well of pain and connect the reasons for getting triggered at work, beyond what was just "the way it was" for others. It was as if I had a casket of unfinished business with my parents that I thought I had buried. But I had to open it to see their ghosts and how the resemblance of them in the politics of the organization had so terrified me. I finally wrote in my journals the things I wish I had done and said at work. I reminded myself of the truth I told each of my parents near the end and that they received it, especially my mother.

After revisiting these personal and professional situations from the lens of grief, I am astounded by my persistent desire for things to be one way and my refusal to see why they couldn't be, and by my inability to take in all the good feedback *and* keep out the bad. I tried to understand integration intellectually and how I could achieve it. However, psychologically I was all-or-nothing in my sense of things. It's like holding hands with a friend while walking and not letting go when it's time to leave and wave goodbye—you don't get too far. I wanted to "flip the switch" all at once and be well and whole. Maybe it makes sense that I have my eye condition. If the body reflects how we think and what we say and do, I have been psychologically blind to my mixed feelings and have refused to believe I was deprived of an emotionally healthy childhood. I only wanted to love my parents and not hold them responsible for the consequences in my development. I left home, got married, got divorced, got academic degrees, had a career, and another, but did I ever really leave them, separate, and individuate? Perhaps that's the deeper reason I couldn't leave jobs ending well; I didn't feel allowed to move on. Being raised not to express feelings, expressing grief was too much of a stretch. Even though I felt terrible when betrayed, it was worse to contemplate betraying others: my parents, or my bosses who served as their stand-ins. I didn't want to go into the darkness temporarily in order to let the tears of grief water the ground of growth. With expert support, however, I finally was able to tolerate the necessary pain of the grieving process. Then I knew I better get to know my other feelings as well.

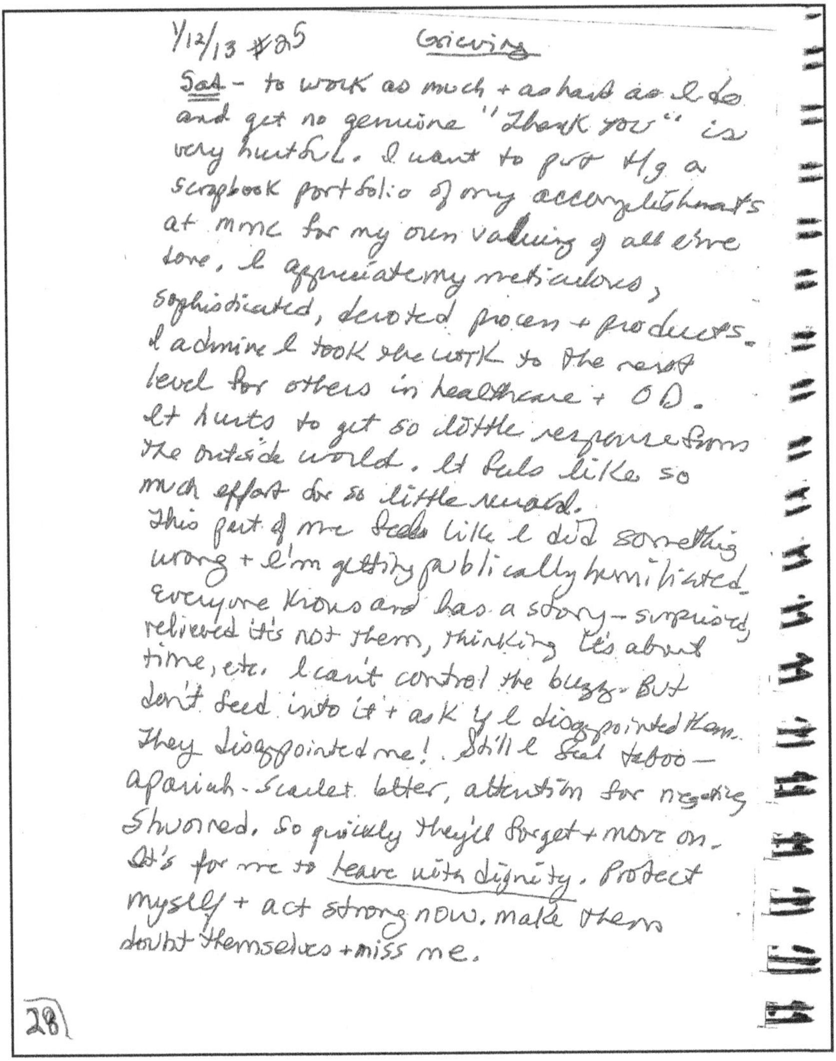

1/12/13 #25 Grieving

Sad – to work as much + as hard as I do and get no genuine "thank you" is very hurtful. I want to put tog a scrapbook portfolio of my accomplishments at MMC for my own valuing of all I've done. I appreciate my meticulous, sophisticated, devoted process + products. I admire I took the work to the next level for others in healthcare + OD. It hurts to get so little response from the outside world. It feels like so much effort for so little reward.
This part of me feels like I did something wrong + I'm getting publically humiliated. Everyone knows and has a story – surprised, relieved it's not them, thinking it's about time, etc. I can't control the buzz. But don't feed into it + ask if I disappointed them. They disappointed me! Still I feel taboo – a pariah – scarlet letter, attention for negative. Shunned. So quickly they'll forget + move on. It's for me to leave with dignity. Protect myself + act strong now. Make them doubt themselves + miss me.

28

Image 39: "Grieving," working through feelings of loss and humiliation.

CHAPTER FIVE

Feeling

Healing is coming to terms with things as they are.
—Jon Kabat-Zinn

"THERE"

All my life I wanted to be somewhere I wasn't. At the same time, I wasn't exactly sure where I wanted to be. I just knew where I was wasn't "IT." When I took the battery of inventories in high school, the counselor, explaining two of the most noteworthy findings, said, "Your results show an extreme lack of contentment and also an extreme desire to help others." The irony of being dissatisfied with my own life while wanting to direct my energy toward fulfilling other people's needs was lost on me at the time. Years later, when I interviewed the women in my study, I was in my forties and still searching, unsuccessfully, for contentment. I explored with them my desire for a "THERE," a destination of calm, confidence, and contentment where I could finally end, or at least pause, my search. Uniformly, these successful businesswomen assured me there is no "THERE." It's all a process: enjoy the journey. An interesting concept, I thought, but I prefer closure and sure things. So I was deeply disappointed and discouraged to hear what these women, my role models, affirmed. How could all my searching for the final reward be for naught? How could the searching itself, which was so painful for me, be the point of it all?

After interviewing the women and writing up my results, I still needed help finding my voice for the final chapter, in which I had to summarize the significance of my research. Peter Vaill, my committee chair, spent two hours on the phone encouraging me to just write what I thought and felt. My fingers would tell me what to write, he said, and my intuition remembered more than my notes. He told me I didn't have to come up with a fancy model or seven-step approach to becoming like these successful women. I just had to hold them up as models. The experience was so freeing and new I ended the document claiming it was a "*labor of love and work of art.*"

Upon submitting my dissertation, I was told my work had far exceeded my committee's expectations. Then, they offered me something I felt put me "THERE," or at least in the "THERE" zone. I was told that, rather than defend my findings in a public setting prior to becoming a doctor of philosophy, I would be given the rare opportunity to present a colloquium. That meant when I walked into the room, I would immediately sign the formal document that decreed I be granted the doctor of philosophy degree and be welcomed for the first time as Dr. Kaplan. I would then give a talk and field questions—with the pressure already off. Suddenly, I had morphed from the "cute little girl" in my father's eyes to being a scholar whose work was "sophisticated." Suddenly, the dismissive competitive judgments of my mother had given way to hearing my work was a "page-turner." I finally saw the person I longed to be in the mirror.

Reflecting on how I had accomplished this achievement, I noted that I had taken myself seriously, completed exquisite work, and been delighted with the evolving process. I had become a researcher who could finally enjoy my methodical and conceptual approach. Instead of skimming the surface of the content, as I had in the past, I had immersed myself in the wisdom of the women I interviewed and found unique ways to capture their essence. As I mentioned in Chapter One, I created one-page Poem Portraits using language that evolved from our intimate conversations, with titles such as "Seeing Full Pictures with Intense Integrity," "Ever Public and Private," and "Social Justice and Those Who Refuse to See." I then wrote a group poem and assembled a collage (see Images 7 and 8)—my own creative and efficient step of "data reduction." Image 40 shows one of the poems I identified with in terms of always looking to the past and then worrying about the future.

Seeing Life in the Rear View Mirror

I have always been ahead of my time.
It has been profoundly interesting to me
to follow my intuition, then look back and see
what I was doing a few years ago, is now
front and center. It's not a trend when I start
to do it, but it is by the time I'm done.
I was born right before the baby boom generation.
I have to look in the rear view mirror
to understand myself in retrospect.

I feel like a pioneer, like an oldest child.
Always the first one and making it up
as you go along. You break ground
every time you do anything, just as in our field.
After the people invented OD and started
doing it, we were the first generation to get trained,
to experience the field once there was one.
That is sort of special too, in its own way.
We know all the great stories and intrigues.

We were the young women at the workshops
they were chasing around the hotel!
Women in OD started with a sign in the ladies room,
talking about no access to leadership structure.
The question of whether women ought to be on the program,
to have influence, never even came up. These issues now
are ridiculous. We're so mainstream, we're in danger of
over powering the profession and weakening the field.
It has all really changed, yet it's also full circle.

I was the first woman to get a Ph.D. in my graduate
department. I did management training for women
before it was ever done. I did race relations training
which is now called diversity. I was on the ground
floor of wellness and AIDS education. But somehow
I'm always behind the scenes, never front and center.
I have credibility, respect, a variety of interests, but
no niche, no national standing, and I feel blocked.
It's like the shell game, I look under each one, but

it's not there, it's inside of me, a piece that is missing.
Like the Lone Ranger, the masked women who rides in,
solves a problem, and goes off into the sunset. No visibility.
I want to do something substantial enough that the field
is farther forward than it would have been without me.
I have the capacity, I just don't know how to get there.
And then, when does my lazy part get to have expression?
And what kind of old lady do I want to be?
Do I have to wait to look in the rear view mirror?

Image 40: Poem Portrait, "Seeing Life in the Rear View Mirror."

The joy of this experience became what I wanted again and again in my career and for the rest of my life. However—and by now you know there is always a however with me—without the support of my committee and a clear direction, I floundered. They had not signed up to be joined at the hip with me once I accomplished the university's requirements. In fact, at the end-of-year party for graduate students, the department head joked to me that doctoral students don't get tenure—funny, and terrifying. I loved my doctoral journey so much, I took ten years to complete it. Then I was forced to reenter—and navigate—the real, nonacademic world. Driven to make money and not let my degree go to waste, I went on interviews and joined training groups for contract work. I hated it, but I made myself keep doing it. After all, this was part of the journey, too, right?

The problem was I didn't know how to keep the excitement going, and I had fallen into my old trap. I was looking for a "THERE" for my first job in my new career rather than seeing a long career as a continuous evolution of self. I had loved interviewing the women, as it played to so many of my strengths, and I missed doing the in-depth research, to which I was also well suited. Peter was the one who'd made me stop at thirty-two. Normally with this type of research, once you see the pattern, you can stop collecting data. But each successive story was so fascinating and unique to me, I could have kept going indefinitely. I knew the point of graduating was to practice or teach, but I wondered if I didn't just want to interview people for a living, as radio or podcast hosts do, such as Terry Gross on *Fresh Air* or *On Being with Krista Tippett*. Another option that occurred to me was forever doing literature reviews on selected topics and publishing them, as Maria Popova does so eloquently and accessibly on her blog *The Marginalian* (formerly *Brain Pickings*). Of course, I forgot how much the real magic for me is facilitating groups that go beyond what any individual could accomplish on their own—that helping others come together to find their "THERE" was some of the most meaningful work I could do. Though I didn't understand the reasons then, OD was actually a good choice for me.

Finally, in 2005, after my first six months in the new job in Brooklyn and ending the physician program at the other medical center, I declared my "THERE" as being less tentative and discovering my very own authentic base of power. Later that year I realized, by that definition, I was "THERE," but being there wasn't what I had thought it would be. This was a major shift. It wasn't about being perfect, but to bumble and stumble through continuous improvement. "THERE" was realizing everyone sees both sides of me, my strengths and my agony. I no longer had to be paranoid because there was nothing to hide. "THERE" was enjoying my brilliance, accepting when I needed help, and getting help before things reached a crisis. "THERE" was letting myself know the truth if I promised not to do anything about it impulsively. "THERE" was preparing twice—the structure *and* the connections—my truth and how to express it so it could be heard. "THERE" was giving myself unconditional acceptance no matter where I was or what was going on. Through stops and starts, my understanding of "THERE" continued to evolve, until I finally felt I occupied the space, rather than obsessing over the quest of reaching it.

Before my fifty-sixth birthday I declared my "THERE" was being totally committed to my integrity and healing. My fourteenth journal was titled, "Committed to My Integration: Accepting Only I Can Change How I Feel About Myself." I acknowledged I was fighting for my eyesight at every level, to accept my darkness so I could see. Again, I reminded myself that "THERE" was having a stable inner adult who was self-accepting and mutually respectful no matter what had happened or how others reacted. This was perhaps the hardest life lesson for me to incorporate, as evidenced by how many times I repeated it over many years. For example, I found an index card I had put in one of my journals when letting go of all my files and piles in preparation for our move. Robyn had decoded what I really meant when at six years old I'd stood at the side of my parents' bed and asked, "*Am I mature today?*" She said what I meant was, "*Are you accepting me today?*" Robyn explained I was still trying to be beyond criticism, and I agreed, that was exactly what I had wanted (31; 98).

Looking back, I can see that when I was struggling with my increased leadership visibility in the workplace, my "THERE" was to find the truth of my dilemmas and resolve them honestly. "THERE" was also taking risks outside of my comfort zone (31; 30). I wanted a year of knowing my true needs and arranging my life to meet them. A quote I saved perfectly acknowledged my soul's journey: "I may not be there yet, but I'm closer than I was yesterday" (27; 4).

In 2007, when I started my monthly writing weekends (Journal 17) I aspired—and gave myself permission—to do exactly what I loved. It had finally dawned on me that my negative litany of thoughts would never get me "THERE." When in that dark place, I always thought: "*I'll never get what I want, nothing helps, I'm a wreck, I can't get to the bottom of it, and I hate myself and my life*" (17; 47). I know some of you have experienced similar feelings. So I challenged myself: What if I acted as if I believed I *would* get everything I wanted, just in God's time, not mine? This was my version of "fake it 'til you make it," but I would argue it was a totally authentic act. I'd say: "*Everything is happening not to me but for me. I'm fabulous, look at all my role models. I am at the bottom of it, and it's releasing and transforming now. I love myself and my life because I'm getting my body back, discovering who I am and what I want, and staying on top of my work. I am writing my story and sharing my wisdom.*" Though I was never one to believe in affirmations, this was worth a try, and the results were encouraging.

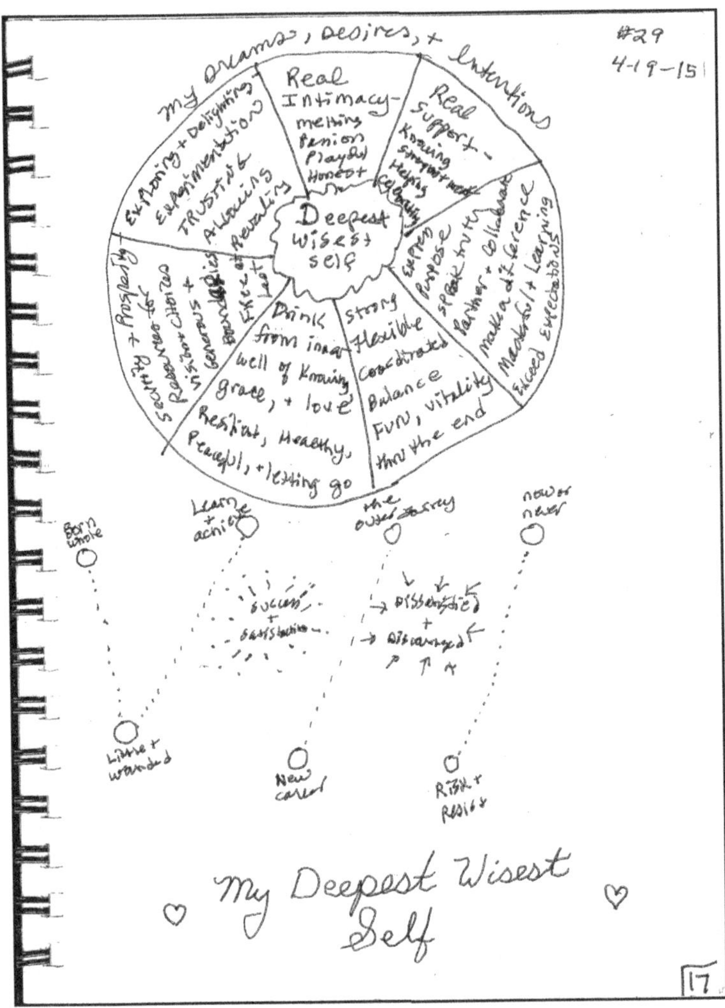

Image 41: My Deepest Wisest Self.

In 2015, when I was preparing to present my follow-up research at the national OD conference, "THERE" was listening to my Deepest Wisest Self for my dreams, desires, and intentions (29; 17). "THERE" was relaxing into my redemption and reconciliation, symbolized by a big sculpture in a park in California I happened upon—when taking a breather from helping my mom—of a man peacefully resting in the sun

(29; 27). (See Image 42.) It was so different from an earlier symbol of my feelings I had encountered in a park in Washington, D.C.: a sculpture of a man half buried alive—a character with whom I had resonated for years (24; 120). (See Image 43.)

Burying myself alive was such a dominant feeling for me. I felt so burdened by all I had to do, and work was just about all I had time for. Yet, you know by now how determined I am, and I wouldn't let hating myself or my life stop me from meeting expectations. The fact that the sculpture was called "Awakening" made me hope that one day I, too, would emerge from the depths of despair and reenter the world of the living. But first I would have to get underneath "IT" if I was ever to understand and change.

Image 42: My photo of David Phelps's "The Dreamer," Civic Center Park, Palm Desert, California.

Image 43: "The Awakening," by J. Seward Johnson, Jr., at Hains Point, Washington, D.C. Photo: William F. Yurasko, CC BY 2.0 <https://creativecommons.org/licenses/by/2.0>, via Wikimedia Commons.

"IT"

People say that what we're all seeking is the meaning of life . . . I think that what we're really seeking is an experience of being alive, so that our life experiences on the purely physical plane will have resonance within our innermost being, so that we can actually feel the rapture of being alive.

—Joseph Campbell, *The Power of Myth*

The only hope for changing my life was to define and then redefine the words that had been defining me for so long. If "THERE" was my desired destination, "IT" was the undesired stimulus for my endless searching.

"IT" makes me miserable and is how I suffer. I always resonated with the line from Woody Allen's classic, *Annie Hall*: "Life is divided into the horrible and the miserable." As I see it, the horrible is real hardship and tragedy: growing up in poverty, homelessness, enduring sexual and emotional abuse, having a terrible skin disease that hurts and can't be treated. But misery, ah, that is self-induced and comes from the inaccurate beliefs and stories we make up about ourselves. It is like adding too much salt to every dish we prepare and ruining it. Misery is never really learning and growing but instead being stuck in an endless loop with much energy but no solution. Misery is always complaining and blaming, usually beating ourselves up. Misery can be elevated to a humorous art form and way of life, but unfortunately in my case I never saw the humor. The joke was, literally, on me.

While Patrick and I were watching stand-up comedians auditioning for *Britain's Got Talent*, I saw something amazing. People with severe disabilities, one unable to stand, one with literally no voice, and another with autism, were somehow able not to take their challenges so seriously and actually reshape them as positive qualities. They laughed at themselves and used their difficult circumstances to create scenarios that were genuinely funny, even more hilarious than the other contestants. They turned their physical difficulties into something not horrible or miserable but honorable and valuable. They didn't feel sorry for themselves and give up. They exceeded what their parents, teachers, and friends expected of them. They loved themselves and their lives, using everything they had been given, not focusing on what was missing. They did not indulge in misery but instead turned their hardships to advantage.

Since "IT" made me so unhappy, I always wanted to get rid of "IT." "IT" would yell, "You deserve to be punished, you are too big for your britches, I'm going to cut you off at the knees. You will never have your heart's desire" (22; 119). I wanted to strangle "IT," to finish it off once and for all.

Others have had a hard time being in "IT's" presence, too. "IT" refuses to let in the confidence a boss has. "IT" hears the same therapeutic interpretations time and again but does not use them to take effective action—another example of the response barrier. Those impatient with their own weaknesses can't stand being around someone else's obvious display of tentativeness and indecision. Colleagues will criticize rather than empathize or look at their own patterns. In my case, they would say, "Get over yourself, let go, move on, and just do it" (12; 31). Once at an intensive management retreat, where I assumed the leader would have empathy for our shortcomings, she assigned small groups, carefully selected, to act out our default modes of operation. My partner and I were to act like celebrity twins, self-absorbed and superficial. The point was to stretch our awareness of what she called our "nerdier" parts and thereby own our less attractive qualities. By doing so, we would become freer to commit to being more grounded and centered. My partner and I enacted our roles and ended by reading love letters we wrote to the nerdy parts of ourselves. Everyone laughed and clapped, but I wasn't sure either of us really changed in awareness or our behavior. The whole thing only made me feel worse about myself.

Many mentors and therapists have defined my "IT" in an effort to free me. They saw it as perfectionism, looking outside myself for approval, and resignation that I'll never change. Professor Harvey called "IT" my "Jablonksi," which he defined as "those areas in which anxiety or other factors threaten integrated self-awareness and self-enhancing action" (31; 38). I wrote in my study plan to work on those issues, which included: "difficulty setting priorities in relation to use of time;

obsessive and perfectionist tendencies; dealing with anger and criticism; balancing needs for individuality and intimacy; trusting my ability to make decisions and think critically; unrealistic self-assessment and self-regard; and realizing and using my personal power." A tall order, for sure. I have worked on these issues in various ways and with varying degrees of success since then.

I have come to appreciate that "IT" is a self-protective habit I took on never to excel too much and threaten my parents or evoke jealousy in colleagues. As a child I needed protection from the impact of my parents' narcissism, but those coping mechanisms, so necessary as a child, didn't serve me well as an adult. "IT" is how I raised the drawbridge on every accomplishment and started over, sadly, not building from the launching pad that could have helped me soar (26; 87).

"IT" is the conviction "I can't," and I believed it was true because of the evidence that I was not enough (9; 16). My critical voice told me I wasn't mature enough, confident enough, good enough at work, perceptive enough to hear all my parts, integrated enough, organized enough, earning enough, or intimate enough. "IT" is the broken record that says, "I can't do it, I can't hold my own, can't face others, can't succeed, can't have and don't deserve deep satisfaction" (16; 86). "IT" is looking for others to give me my sense of approval and acceptance (20; 3). "IT" is the anguish, the waiting, the wishing and hoping, the believing, the determination, and knowing it is not going to happen, it didn't happen, it won't happen—ever (20; 3).

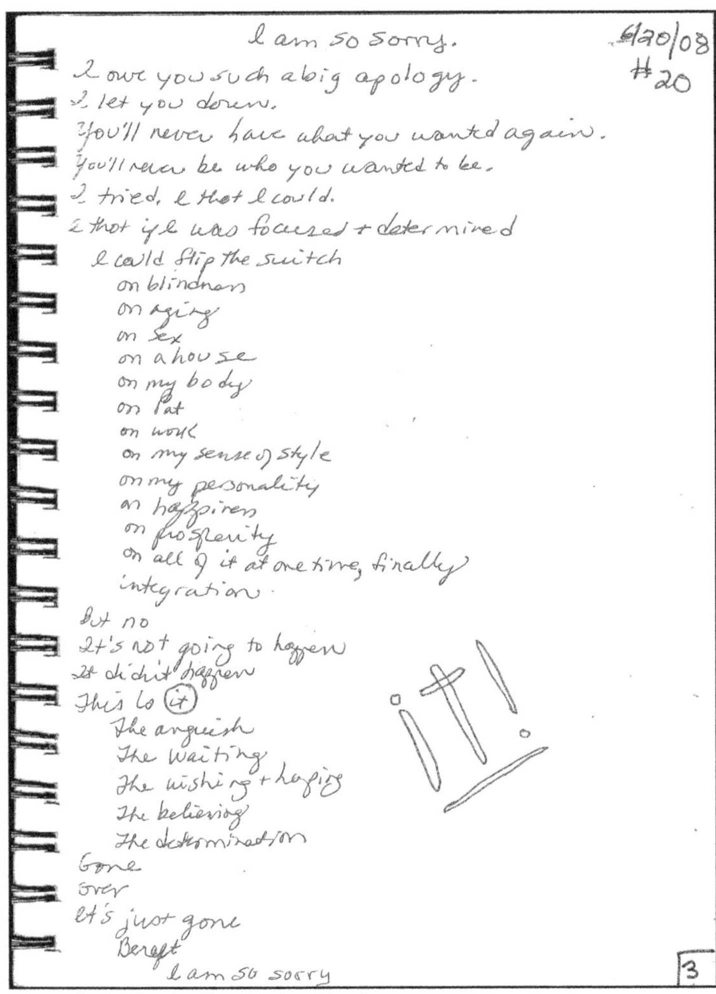
I am so sorry.
6/20/08
#20
I owe you such a big apology.
I let you down.
You'll never have what you wanted again.
You'll never be who you wanted to be.
I tried, I thot I could.
I thot if I was focused + determined
I could flip the switch
on blindness
on aging
on sex
on a house
on my body
on Pat
on work
on my sense of style
on my personality
on happiness
on prosperity
on all of it at one time, finally
integration.
But no
It's not going to happen
It didn't happen
This is (it)
The anguish
The waiting
The wishing + hoping
The believing
The determination
Gone
Over
It's just gone
Bereft
I am so sorry
IT!
3

Image 44: I am so sorry for "IT."

Ultimately, "IT" sprung from still wishing I never was wounded in the first place (27; 89). It's like having an accident that causes quadriplegia or being born with cerebral palsy. If we don't accept the wounding, we can't find our wholeness in spite of handicaps. I couldn't feel my soul's longing because I was wishing for something that couldn't be undone or erased. "IT" is holding on to repressed anger and taking it out on yourself. The truth and history of my "IT" was first revealed in a candid childhood photo of me (see Image 45), taken by my grandmother, where she caught me not smiling.

Image 45: A photo taken by my grandmother shows my inner sadness.

When I first saw the photo as an adult, I was taken aback—here was the proof. I saw little me looking inside myself, not smiling. I was wearing a robe and sitting at a table with my head resting on my folded hands. My eyes and expression were sad. When I was teaching at a university in 2006, a perceptive student told me privately after class that she could see sadness in my eyes. I didn't know my sadness showed; I thought I was doing a good job of hiding it. I hid it so my parents wouldn't be upset and then I hid it from myself, which only made me more confused and unhappy. Then, I knew I had to get to know my true feelings and contain "IT." At work, I remembered Robyn telling me my little ones inside were never going to grow up, nor were they ever going to go away. It became my job both to listen to and protect my inner self with more adult, effective coping mechanisms, as well as actively deal with "IT." Perhaps my inner self was stronger than I thought, but that was something I still needed to discover.

"IT" is why I would bury myself alive with too many projects, books, piles and files, priorities, obligations, and clutter. "IT" is why I would gain and lose weight, start and stop exercising, forget to take care of my environment, and not consistently do the things that would make me feel healthy and good about myself. One day, I made a chart of seven of my main issues on one axis and asked myself questions on the other, filling in my response in each cell. (See Image 46.) In the last line I felt I cracked the code: I needed to face, know, feel, allow, grow, do, and be "IT" (22; 121).

Issues	Weight	Food	Exercise	Sex	Finances	Order	Beauty
Sx Present	over 150 lbs. Biggest belly ever.	Eat whatever, whenever.	Avoid as much as possible.	Refuse, No bodily desire.	No debt. But spend too much.	Piles + Files, undeleted emails not neat + tidy	Black clothes
Best in Past	117, lean + fit. Lawless 3yrs 2001-4	Fit for Life, cooked gourmet	ran marathon, did triathlons, walked to work.	michael angelo easy, satisfying, creative, real, sustained	NOW is BEST!	Mt. Sinai w/ organizer ♀	36-casual + dressy sense of style
WANT Future	117-122 lean + fit + Healthy.	eat mindfully, soulfully. cook healthily.	yoga, walk, wts with desire + joy.	Real intimacy With Patrick. soulful + loving	Save more. Earn more. secure + generous	Have what need Quickly + easily restore order.	Sense of Style, Professional, Casual Sophisticated
WHAT IT WILL TAKE	Patience	Presence	Sensation	Acceptance	Focus	Convergence	Divergence
Let Go OF (Keeps in place)	Hiding, safety of protection, not caring	Emotional eating convenience, impulsivity	Inertia, denial, not scheduling	Fear of disappointment, comparing, Regret, Grief.	Procrastinating, Wishing for magic + no effort.	Decisions again, not making time to deal with	Invisibility, Getting too much, NOT Being 45.
How CAN I Cultivate	SAFETY	COMFORT	ENERGY	Desire	Willingness	Tolerance	Grace
Underlying Cause	[illegible] of work + Managing Visibility	Reward self for work effort	Don't want to Leave work	No energy left - solitude	Spend on vacations to Renew	Too much work to deal with	DON'T want more attention
IMPACT of work	Is healing to me + mm[illegible]	Restaurants in neighborhood	Few places + classes around	more masculine than feminine	Salary + security	More to read, write, do, + file	Easier to have 1 look
Stress	Behind Incomplete Disappointments	Hungry Anxious	Starting over	Flinch Embarrassed	Risk Bad Credit, Retirement	can't find things overwhelmed	NOT PUT TOGETHER clothes too tight
COPE	Lists, Bracket, Swim with sharks Journal/Inquiry	Pause, bring snacks, plan	Go slow	Breathe, eyes, Tantra practice	Expert support	MAKE TIME b/4 + after projs	Laundry, cleaners, shop
Hungry for	my body, Sanity, sustained	Creativity, peace	JOY Look forward to	Arousal, SYNERGY	Prosperity, Abundance	Aesthetically Pleasing	My Face, COLOR
ADVICE from Lane, RN	Love your self	Eat well, [illegible]	Yoga, Dance	Let people in	Life is short	Keep up with friends	Let yourself shine
21 KK	Face IT	Know IT	Feel IT	Allow IT	Grow IT	Do IT	Be IT

Comment + Contrast

Inquiry - I want to know more about the issues I continue to struggle with: wt, $, sex, [illegible], order. I'm curious if the underlying issues are similar and if there is something for me to learn that will help me move toward greater wholeness, integration, + peace — my soul's longing

TRUE HUMOR — 3/30/16 #22

Image 46: Cracking the code of core issues.

I learned I had to stop avoiding my wounded core as if it were a tumor, and instead to touch it lightly to see what was underneath. To go through it, not around it, in order to dissolve, metabolize, and release "IT." To realize "IT" doesn't have to persist. It was time to discover how "IT" got constructed and explore how to deconstruct it. Perhaps by understanding "IT" I would finally find my power.

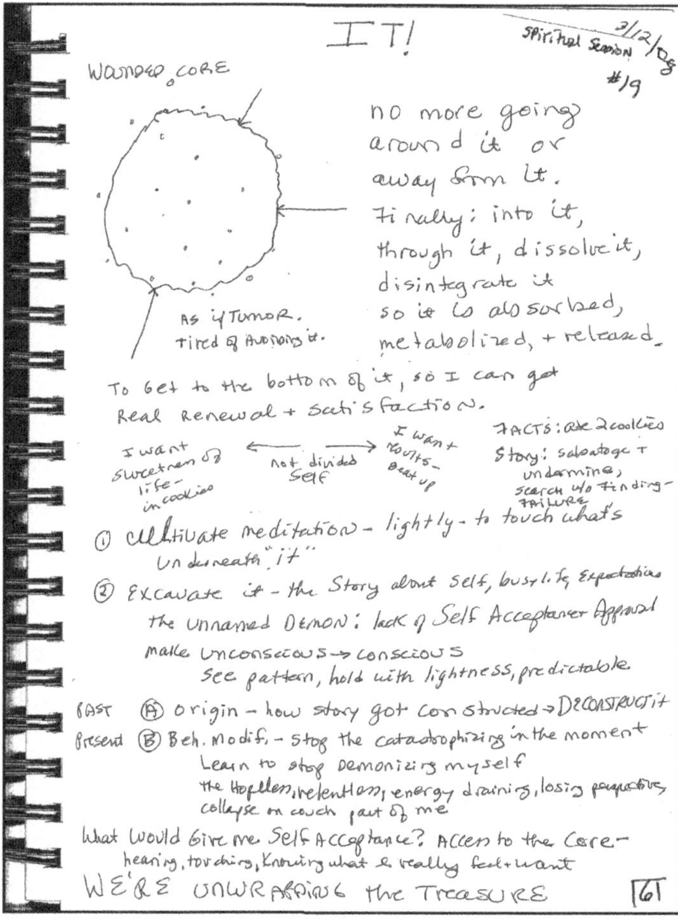

Image 47: Touching "IT," my wounded core.

This awareness was the beginning of hearing a voice inside that was more me, a part of me I called HER. Once I found HER—the little ones inside I had ignored and disparaged—I began to take HER out to really learn, be present at work, and take her intelligence seriously. I had HER meet people who enjoyed and encouraged HER and made HER feel alive and safe. She began to put "IT" in its proper place.

For so long, my fear of grieving prevented me from facing what I had given up by searching for perfection and not accepting being less than my expectations in any moment. With my prior tendency for procrastination, I finally decided the grief of regret would be so much worse if I waited to reconcile with myself until I was on my death bed. I began to face the less acceptable parts of myself and get to know them better (16; 87). I had feared my unmet need for recognition would be met unconsciously through illness or something ugly. I tried, without actively trying, to get rid of "IT" through fat, accidents, name-calling, and mess. Instead, I had to face unattractive parts of myself head on to grow intimate with them before I could ever heal and integrate. These included:

> **The persecutor/abuser/aggressor** who is angry and critical and hates my victim part, beats myself up, makes things worse, berates me and keeps me stuck, expecting I should do things perfectly or else get punished.
>
> **The victim** who says, "I can't," is afraid, worried, little, very sad, shut down, pretends and placates, inviting attack. She resigns herself, avoids conflict, accommodates, lacks confidence, is weak and vulnerable.
>
> **The saboteur** who attracts negative attention through delay, denial, distraction, forgetting, losing things, accidents, disconnection, and rebellion. She uses "negative control," meaning if I can't have what I want all at once, then I can guarantee failure and feel better that at least I was the cause of my humiliation, disaster, disappointment, embarrassment, and massive self-hate.

The persona of the good little girl, always trying to please, determined, devoted, and overprepared. She also lets herself be seen as messy, miserable, impatient, unrealistic, and self-absorbed.

These four inner voices and outer behaviors were—and still are—evident in situations that cause me unease, embarrassment, and pain. If I stop to reflect, in the privacy of my journals, I can distinguish who was taking an active role. Then I can think about how I could have done something more effective, dare I say, coming from a more authentic, integrated, centered, and grounded part of me. It takes practice and discernment, but step by step there are clues to understanding how to deconstruct "IT."

I saw that in searching for "IT" all these years (19; 31), I was really searching for:

Permission to listen to myself and be myself.

Acknowledgment of my shadow and how I collapse into the negative.

Choosing to enjoy who I am and share what I do have and what I can do.

Letting go of my relentless attachment to the past, of misery and beating myself up.

Asking for help to accept my imperfections and take action.

Having faith that my soul issues are why I was born, and I am protected and guided on my journey.

Being grateful for all who are there for me and all the blessings I have received (29; 19).

Finally, I had these core insights (16; 99):

My misery can go away, but not HER.

My dad, some of the doctors, and many senior leaders hate HER because they won't own their own vulnerability.

My mom and people like the CEO know HER and seduce HER out, but then they humiliate HER in public.

My job is to accept HER and not abandon HER or beat HER up.

Envy and comparisons, and worry I'll never reach my potential, is my work self (persona) trying to get love when and where it is not available.

Recognition that leads to inflation will lead to being banished or punished, therefore I have to give recognition and approval to myself.

Being mean and antiseptic when I don't meet my perfectionist expectations is not effective.

Disconnecting from myself as retaliation, when I have been unrealistic and naïve, must stop.

Integration for me includes letting responsibility be born from love and creativity born from grief.

My Deepest Wisest Self will guide me to make meaning of my work, choices, relationships, and life (27; 106).

I began to understand that I used "IT" as a kind of nervous tic to ward off aggression (11; 36). "IT" was why I would put myself down before someone else did. But I discovered that bullies thrive on that victim mentality. I would have to learn to use boundaries, own my own aggression, and express anger; to stop looking for the one "Aha!" moment that would make me all better, once and for all; to deeply accept my wholeness, my light and shadow, and change "IT" to desire (11; 53). I knew what I had to do, but as always, easier said—or known—than done.

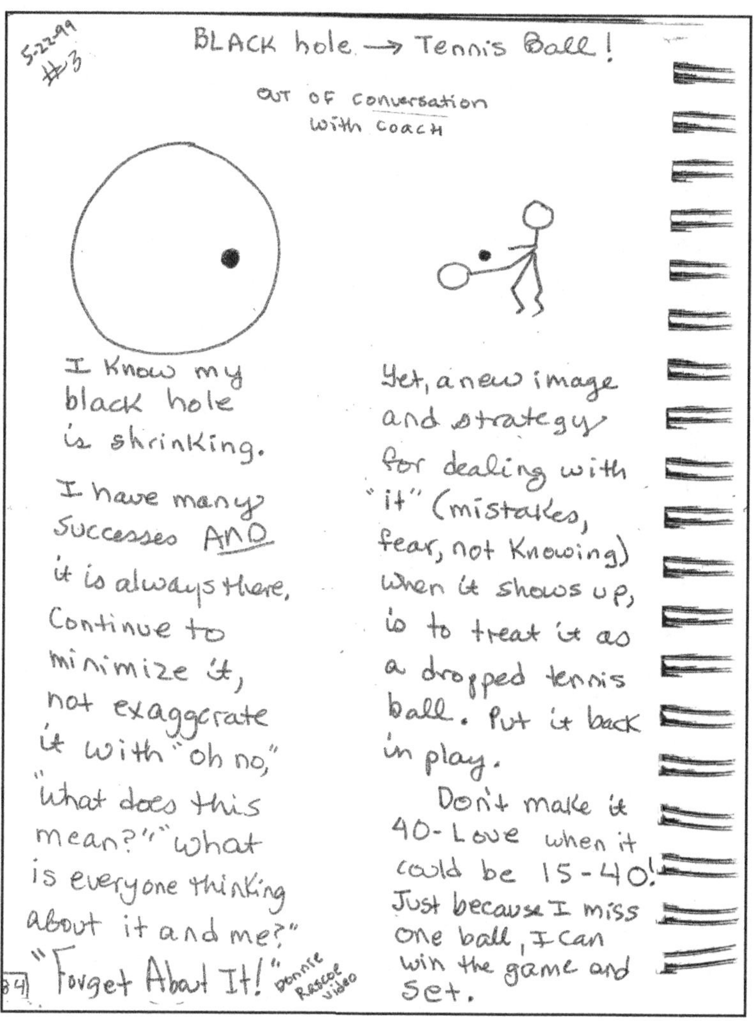

Image 48: Dealing with "IT" at work.

Anger

This being human is a guest house. Every morning a new arrival. A joy, a depression, a meanness, some momentary awareness comes as an unexpected visitor. Welcome and entertain them all . . . The dark thought, the shame, the malice, meet them at the door laughing and invite them in. Be grateful for whoever comes because each has been sent as a guide from beyond.

—Rumi, "The Guest House"

If you knew me, anger is not something you would associate with my personality. I am generally positive, enthusiastic, compassionate, and kind. Perhaps my unacknowledged feelings would leak out at work, but colleagues said I seemed "off," not angry. But if I track how my experience of anger has changed through the journals, it tells me why and how my wholeness was lacking. The story my parents would always proudly tell was what a perfect child I was. As a baby I didn't cry; I slept when I was supposed to sleep. They would wonder out loud why other parents complained when I was so easy. Then Mom would remind us that growing up she was frightened by her parents arguing, so she and Dad decided never to yell. Well, you can decide not to yell, but you can't decide never to feel upset with your child. That's why it became confusing when I could pick up on my parents' anger toward me, even though they consistently denied it. Mom expressed anger, or rather repressed it, through being annoyed and irritated; Dad with impatience, saying, "come on, come on."

In sixth grade I had one of my girlfriends over, and I was playing my guitar sitting on the bed. She spotted my plastic baseball bat in the corner of the room and started swinging. Next thing I knew she had unintentionally bashed the side of the guitar and broken it irreparably. Embarrassed and scared, she left abruptly to go home. I told her it was OK, an accident, don't feel bad, but as soon as she left I started crying. My parents called to me from their bedroom, never coming to see what had happened. Dad asked, "What's wrong?" But when I brought in the destroyed guitar, Dad didn't ask how it happened, berate me for breaking it, or comfort me with an assurance he'd replace it. Instead, he said, "Why do you have to be so emotional?" and invalidated my response completely. Mom looked at me sympathetically, but she didn't reach out with words of wisdom or offer any relief. I would have to wait until I met Patrick to know what being enveloped in someone's arms because you are hurting felt like. It was irresistible to feel that understood.

Another searing incident occurred, and reoccurred, during high school. It seemed we didn't like to shop as a family, so twice a year we adopted the "get it done" strategy. The day would come when Dad said I should go buy some "clothes for the season." He never told me how much I could spend or how many items I could get. It was always just "get what you need." I would try on each outfit in a mock fashion show while Dad sat in the living room and approved. When, at the end, I brought in the pile of clothing, he would scold me for choosing too many things and pick one item to return. Looking back, I think he was upset I was growing into a young lady and was scared of my budding sexuality. But in terms of money, he never told me what his budget was. A healthier parent might have taken the opportunity to set a spending boundary, or even emphasize quality over quantity. But as a narcissist, he couldn't imagine why I wouldn't do what he would do and intuit his rules without him having to say anything. This took all the joy out of shopping and constituted a pattern in other areas as well. I would always ask what the limit was on a dinner out or some other expenditure, but he would never say. I had to learn to hold back, look for nonverbal cues, and try to figure it out myself. Once he was mad because I asked him how he earned a living as a doctor, in terms of charging patients and providing for the family. He refused to respond, as if it was a secret and I was not to have an inquiring, practical mind that might be thinking of how I would eventually take care of myself. Since I was to be taken care of, in his view, why bother my pretty little head with such trifles?

Mom had this way of giving me feedback as a putdown: "You're so conceptual." I'd feel disappointed and, dare I admit, angry, when asking for advice and getting platitudes in return. She seemed to be quoting something she learned in therapy, as in "what was, was." But she'd say it with a Yiddish accent, "Vhat vuz, vuz." Yes, I needed to not live in the past, as did she, but her words lacked any emotional connection or intent.

My journals show my buried emotions and what messages I picked up. With the grief counselor I discussed in the previous chapter, I was able to get in touch with how persecuted and victimized I felt. The images I found and the words I wrote tell a very different story than the perfect child from the perfect family. No wonder I decided I never wanted anyone to feel as badly as I felt, causing me not to express anger or even admit to feeling that emotion.

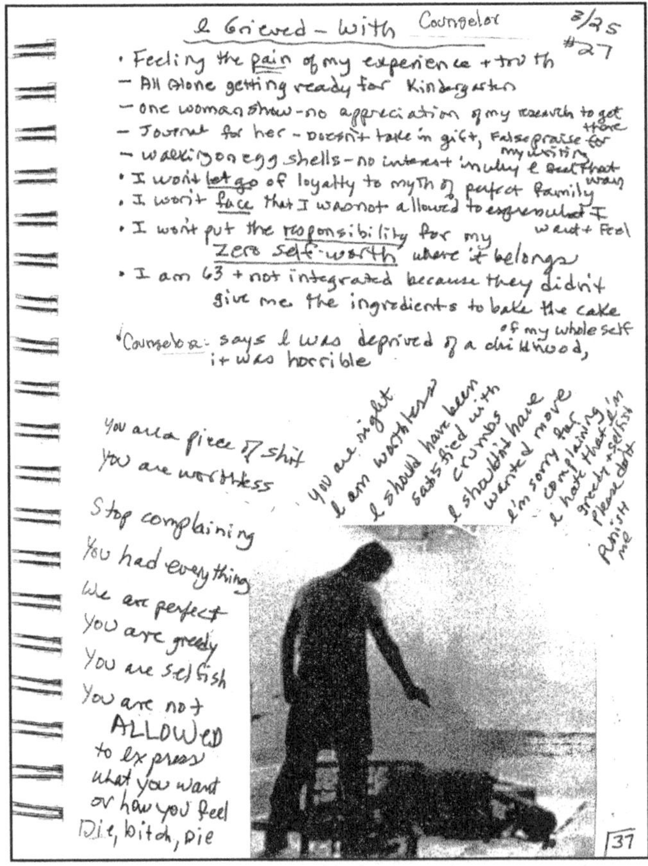

Image 49: Shutting down from angry messages I received.

A Total Biology practitioner I went to after the car accident reminded me of the denial of anger in our family. She said it was healthy I was angry because I didn't get the love and care I needed as a child. She helped me realize that as an adult, I no longer had to stuff it as if it was unacceptable. I needed to take down the protective wall I built and express what was dark in my soul. Go to the experience of abandonment and feel the rage and hurt of being misunderstood and unloved. I needed to see that I was not the center of my parents' life, and I did not have a nurturing nest to grow from. Feel it. Then release it. Because I'm an adult, I have tools, and I don't need my parents' approval, guidance or love (13; 56).

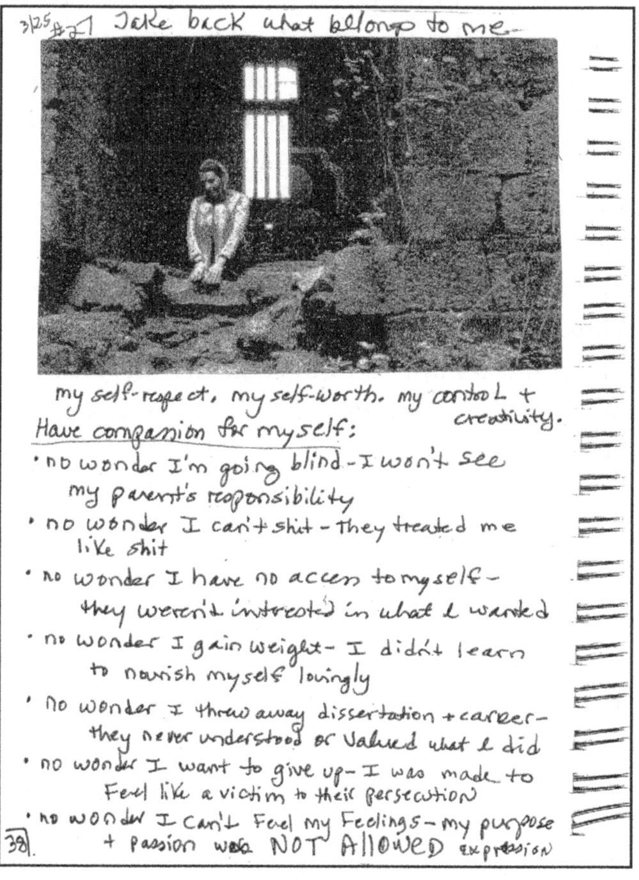

3/25 #27 Take back what belongs to me-

my self-respect, my self-worth, my control + creativity.

Have compassion for myself:

- no wonder I'm going blind - I won't see my parent's responsibility
- no wonder I can't shit - they treated me like shit
- no wonder I have no access to myself - they weren't interested in what I wanted
- no wonder I gain weight - I didn't learn to nourish myself lovingly
- no wonder I threw away dissertation + career - they never understood or valued what I did
- no wonder I want to give up - I was made to feel like a victim to their persecution
- no wonder I can't feel my feelings - my purpose + passion were NOT ALLOWED expression

38

Image 50: "Take back what belongs to me."

Prior to this type of healing, my first husband and I decided we, too, would never express anger, effectively repressing it and eventually causing the silent tension to drain the life out of our relationship. Now, Patrick and I decided to do things differently. He has helped me unlock my anger in healthy ways. I was relieved to realize I was no longer the pleasing, self-blaming and sacrificing child with him. I often treated Patrick the way I was treated: negatively, aggressively, and meanly—because I knew he could take it (2; 77). But unlike me, he would rather be angry than sad, easily expressing his displeasure as a corrective whenever he felt it. Then, for him, it would be over. For me, this was a shock. At first, I felt he had energetically vomited all over me, and it would take hours or days for me to clean myself off. But then, I realized how suppressing my feelings wasn't serving me, and I freed myself to speak up more and allow him to be his true self. Where we go in a conflict doesn't feel comfortable at the time, but letting the conflict play out has produced lasting benefits for deepening our understanding of each other and healing from our similarly challenging pasts.

A typical example is when we would have an argument—maybe about him not feeling respected when I left piles on the counter, or me not needing his help and wanting him to apologize for hurting me in some way—just before we were meeting friends. Once we were with others, he would flip to being outgoing and social and act as if nothing had happened between us. But I couldn't shake the feelings and he would ignore me, which was code for him being mad I couldn't bounce back as quickly and easily. For me, his cold shoulder added insult to injury. Once we got home, we would process the dynamic, each sharing our truth. It was extremely uncomfortable, but eventually we got to the other side and could hug and laugh at how ridiculous we were.

Looking back at my career, I realized that since I stifled my anger, my aggressive energy was often expressed through overachieving and turning my rage against myself. This had some benefits but many more costs. I would rather be depressed than angry, victim rather than persecutor. Yet, integration is finding a way to navigate both poles of any extremes. Not perfectly, but with willingness and awareness. Perfectionism is poison and a way to stay stuck in powerlessness. Being willing to aim lower and explore what is possible is a risk worth taking. For example, when I was obsessing about how to meet the needs of the managers in the training program my partner and I designed, one of the managers teased me in the privacy of her office. She gave me her sage advice, which I use to this day: "There is no bar so low I can't meet it." What she meant was, if I would lower my expectations, it would be good enough. What I received as a bonus was that creating less pressure opened a space for me to be both/and rather than all/nothing. As in, I could *both* create actions to implement objectives of the training session *and* hold space for spontaneity and connecting with the managers in real time. I moved into territory I hadn't known existed.

Minor rebellions signal anger to me, when I'm procrastinating, shutting down, or being pissy (call it fussy, snippy, cranky, or crabby). If I remember, I ask myself "*Tell me what is wrong and is there is a way to be more direct with my feelings?*" For instance, instead of stewing, could I cancel an appointment I feel is interrupting my creative flow, or could I decide to tell someone the impact their behavior is having on me?

A breakthrough came when I could witness someone's anger and not have it be about me. I could observe the rise and fall of the emotion and have compassion for their pain. Two quotes in my journal (32; 88) resonated with me and provided insights:

> What we have named as anger on the surface is the violent outer response to our own inner powerlessness, a powerlessness connected to such a profound sense of rawness and care that it can find no proper outer body or identity or voice, or way of life to hold it.

This quote from David Whyte, an English poet, helped me understand that anger is an expression of deep caring and also helplessness, giving me insight about the other person and empathy for them. I could imagine having compassion instead of just fear, hating it, and wishing the expression of anger would stop.

Then, I saved in my journal what my therapist Robyn wrote about what happens when someone has a meltdown:

> When we share intense emotions, its energy is like a tuning fork: it resonates similar emotion in the person listening to us. If they aren't in touch with or are actively avoiding that emotion in themselves, listening to us stirs up unpleasant/disturbing waves in their psyches. Their attempts to "help *us* feel better" may, more likely, be seen as their attempts to shut down the feelings in us that are resonating so unpleasantly in them so that *they* can feel better.

An example of how I used these insights happened one night when many of Patrick's beloved CDs fell to the hard floor and broke. In the past I would have hated his anger over the incident and wanted him to stop expressing it. But with the first insight, I could see how helpless he must have felt because he cared so much for his collection of music. I then privately sent him loving energy. I didn't try to problem solve or offer platitudes. I didn't try to help, only getting in his way and making things worse. Instead, I used the experience to see the places in me that were hard to deal with and witnessed him with love and compassion. This wasn't about me. What a triumph!

The thing is, I always wished I could read about how others actually experienced and dealt with their emotions. Because we weren't to talk about feelings as children, my feelings seemed to get lodged in my body and I didn't know how to get them out. I tried to avoid expressing anger but wished I could let it escape and hated not knowing how to be more skillful dealing with it in myself or others. That led to reading extensively on dealing with anger and conflicts. Still, those books seemed too logical and removed from actual experience, not connected to the angst I felt so acutely. Words on a page can only do so much to capture feelings in the heart and soul. I studied how I dealt with frustration, unhappiness, being mad at myself, not feeling safe, and bullying.

But better than trying to analyze my reactions, I tried to build on experiential learning. In 1995 I attended a three-day workshop about receiving the raw emotion of anger. In pairs, one person would yell, less with words than with deep sounds and intense facial expressions. The receiver's job was to stand there and let the emotion wash over them. To do nothing. To not try to control it, run away, retaliate, or dissolve into tears. Then we reversed roles. More practice like this would have been truly helpful, but I knew of no other offerings. Yet, little by little, I tried to risk growing into facing and dealing with anger, in both myself and others.

For example, when I was betwixt and between jobs, and lost about what to do next, a close friend told me she hated to see me drowning in sorrow. She said I needed to get angry at bullies instead of taking it out on myself. She taught me what she had finally learned when leaving her abusive husband: "Even if I did things to cause it, even if I can understand his reasons, the behavior is unacceptable and has to stop."

Seeing how such a gentle soul as my friend finally gathered strength, stood her ground, and got out of a bad situation was very instructive for me. It led me to self-talk that enabled me to own my anger and gain perspective that had been invisible in my buried emotions. Even if I didn't express my anger to the actual bullies, the energy moved me forward to explore options and get unstuck (26; 62).

Then there is what I called "facing my fiasco." I went to a recommended financial planner to get assistance in creating a budget. However, in no time she began shaming me about buying too many books. She said I'd have to give up my dream of a house in the woods because I needed money for retirement. She said I wanted things because I felt deprived. I was appalled at how someone I was hiring was scolding me, and I certainly didn't feel she could help me. I ended our session with composure, but as soon as I got home, I sobbed for hours, releasing the emotions, especially anger, I had felt during the meeting. How dare she talk to me that way . . . the way I talk to myself! But the situation was instructive; it showed me my boundary. I decided I only wanted to work with people who understood me, listened, and helped me make integrated decisions, rather than legislating them. I know what yes feels like, and this woman was a definite NO (18; 67).

Reviewing my journals showed me shifts in dealing with anger: how I started hating my past, not me; how I had dreams where I was appalled at not expressing my rage and sick of not owning my truth; how I learned to help people feel safe so they could then hear my thoughts and feelings about holding them accountable. I began to accept anger as a real and valid emotion, linking it to waiting (weighting) for my life to be handed to me, for others to meet my needs, waiting for the convenient time, for others to change. Denied anger was the bell jar that stifled my aliveness and prevented "going for it." I eventually decided to meet anger with curiosity and see, as Rumi says, if I could welcome all my emotional guests and learn what they had to teach me. That led to me wondering what actually triggered my emotions.

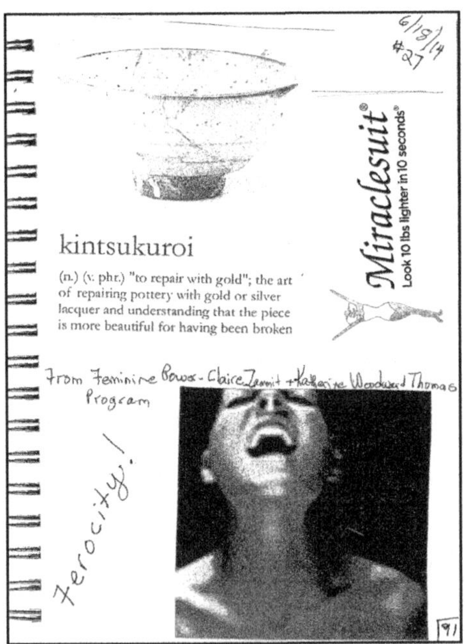

Image 51: Imagining expressing ferocity and repairing what's broken.

Triggers

What got you here won't get you there.
—Marshall Goldsmith

Inside my very first journal, I drew a colorful picture of a clown with the title, "Please don't push my buttons." Each button on the costume had a different trigger. At that time, I identified them as: "see me, anger, rigid, criticism, what if, and abandonment." Wishing I didn't get triggered, I was attempting to at least get to know my buttons so I could anticipate them and perhaps not get so triggered by them. Reacting to triggers made me feel badly about myself, like the song "Cathy's Clown" by the Everly Brothers. Rather than being about a jilted boyfriend, I took the lyrics to be about my discordant relationship with myself. Why didn't I realize everyone had buttons? Or pay attention to their reactivity, instead of beating myself up? It would be a long time before I could give myself credit for trying to be self-aware and handle my emotions better, and years before research and the practice of emotional intelligence made such behaviors important in the work setting and for successful leadership.

Image 52: "Please don't push my buttons."

I am now quite aware of other buttons. Feeling not listened to is always a trigger, be it with my husband, a colleague, or a repairman. Another to be counted on is when my computer freezes, or some other technical fix is needed in the house. I hate it when friends or family disconnect and won't say why. More frequently it's fearing I'll be late for a commitment or interrupted in my flow when engrossed in writing, a project, or movie. Losing things drives me crazy. Hearing words that make me feel diminished, like "cute" or "little," brings me right back to my childhood. Worst is when I give myself a hard time because I worry I said something that made someone else feel badly and would damage our relationship. In any of these situations when I am triggered, I am not at my best. I might start talking loudly, being snippy or confrontational, getting distracted, or stewing in silent frustration. Usually these responses are fairly easily remedied with a walk around the block, making something to eat, taking deep breaths, and trying to find the humor in the upset. If nothing works, crying and hiding in bed, pulling the covers over my face, soothes me until the energy passes.

During my years as a leader of culture change, I found examples that captured my growing awareness of other triggers at work. My approach to self-discovery is to be meticulous with analyzing real situations. Documenting them makes me face the facts of what happened. If I am ever to improve, I know I have to tolerate the uncomfortable feelings, admit the awkward moments, and think about what I could have done differently. At least, by lessening my perfectionism, I can learn to anticipate my triggers, even as I wish I didn't still have those buttons to push. Here, as with anger, are situations that I am making transparent for the benefit of those of you who have missed getting mentored and supported in your own work and personal lives. Some I eventually mastered and deactivated, like disconnecting the wires on a light switch. With others, I just had to accept that they may surface and keep trying to be more adept in my responses.

Here are nine examples of how I got triggered at work:

Something was unfinished. It would be like a blinking light demanding attention. Then, once completed, it was off my list and I'd experience momentary calm and relief. Until the next demand took its place. This was an addictive cycle that provided no satisfaction: avoid, resist, push through, do it, be tired and disappointed, waiting for the next assignment with my empty promise not to repeat the cycle (10; 10).

Feeling I was being disloyal to my parents' view of me. It was clear to my body workers that I had the skills to help others but needed to use them on myself. My body responded positively in each new position, as if saying, "I'm going for it." But it was as if my lack of organization, gracefulness, and confidence was designed to guarantee dissatisfaction and keep me tied to my parents' view of me. Instead, the bodyworkers asked, could I free myself from their distorted vision and live the truth of who I was—courageous, compassionate, and competent? (10; 37).

Being dominated, micromanaged, and rushed. The outside consultants who were the eyes and ears of the CEO acted as if I needed to be pushed and structured to take action. As my father often did, I would say to myself, "Don't tell me what to do." Even though I was aware of my resistance at times, it was mostly because I hated starting projects. But once I understood what I was doing, grasping the pattern in the individual steps, there was no stopping me. Eventually, when I finally spoke my truth to the consultants, we began treating each other as equals in different roles (10; 24).

Others were being creative, productive, and honoring themselves, and I wasn't. Especially if their efforts were seen by others and led to promotions or other opportunities, I might feel sorry for myself. Once I wrote a snippy, self-righteous email to someone—not the one for whom I felt envy, because I hadn't acknowledged my feelings. Instead, I acted them out. Over time, I learned to slow down whenever I felt anxious, rather than rush to take action impulsively in order to get rid of my toxic feelings. Instead, I learned to use uncomfortable feelings as clues to my true desires and to inspire myself to take the next right step. Impatient with how long my process often took, I would remind myself it might be because I tended to do things deeply and widely, not superficially and transactionally (10; 134). Also, everyone's journey and time frames were different. I needed to stop one of my worst habits, that of comparing myself unfavorably to others (11; 5).

People who overreacted and were unpredictable. I dreaded meetings and left every conference room feeling marginalized and devalued. I hated being in an expanded space and then energetically having my balloon popped, especially in public. I hated leaders being political and inauthentic. I hated all the blustering. I practiced expecting the unexpected (like improv), not making the other person's behavior be about me, and learning more about the political frame of reference. I practiced not making things worse by "putting a spin on my wobble." (See Image 53.) Also, I learned that some people who acted all puffed up and critical of others were really more sensitive than they let on. It relieved me to observe how "they could dish it out but couldn't take it" (11; 6-7).

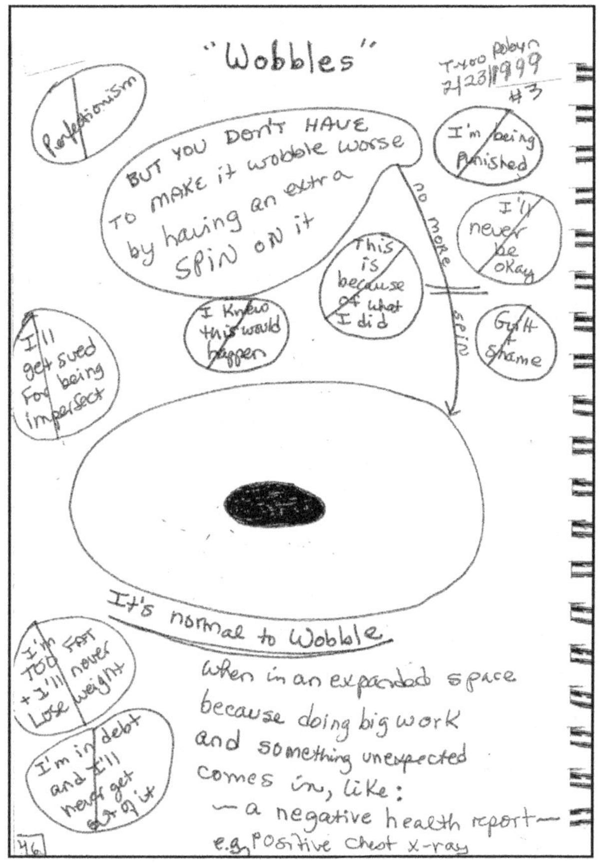

Image 53: "Don't put a spin on your wobble."

People who controlled, manipulated, undermined, and were not held accountable. There was no reason I had to like being treated disrespectfully. My job was to learn to speak up with respect and not protect those who humiliated me. My default was to act from the fearful little girl who wasn't doing a good job. That confused people and put me in the middle, where I did not want or need to be. Nevertheless, not everyone came from integrity or valued what I valued. Choosing my battles was another lesson (11; 111–112).

People who acted smug and didn't appreciate my expertise and style. I finally observed this ongoing dynamic with repeat offenders and decided to raise it, providing emotional safety. Then, I asked them why they acted as if they didn't trust me. I told them they acted as if I was doing something to hurt them, the client, or the institution. I heard them attributing bad motives to me and I didn't feel I deserved it. They certainly were not bringing out the best in me. That truth cleared the air and they apologized and offered different options for working together. Real progress (15; 10).

Fear of being scapegoated, humiliated and rejected. A boss was going to confront an employee, whom I knew was aggressive and not open to feedback. The boss asked my opinion of her, since the employee often denied, blamed, and withdrew when criticized. Being aware of the upcoming conversation, I was more upset than the employee was. I was feeling overly responsible for her pain and protected her by not speaking up. I also liked times we collaborated and would miss her if she left. The outcome, according to the boss, was that she owned part of her behavior this time, but it didn't change my upset anticipating her anger in the future. Turns out I felt relieved when she finally left and moved on (16; 24).

Feeling hurt and not knowing what to do about it. My spiritual therapist helped me see the reality of two types of hurt: unintentional, from people we love, and reactive, from people with whom we don't feel safe or know well. With the second group we might be moved to retaliate. With a colleague who led with haughtiness, the therapist helped me instead wonder about that person's insecurity and lack of awareness. Finding compassion, I considered that perhaps she acted superior to keep people away and not be vulnerable. If so, I reasoned she must be hurting inside for her to use that defense. Asking myself how I could react differently, I looked for ways to build a bridge each time the situation resurfaced (21; 111).

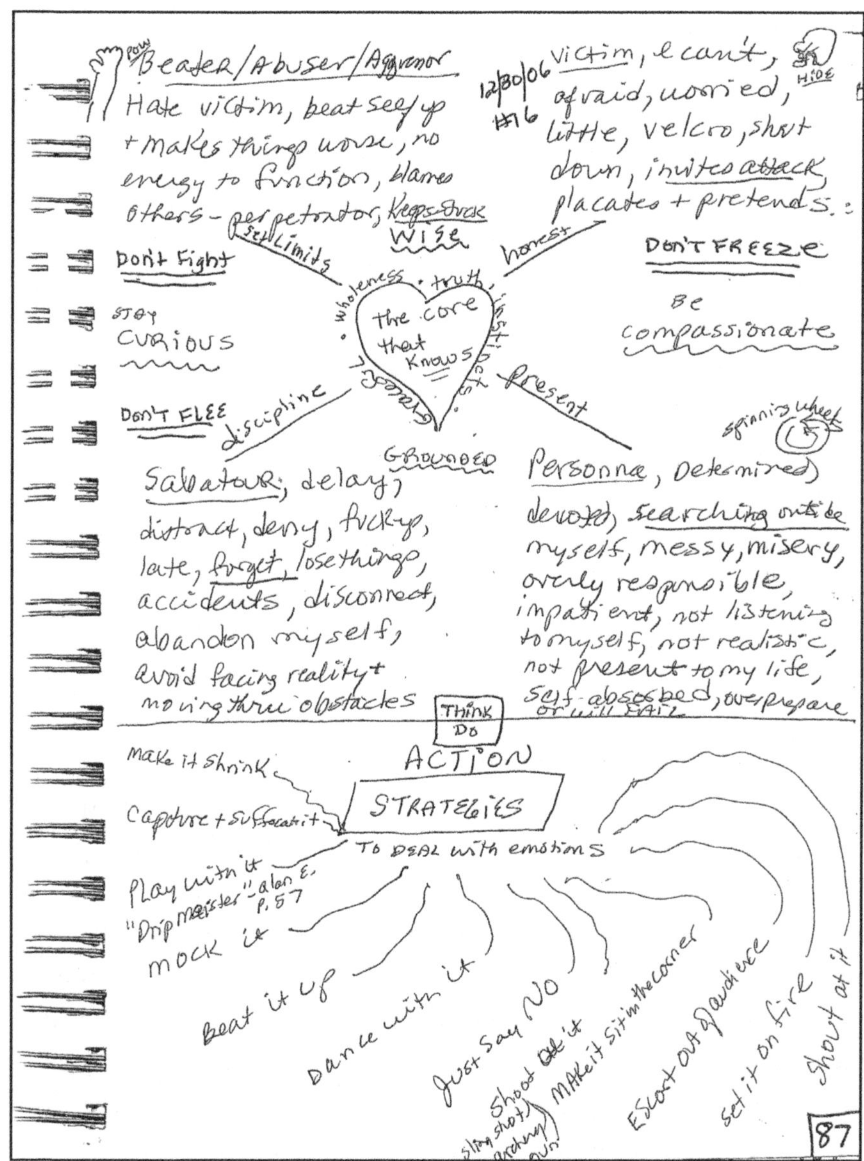

Image 54: "Fight, Flight, or Freeze."

Here's what I have learned from examining situations where I have been triggered. Due to the unacknowledged trauma I experienced as a child, when later terrorized and triggered, I reacted as our nervous systems are programmed: fight, flight, or freeze. I relied on flight and freeze in response to other people's fight (16; 86). Because of my default "*I can't*," I told myself too often that I couldn't face others or hold my own. But what I was learning was that even though at the moment of conflict, when I thought whatever I was feeling was the most real and true thing, it really was only a part of me, not the whole of me. I had other parts that could stay curious and see that when others needed to let off steam, it likely wasn't about me. I then needed to use whatever strategies I could to stay grounded and keep breathing. Over time I could play with my fearful frozen self and not take it so seriously. Imagine if I could even find some humor in the scenario, rather than scaring myself with how heavy and stuck I felt? My main strategy was to pause, be with my feelings, then ask myself how to handle the situation, and most critically, let it all go and move on. The most important step is to pause. It breaks the stimulus-response habit. It gives the nervous system time to quiet down and not react emotionally. Taking time to intentionally breathe helps short-circuit instinctive and not reasoned responses. Then after the rest of the steps, my key word for the last step was, "*Next!*" (13; 56).

When coaching clients who were triggered, we would question whether their problem could be a projection of disowned parts of themselves. As has been said, "If you can spot it, you've got it." With leaders whose main concern was being in control, I saw how detrimental unfettered aggressive behavior was on employee morale. To help leaders grow and the organizational culture change, it was my job to speak my truth respectfully, using boundaries and political savvy. I had knowledge and compassion for them based on my experience. At the same time, until those capacities were more solid in me, I had to take care of and mentor myself.

I knew having boundaries required awareness of self versus others. When I was young, I was desperate to have my strengths and weaknesses mirrored to me. With my parents focused on themselves, this process got inverted: I became skilled at mirroring them and others. I unconsciously smiled most of the time to keep people attracted to me, but I discovered I didn't fully connect with others if they told me something about myself that I wasn't ready to hear. Giving off a need to be seen as perfect, I knew, of course, that I wasn't, but I was afraid to find out the impact of my behavior on others. Therapy provided some of that important information, and learning about group dynamics helped fill in more blanks. Similarly, I observed that not everyone was on the path to learning about themselves; some had other core motives, such as power and control. With this perspective, it was easier to understand where others, by whom I was triggered, might be coming from and, at the same time, stay separate from their negative influence and manipulations. I once had a coaching client who always wanted to be right. He never could see when he delivered information that wasn't his to share, because he wanted attention that he thought would show him to be worthy of more power and a promotion. It was my responsibility to keep focusing on the goals and opportunities in fraught situations such as this one with as much curiosity, respect, and grace as possible.

As Hermann Hesse said, "If you hate a person, you hate something in him that is part of yourself. What isn't part of ourselves doesn't disturb us." Getting to know these repressed and rejected aspects is not easy and cannot usually be done alone. It requires exploring childhood trauma with a qualified professional to discover the origin of patterns developed to protect the child from punishment and the consequences of certain unacceptable behaviors in the family. Determined to unearth my shadow, I was always in some sort of therapy and healing practice. In the beginning I would have been happy if I could have figured out a way to just "seem together" without doing the hard work of really facing myself. Later, I decided I didn't want to take "a spiritual bypass," as if enlightenment could come from just focusing on the positive and repeating affirmations.

One way to go deeper was to explore my response to triggers and to ask myself why I was reacting in an unhealthy and unconstructive way. The process involved backtracking through emotions to memories and early programming. Another reason I wanted to do this inner work was professional: to help build communities in organizations that were more aware of themselves and didn't project evil motives on others to justify meanness or emotional violence. For example, graduate students in the course I was teaching on gender in the workplace would bring in tricky situations, such as being accused of relying on white women's privilege or suffering from stereotypes preventing women in academia from achieving leadership positions. I used all this information about triggers and organizational dynamics to unpack their beliefs, feelings, and options. By not being as afraid to face the dark side of individuals and organizations, I strengthened my leadership and ability to coach others in the classroom and at work. The more I could accept myself, the more I could help others with their own dilemmas.

CHAPTER SIX

Accepting

Healing may not be so much about getting better, as about letting go of everything that isn't you—all of the expectations, all of the beliefs—and becoming who you are.

—Rachel Naomi Remen

Me, Warts and All

One of the dominating themes in my journals is the need to understand my strengths and weaknesses, warts and all. Coming out of childhood with a shaky identity and unstable foundation, I was inordinately sensitive to feedback from others, both positive and negative. I sought friends and colleagues to affirm what they saw in me so I could piece together who I was. If someone said something positive and meaningful, it filled me up but—with the leaks in my vessel—didn't last. When given a negative, I would swallow it whole, then regurgitate every negative judgment I never let go of. I was long overdue to have an internalized sense of who I was, based on accurate mirroring over time, but this self-image was something I struggled to form. That is why so many journal examples swing from elation to despair.

After a while, it becomes both boring and bewildering to read over and over the same things. From the solid ground I'm on now, I marvel at the teeter-totter of my emotions and unstable sense of self. It's frankly embarrassing. But this is the consequence of lack of mirroring from narcissistic parents. Friends and colleagues would say: "You're brilliant." "You're too sensitive." "You're so creative." "You are too perfectionistic." "Your desk is messy." "You need better boundaries." "You are a talented gem; we are lucky to have you." Now I know it's all true; it's the total package of me. But for years I couldn't believe the good, hated the bad, and barely tolerated the ugly feelings, as if walking by a distorted mirror in an amusement park—which was anything but amusing. Slowly, with both/and perspective, I began to really listen and absorb the messages from others.

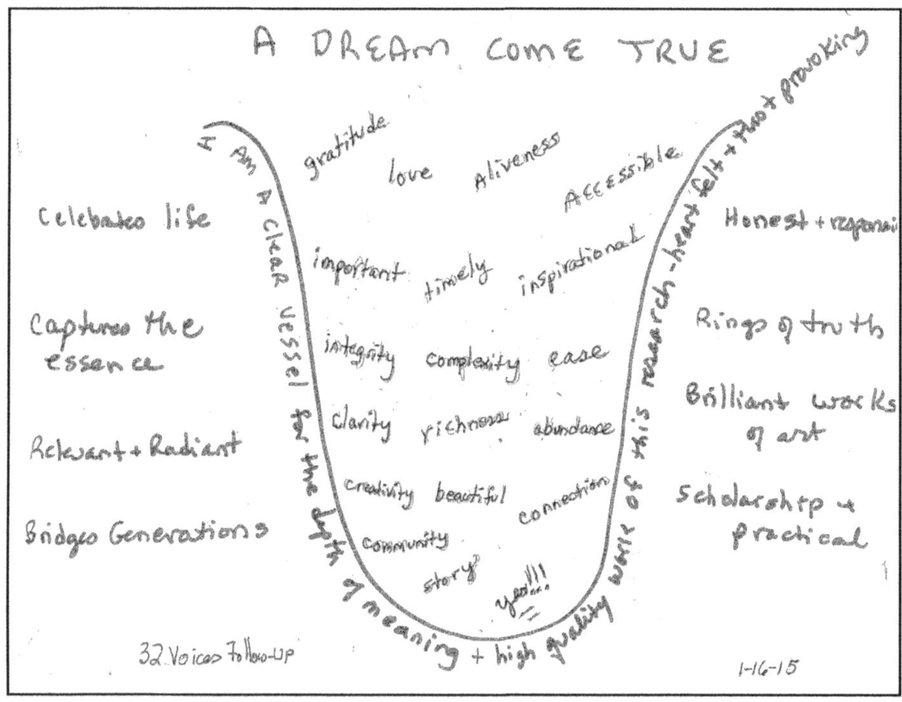

Image 55: "A Dream Come True": being a clear vessel.

Perhaps the feedback that has meant the most to me was from one of the women in my doctoral study. She was also in a workshop where I introduced my research in 1994, and she presented with me the findings of the twenty year follow-up. She called my first study "exquisite" and my follow-up "significant." As those two pieces of work represented the bookends of my academic career, her praise led me to believe in the impact of this accomplishment, which I couldn't see myself. After the presentation, I walked into the ladies' room, where a participant had been telling my second copresenter what she saw in me. Seeing me, the copresenter said, "Tell her directly." The participant held up a mirror showing attributes no one has ever told me about so directly. "I have never seen anyone with all the qualities you have, all at once," she said. "You are engaging and authentic, analytic and brilliant, intuitive and creative, methodical and determined, and clear and expressive" (29; 95). I was floored. It took time for her experience of me to sink in, even though we received a standing ovation and outstanding scores and comments on the formal evaluation of the session (29; 140). How could I be so unaware of myself and the effect I had on others?

Later, when debriefing the experience of collaborating for this workshop, the copresenters offered additional feedback. Because their positive and negative comments were balanced, I was better able to absorb them. One said she was glad the template she offered was helpful with structure, but noted she often had to be patient with me while I processed how to put the design in sequential order. The other wondered why I needed three conference calls to design the workshop. She never could afford that much time and perfectionism in her other work. She suggested I work on "good enough," similar to the advice I had received about lowering the bar.

Patrick was an experienced external OD consultant with his own firm, The Consulting Group. While he became an OD professional because of my encouragement and support, by this time he could reciprocate, as he understood my work tendencies intimately. He was proud of me, but also knew that for me, recognition was problematic. He hoped I'd go forward with grace and for the love of the work. He'd seen me go backwards, beat myself up, or sabotage myself enough times, and he hoped I would avoid that. He advised being positive, grateful, and focused on the future. Over our years together, many of his significant insights and recommendations appear in my journals (29; 102):

> My future won't be handed to me; it has to be created and developed by me because it has never existed before.
>
> Patrick always saw that I lacked confidence and tried to support me with his love and perspective. However, it was frustrating for him to see the same issues over and over. He said I needed to find my core and ask myself: Why don't I feel it? Who am I? What is my drive? What is my resistance? When will I stand alone?
>
> He believed I would have a bright future. I am "somebody." Identify who that somebody is and how I can help others go forward with what I have learned.
>
> Be resilient. Own my force. I am brilliant, strategic, influential, and dynamic. Let others see me as he does.
>
> Be grounded and own my opinion. Figure out what's my word. Is it integrator? Then stand for that.

I was appreciative of his feedback, and I reflected on it. Although I never quite created the future he held as a possibility, I am deeply grateful for his love and partnership. I was also thankful for my friends and colleagues who shared what they saw as my strengths and weaknesses. One of the problems with finding my core was that I couldn't *feel* it. Peter Vaill used to say to me that with my encyclopedic knowledge, I shouldn't read or write anything I didn't feel. If I didn't lead with my heart, my work would be sterile and boring. When I connected with my feelings, I was creative and brilliant and others could benefit. My dilemma was that I could process things intellectually—all the observations, advice, suggestions, and insight from others—but the issue for me was not intellectual. It was emotional. As a smart person, I would have thought my way out of not holding on to my strengths and weaknesses if I could. I needed to feel my way out of it, to shift how I felt about myself.

You must know, too; we can't just tell ourselves to see ourselves differently. It's like when I was learning to play Frisbee. I thought I was doing what my friends explained, but my body wasn't cooperating. I couldn't feel what their words and instructions meant. That disconnect is what happens when we have had early emotional neglect and lack of mirroring. We have to eventually experience a paradigm shift of the self. In my case, I first had to believe I had a self, then that my self was valid and worthy, and further learn how to use it successfully in any given situation. That's not an easy thing and let me remind you, it is not linear. Yet, it's worth the effort of not giving up, no matter what. Otherwise, what's the alternative? That's actually why I am taking the risk to write this book. If any of you feel your sense of self is slippery, you can't hold on to it or find it, and you too are baffling to your friends, family, and colleagues, please know you are not alone. There is at least one other person who has felt that way, and she put herself together by reading her own words, thoughts, and feelings, her own journal entries, again and again. By reviewing "My Wise and Wonderful Black Book Series," I finally had enough clues to connect the dots. I was *becoming visible to myself*, even if I wasn't going off into the sunset with a shiny new plan.

Connecting the Dots

Unbelievably, I didn't start figuring out who I was based on my own archeological dig until participating in my seven sisters "Pleiades" storytelling group in 1993. I was forty-three, in the dissertation phase of the doctoral program, and searching for clues on how to understand the collective story of my thirty-two completed individual interviews. The facilitator said we first had to identify and "map" the story we most related to in *Women Who Run with the Wolves* by Jungian analyst Clarissa Pinkola Estés. We had to buy a journal and write in it throughout the group experience. I added notes on movies and books I liked, my own poems, some of Cathy Guisewite's *Cathy* cartoons (remember those?!), feedback I received, insights from mistakes and conflicts, issues with money and time, and anything else that seemed relevant to my journey. In particular, I took notes on the creative process and applied it to my dissertation progress and challenges. The permission and guidance unleashed my creative expression with collage and an emotional freedom I had never before enjoyed.

The story I resonated with was about Vasalisa the Wise, a little girl who loses her young, loving mother. On her deathbed, the mother gives Vasalisa a little doll, telling her always to keep it with her, always to keep it hidden, and always to consult it when she needs advice. When her father remarries, her stepmother is predictably evil and her daughters predictably jealous. They treat Vasalisa cruelly and ultimately conspire to send her out into the cold, dark night for a fire ember. This requires a dangerous journey into woods inhabited by the witch Baba Yaga, which will surely lead to Vasalisa's death. Consulting her doll at every turn, Vasalisa manages to confront Baba Yaga, who demands that she complete nine impossible tasks. After she succeeds with the help of her doll, Baba Yaga sends her home with a fiery skull, which burns the family and house to the ground.

The story resonated with me because the innocent girl had to accept the circumstances of how she was treated. Her weak father allowed exploitive and exclusionary behavior from the wounded feminine influence in their house. While frightened, Vasalisa symbolically goes on a journey to the unconscious. There she faces negative forces both in the world and within herself. Learning about her shadow in a way she wouldn't have if not for being mightily challenged, she trusts her intuition (and her mother's advice) and stands up to the intimidating authority figure, Baba Yaga. By seeing the light of who she is in the underworld of her psyche and soul, she becomes a whole person who can use what she knows to go forward in life with confidence and potency. No longer naïve and heeding the counsel not to ask too many questions, she understands the power of seeing the truth and not letting herself go back to being unaware. It was not an easy path, but the power of her story made me feel that one day I could complete the difficult tasks I had to encounter to become whole. This story still lives inside me and has provided at least one map for my own inner journey.

Image 56a: Mapping the story of Vasalisa.

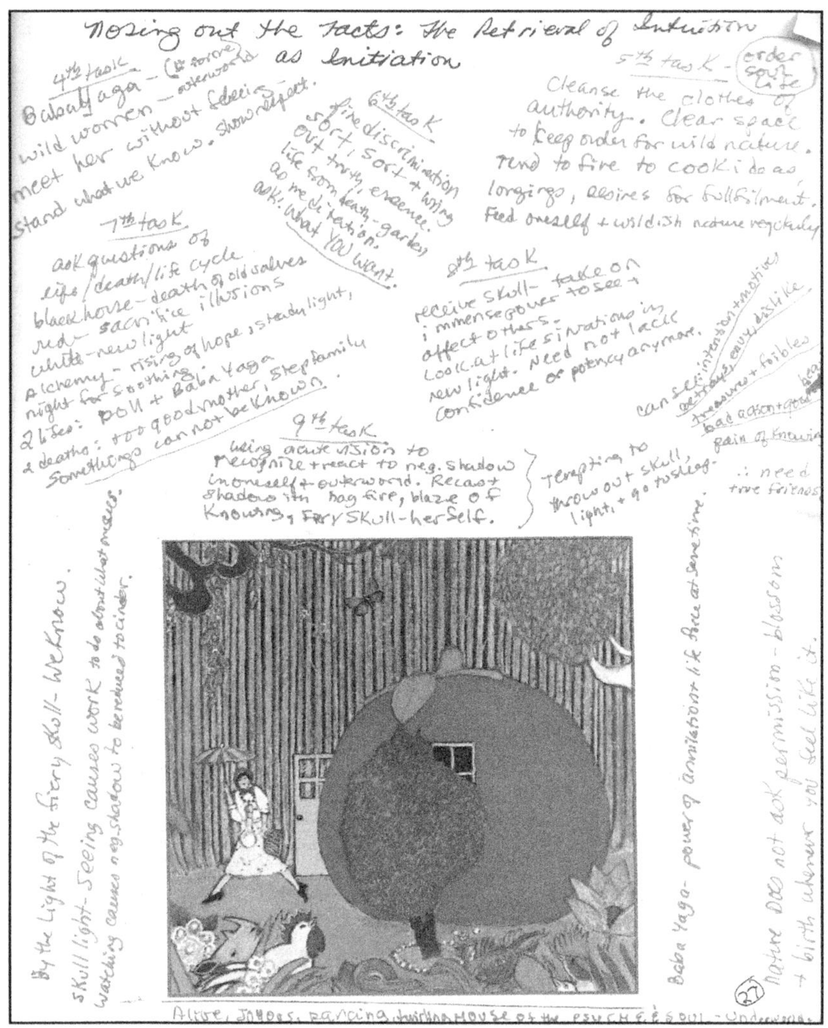

Image 56b: Mapping the story of Vasalisa.

In an effort to embark on knowing and seeing myself in a new way, I used my conceptual skills to categorize what I observed when I looked in my own mirror of introspection. I made up names and personalities for each aspect of myself, imagined their appearance, and also assigned each aspect a song to remind me how to tame and integrate each of my four oh-so-different parts with a little humor:

Taskmaster: My Taskmaster is the "work mode" voice always beating me up. It values achievement over everything else, including health and happiness. It feels like masculine energy and dresses in a conservative black suit, peering over bifocals at me in a cautioning judgmental scowl. The Taskmaster says: "Tell me I'm prolific and productive," "If I don't excel and perform, I'm nothing," and "Go faster, don't let people interfere with your plans." Then, he berates me for being stupid and not fast enough, making me hate myself and act critical and complain. His purpose is to keep me driven and motivated, but he lacks a sense of balance. He's like a pianist who only plays one key over and over. He requires that I develop aggression, realistic time frames, and internal expectations. The way to tame the perfectionistic Taskmaster is to ask for support before becoming exhausted rather than magnify self-doubts and weaknesses, and to focus on power and priorities. Song: Frank Sinatra's "My Way."

Poet: My Poet tries to open me up through nature and solitude to express myself creatively. She loves symbols and is athletic and artistic. There are never enough books, ideas, or adventures for my Poet to read, consider, and experience. Clearly feminine, she likes to be seen in running shorts or cute sundresses, forever young and spunky. She's my wild woman, idiosyncratic and expansive. The danger of listening to the Poet is becoming naive, impulsive, and inflated. Like a boat sailing blithely without a rudder, the Poet is not connected to reality and unaware of the dangers ahead. Immersed in the creative process, she is inattentive to mess and piles. Her purpose is to connect me to the mystery of life and my unique way of processing it. She's also the part that appreciates Grace and images. She requires that I create containers bounded by time and resources, not believing I can "count to infinity." While in my "own zone," the way to tame the Poet is to stay grounded so she won't cause me to crash. Songs: "I Won't Grow Up" and "I'm Flying" from *Peter Pan*.

Drill Sergeant: My Drill Sergeant wants plans and to check everything off his list to keep control and order. He keeps a barrel around himself to live a restricted, safe, and orderly life. A trouper and obsessive, he likes swinging arms to keep distance while making clear "whoever gets in my way is going to get it." A total tough guy, the Drill Sergeant makes agendas happen and follows through no matter what. Taking everything seriously, he is defensive and makes decisions without feelings. When challenged, he goes to fight or flight. Previously a Boy Scout (his motto is "Be Prepared"), he now resembles a policeman or wears his military uniform, replete with steel-toe boots, and swings a baton. The purpose of the Drill Sergeant is to keep me organized and reliable. But to avoid me being seen as an "ice queen," he needs to be more subtle, less controlling, and aware of not alienating others. The way to tame the Drill Sergeant is to not harshly confront others about punctuality and agreements, but instead realize it's not always "my way or the highway." Song: "I'm Late" from *Alice in Wonderland.*

Romantic: My Romantic is sensitive, wants caring and connection, and likes to go with the flow. Vacations, going out to dinner, making love, and just having fun are some of her favored activities. Her preferred mode is receptive and passive, loving to sleep and dream. Definitely feminine, she wears long flowy dresses, delicate earrings, lipstick, and nail polish. Not caring about being fat or lazy, she just wants to communicate for comfort and clarity. The purpose of my Romantic part, my beautiful inner rose, is to have loving relationships. However, she is often in danger of merging with others and getting swept away and, as a result, requires some awareness of boundaries and realistic limitations. To tame my Romantic, I have to remember not to be too personal, dramatic, or overly focused on pleasing others. Song: "I'd Do Anything" from *Oliver!*

Being able to distinguish these discrete parts of myself provided a sense of relief: I was finally getting to know myself better. But this was only the first step. I quickly realized I needed to integrate all these aspects of me into a coherent whole—a true self. Otherwise, I would be unable to navigate and resolve the endless conflict among their various intentions and distinct modes of operation. Now I know why I used to think if someone wanted to know me, they'd have to see my whole closet, because on any given day, what I wore wouldn't tell the whole story. (I used to say I had, like the ad in *Seventeen Magazine*, "The many looks of Bobbie Brooks.") I didn't know if everyone had such a rich diversity inside that wasn't completely visible and not understood in its entirety. I imagine other people's parts go by different names and appearances, yet they recognize in themselves the same challenge of finding unity among the many voices.

Clearly, I was really a piece of work and had to challenge myself to learn to negotiate with my parts—for achievement, control, adventure, and love—as I would with building a team at work. Was there, for example, a way to be "both/and," both creative on weekends and focused on work during the week? (17; 63). The need to integrate is why I chose the yin and yang circle as my symbol for 1994 after completing my PhD: to attract and focus on wholeness (Image 5). Yet, wholeness is not a permanent destination and also involves integrating the shadow, the unknown dark side of the personality, one of the important tasks for Vasalisa. As defined by Jung and others, the shadow is instinctive, irrational, and prone to the unconscious mechanism of projection. Still a meaningful symbol for me today, wholeness is not something I could have expected to achieve at the end of one year. In fact, I had the same basic list of "Top Ten Goals for 1999" all the way through 2012 (31; 48).

It turned out that before I could accept myself, I had to own my shadow, which I named "depressive core," and dispute "My Sad, Sad Story." Like a worn-out stuffed animal, it was old and familiar, but no longer comforting. Or I could see it as a broken record repeating an endless refrain: "Everyone can succeed but you; you are doomed to making a big deal out of everything; you are impenetrable, inconsolable, and unchangeable." Or I could view it through the lens of a myth like

Sisyphus: "You are forever consigned to push the rock of achievement up the mountain, only to have it always push you down again." "You can't get THERE from HERE." Or I could put myself on the stand as a witness for the defense—of me: "You will always attract prosecuting attorney energy to prove once and for all that, despite your accomplishments, you have no basis for a competent practice at anything. You deserve to be publicly humiliated and banished in infamy." Or I could imagine my epitaph: "She fulfilled her destiny: Failure to Thrive." The ghosts will cheer with glee, saying, "That's right, you are NOT ALLOWED. We will always take what you want from you."

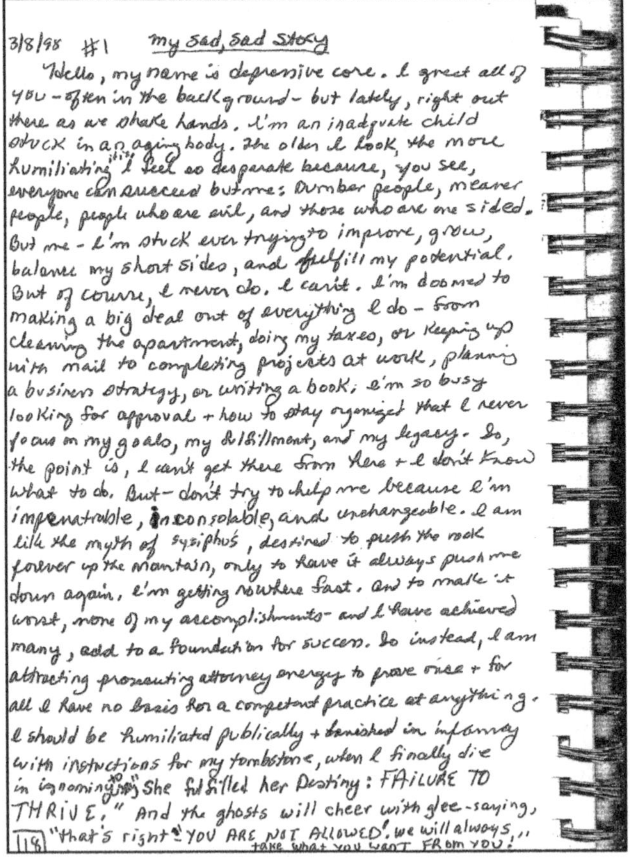

3/8/98 #1 My Sad, Sad Story

Hello, my name is depressive core. I greet all of you – often in the background – but lately, right out there as we shake hands. I'm an inadequate child stuck in an aging body. The older I look, the more humiliating it is. I feel so desparate because, you see, everyone can succeed but me: dumber people, meaner people, people who are evil, and those who are one sided. But me – I'm stuck ever trying to improve, grow, balance my short sides, and fulfill my potential. But of course, I never do. I can't. I'm doomed to making a big deal out of everything I do – from cleaning the apartment, doing my taxes, or keeping up with mail to completing projects at work, planning a business strategy, or writing a book; I'm so busy looking for approval + how to stay organized that I never focus on my goals, my fulfillment, and my legacy. So, the point is, I can't get there from here + I don't know what to do. But – don't try to help me because I'm impenatrable, inconsolable, and unchangeable. I am like the myth of Sysiphus, destined to push the rock forever up the mountain, only to have it always push me down again. I'm getting nowhere fast. And to make it worst, none of my accomplishments – and I have achieved many, add to a foundation for success. So instead, I am attracting prosecuting attorney energy to prove once + for all I have no basis for a competent practice at anything. I should be humiliated publically + banished in infamy with instructions for my tombstone, when I finally die in ignominy: "She fulfilled her Destiny: FAILURE TO THRIVE." And the ghosts will cheer with glee – saying, "That's right! YOU ARE NOT ALLOWED! We will always take what you want FROM YOU!"

118

Image 57: "My Sad, Sad Story."

As soon as I wrote "My Sad, Sad Story," I had a need to challenge it and stick up for myself. I was angry and argued that I should be allowed to be me, warts and all. I was sick of being perfectly miserable. I wanted to go for it—my passions, dreams, even my mistakes—*my way*. Even then, another part of me in the dialogue would resist, saying "she's not ready yet, she hasn't lost weight, gotten out of debt, or created a plan." But a wiser part was willing to risk not "waiting until" all her objections were addressed and resolved. That really got another part scared, accusing her of being too big for her britches and catastrophizing terrible outcomes. Yet, the hidden but budding wise woman was committed to healing the world and living from her Deepest Wisest Self.

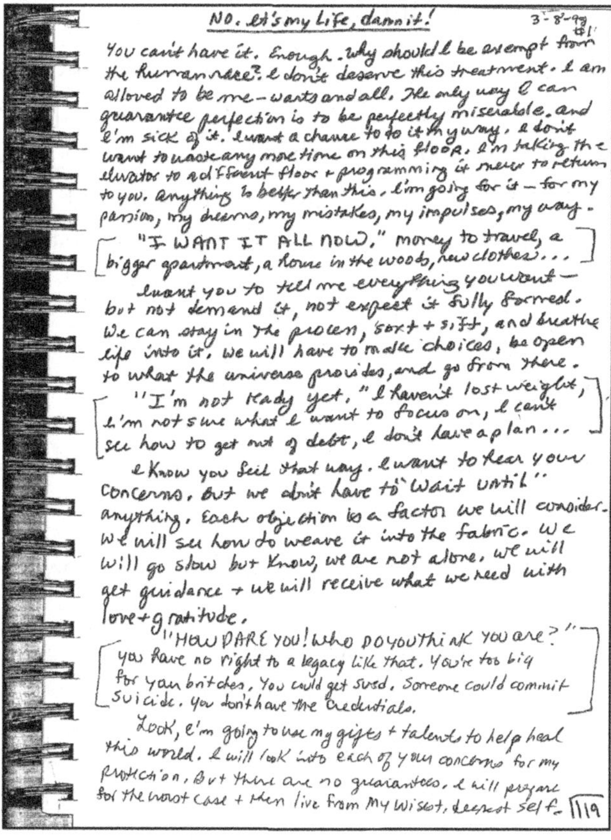

NO. It's my Life, dammit! 3-8-99 #1

You can't have it. Enough. Why should I be exempt from the human race? I don't deserve this treatment. I am allowed to be me—warts and all. The only way I can guarantee perfection is to be perfectly miserable. and I'm sick of it. I want a chance to do it my way. I don't want to waste any more time on this floor. I'm taking the elevator to a different floor + programming it never to return to you. anything is better than this. I'm going for it—for my passion, my dreams, my mistakes, my impulses, my way.

"I WANT IT ALL NOW." money to travel, a bigger apartment, a house in the woods, new clothes...

I want you to tell me everything you want—but not demand it, not expect it fully formed. We can stay in the process, sort + sift, and breathe life into it. we will have to make choices, be open to what the universe provides, and go from there.

"I'm not ready yet." I haven't lost weight, I'm not sure what I want to focus on, I can't see how to get out of debt, I don't have a plan...

I know you feel that way. I want to hear your concerns. But we don't have to "wait until" anything. Each objection is a factor we will consider. We will see how to weave it into the fabric. We will go slow but know, we are not alone. We will get guidance + we will receive what we need with love + gratitude.

"HOW DARE YOU! Who DO YOU THINK YOU are?" you have no right to a legacy like that. You're too big for your britches. You could get sued. Someone could commit suicide. You don't have the credentials.

Look, I'm going to use my gifts + talents to help heal this world. I will look into each of your concerns for my protection. But there are no guarantees. I will prepare for the worst case + then live from My Wisest, deepest self. 119

Image 58: "No. It's My Life, damn it!"

With depressive core distracting me from a realistic sense of self, it was noteworthy that colleagues who knew me well saw me differently. I was able to connect more of the dots when I reflected on the gift I received at work on my fiftieth birthday. It was a journal from my boss and coworkers that ended up being significant during my journal series review. They knew I kept journals and they also knew I didn't see myself as they saw me. In their honesty and kindness, they wrote: "You are a gift beyond words, you bring delight to all who know and work with you, you are willing to teach and learn, you are enlightening and authentic, full of generosity and love, power and presence" (31; 46-47). Was it OK for me to believe them?

They went on to write, "If I could give you anything, it would be . . .

> An **adventure** to a faraway place with exotic fragrant flowers that catch your nose through a warm breeze, with an expansive vista with majestic mountains . . . where you would feel relaxed and comfortable. Even though people you meet are not familiar and don't speak your language, you would feel a spiritual bond. You would feel exhilarated and challenged to explore, try new things, and taste the unusual delicacies.
>
> A **boomerang** so you could receive the same gifts you give so generously to others: kind acceptance of all parts of us (blemishes and all), belief in our abilities to create our future, and creativity to make it fun. You are precious.
>
> A clear **mirror** in which you see, without a doubt, your gifts, talents, skills and beauty—and know these are available to you always. Life is a blessing, listen and stay fully engaged. You are open to relationships and are a creative genius."

Somehow, they were able to predict my future, though it took me a while to get there. I now am living the adventure, using the boomerang, and finally looking in their mirror to see the me they saw.

Through my later work, I learned to own my strengths by observing myself and expressing who I am in my own words, not from an inventory or other conceptual tool. I knew I was good at follow-up; I trusted the organic inner knowing and outer alignment; I had a trustworthy intuition; and I knew when and how to be efficient. My type of efficiency was the "simple elegance" to find and express the truth of complexity so others could make changes. Like the malachite rock on my meditation altar with its deep imperfections, I was starting to accept that my flaws and quirks were part of the whole that I was. The darkness was not to be gotten rid of, but instead held to the light to examine (8; 65).

As my boss at Maimonides prepared to retire, she tried to prepare me for life as a vice president without her as a buffer. We had regular "walk and talk" sessions after work to help me with the transition. But I was nervous. Without her as a counterweight, I worried the whole senior leadership team would become unbalanced. To cope with my anxiety, I remembered that balance existed inside myself, not only between my dark and light parts, but also in the dynamic of the three elements I had discovered in my psyche: my "Poor Little Girl" who tries so hard to be perfect, wants to be invisible, and never disappoint anyone; her "Evil Twin" who hates and sabotages her, wants to be visible in her misery, and attracts negative attention through scapegoating, shame, and blame; and the "Wise Woman" who feels fortunate to have experiences that lead to healing. *She* can see the power of the Evil Twin and the sensitivity of the Poor Little Girl, taking the best qualities of each for herself. *She* can integrate different voices and offer gifts with awareness. *She* treats others with respect and expects to be treated with respect. *She* is able to own her gifts publicly and receive recognition and gratitude.

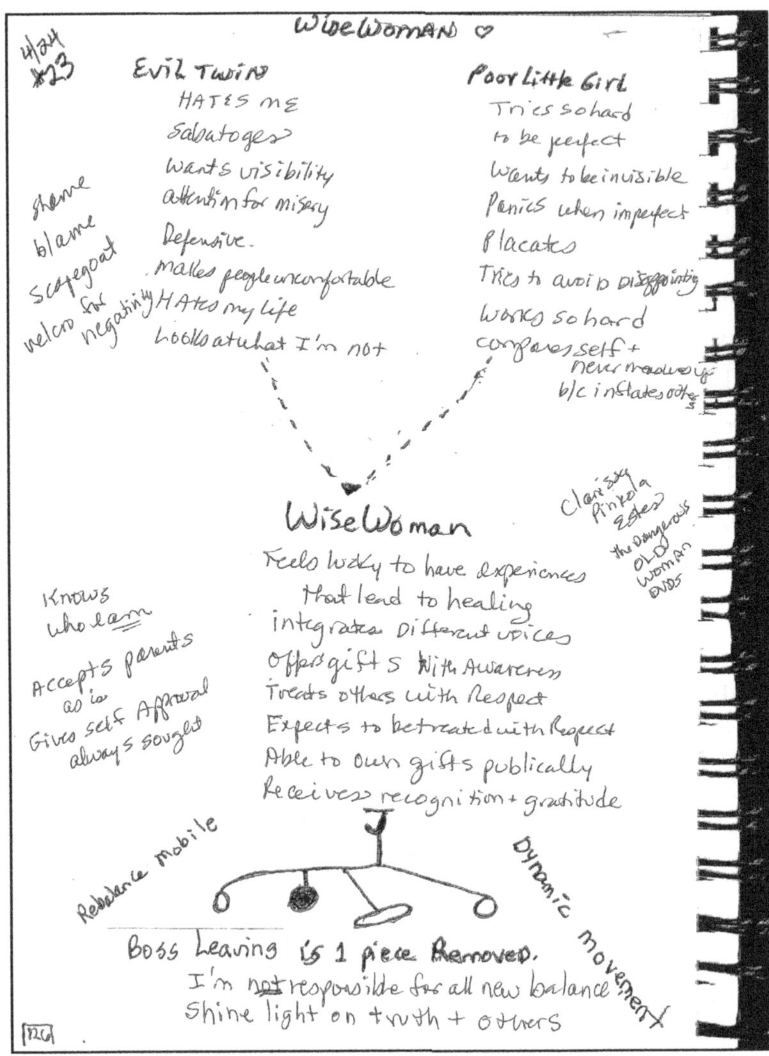

Image 59: Discovering my "Wise Woman."

The result of my work was reconceptualizing my self and embracing the new, fully integrated me. At my best I am a "story gardener" who both plants seeds and cultivates the soil so others can grow to their full potential and heal (4; 107). Analogous to photosynthesis in the actual garden, I used my imagination and capacity for synthesis to metaphorically nourish people and projects. This was evident when designing programs, coaching individuals and teams, and when giving the women in my study a new way to see themselves. That is why when I read them their unique Poem Portrait over the phone to make sure they felt it fit, they often cried. Just as flowers bloom when they are ready and in their unique splendor, people blossom when given the right type of care, conditions for success, and consistent attention in any weather.

Other metaphors that describe how I work include being a "choreographer" who embellishes and enriches the dance others are doing (12; 69). I am also the "weaver" to other people's warp (9; 125). I am a "bridge" between theory and practice, and as I was described for an external consulting job by my first boss, "a gentle soul who gets to the heart and soul of the matter" (4; 108).

It seems inconceivable that so much of this feedback and introspection didn't give me confidence and ease. The question is, what would it take for me to use the information about knowing myself to take action in line with my best self? That is where the need to authorize myself, or give myself permission, comes in.

Authorizing Myself

When I dare to be powerful—to use my strength in the service of my vision, then it becomes less and less important whether I am afraid.
I have come to believe over and over again that what is most important to me must be spoken, made verbal and shared, even at the risk of having it bruised or misunderstood.
The quality of light by which we scrutinize our lives has direct bearing upon the product which we live, and upon the changes which we hope to bring about through those lives.

—Audre Lorde

Inspired by these quotes, I was determined to absorb Lorde's wisdom and act on it through my leadership, publications, and journals. One of my mentors on my doctoral committee was always confounded by my lack of confidence when she saw me as so talented and intelligent. When said I felt "fat, ugly, and stupid," she said, "Wait until you get to be my age, then you can add 'old and poor' to the list!" (I would later add another letter, U, for being unsatisfied, and sigh, "OPU.") This mentor countered that my patience with observing processes and making sense of their meaning reminded her of the foremost woman research scientist who studied genetics in maize, Barbara McClintock. I had never heard of her but found she received the first unshared Nobel Prize in 1983 for her discovery of transposition. When I read her biography, *A Feeling for the Organism* by Evelyn Fox Keller, I was amazed at being given such a deep compliment and couldn't imagine I deserved it. The professor then asked me, "When are you going to authorize yourself?" I had never heard that phrase and certainly not applied to me. I figured it meant something like being the author of my life. I felt as if she was saying I'm not inadequate, but it's up to me to value and empower myself. Her reframe was both a priceless gift and a worthy challenge that took me many years to accept.

Part of the reason it didn't even occur to me to be the author of my life was that I was raised to feel I didn't matter. I couldn't say, "look at me," because my narcissistic parents got there first: narcissists only want you to look at them. I remember a scene as my friends began having children. We would be lounging around their apartment complex swimming pool, and their kids would continually shout, "Look at me, Mom!" Maybe they had just made a somersault into the water for the first time and were so excited. No matter what my friends and I were talking about, their mother would consistently look up, smile, and say something like, "That's great, honey. Do it again!" I realized I never had that experience and never would.

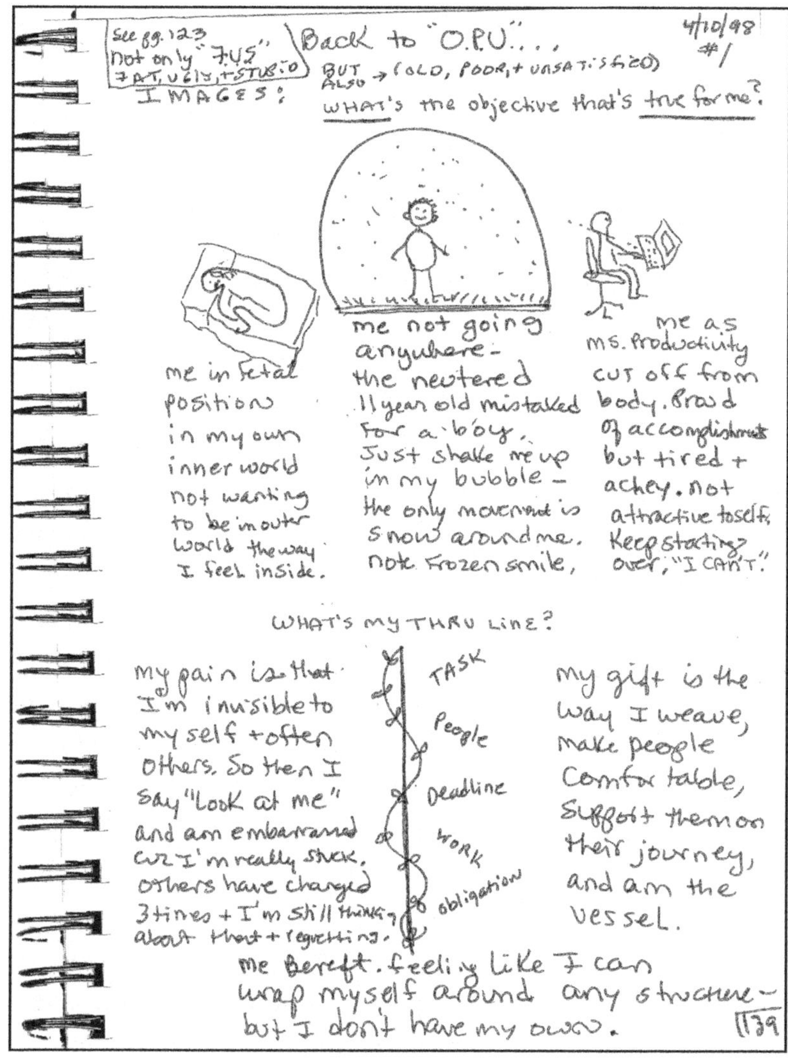

Image 60: Old, Poor, and Unsatisfied (OPU).

Authorizing myself took a number of steps from after I left the doctoral program all the way until my parents died. At the time, I actually didn't see these situations as forming a pattern of self-authorization. Now, looking back, I can identify stages of my process, which are naturally going to be different for each individual.

My first step along the path of self-authorization came from a dream in 1998 I found in my journal. In my awake emotional life, I was contracting after expansion—my predictable pattern any time I showed up in the world and then needed a bit of rest before courageously forging out again. In my nighttime sleep I saw the image of a simplified Ferris wheel. While some of the arms were high in the sky, as the central wheel rotated other arms dug into the earth with claw-like appendages. I interpreted the message of the dream as my need to dig down into the dirt of my soul to get more material to integrate and bring into the light (2; 113). This type of wisdom and advice was so different from the work mentality to keep going in a straight line, consistently hitting targets with even energy and prowess. But rereading this entry, I still can feel the quiet inner pride of beginning to listen to and trust my newly discovered self.

A few months later, I was spending the weekend alone in Brooklyn, sitting at my light wood round table, staring out the window, struggling to write on my laptop. However, I had had a big week of showing up in the work and then getting triggered. Luckily, I remembered the two-pronged practice Robyn and I created when I had just started working at Mount Sinai. Now it was my job to hold my scared little "I can't" selves safe along with my "in the world" mover and shaker. I reflected on how I moved through the layers by trusting myself. A breakthrough came when considering my love of aesthetics. Instead of beating myself up for not producing paintings and poetry, I had a shift in perspective and saw that what I was doing in my life was actually my art. How I tended my body, my apartment, and office were each a creative expression. Going on a long walk in Central Park, getting a manicure, and buying a new comforter for my bed were each examples of my love of aesthetics. My work, relationships, and projects were also a form of art. In other words, *my life was my palette.* While my art wasn't on exhibit in a gallery, my actions were on display to those impacted, and they were very satisfying to me (3; 79).

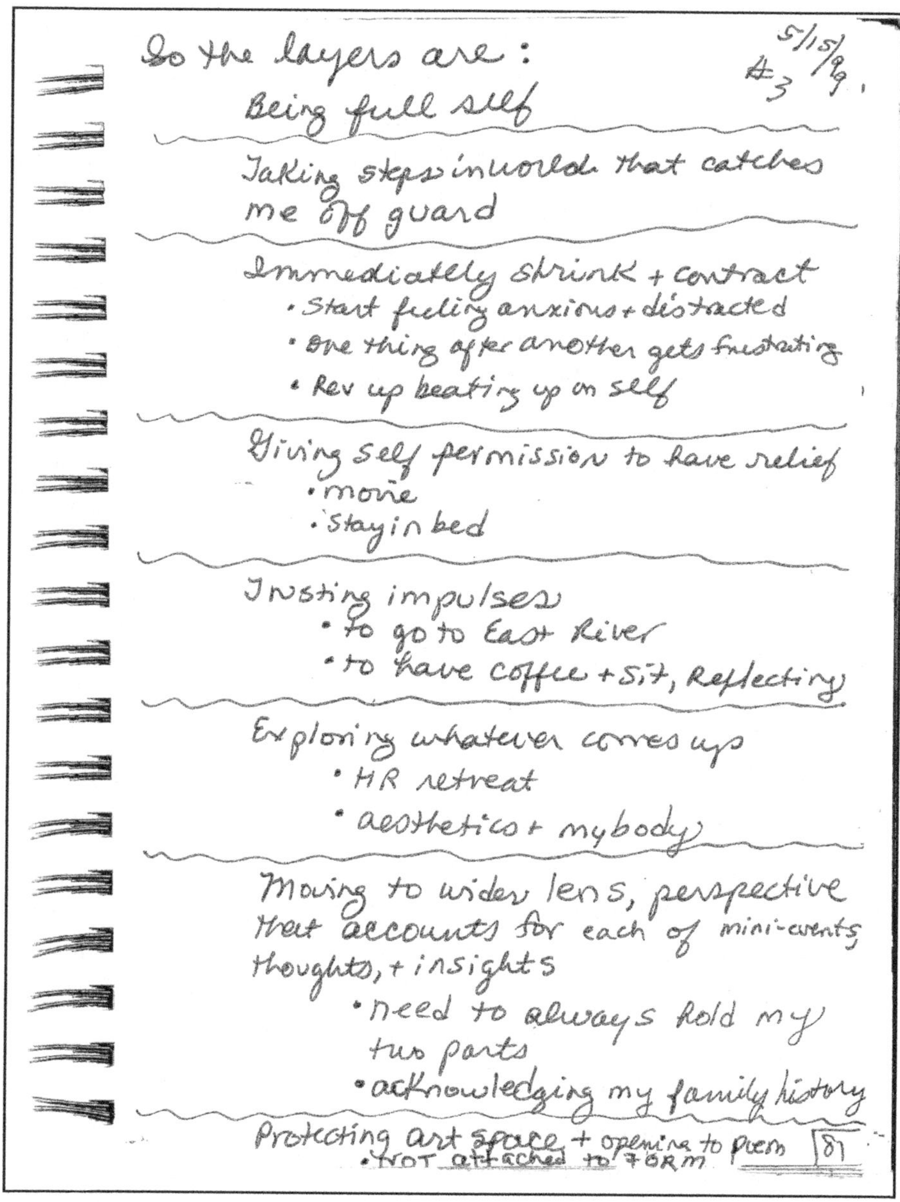
So the layers are:
5/15/9
#3
Being full self
Taking steps in world that catches me off guard
Immediately shrink + contract
• Start feeling anxious + distracted
• One thing after another gets frustrating
• Rev up beating up on self
Giving self permission to have relief
• movie
• stay in bed
Trusting impulses
• to go to East River
• to have coffee + sit, Reflecting
Exploring whatever comes up
• HR retreat
• aesthetics + my body
Moving to wider lens, perspective that accounts for each of mini-events, thoughts, + insights
• need to always hold my two parts
• acknowledging my family history
Protecting art space + opening to poem
• NOT attached to FORM
81

Image 61: Layers to trusting myself.

Another important shift in authorizing myself came about four years later when a passage in a parenting book described the stage where I got stuck in childhood as being all about authority. Children need to separate from their parental attachment in order to individuate. My therapist elaborated that this stage was all about the parents establishing rules and structure as well as helping the child deal with frustrations as they occurred. The work was to distinguish the image of perfection from the reality of imperfect parents and children in an imperfect world. Through therapy, we were reknitting the dropped stitches and providing the insights and corrective experiences to heal (16; 80). In practice, that meant I could risk becoming more myself before expecting to have strong interpersonal relationships (9; 26).

A similar idea was offered in an extended workshop I attended on Whole Systems Change two years later. The coleaders reminded us that "differentiation precedes integration." This was so simple, and also astonishing. A bell of clarity sounded in my brain, and I felt a calm knowingness come over me. Then I took the statement apart. On one level it means to clarify thoughts and feelings before taking action, to ground yourself before connecting with different social roles and contexts. For organizations, it means each team and department needs to have a voice in order to make the most informed decisions. In collecting data, it means analysis must be done before synthesis. How this affected my journey of self-authorization was to normalize coming apart before coming together. To realize we are always in motion, in different stages and paces. The more I could let myself and others be where we were, the better the combined outcomes would be. As the facilitators said, "We are working with seasons and can't rush winter into spring. Transformation takes time, changing the world one meeting at a time." For me it meant being the integrator inside myself as I was the integrator in my work role, to give myself permission to hear the negative parts in order to strengthen the whole (16; 39).

Since my work was about culture change, it was bigger than my own psychodynamics and gave me something to reach for. I could be both a mirror to others and their teacher, perfectly matched to learn and grow with the institution. Speaking up in meetings, I authorized myself to state my opinions so they were heard; in contrast to feedback I got on a management retreat, finally my words were landing with more of a "gong than a ping" (12; 31). As they said on *American Idol* and *The Voice,* I strove to find the right song and make it my own (19; 35). I relied on a mantra that helped me prepare for work and think through what could go wrong, which really worked for me: "*Hope for the best, plan for the worst*" (16; 26). Facilitating the Schwartz Center Rounds, I found my voice in each case a given department presented, giving it a title and preparing stimulating questions for the audience during the debrief.

Deciding I could refuse to be publicly humiliated, I practiced not deferring to authority (19; 77). When a senior leader attempted to take the conversation in a nonproductive way, I skillfully held my own and asked a department chair in the meeting if he ever felt the vulnerability we were discussing. The room held its breath for the risk I took, but he actually shared some feelings and became a role model for others in revealing feelings related to the theme. That meant I was standing up to Baba Yaga, the critical task in the Vasalisa story. Rather than freeze when I expected myself to know how to do something without having done it before, I realized I needed to experience it first and learn in the doing of it (19; 35). This was not only true at work but also in my personal life. My spiritual counselor urged me to make Patrick aware that when I felt there was a void, I acted mean, and didn't like his "Incredible Hulk" angry energy in return. We needed to make our relationship a joint endeavor that we'd only be able to move through by doing it together.

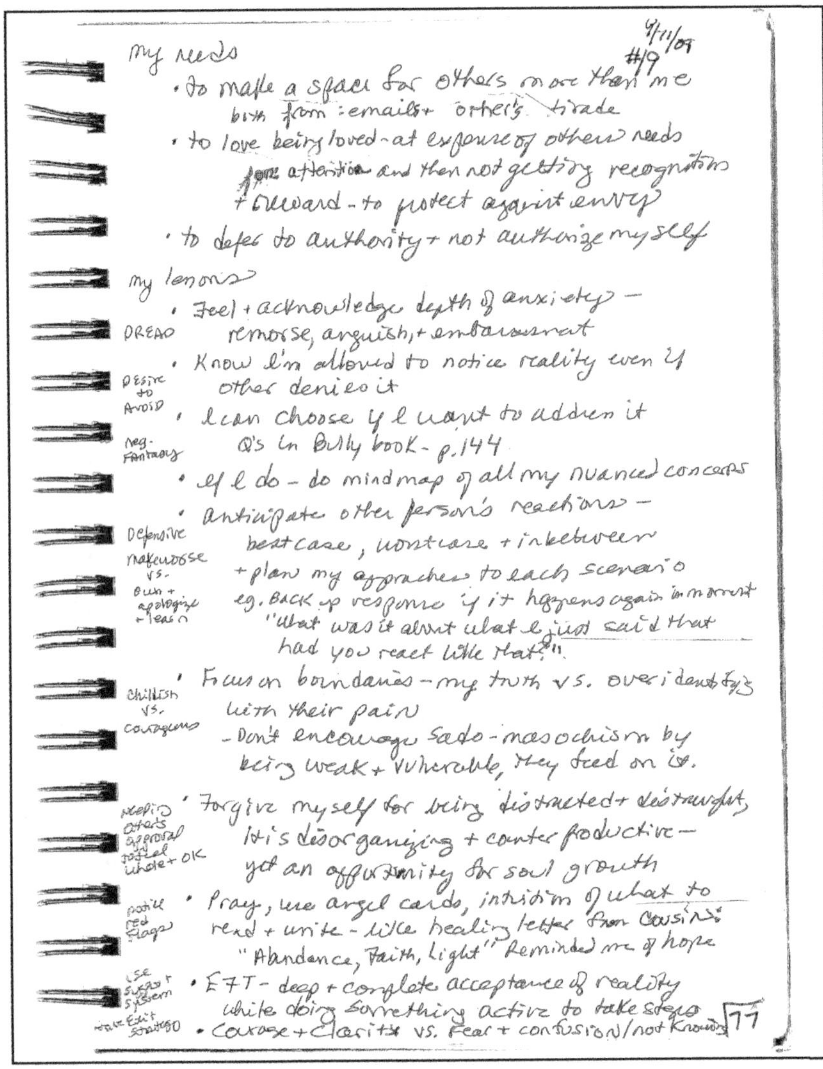

9/11/09
#19

My needs
• to make a space for others more than me
both from: emails + other's tirade
• to love being loved - at expense of others needs
for attention and then not getting recognition
+ reward - to protect against envy
• to defer to authority + not authorize myself

My lessons
• Feel + acknowledge depth of anxiety -
DREAD remorse, anguish, + embarrassment
• Know I'm allowed to notice reality even if
DESIRE TO AVOID other denies it
• I can choose if I want to address it
Neg. Fantasy Q's in Bully book - p.144
• If I do - do mindmap of all my nuanced concerns
• anticipate other person's reactions -
Defensive make excuse vs. own + apologize + learn best case, worst case + in between
+ plan my approaches to each scenario
eg. BACK up response if it happens again in moment
"What was it about what I just said that
had you react like that?"
• Focus on boundaries - my truth vs. over identifying
Childish vs. courageous with their pain
- Don't encourage sado-masochism by
being weak + vulnerable, they feed on it.
Needing others approval to feel whole + OK • Forgive myself for being distracted + distraught,
It's disorganizing + counter productive -
yet an opportunity for soul growth
Notice red flags • Pray, use angel cards, intuition of what to
read + write - like healing letter from Cousin:
"Abundance, Faith, Light" Reminded me of hope
Use support system • EFT - deep + complete acceptance of reality
while doing something active to take steps
Have exit strategy • Courage + Clarity vs. Fear + confusion/not knowing

77

Image 62: My needs and lessons.

What also was helpful was corresponding with my mentor, Peter Vaill, throughout the years. Peter constantly tried to show me my worth. He believed in me in the doctoral program. When I was publishing my second article on my study and needed encouragement, he was there, and again when I was designing the twenty-year follow-up study. Each time, he'd resend the poem he wrote about me, because it was always true. No matter how nervous I was exploring the next challenge, he knew I had courage, even though I still didn't (28; 56).

In 2009, while struggling to write an article on the enduring wisdom of the women in my study, I received an email from Peter saying, "It seems to me, though you didn't ask, that it's about time to just say goodbye to your angst, keep 'going for it' as you always do, stop second-guessing yourself. You're at your best when you just follow your heart. As the poem says, the abyss is not your angst; that's the reality of your life circumstances because you're a daring woman; and you work on things ahead of which there are real abysses" (22; 66). Since he believed in me, when he knew me so well and he meant so much to me, I slowly began to believe in myself, too, and I published the article.

Evidence of progress appeared one day in a leadership meeting with the CEO at the medical center, with whom I often felt intimidated because she was so quick to read the room and attack the weakest link. When she mentioned my work partner was at a breakfast meeting—which I had also attended—I spontaneously said, with humor, "What, am I invisible?!" Everyone laughed, and I had made my point without being obnoxious. My boss said my comic timing was impeccable and natural. I told her I was tired of being invisible, I wanted my contributions noted and my truth heard. As in a recent dream where I had crossed the line, I affirmed to my soul, "*I will not be blind to myself anymore*" (20; 14).

I was seeing more and more that when I stuffed down my negative feelings and bad qualities, I hid my positive traits and good moments as well. We think compartmentalizing our emotions is a neat, organized process, but it is messy and inexact. We often end up losing things we want to keep. During a body work session, enjoying being connected to my body, I said to myself what had once been said to me, "You should have been a dancer!" (20; 67). But then I realized I am more of a choreographer at work, and that was even better for me.

A great moment came was when I naturally authorized myself with my parents. No sooner were Patrick and I back from a vacation to celebrate my sixtieth birthday in 2010 when, to my surprise, Mom and Dad decided to put their house on the market without telling anyone. Because of their age, I think they were taken advantage of. The house was priced low for its prime location, and it sold in one day. I wish they had called me and my sisters so we could have guided them. They also agreed to a sale contract that had them leaving in thirty days. As the deadline approached, they became increasingly depressed, anxious, confused, and in conflict. My heart felt their pain. Hearing their voices on the phone, my husband encouraged me to go see them and not have regrets, as he did with his own family.

I called both my sisters, who had been in touch with our parents, and they validated that Mom and Dad were a mess. If I felt called to respond, they said I should go ahead. When I phoned my parents, Dad answered and said it was a difficult time, a big step for him. He didn't usually admit emotions, getting angry if anyone offered help, so I spoke from my heart. "I hope you don't get mad at me, but I ache for you and Mom. I feel like I could help. I want to see you. Would that be OK?" He responded, "I'm touched. When are you coming?!" I made plans and he sent a brief email saying Mom was also very pleased. Even more so, I realized I didn't need my parents' permission to reach out to them and offer help.

They picked me up at the airport, and over lunch at a restaurant they confided how miserable they were. I observed them attacking each other, a rare occasion in their dynamic, and I said, "Hey, we need some ground rules here. You have different styles and under stress they get more pronounced." I was able to take the reins and help them through it. On the way back from the bathroom, Dad said to Mom, "Would you give an old man a kiss?" It was a sweet way to reconnect and go back to their house.

Over the next four days, I witnessed how Dad barked orders, like the doctor and delegator he was. Mom lost her center, got emotional, and shut down. I spoke to each of them individually about my fears for them and surfaced their fears and pain. I was the facilitator for them that they never were for me. Together, we discussed transitions and how to go from the old to the new. Visiting the Atria Hacienda, their retirement residence, it was hard to see so many people with wheelchairs and oxygen tanks in the dining room. Dad said it made him feel like a patient, not the doctor he had been his whole career. But Mom said she felt reassured they would have medical help if they needed it. The setting was gorgeous, and their apartment was small but of quality. I became like the general contractor, measuring walls and figuring out how many paintings and which furniture they had room for. Mom took on the role of organizing tasks and writing them in a notebook. Dad monitored their pace so they didn't do too much at once. I flew home and called each night for their progress report. They made the transition in time and in more harmony. I was so pleased I could offer comfort and guidance for their next phase of life. With my expertise at work with dynamics and processes, I sensed I could confidently help them. Authorizing myself was a huge step for me. And I was aware that the process of reversing parent-child roles had begun (23; 21–22).

My Mission

The two most important days in your life are the day you were born and the day you find out why.

—Mark Twain

Most organizations are familiar with trying to articulate their purpose, vision, and mission. Purpose is why they exist, vision is what they want to accomplish, and the mission supports both by succinctly saying how it will achieve the vision. Strategies then are a series of ways to use the mission to achieve the vision, and goals are statements of what needs to be accomplished to implement the strategy. While this often seems like gobbledygook to most of the employees, the aim is to align everyone on a shared roadmap toward the future. If clear on the mission, then it's easier to articulate core values, make decisions, allocate resources, and set priorities. These same elements are often used for career development.

Searching for my mission was perhaps a sneaky "THERE" trying to seduce me into finding the one everlasting statement to ignite my work and legacy. Even though I always say how I trust the organic process, some part of me insisted on finding the answer first and then implementing it, quickly and once and for all. That part does not tolerate ebb and flow, evolution and change. It is aligned with my father's intolerance for process. It is my shadow self, the quantitative researcher looking for a hypothesis to prove. While searching for my mission sounds like something my head wanted, my heart was adamant that I needed to know it, to feel it, to have it, to live it—my sole purpose and passion. I wanted to live by Picasso's words, "The meaning of life is to find your gift. The purpose of life is to give it away." And though I thought for years I had failed at this, the journal entries about my mission told a different story: I *did* give my gifts away. It seems the part of me that wins out is the one experiencing life, with all its surprises and synchronicities, and then accepting what that means for me, my work, and my mission.

During the first year in my new field of OD, my mission was revealed through Grace—the synchronicity of the universe conspiring to help me. My boss could not attend an outside meeting at an institute interested in learning about how OD could align with their goals: to train actors and sponsor businesspeople to be more creative in their work. So he asked me to attend in his place. At the meeting, as a form of introduction, I fielded questions about my background. I spoke about my research, including the collages and Poem Portraits I created to better understand the women I studied. The director leading the meeting smiled and said, "You don't know that you created art, do you?" Of course, I didn't. We went on. As the meeting ended, he asked me if I would be interested in having a gallery opening with my art and live presentations of my poetry with fellow actors at The Actors Institute. Shocked, I said I would think about it and get back to him. What would be a no-brainer for most aspiring professionals, for me created a conflict. Would my boss be upset or jealous? Was I ready to be visible in this way? Could I actually do it well and not jeopardize my day job?

Here's how I decided. At this time, my sister Karen and her husband had offered me, as a graduation present, a stay anywhere in the world where their timeshare was available. While I had studied women and valued leading from the feminine, my work experience was now decidedly masculine. The medical environment is based on hierarchy, logic, and authority from the top, not webs of connection. To balance and not forget my core, I decided to go to Malta, an island that honored the feminine through its ancient goddess sites. While there, I read a book I had selected for the trip, one of the most sensitive and insightful examinations of the feminine, written by a professor of English literature, Tom Absher. His book, *Men and the Goddess: Feminine Archetypes in Western Literature*, illustrates through ten male characters in search of wholeness, how both men and women have been victims of patriarchy and blinded by the negative effects of male-dominated values. Through his analysis of these classics, I found the confirmation I was looking for: I should enthusiastically say yes to the opportunity the director had offered before I left. If his stories have meaning for men as well as women, then they had relevance to the male-dominated patriarchal medical centers in which I now worked and needed to help lead.

What ensued was an intensely exciting collaborative project. The director became my partner in the endeavor from start to finish, teaching me through his example how to create strong partnerships at work. He asked me to bring in my written Poem Portraits so we could select an actor for each one. Since he knew the actors in training, when I described the individual stories from the interviews, he paired each story with the right person. We had practice sessions that made the stories come alive.

Prior to the opening, this partner hung in the gallery each of my art-sized Poem Portraits and collage images (Image 19). We sent out invitations, calling the event *32 Voices: A Multi-Media Project about Women and Their Songs of Struggle, Success, and Self.* I had hired a graphic designer to create the invitation. It was her idea to list the title of every Poem Portrait, using a different font. Like the women themselves, each was different and together created a pleasing image to the eye.

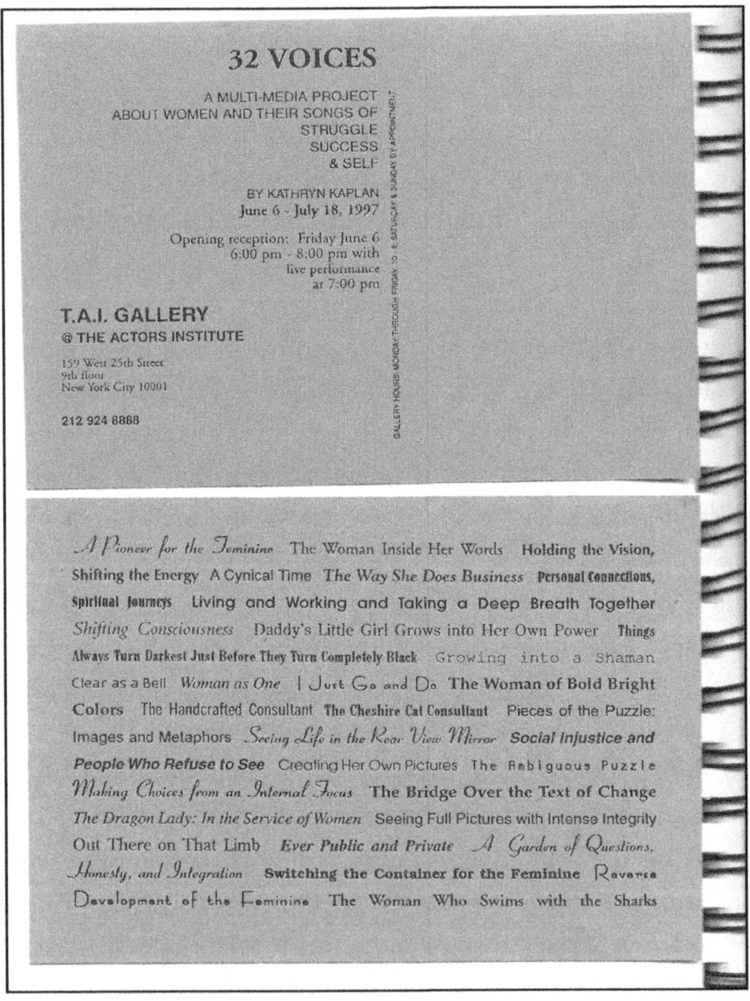

Image 63: Invitation postcard for my exhibition 32 Voices.

We set up the exhibit in a not-big-enough multipurpose room with folding chairs. The building was old, with no air conditioning, and with the summer heat, its big windows were thrown open, letting in the honks and screeches from taxis outside. The room was packed with people. Each of the twenty-six female actors stood in front of their assigned Poem Portrait, hung on the white plaster walls. One at a time, they brought each piece to life. Everyone was thrilled, and a standing ovation was followed by a Q and A session. The audience couldn't believe I wrote all the Poem Portraits and that they were about women other than those in the room. A woman in a flowered work dress with a black suit jacket shouted out, "Where is your book? We need it!" I felt encouraged and validated, and also somewhat overwhelmed because I knew I was not sure how to write it for a larger audience. Yet, the event was so successful, the director scheduled two more performances and kept the gallery open for six weeks. The experience confirmed my sense of my most alive self, fulfilling the mission "*to create in-depth, multimedia, meaningful, collaborative projects.*"

Rather than constructively seeking help to turn my creative work into a book, I reverted back to searching, wanting to find my mission for OD work—as if I hadn't already found it. The Actors Institute was expanding into offering workshops linking acting and business. I took a number of courses. In 1998. our class was guided to write what the facilitators called a "manifesto." The vision statement I came up with has stood the test of time. Back then, my mission seemed too risky to put forth, but writing it down supported me in living into it over the years (2; 53).

My vision was listening soulfully and expressing artfully. I set my mission in verse:

That I am ever deepening my relationship to myself—
I look inside for meaning to my life
I reach and stretch for that which my soul longs
I let myself get all the help my precious being needs
I realize that to be vulnerable is a strength
And I believe in risking being real over and over.

That I carefully develop my relationship with others—
I surround myself with people who care
Who see me as I really am and embrace all of it
Who help me heal and are on their own journey
Who encourage and stimulate my creativity
And who appreciate and require my gifts.

That I am an artist and my life is my palette—
I trust the universe and myself as a vessel
I am willing to speak my truth
I am open to new forms of creation
I remember the possibility for magic and Grace
And I know my art comes from being fully present in the moment.

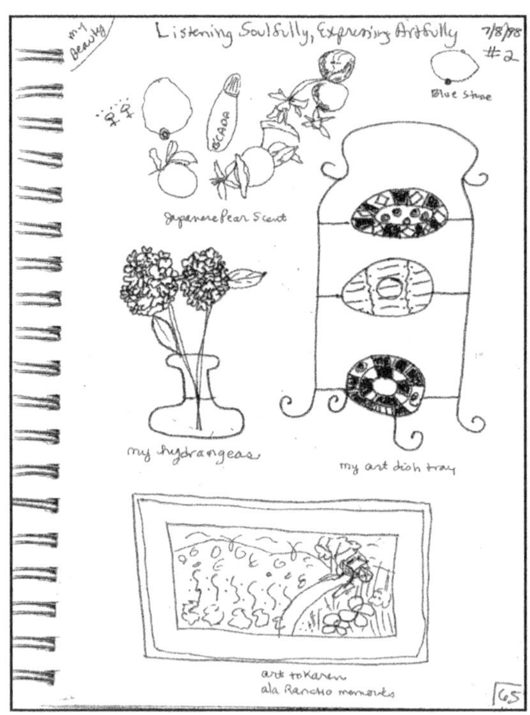

Image 64: "Listening Soulfully, Expressing Artfully."

Reviewing my journals, I saw examples of how I was helping people at work deal with the pain they experienced in conflict situations, and how my familiarity with my personal pain helped me know how to help them. By 2001 I realized, "*My pain is my purpose*," a way to turn my difficult experience into my special offering, authorizing myself with my secret sauce, for those who didn't know how to leverage their own pain. In a classic reversal of the adage "hurt people hurt people," I was able to break the cycle (7; 58). Because of this new awareness, I was able to hold my own during a weekend OD special interest group meeting on racism and white privilege. I was the only white woman; in the group were a gay white man and several African American women. While they each defined their OD practice through the lens of social justice, I said my lens was the pain individuals experienced in an organizational context. Raised in a largely white homogenous suburb, I viewed oppression as a personal and family dynamic. I wasn't aware of white privilege until I interviewed the women in my study. They explained how racism and other forms of prejudice were ongoing systemic issues they addressed in their consulting practices. I followed up by attending special workshops designed to address racial issues in the workplace. I read extensively on power differences among racial groups, white women's collusion, and the real risks in challenging the status quo. I always believed in a diverse workforce and society and was committed to help myself and others grow on this path (8; 136).

In 2004 I wrote that my soul's purpose was "*to see and be who I really am—in order to save my sight*." It was a battle worth fighting (9; 106). By the following year, through ever-stretching with ever-challenging assignments, I knew I had to keep leaning into the new places. As always, my only question was how hard I would make it and how long it would take. My mission was personal: to make sure every week I made "*time for work, my husband, and HER*" (10; 7).

Once, after coleading a team development session at Maimonides Medical Center, two of the participants came up to me to affirm my contribution. Even though my male coleader had been more forceful and dominant, they said, "You create an environment for people to learn."

Bringing out the best in people in this way seemed an additional mission for me to remember and value (11; 63). I didn't have to be the most charismatic in order to make a difference in other people's lives.

Then, I went to an advanced management retreat for OD development. One of the points of the experiential learning was to emphasize that there are parts of ourselves that never change—and they don't have to. The strategy promoted was to not let the damaged parts lead, but rather to use tough love, boot camp, or whatever it took to be our most mature and effective self. However, my little ones inside felt like those options were designed to obliterate them. They got scared because my leadership position required me to be so visible. But since I knew the little ones never would grow up, they needed to feel accepted and valued. I decided I was put on this earth "*to heal and live my soul's purpose*" (12; 47), and I could do this through my mission "*to help create authentic community*" (18; 12).

During the review of my journal collection, I decided to look back at my "too big" journal (before I found my right size and began the Black Book Series) and found something significant I had totally forgotten. In 1994, after the PhD and searching for my next steps, I had asked, "What strands want to come forward to weave a new pattern for my life?" To my amazement, I had done them all over the course of my career:

> Helping women find their voices and express them in new forms in the world.
> Empowering women from a spiritual focus.
> Making women visible.
> Taking the journey toward wholeness.
> Bringing the deep feminine into organizations.

This commitment to furthering women's leadership was demonstrated over several years by consulting with Mount Sinai's Women's Faculty Group and designing and delivering a course on gender in the workplace at NYU's Wagner Graduate School of Public Service. Both became a platform for helping scientists and students become aware of the reality of patriarchy and to show up as perceptive, strategic, and skilled leaders within that context. I gave presentations, designed activities, and assigned readings to surface differences in feminism between white women and women of color, how men and women's use of power were perceived, and how to strengthen wounded feminine and masculine energies for work. We practiced effective communication styles and learned to identify "stoppers," a term coined by psychologist Anne Wilson Shaef to signify maneuvers used to stop women from threatening the status quo. We examined systemic issues of racism, sexism, and ageism, and how stereotypes bias women's advancement. We affirmed how important allies were when making change on the individual and organization level, an ongoing and often emotional process. My mission from this time was to help the women be true to themselves as leaders, using their vulnerability as a strength.

In retrospect, I wish I could have reassured my ever-seeking self that I actually was living my missions all this time; that they changed as my circumstances changed and in response to the challenges I was facing, that they were enough and I was enough. All my mission statements are true, but not necessarily simultaneously or equally. I didn't know what I needed to integrate further self-acceptance was an awakening, which I experienced when going deeper into my relationship with my family.

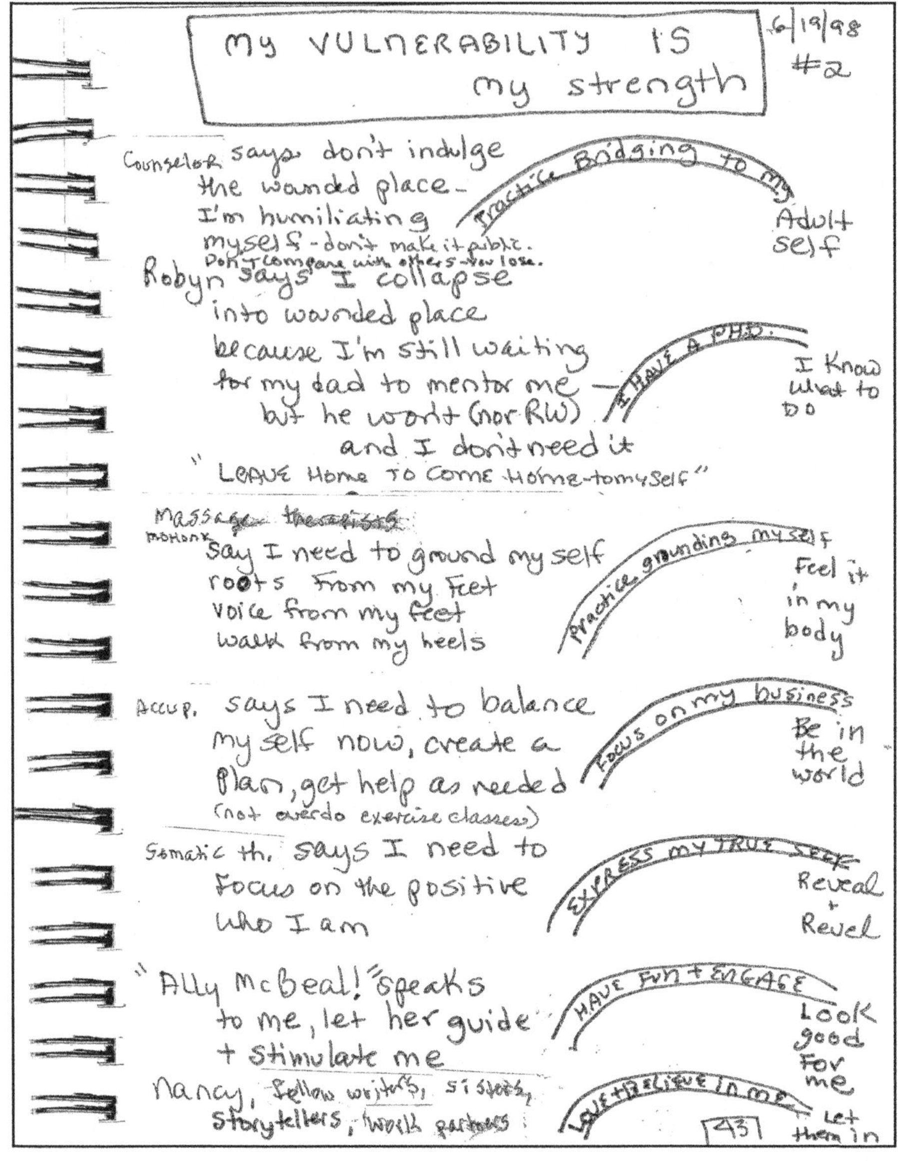

MY VULNERABILITY IS
my strength

6/19/98
#2

Counselor says don't indulge
the wounded place –
I'm humiliating
myself - don't make it public.
Don't compare with others - you lose.
Robyn says I collapse
into wounded place
because I'm still waiting
for my dad to mentor me –
but he won't (nor RW)
and I don't need it
"LEAVE Home TO COME Home-to myself"

Practice Bridging to my
Adult
self

I HAVE A PHD.
I Know
What to
DO

Massage therapists
Mohonk
say I need to ground my self
roots from my feet
voice from my feet
walk from my heels

Practice grounding myself
Feel it
in my
body

Accup. says I need to balance
my self now, create a
plan, get help as needed
(not overdo exercise classes)

Focus on my business
Be in
the
world

Somatic th. says I need to
focus on the positive
who I am

EXPRESS MY TRUE SELF
Reveal
+
Revel

"Ally McBeal!" speaks
to me, let her guide
+ stimulate me

HAVE FUN + ENGAGE
Look
good
For
me

Nancy, fellow writers, sisters,
storytellers, work partners

LOVE + BELIEVE IN ME
Let
them in

43

Image 65: "My Vulnerability Is My Strength."

CHAPTER SEVEN

Awakening

To live in the hearts of those you love is never to die.
—Hazel Gaynor

My Mother

This was Mom's favorite quote as she contemplated her mortality, and she shared it with her daughters frequently. In contrast, Dad, who was twelve years older, would say in conversation, "If I die . . ." Even though he died three years before my mom, I have chosen to write about her first. It's almost cliché to say that many psychological issues are rooted in the relationship with the mother. And as a feminist, I am not comfortable placing all the blame there. But as an adult who was for years unable to reach my full potential, I had to start somewhere, even reluctantly. In fact, back when I was with my first therapist, a psychoanalyst, I rebelled against talking about my mother because I felt I had nothing to complain about: our family lived a privileged, financially stable life. I was grateful to my parents and because of how much I loved them, I never wanted to betray them. The only hook was my therapist actually reminded me of my mother: thin, attractive, and most of all aloof, with that dismissive look on her face. She and her interpretations triggered me.

Perhaps that's why I have few lasting memories of those seven years in psychoanalysis. But what I remember is critical. First, she gave me a visceral understanding of transference and countertransference. She not only evoked a similar reaction to what I had with my mother, but she also treated me in the same disparaging way. My husband at the time wondered why I stayed, especially given the expense. But just as I was unable to fire the employee who ended up undoing my first job, I was unable to fire my therapist. She also had set a rule (clearly in her own self-interest) that I couldn't make a major change until we finished the psychoanalysis. My goals were to decide about my marriage and my career. But after seven years, I wasn't able to make those decisions with her, so I finally quit. I sought out a male psychiatrist who had served my friend Nancy well, and within a year he helped me decide to move on in both spheres. One day I made an appointment to go back to the first psychoanalyst for one session and give her the news of my decisions. Her snarly response, "The unlived life is not worth examining," was the reverse of Socrates' famous dictum and showed her disdain, revealing that she had been, of all things, bored with me. What a waste.

The only other concept that stayed with me from her was "negative control." She suggested that when I was anxious, since I couldn't guarantee success, I felt more in control if I sabotaged myself and guaranteed failure. Over the years, I found that reflex to be my tendency and learned to curtail it. But where was she when I needed help understanding the source of my anxiety and effective strategies to lessen it? Why didn't she help me navigate my emotions and express them? Unfortunately, I believe my unhealthy dynamics got solidified, indicating that what I experienced at home with my parents was the dominating pattern in my life. It remained for me to uncover these dynamics, then change them with other therapists and healers over the next twenty-five years.

The therapist who helped me the most with my family patterns was someone who had experienced the same kind of mother, perhaps worse. Robyn had done extensive inner work and discovered her own wisdom, reflected in original quotes that had great applicability and resonance to me and others. These included gems such as, "Go only as fast as your slowest parts feel safe to go." "Rest is a sacred act." "When you can let yourself really accept who and how you are . . . no one else will have much problem with it. Practice letting yourself just be." And, when overwhelmed, focus on "the smallest slice of now."

Regarding my mother and father, Robyn helped me see:

> How I acted a mess to stay connected to my parents, protecting them from the messes they made and could never admit.
>
> When I stopped being mad that my parents never loved and accepted me or knew me the way I wanted, I would be able to let in all the love from others. Instead of my anger forming a moat around my closed door to life, I could put down a drawbridge and open the door to love and life (Image 11).
>
> I felt rejected by Mom when I tried to console her. I had compassion for her; now it was time to have some for myself (3; 18).
>
> Being miserable punished my parents but hurt me more (9; 118).

She also helped me reflect on and assess my past dynamics so I could focus more on the here and now, on how to deal with these patterns when they showed themselves at work and in my intimate partnership:

> My early lack of consistent bonding led to my low self-esteem, creating a false self, and relating to my parents primarily.
>
> By age six my complex was established: I couldn't have happiness because I believed my parents had it all. My role was to make them feel good, so I pretended to be happy and strove to achieve, while splitting off feelings of loss and vulnerability. In contrast, my parents projected their weaknesses on to me, which I accepted so they wouldn't have to feel them and could disown them.
>
> By high school I didn't trust myself and began actively looking for outside counsel on making decisions about college, career,

and marriage, because having a sense of direction and closure made me feel I had a secure base.

Once settled, I was aware of my private and compelling emotional life and searched, through working with a series of therapists, for the missing pieces and reasons for my inadequacy and unhappiness.

I gained additional insights, such as:

I was told to build my muscles to differentiate from my parents and self-soothe when fussy.

I learned Mom taught me not to trust myself because she didn't trust herself.

Craving real connection, I hated when Mom was being superficial and just offering platitudes.

Even though Mom sometimes called me her "authentic eccentric," as a way to make sense of how different I was from her, she really preferred others. To her, I was invisible and forgettable, which I internalized and played out over and over at work (16; 84).

I was made aware I didn't take care of my body because then I would be like my parents, selfish and self-absorbed. But I was cautioned to stop both envying and criticizing them (17; 16).

These ideas may seem obvious to some of you, but if you have ever been in therapy, you know these nuggets don't come easily or consistently. Only by circling around the same issues again and again can the therapist identify your patterns and make helpful interpretations and recommendations. For me to realize there were reasons for my behavior that I hated and was embarrassed by—being messy, being miserable, ignoring my body—required that I start to give myself compassion. I had no idea I truly had experienced neglect and that I was desperate for emotional connection. As the oldest daughter, I thought I should know how to function effectively, but I didn't and didn't know what to do. I felt like I was born guilty, and that fact made me overly responsible. So it was a great relief for my therapist to validate that I did lack early bonding—and that its absence had consequences. Remember, I thought my parents were perfect, and retained few memories of my childhood, blocking out the rest. When my husband Patrick wrote his childhood memoir, I was astonished at the detailed scenes and stories he recalled and wrote about with vivid emotion. He thought I should do the same, but only through years of therapy was I able to piece together my key moments and feelings when growing up. In obliterating the painful ones, I'd lost many of the pleasant ones, too.

A revealing reflection was when I asked myself what kind of mother I had been to myself. The stimulus was preparing for a weeklong leadership retreat at Harvard, with my boss sponsoring me to enjoy a deep dive into leadership with the best of the best. This should have been exciting, but you know me, I was anxious and shutting down. My negative fantasy was that I wouldn't measure up to all the other attendees, my case study wouldn't be as good, my comments wouldn't be as insightful. I had been in this emotional place before, obviously, and rather than be in the moment and let myself learn, I was sabotaging myself yet again. Sure enough, once there, in the cavernous auditorium with bright lights, seats arranged so everyone could see the leaders on the stage, and the smell of prestige in the air, I was almost immediately triggered. One of the coleaders was provocative, like my mom, while the other was passive and kind, like my dad. I knew the latter leader wouldn't protect me from getting publicly humiliated when I scapegoated myself for not being perfect and the best participant, so I was doomed from the start. I lacked the capacity to guide—or effectively mother—myself through this challenging situation. Instead, I seemed determined to act out my childhood response to my internalized parents rather than be a better adult parent to myself in the present.

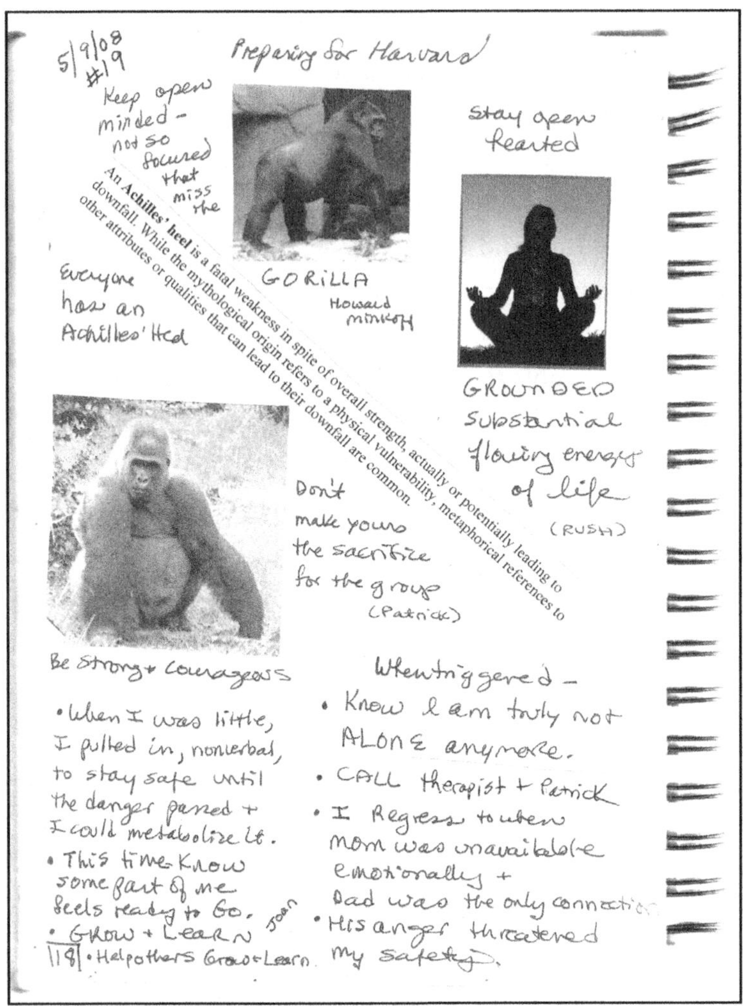

Image 66: Preparing for the Harvard conference.

By the end of the week, I experienced a transformation. I was able to go home victorious because I managed to stay in the moment and do a stellar job of teaching in our small group by handling dissent and using the new strategies effectively. I was praised for my "calm power" and creating a "holding environment" (19; 133). This familiar pattern was by now predictable—I had to suffer first before proving I was worthy, to hide in the depths before rising to the occasion. Prior to this part of the curriculum, I had reached out, crying, to one of the small group facilitators for support, because I was using my old mechanism of "negative control." I was ashamed and mad at myself for not mothering myself when I needed it most (19; 120). That's when I was forced to focus and reflect on the self-mothering tendencies I had successfully used that week:

Abusive: beating myself up for wasting time

Uncompassionate: fearing having my vulnerabilities exposed

Neglectful: not exercising, eating late at night

Indulgent: going out to restaurants for wine, desserts, and excess

Detached: not asking for help on technical equipment

Nurturing: loving the tulips, bringing music, staying safe

Healing: giving myself advice to accept and approve all of me, not allowing self-sabotage and sacrifice, monitoring my ego like a puppy on a leash, forgiving myself, realizing everyone has baggage, no one is looking at me as critically as I am, and affirming my courage

My self-mothering skills hadn't developed because my mom fit the pattern of the classic narcissist: she was all about her own needs, feelings, schedule, activities, and timing. It used to surprise me when, all of a sudden, she complained that she was tired or hungry, as if those states had never happened before and she couldn't sense or predict them. That is probably why I'm such an anticipator. Deciding on a restaurant took my parents forever, which resulted in me being a planner to avoid that kind of distress. Once at the restaurant Mom could be as cold, dismissive, and rude to the waiters as to any of us. Then, she could suddenly be fun and funny if it served her. She could never bear other people's sadness or struggles. And I knew full well never to make her feel inadequate. It would be "off with your head" if you asked her what was wrong or told her what was wrong for you (16; 34).

It was always hurtful and disappointing to get birthday cards just signed with their names. I wasn't expecting a check, but Mom and Dad were both artists and writers; couldn't they have done something expressive? The cards felt so empty and also disingenuous (8; 59), especially as I always went out of my way to find unique and thoughtful gifts. My husband Patrick loved my parents, and they loved him and later relied on him. But he also witnessed how they devalued whatever I did for them, leaving me feeling damaged. After a phone call with Mom and Dad that didn't go well for me, he was upset about how they didn't see or want my love and care. That night he woke up in the wee hours with a creative response for my mom's upcoming birthday party. His idea would serve as a way of setting her straight in a humorous way that she would probably appreciate. We would write a story about her. We would replace the "Sam I Am" phrase from Dr. Seuss's book *Green Eggs and Ham* with "The Fran I Am." It was brilliant. Over the next few months, we worked on changing the poetry, but my changes had a hostile edge because of my resentment at not getting what I needed as a child while Mom was off being creative. I never could have created this revised book as a gift for her alone. Patrick, not having the childhood history, but being extremely observant and always respectful, took the lead in moderating my contributions while preserving their essential message. As he responded to the illustrations with new text, I filled in the facts and edited the story. We both glued pictures and dialogue until it was finished. Here's an example of the truthful humor:

Can't we join the fun?
Does it have to be just one?
Let us in, let us see your creativity.
We want to know how you start
one of your creative pieces of art.

I cannot create with eyes upon me
I must escape to the studio I adore so fondly.
I will be back soon, just wait for me
Then you will see the Fran I Am and
The Fran I'll be.

Image 67: "The Fran I Am."

We presented the gift to her and she stared down at the pages, surrounded by her family. We said, "You can read it later." She said, "I'll read it now." We could hear Karen gasp as the story unfolded. Everyone was holding their breath to see if Mom would be offended by the truth beneath the words. When she finished the book, we were practically trembling. "I love it," she said, "it's a true story, and I appreciate the humor" (8; 91). To our surprise, on our next visit, there it was on display on a beautiful, sturdy, tarnished brass stand. Did she put it on display because she felt we had seen her, or because she loved my husband? Maybe both.

Image 68: My drawing of one of the art studios to which my mother was constantly escaping.

It is also important to me to acknowledge the joy Patrick and I often felt with my parents. I have photos of them dancing in the kitchen of their apartment to jazz music we brought and they loved. Once my mom actually let me shine publicly. She was leading a women's group at their first retirement community, when both my parents were still well. She had written a piece called "Life After Stilettos" about women aging, and then facilitated a conversation with a circle of about thirty women residents. She actually introduced me and let me contribute to her process, and then praised me—a first (24; 20). I felt so seen, and I happened to be thin and dressed in a flowered layered skirt and hot pink camisole—an outfit surely my Poet had picked out. Of course, nothing lasts, not my weight, her health, or this recognition, but it remains a great memory.

As my parents aged and couldn't travel anymore, I asked if I could visit them on my birthday. Dad said, "That would be the gift of a lifetime" (17; 74). I finally understood that neither parent had more to give, it wasn't personal. They were disconnected from their own pain and responded with detachment and superficiality (21; 40). By observing them in the retirement home, I took away positive lessons to help with my own aging:

Definitely exercise: it helps with balance and getting up and down

Stay organized: simplifying makes the environment more tranquil and inviting

Feed passion: it makes life worth living and you more interesting to others

Save money: necessary for retirement, extra health costs, and peace of mind

Be a good person: handle relationships with care and integrity, especially with my husband

Did I forget to add humor? When Mom sent her "Five Wishes" to her daughters for her desires for health emergencies and death, she included three hilarious photos. She titled it, "How Quickly the Years Pass." The first was with little girls holding hands, looking out at the water on the beach. The second was with hot young women and their long, gorgeous hair, bent over the railing wearing short shorts, exposing their sexy buns. The last was five elderly women hiding their faces and unfashionable blouses, bent over, exposing their big butts and fat dimpled legs! (31; 131). Mom could also be poignant, especially at the end when she told my youngest sister Robin, "I don't ever want to grow old again" (28; 106).

About ten years earlier, Mom wrote her fictionalized memoir, *The Prettier Sister*, which included passages I found very insulting. Her story had twin daughters, one of whom slept with the husband of the other sister. I don't know where she came up with that concept, but it felt horrible to wonder if she even unconsciously thought of me, or any of the sisters, that way. But by the time she was "at the last stop before the last stop," as she had written in an essay, I read her book a second time. Mom had again fainted while I was with her and had to go briefly to the hospital. Interestingly, she only fainted and had to go to the ER when I was visiting her or she was visiting me. They never found a physical cause, so I can only infer it was related to our relationship, something she never owned or expressed. When she returned to assisted living this time, I had finished the book, and I had nothing but empathy for this woman's pain and darkness. I also thought that if she realized the ugly way parts of her story portrayed her, she would have already died. Her book reported the main character enduring early sexual abuse from her father (based on my mother's stepfather), as well as demonstrating repeated cruelty to her prettier sister.

As a writer and in life, Mom's psychological defense was to express herself and then deny it. Many of her old friends called her to criticize her book saying, "How could you say anything mean about your wonderful parents?" She'd say, "It's a novel" and then never talk to them again. She never told any of the immediate family the truth behind the book. So I was chagrined to read an entry in the virtual ceremony my sisters and I created after she died, integrating anecdotes and photos from friends and family about their beloved Fran. A distant relative had only heard of Mom through her writing and was eager to meet the woman who wrote such a "bare, bold, uncomfortable story." It turned out that when she'd asked Mom about the book, Mom finally admitted, "Write it? I lived it." I felt punched in the stomach and betrayed by her many years of withholding the truth from me.

I had much unfinished business with my mother and though there were risks, I was eager to resolve it. Had I still been working full time, I would have missed the extended visits and tenderness in finally just spending time together. After Dad died, I expected Mom to love her independence and be even more creative. Instead, a year later, after the celebration of my father's life with friends and family, Mom declined physically and lost interest in art, writing, and her daily walks. She isolated herself from the retirement community, where she had enjoyed many friends. One evening, I got a call that Mom was being transferred to a rehab facility because she was not well. Since a consulting contract had just fallen through, my husband encouraged me to go help her. I left the East Coast, flew to her on the West Coast, and ended up staying a month.

When I arrived, she was so confused that my sisters and I decided she needed more care than her current living situation. I ended up making the move for her to a full-care assisted living facility, with Karen, her husband Carey, and Patrick helping toward the end. While with Mom, I excitedly created a journal for her, just like the type I used, with pages on her doctors, names of staff and residents, timeline of phases, and things to do. I brought over from the other apartment all of her clothes and piles of manuscripts, putting them in her living room closet in case she ever wanted to write again or read what she had written. I also organized her apartment, filling her bookcase in the living room with all her special keepsakes and treasures. She said she liked looking at these shelves filled with her favorite books, colorful trinkets, and photographs. I set up her kitchen table area to be used like an office space, where she could find all her pens and pencils, and could write or draw. On the wall was a corkboard where I hung all the important pages I had typed up for her with her doctors' names and phone numbers, as well as how to contact her friends and family. I enjoyed and was proud of my efforts to help her feel organized and more settled. She was not expecting this kind of help, and I was glad I could momentarily put a smile on her face. She asked, "Why are you so good to me, I don't deserve it. I wasn't this good to you." "I know," I said, "I love you and it is my honor and joy to be here for you." She didn't hug me, but she looked stunned and swallowed, her face pinched, as if, for a moment, she felt the magnitude of what I felt and expressed.

My sister Robin, fortunately, was able to replace me after my month with Mom, and she stayed for six months. When I asked her how the journal was working out for Mom, she shared that Mom never used it. This upset me, causing me once again to feel rejected. But Karen validated my worth, and all my loving efforts to help our mother by saying, "Kathryn, you had a vision and it came to fruition. You did more than enough. And you are enough!"

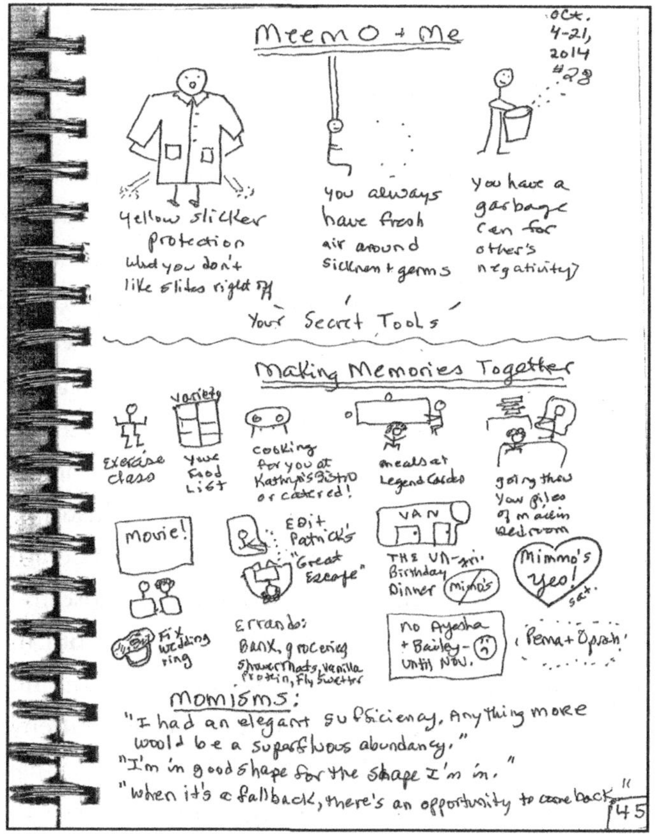

Image 69: "Meemo + Me."

Robin decided we needed a place nearby where we could stay to make it easy and affordable to take care of Mom until the end. Mom said the family apartment she found was the best thing we ever did. As the sisters rotated coming in from out of town, I helped us become a caretaking team, using our different strengths and availability. I made sure Mom led with her pace, desires, and decisions. Once as I was leaving, she said she learned compassion from me. "You helped Dad die and me live." I was astonished, as I always was by her rare moments of self-awareness and even rarer expressions of gratitude. She said I gave her more love and attention than she ever had or deserved (26; 44). Nothing was more meaningful and healing to me. It made up for much of what I didn't get as a child.

Every time I came to the door of her room, she greeted me holding her bright fuchsia walker saying, "I adore you." It was jolting and a little hard to take in, after never hearing those words in all the years I'd known her. On one six-week visit, I saw she was seriously declining and beginning to slip away. I helped her get ready for lunch, wheeling her into the dining room propped up with pillows, and keeping her company, as she insisted. I organized hospice and wrote instructions to help the staff meet her needs when one of us wasn't there. It was heart-wrenching to see her so weak and helpless. I dug deep to bring my long experience in healthcare to this personal situation. At work, to engage staff in having empathy for patients, we'd say, "What would you want if it were your mother or brother or other family member needing this care?" Well, despite our history, it was my mother, and now I was putting such a scenario into practice.

I stayed present because I knew I was getting an "up close and personal" view of end-of-life realities. We all know everyone dies, but it is so hard to actually factor in and plan for our own deaths. On one hand, it was easy for me to give my mother care because I had natural empathy and was observant of her needs. On the other, I confess to having moments of resentment for her not being the loving mother I needed as a child. I understood she was unable and not just unwilling, that her emotional history made her push me away, but that didn't make it hurt any less. As an adult, I saw how dismissive she could be of others, friends and family alike. Bottom line, she was the mother I had in this predicament, and as her daughter, I had no intention of letting her down.

Always checking in with the sisters when we had decisions to make, each affirmed our loving presence and support. As one of the cards framed in the family apartment declared, "One day she woke up and understood we're all in this together." We continued to be a team even after Mom died, when we went through her belongings and the apartment. We came together as I facilitated a circle with the residents to honor my mother and tell stories about her. I was so grateful to have the space and skills to express my mission to create community with the sisters, the assisted living residents, and extended family. I believe this was the universe letting me do what was most important, even though it involved being hurt when having to leave my job.

After so many years with me working and Mom involved in her art business and writing projects, I couldn't believe the satisfaction of our just being together. Watching television, looking at the garden, talking about her friends and memories was so nourishing for each of us. How could this time be so different from my childhood? Was it that dependence and impending death gave my mother perspective? Yes, she listened to Pema Chödrön CDs a lot and would call Karen to have nightly debriefs with humor and insight. Was it also that I was different? I think so, because not working at the medical center, working through my grief, and having flexible time made me realign my priorities. I felt like my whole life I had wanted but been unable to help her, be involved with her. I wish it had happened earlier rather than later, but I cherished every moment. We laughed at silly comic DVDs I brought, and just hung out together so comfortably. She'd dictate and I'd write letters to her friends. I bought games that were good for cognitive stimulation for us to play. The friends she ate with played poker after lunch, so I created a simple way for her to join in and get the camaraderie left behind at the first retirement home.

The truth was, I had been available to her in this way for years, but she had never wanted my companionship. It was painful to think of all the lost opportunities for mother-daughter bonding, caretaking, and joy. Only once, when she had breast cancer surgery, did she let me buy her blouses with double pockets to hide her missing breasts. It was just so hard for her to be vulnerable or real. The significant difference now was that I was able to hold both/and awareness instead of the all-or-nothing zigzag of my youth. I knew exactly what to expect from her. I didn't count on getting anything more than that, but when she did open up, I was ready to receive and enjoy the blessing.

As I learned from my first marriage and divorce, it takes two people to have a relationship and only one to end it. I couldn't do both parts with her; Mom had to meet me and most of the time she couldn't and wouldn't. So with all we were experiencing by just being together, I was always waiting for the disapproval of a suggestion with the irritation she had mastered. Of course, she delivered.

Then, one day I entered her room and she was on the floor, wedged between the nightstand and the bed. Grateful to be the one to find her, I was frightened to see her reduced to such a vulnerable and potentially dangerous position. I also felt an energy jolt, confident I knew what to do and could help her. "What happened to my little mommy?" I asked gently, getting down on the floor with her, looking tenderly into her eyes. My first intention was to make sure she hadn't hurt herself and see if she was confused. I asked her, "How did this happen, Meemo?" She pointed weakly to the wheelchair and the bed but couldn't really explain. Her demeanor was so sweet and peaceful. I knew the end was near. I also felt that if we'd had this type of mutual rapport when I was growing up, I could have been a mother, too. So much wasted time. So much sacrifice. It was as if I was being a nurturing mommy to a hurt child, and it felt so natural and loving, as when my cousins asked me to create the birth announcement for their first child. I had the love inside me to be a mother, I just couldn't allow it for the reasons I've explained. And given how long it has taken me to write my story and heal my wounds, I know it is still the bittersweet, correct decision.

Image 70: My drawing for my cousins' baby announcement.

The hospice counselor said it would help each of us to forgive anything that might stand in the way of a peaceful ending. I didn't really know where to start. I know I had begun the process of forgiving my dad, but Mom and I still had so many unresolved issues. And was there a risk, by bringing them up, that I might make things worse? Stuck in my mind more than my heart, I struggled to find the perfect thing we most needed to clear up between us. I mulled it over but couldn't put my finger on it. The next day visiting Mom, I acted on an impulse and did something I never had done: I climbed in bed next to her. Then, it just rolled off my tongue when I said to her, "I apologize for being less than the best daughter." She said, "You? Can you forgive me? I wasn't the best mother." I reached for her hand and said, "We were perfect for each other."

Another day, more lucid, she asked what had happened to me at work. I had never brought it up and neither had she. But time was running out, it was up to me to tell my truth and see if she could actually grasp it and have empathy or at least insight. Was our dynamic finally changing? I took a deep breath and briefly explained that some of the issues we had with each other, I also had with the CEO. Mom said, "You have the nicest way of blaming me." Not exactly an attack, but she managed to make my work troubles about her feelings, and it remained to be seen how this interaction would play out.

The next morning, I got my answer. She was more confused and said she'd had a dream about me. She said I was trying to strangle her, but she wouldn't let me. This really threw me for a loop. Later in the day she was clearer, and I found my bearings. I realized it was true—she was fragile—but I forgot that in the end, she would always take care of herself and was not going to let me hurt her. It was a relief, both that I spoke my truth and that she accepted it and wasn't damaged by it. I had to wonder, if I'd taken risks earlier in our relationship, would we both have survived, learned from them, and evolved? I'm not one to dwell on could-have-beens, but it made me wonder if there might possibly have been a better way between us.

Once when I was young, Mom and I were in a beauty shop and a teenager was railing at her mother. It was ugly and we decided right then we would never do that. I didn't realize at the time that through my work and therapy, I would come to see the value of healthy conflict and get good at helping others through it. Too bad I couldn't authorize myself as a teenager to act like a teenager. I also see now that in a sense, Mom and I never changed from who were each were as people. The shift was that I no longer let fear stop me and she finally stopped letting my attention go to waste.

I went home, and Karen and her husband came for a poignant final visit. Then, I got the call that signaled the end. Saying goodbye when you've had a conflicted relationship is particularly hard, because you have to acknowledge the problems alongside the good memories and moments. Otherwise, it isn't honest and real. I also found it hard not to know if this was really the end or a false alarm. I made early morning reservations to fly right back, and I was so churned up that I ran to buy bottled water for the flight and arrived at the gate after they had just closed the door. Rescheduled for the next flight out, I had plenty of time to reflect on the reality of our relationship in all its texture and complexity.

When I arrived, Mom was being wheeled to her room and when she saw me, she couldn't figure out why I was there. I told her I was informed she was failing and I wanted to be with her, to help her feel safe and loved. The assistants put her in the bed and she never got up after that. I sat next to her quietly, hoping my presence was a comfort. She couldn't keep her eyes open, so when I said, "I'm going to be as loving as I can, but I know it won't be perfect," she chuckled and squeezed my hand. With Mom's eyes still closed, her granddaughter drove two hours to be able to hold her hand and say goodbye. That night I slept on the couch, but Mom never again opened her eyes, which upset me terribly. In a way, her eyes had been closed to me, to really seeing me, my whole life, and I wanted one last eye-to-eye proof we were connected. But I suppose that was about me. Maybe Mom had all she needed. When she took her last breath, I couldn't believe it. As much as I had known it was coming, I was wracked with guttural sobs. It shouldn't have surprised me. No one ever meant to me what my mother did, and I was and still am glad to finally feel that love in all its entirety.

My Father

As long as we take ourselves to be the child who was hurt by an unconscious parent, we will never grow up. We will keep looking for the parent who never showed up and forget to see that the one who is looking is no longer a child.

—Geneen Roth, *Women Food and God*

In order to grow up and get unstuck from my childhood, I had to learn it was not my job to take care of Dad's emotions or Mom's moodiness. Similarly, if one sister wanted something, it didn't mean she had to get it or I had to give it to her. If a sister was controlling or judgmental, it didn't mean I had to respond in kind. I was starting to understand that people get to have their own reactions and I am responsible for mine. Again, obvious to some, but for me, a revelation (11; 117).

My dad was usually very healthy, never seeming so much older than my mom. He ran daily until he shifted to the treadmill at the gym. We called him our Renaissance man, who never complained after he retired when aging gradually affected his physical and mental faculties. We watched as one by one he had to give up golf, bridge, reading, writing, crossword puzzles, driving, and finally, calculating the tip at a restaurant. He had loved being a doctor and was loved by the staff at his clinic and the hospital because of his excellent care of patients, quiet unassuming manner, and unexpected dry humor. But he was loath to face his vulnerability as a patient. When Dad had quintuple bypass surgery in his eighties, he pointed to a pad of paper and shakily wrote to me, "I'm scared." When he was able to speak a few days later, he said he was sad because he was afraid he'd never get well. I then knew he saw me as someone emotionally available with love and empathy for him, even though he had rarely, if ever, been able to offer that to me. Once recovered, he sealed over. Later, I had to face the reality that he was never going to open up or be fully open to me; it wasn't my fault, that's just who my father was (8; 92).

Dad had ample vehicles for self-expression: as a sculptor, through his Plexiglas art, and later through his writing. Though he never wanted to talk about what his art or stories meant, to me they were sensitive and evoked emotion, like his large bronze rabbi that was later bought by a famous temple in Los Angeles. He was also a gifted storyteller. After he retired, he would wake up from a dream and write the story down by hand on a yellow pad, never needing to revise it. Mom was annoyed, because she said, "All writing is rewriting." They both participated in a writers' critique group, and Mom typed his stories and shepherded their publishing into two books. Once I interviewed him and wrote his own story, but he didn't like that I used his words to create a Poem Portrait and seemed dismissive of my effort. He continuously thwarted being known by me except as *he* wanted to be seen and known. Nevertheless, we liked to discuss articles we read in the *New Yorker*, and later, laugh together with my husband over episodes of *Curb Your Enthusiasm*.

I had spent my whole life nudging, prodding, inviting Dad to be more emotionally open, even buying him a journal, to my sisters' chagrin. As the oldest, I held on tighter and took longer to give up. After all, I had wanted to be a doctor like him and have the financial stability to provide for those I loved, as he did. And eventually, I achieved it.

One vivid phone call stands out when, in graduate school, I was still trying to get my needs met from childhood. I called my parents' house crying. Patrick overheard me telling my father, during work on my dissertation, how scared I was that I just couldn't do it. My father replied, "I'm going to play golf. Goodbye" (13; 21). Patrick was appalled, not at my father, but at me, for deluding myself and expecting something I was never going to get. When, if ever, would I learn? What I was hoping to hear was my father's encouragement and love for me. If I was the apple of his eye, as he told me, why didn't he want to help me? If he could have just said something like, "I hear you, honey. It sounds like a difficult time, and I know you can do it," I would have felt satisfied, acknowledged, and energized to return to my work. He could have said anything, instead of dismissing me. After the call, I felt I had a right to feel disappointed by him—and in him—but Patrick called me on it, letting me know the only one responsible for my disappointment was me.

Relentless in my pursuit for some notice of me and my needs, I begged Dad to write me a letter when he was retiring from his practice and pass the "Doctor Kaplan" baton to me. He complied with a handwritten note on his medical affiliation letterhead from October 1992, two years before I graduated:

> Dearest Kathy,
>
> Today is the start of the last month of my career as a practicing physician. It's been a good career which I have enjoyed and functioned with pride; and for a variety of reasons I have loved being "Doctor Kaplan."
>
> So with these thoughts, I toss the mantle of "Doctor Kaplan" to you, a most worthy recipient and I hope you have as much fun and success as I have had.
>
> It was a wonderful weekend we spent with you. I love you with all my heart—you are the greatest.
>
> Big D

I was grateful to get the letter and have saved it for all these years. But it was also bittersweet, so let me decode it a bit. He casually "tossed me the mantle," requiring me to catch it, rather than "bestowing" it on me with any sort of ceremony. He could have said I was honoring him by taking it up and he was proud of me. Instead, there was a subtle put-down because I knew he didn't really think I'd have the level of fun and success he did. Further, I was only "the greatest" because I made him look good over that particular weekend. With my parents, you were only as good as your last performance. He obliged my request for the letter, acknowledging me on the surface, but like my mother, the subtext was still all about him.

Later, when I got my PhD, Dad still didn't consider me a real doctor, and he applied the same logic to his PhD granddaughter. Although he gave me a graduation party, he never took time to read the Poem Portraits I had on display as part of the celebration. He didn't understand why these women would reveal their vulnerabilities like that. Yet, after eight years in my new field, he did encourage me to go on a job interview for an expanded leadership role, but not because he valued what I did. He wanted me to get more recognition so he could tell his friends something that reflected well on him. This is the hallmark of narcissism. Out at dinner one night, I told him how frustrated I was after again he asked,

"Are you getting recognition?" Why couldn't *he* give me recognition? And how could I feel I deserved to get it externally if I rarely got it from him or my mother? He never truly appreciated my work, even when I was helping physicians become better leaders. ("Hello, Dad?") Nor did he recognize my accomplishment when my surgeon partner and I received an award for raising the caliber of physician leadership throughout the institution, and especially for our ongoing work on the Code of Mutual Respect (21; 113). The saving grace was my dear Patrick witnessing how sad the whole dynamic was. That made me know this was all real, that it wasn't me, that I didn't make it up.

Then, I had an experience of agony after a visit with my parents. I was distraught and deeply hurt that I was still not getting the love from them or any recognition for all my accomplishments. When I arrived at their home in the desert, to keep burying my pain, I decided to stay passive, go with the flow, and not let them know how upset I was, just as I'd always done. We'd sit in their light and open living room on the wraparound couch, each reading a magazine. Surrounded by floor to ceiling art and sculptures, we inhabited a stimulating environment in contrast to the emotional desert of our communication. If I ever had spoken my truth and expressed my anger, hurt, and distress to or about them, not only would they have been shocked, but I actually feared they may have asked me to stay at a hotel or leave altogether. Instead, we were, as always, the perfect family, it was going to be the perfect visit, I would be the perfect child, and they would maintain their roles as perfect parents. A complete and perfect fiction. But I must have done something my father disapproved of, because at some point he acted insulted, irritated, and withdrawn. I didn't know why, and he didn't tell me what I had done. And of course, I didn't dare ask. I was frustrated with not attempting a real relationship, but why couldn't I see, as Patrick could so easily, that nothing was ever going to change? If I didn't mirror Dad perfectly, I wasn't worthy of his attention. It was all about what I gave to him, and he was extremely hard to please. By the same token, it really wasn't my job to make him happy or manage his emotions, though it took me a long time to learn that. When I got home, the pain of that visit wouldn't leave me. Why couldn't we all just speak our truth?

Image 71:My drawing of my parents' living room in their Chicago apartment, which looked nearly the same in their desert home.

It then became obvious to me where my fear of disappointing others came from. My father was always disappointed and critical of my moods, vulnerability, and process. This was the imprint he left on me. True, doctors are trained to be detached, invulnerable, and decisive. But he wasn't my doctor. He was my dad, and his job as a parent was to grow a child, not treat a patient. He was, apparently, incapable of seeing me for my potential or my gifts, only for how I reflected on him. He consistently misperceived my intentions toward him. This lack of congruence between us was extremely upsetting, and though I tried a million ways to get in sync, nothing ever worked. The truth was, I didn't really exist except to meet his needs. But it was unbearably painful to see and accept that, so I became determined and devoted and maintained the myth of perfection so as not to feel the pain and truth of my aloneness, abandonment, and rejection (16; 33–34).

Image 72: A collage reminding me to live my life for myself, not in search of my parents' approval.

When my parents felt good, they could be generous and had the means to be. I remember Mom's parents, Grandma and Pop, as always giving when they came for our ritual Sunday brunch, bringing bags of bagels, lox, cream cheese, and salami, but most of all, love. Pop was a teaser, dressed to the hilt in his hand-tailored suits flaunting their patterned silk linings. I loved to look into his beady eyes and laugh at his silly jokes, which he repeated ad nauseam. My grandma, an impeccable dresser and a classy lady, had her hair and nails done every week of her life, even eventually in the nursing home. I used to try to find sophisticated sweater sets like hers when I was consulting. Although she was not admired by most of the family, she was someone who understood me and invested in me. I don't think she knew I didn't get the love she gave from my parents. That is why I dedicated my first book to her. If I called her crying at any age, I knew I'd be embraced and emotionally safe. She was the only caring female nurturer I had. My earliest memory of her showing me real love was when Mom and I came to visit once during the day. The drive was too far for my little bladder, so when we arrived at their small apartment, I asked to use the bathroom. But Pop liked to watch his six-inch Sony television while sitting on his throne for what seemed like hours. Classy, elegant Gram quietly took me into the kitchen and helped me pee in the sink! No judgment. No shame. Then she opened the cupboards to give me her standard treat: homemade chocolate pudding, still cooling, with the skin on top.

When in high school, I was president of Girls Club, and that meant Dad was to say a few words at the annual Daddy-Daughter Dinner Dance. He was shy and hated speaking in public, as he had to do for my bas mitzvah when I was thirteen. I think he actually resented me for bringing him into uncomfortable public situations. His reticence made me uneasy that we weren't performing our parts perfectly, and I eventually took on his nervousness, when I might have been enjoying the group social experience. Nevertheless, he was more forthcoming one-on-one, and we continued daddy-daughter outings from time to time after I moved away as an adult. Once when he visited me in New York, he invited me to dinner and a Broadway play, Martin McDonagh's *The Beauty Queen of Leenane*. I have no idea why he selected this play, but it turned out to be significant for me. The daughter had a difficult relationship with her narcissistic mother but still took care of her in her old age. When her mother died (spoiler alert: murdered by the daughter), she knew she would never leave the house because she had lost all hope. I found the play sad because in the daughter's old age, no one would take care of her and she would die alone and miserable. For years after seeing it, I feared I'd be like the daughter who, when finally free to emotionally leave her deceased but often mean and controlling mother, I would become her instead. My ambivalent attachment to my mother was that strong. Did my dad know the deeper meaning of the play? Was he finally trying to make me aware of my unconscious feelings and protect me from them? How come I kept hoping for a reckoning like this but couldn't get it through my head that he would never go there? He was even more black-and-white than I was. Eventually, I came to a profound understanding that my father was not only emotionally shallow, but also, in the words of Tom Absher, "stunted by his own inner emptiness." He projected that emptiness on to me, and I took it in as my own, showing again, I *can* take things in, as long as they are negative attributions. Our conversation after this emotional play proved our pattern. He discussed how hard it was to understand the actors' Irish accents, and I went along with it as the salient point of the evening. What choice did I have? (3; 52 and 29; 61).

As the years went by, surrendering to the truth of our relationship, it grew harder and harder for me to please my father with a birthday gift. If I found something I thought would be of interest, I remained wary. My therapist Robyn said if Dad didn't like my gift of a special book and card and was disappointed, I could say something like, "I'm sorry if it's not what you expected and doesn't feel honoring enough." In other words, do what's enough for me and let him have his reaction. She said it was not mean to be matter of fact. Of course, my instinct was to grovel. What was old was the relationship being all about him. My anger was a healthy sign (16; 36). Still, on a visit six months before his decline from kidney failure, I ordered him a one-year subscription to the *New York Times*, which he loved.

At various visits with my husband, my parents would say or write that I "was their joy" and "made them feel like royalty" (11; 44). Dad said, "You're my prize." But the words seemed hollow, and I didn't feel it (11; 43). Perhaps because he never treated me as a prize? This numbness accompanied the realization that I had never influenced him, and that made me feel the relationship was one-way and would never grow. When he was ill, I told him I would miss him so much when he was not with us. He said, without humor, "I'll miss me, too" (8; 92). He would later say, "Don't forget me," but never expressed that he wouldn't forget me and what I meant to him.

Karen, on a visit with Mom and Dad, saw how miserable Dad was in the rehab facility. She realized there would be no rehabilitation; he would die there alone. Mom refused to walk the block to spend time with him there, and I didn't understand why. Karen convinced Mom it was only right to bring him back to the apartment for hospice care, and Karen made it happen. Once Dad was back in the apartment, and Karen and her husband had left, Mom called me to express her anger at all the caretakers coming in and out of the apartment. I asked her when I should come. She said, "Come any time." I arranged to leave work and flew to California the next morning. Upon my arrival, Mom was visibly irritated, although she was glad to see me and greeted me with a hug and kiss. Having just seen Dad in the rehab facility two weeks prior with Patrick, I was so glad to be there and see that hospice in the apartment was much better for him. He was so frightened, upset at being abandoned and rejected by Mom, and giving into being helpless. They placed the hospital bed by the windows and moved the couch into the bedroom, so upon entering the small kitchen past the counter, the previous living room was unrecognizable, yet it signaled home for Dad. I noticed Mom was snippy and mean to him. When he couldn't hold the hamburger (which would be his final meal) and it dropped out of his hands in the dining room, she made a face of disgust, got up, and told the nurse to wheel him to the apartment. Once there, the assistants changed his diapers for the last time, lovingly calling him Mr. Gorgeous. He was so shrunken, but he still had his wavy white hair and handsome yellow sweater, although noticeably stained. He melted with their attention, even though he loved being called Dr. Kaplan, he didn't correct them by saying, "Call me Dr. Gorgeous." Because I was learning to change my ways and see them differently, I could see from Mom's perspective she was devastated her husband of over sixty years was no longer able to take care of her, never mind himself. I suggested to Mom in an upbeat voice, "Why don't you take the day for you. Go be with friends or go shopping. If anything happens, I will let you know." Relieved, she got dressed with one of her signature hats, and left, shoulders back, racing down the hall to the exit.

During one of my alone times with Dad that final day, I sat next to him while he lay in the bed. The man who hated vulnerability was so vulnerable. Now very thin with deep creases in his cheeks, lips pursed with fear, he looked me in the eyes and said, "I couldn't do this without you." I said, "I know, Dad. I'm here for you to make it safe." Not liking my spiritually tinged tone, he barked, "Kathryn, get me a towel." "OK, Dad, sure." I handed him the towel, not able to figure out why he wanted it. Then he said, "I said, get me my towel!" "I did, Dad." Seeing he was confused, I checked with the nurse who knew him best. She said the end was near. It is common to be angry like this, as one last grasp for life.

I immediately hired a Visiting Angel who came that night and stayed up with him, administering morphine as I dozed on and off in the chair behind her. I told her to tell me the second he stopped breathing. When he died early that morning, it was surreal. The father who had been in my life the longest of any man was no longer alive. He didn't look like himself, his face swollen and grey. Containing my emotions, I went into the other room to gently tell Mom he had passed. She held my hand as I slowly walked her to the bed where Dad lay. We kneeled by his side. Mom didn't cry but said, "I'm so scared. I never saw anyone dead and I never wanted to see this." I took her back to her room where she showered and dressed, and she never came back out until after Dad had been taken to the morgue. It wasn't until then, when I watched his lifeless body leaving the apartment, that I released every ounce of love, disbelief, and sadness I had inside me. By the time Patrick arrived from the East Coast at around twelve-thirty, the hospice bed had been removed, the furniture replaced, and the apartment cleaned. It was like the title of Patrick's memoir, *As If It Never Happened.* We understood my mother's desire to have no trace of death there and were horrified at the same time. It was as if she had banished my father after their lifetime together. Mom then said to Patrick, dressed in her smart pants and another expensive and stylish hat, "Would you like to take a widow to lunch?" With that, she took Patrick's arm and out we went.

When I returned to work after being with Mom, I was both relieved and lost. As Karen said, "the little engine that could, now couldn't." When he died, a part of me died. Dad had been like the sand in the oyster of my soul that stimulated the growth of the pearl, my achievements. But with him gone, why was I trying to excel? Who was I trying to excel for? He lived a long time, and I had many chances to try to establish a true connection with him. I was, of his three daughters, the most like him, and I admired his career, his art, and his stability. I so badly wanted him to see my potential and mentor me, but he just wanted me to stay cute and be taken care of. How could he not have seen that person wasn't who I was? Now I was sad, disoriented, and distracted. He had been, perhaps, my foremost antagonist, and I didn't know who I was, how to define myself, without him. Our relationship was defining to me, and I missed him even more than I expected. In terms of closure, when he said he couldn't do this without me, I felt validated about my instinct to be with him at the end. And when he got upset about the towels, I actually relished his direct and real expression of anger. My ultimate grief was that he wasn't capable of more.

Narcissism

The thing that is really hard, and really amazing, is giving up on being perfect and beginning the work of becoming yourself.

—Anna Quindlen

Over the years, I tried to learn about our family dynamics so I could react differently and break the pattern (7; 30). *Necessary Losses*, by Judith Viorst, was my introduction to healthy narcissism. Based on the work of Heinz Kohut, she explains that narcissism is normal, healthy, important, and a good thing. Healthy self-love enriches and complements our love of others. It is developed early on with parents able to take simple delight in their child, such as when the child shows the parent a drawing and receives their notice, praise, pride, and encouragement. The parents' responsiveness tells the child he or she is not alone. Children naturally go through a stage of needing to be seen as "remarkable and rare," and this grandiosity is modified once they are seen and accepted as the wonderful human beings they are. With the appropriate mix of frustration and love, the child can take in these parts of themselves and develop a positive self-image and sturdy self-esteem (11; 37).

Unfortunately, I didn't have healthy narcissism. Neither did my parents. I was like the children Viorst described who were "suffering from important impairments in their early development" that interfered with their "necessary losses—with the giving up of the needs, defenses, delusions that stand in the way of a robust, integrated sense of self." We both lacked self-love, but my lack created a hole I couldn't fill, while my parents readily filled their emptiness with themselves. This makes sense, since my parents also didn't receive the mirroring they needed as children. Mom's father had died shortly after her birth and her mother was depressed for years. Dad, as the youngest of five children, lost his father when he was sixteen and was left alone much of the time. Their generation was not as psychologically oriented as ours, and in the face of childhood tragedy, they didn't get what they needed for healthy psychological development, so in retrospect, it's understandable they couldn't foster that in their children. But when I was growing up, I couldn't comprehend their self-absorption. Mom complained about how bad she had it, despite having all her material needs met and her moods indulged, and Dad just catered to her. In psychoanalysis I learned why narcissists often treat their children as ornaments to adorn themselves. As Viorst explains, "The unspoken deal is this: If you will bury the parts I don't like, then I will love you. The unspoken choice is this: Lose yourself or lose me" (11; 37). All I can say is that these dynamics, although now understandable, were deeply wounding to me and my sisters.

According to attachment theory, I had an insecure attachment, neither consistent nor nonexistent. The "intermittent reinforcement" convinced me, since I only occasionally received the connection I needed, that if only I tried harder, I could get it right and make my parents see me and love me more (17; 41). In Viorst's words, "Healthy growth involves being able to give up our need for approval when the price of that approval is our true self. It means being able to give up defensively splitting and to integrate our good with our bad self. It means that although we may, in the course of our life, be beset by emotional difficulties, we possess a reliable self, a sense of identity."

Before I could apply these insights at work, Robyn would tell me what people thought of me was none of my business and out of my control. But I didn't believe that. I believed I must be liked and approved of or I didn't feel safe. I worked in a political environment and knew I couldn't afford to ignore other people's perceptions. If they gossiped or undermined, it mattered. Yet, I agreed with her that to sell my soul to feed someone else's' narcissism was exhausting and futile.

As she explained, I needed to stop colluding in my compassionate sacrifices. I didn't have to walk on eggshells and deny my reality so others wouldn't get upset. With narcissists I'm brilliant only if they have center stage. If I'm weak, it is a bad reflection on them. Don't point it out to them, just set boundaries: "This doesn't work for me. I'm not available for this conversation right now." My inner work was to practice stopping my habit of protecting their image of themselves by undercutting myself (16; 35). Easier said than done and a huge revelation.

Another therapist strongly told me that until I figured out these dynamics, I would always attract bullies into my life (17; 62). I hated how true that seemed to be. For example, a colleague at work used her attractiveness and competence to get what she wanted. Everything had to be her way: her privacy, her abruptness, her fun. If, however, you said the wrong thing, she'd lash out. She'd give when she wanted to and was exquisitely sensitive to any initiative taken outside of her control. Again, I felt like I was walking on eggshells with her so as not to upset her, just as I did with my mother. And everyone saw the pattern, not just me. I was told by my boss I didn't need to pretend, protect her, or be manipulated by her. It was a relief to me when my boss agreed I shouldn't become her manager; I didn't have to do the dirty work no other VP wanted to take on (16; 35). Still, I dreaded working with her because I couldn't hold onto myself when she was around. This was yet another example of my family dynamic playing out in the workplace.

A confusing and mortifying experience happened once when I didn't know why I was being perceived as narcissistic. Patrick and some of his family members were out for dinner. When the waitress asked if anyone wanted water, I said, "Yes, thank you, I'm a big water drinker," to let her know I'd like my glass refilled frequently and to take the attention off of me after that. But my husband told me privately, "It's not about you." He said my tone came across as someone who was entitled. I immediately went from having fun to shutting down, feeling upset, embarrassed, and angry at him for criticizing me when it didn't seem necessary. At the hotel he said he was upset with my reaction; if it were him, he would have "gotten it" and been grateful. He said at that moment I seemed so adolescent, so like my mother. I hated having parts of myself I was not conscious of, but it is the benefit of an intimate relationship to hold up the mirror, no matter how uncomfortable. Not being perfectly self-aware was precisely why I hated being a leader, always at risk for feeling humiliated when visibly acting immature.

How is it that in this situation I went from feeling comfortable asserting myself in a casual way to being perceived as self-centered, awkward, and irritating (9; 36)? Naturally, I'd be triggered by being called selfish or narcissistic. But the real dynamic was outside of my control, since it was almost certainly due to Patrick's worry about how his family would judge me for expressing a need, combined with my tenuous hold on the idea that the server was actually there to meet my needs. Years later, I could understand this interaction differently and more deeply based on what Patrick wrote in his memoir. Growing up in poverty, if he was visiting with a friend, and they asked him if he'd like a cookie or seconds at dinner, he would always say, "No thank you," even if he was starving. He'd been conditioned to hide his needs. Directly and easily expressing my need for water was triggering to him, as it conflicted with his family's strategy of denying needs to save face. He had also seen my mother be rude to servers and worried I was following in her footsteps, even though I had a heightened awareness of this pattern. Narcissism needed unpacking as it showed up between us and impacted our families of origin.

Another layer was revealed after I quietly processed a certain dream that disorganized me upon waking. To get myself back together so I could be appropriate at work, I engaged in a series of actions based on previous insights. I was aware that when I berated myself for being tired, clumsy, hungry, lost, or late, it was my mother's critical voice internalized in me. I was unconsciously treating myself the way she treated me, probably to feel a connection with her that didn't exist. I then reminded myself to maintain my dignity and gracefulness at work. I also focused on taking in the people around me and paying attention to the whole context (21; 5). It took concentration because I knew that in a nanosecond I could be back to a memory and not in the present moment.

To build my more centered muscles, I explored with Robyn the critical difference between narcissism and healthy self-care. As Viorst reveals, a narcissist will emotionally beat up anyone who makes them feel upset or uncomfortable. If on the receiving end, a person who has self-care will stay connected to their own truth while having compassion that the narcissist is upset. The narcissist will want you to become responsible for their emotions and abandon yourself. If you have self-care, you will respond by staying in your body with your own feelings, even if it is causing them suffering. It is tempting to placate and lose yourself to make the narcissist feel better. But if you have self-care, you consider that possibly they'll grow from the pain, so you listen. If a narcissist is being rejecting, disapproving, disappointed or uninterested, they would like you to take on their blaming, judging, yelling, or crying. With self-care, before responding, you remind yourself of possible explanations: they have nothing to give to you; they never got what they needed; you are not the only one they do this to; they expect perfection and grandiosity. With self-care you understand you don't have to be available to abuse. You give yourself permission not to continue the interaction (17; 84). I don't know if this comes easily to some people, but for me it wasn't natural or feasible.

What I've learned through repeated experience is narcissists don't know they are narcissists. They don't wear a sign saying, "I'm a narcissist, beware!" But they do leave their signature, and it is in you—in the strings they pluck that alert you to the fact you are being triggered. Once you're aware, then it's your job to take the very best care of your wounded self you can. Sure, you're disappointed it happened again. You thought you had cured it once and for all. But being human, you didn't. You then forgive yourself. You pause and feel fully the uncomfortable sensations in your body. You breathe your connection to your Deepest Wisest Self. Maybe you cry for the little ones inside who feel hurt and humiliated once again. You review your notes on the difference between narcissism and healthy self-care. And you move on.

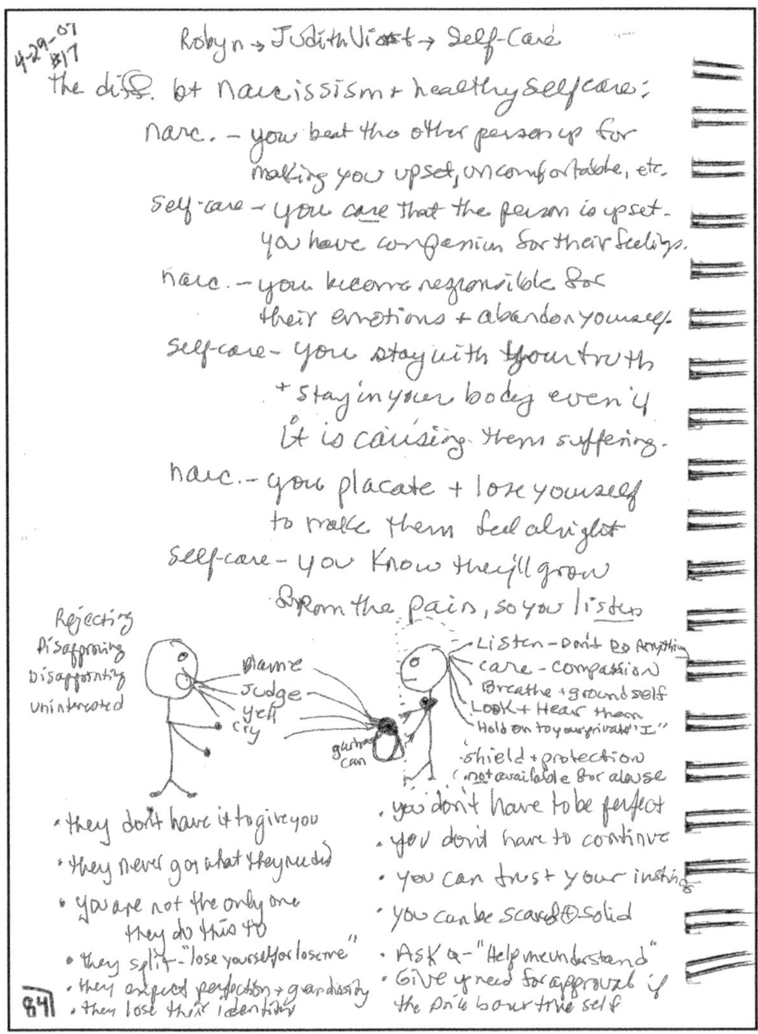

Image 73: Narcissism versus healthy self-care.

Ever the hard worker, I went on to reread McBride's book on narcissism to learn the five steps to healing the unmothered child:

Accept your mother's limitations and allow yourself to grieve.

Separate psychologically from your mother and reframe the negative messages.

Work on your authentic sense of self.

Deal with your mother and your relationship with her in a healthy way.

Treat your own narcissistic traits and refuse to pass on the legacy to your own children.

I did all the book's exercises, including accepting my mother, describing my ideal mother, and owning any of my own narcissistic traits (25; 16–19). It turns out I have two tendencies that perhaps are narcissistic. For example, when an article I wrote got rejected, my first reaction was hurt—a narcissistic injury (26; 66). Endlessly comparing myself to others unfavorably, while desperate for praise and approval, was likely a holdover from seeing my parents get plenty of attention. They didn't give it to me; I wanted it and not having it was hurtful.

Probably one of the unconscious reasons I never had children is I didn't want to pass on the legacy of narcissism. I think, knowing what I know now of myself and narcissism, I made the right decision. However, on reflection, I believe the real inhibiter to being a mother was that I was so hard on myself; I would have worried endlessly about the damage I might have been inflicting on a child, through narcissism or whatever I called my behavior. Over time I have learned to mother myself differently than I was mothered. Where Mom was negligent, I am attentive. Where she was distant and dismissive, I treat myself with presence and understanding. At the same time, I seem to have found what we had in common: we had both been preoccupied with our early and unresolved emotional pain.

What differentiates me from my mother is my empathy for others. I know I am not a narcissist at the core. I focused on finding a diagnosis because I wanted a way to make sense of my agony, but did it really help to have a label, or was it yet another way to demean myself? Because we were raised to believe we were the perfect family, it actually took all this investigation to take the blinders off and reveal the real, imperfect family underneath.

Once I was let go as the VP of OD, the counselor I was seeing for my diminishing eyesight was also astute to my emotional state. She said as a child I sacrificed myself to please my parents and make them look and feel good, part of being in a narcissistic family. When I lost my job, I felt unappreciated, like all the extra work I did wasn't necessary or hadn't mattered. Being let go rekindled early wounds, causing me to become depressed and angry. I wasn't valued, rewarded, recognized, and acknowledged (just as I hadn't been in childhood), so it hurt my self-esteem. But at this point, she said I was stuck and, like a child, having a temper tantrum. She believed I didn't want to work because I didn't want to give myself away again. Unfortunately, by not having an income, I created a crisis. My life was unraveling. Even though I didn't know what I wanted, it was, she said, my responsibility to figure it out. Nothing would be handed to me. I had to reclaim my power, develop boundaries, and express my voice. It was a moment-to-moment practice that was up to me to take on—and I did (26; 66).

I did everything I knew how to do to put together the one thousand pieces of my jigsaw puzzle self in a new way. Still searching and determined to heal, resigning myself to not working and the consequences of the financial stress, in 2015 I sought out one final therapist. This one said I needed to have faith in myself and also gently suggested I look into codependence. I was definitely not interested in reading even one more book or applying one more label. However, she thought if I needed a way to think about my patterns, this might be a more fruitful path. I dutifully read the Twelve Steps and Twelve Promises of Co-Dependents Anonymous (27; 125). A revealing quote I found said, "Codependent recovery is letting go of what you never had" (27; 102). Wow, it took my breath away. I remember walking while thinking about this quote and just shaking my head to really get it, to feel it. Then, I learned how the codependent and narcissist fit together as magnets. I concluded this might be true as I reflected on an example with my mother. Often, when she had a creative idea, such as welding a sculpture from car parts, I would devote myself to bringing her discarded hubcaps I found in a field by my parents' house.

Further, I discovered that "The narcissist has an overpowering need to feel important and special, and the codependent has a strong need to help others feel that way" (27; 102). I considered that this dynamic might have been what made me both successful and invisible at work. I loved helping individuals, teams, and departments find their voice and make changes in line with their intentions. My Poem Portraits were a way of mirroring and honoring others. But I didn't enjoy being the leader with her own vision and staff; I was more comfortable—and effective—being second in command, implementing the dreams and plans of others. I admit, I did wish to be seen and valued for my facilitative strengths and not criticized for not being a more commanding and visible presence. I guess you can't have it both ways, and this dichotomy is probably why I felt like I didn't make a bigger difference in my work and life.

As I looked for other definitions and characteristics of codependent people, I found: "Sacrificing one's personal needs in order to try to meet the needs of others" (31; 120). This one hit me hard. I never realized codependence could encompass so many of my patterns and pains. It is characterized by people pleasing, need for validation and approval, rescuing others, poor boundaries, fear of being without an intimate partner, and denying desires and emotions. It is caused by childhood patterns, emotional neglect, and reversal of the parent-child role. And the description fit me like a glove.

In 2008, I had just received a perfect performance evaluation from my boss who said, "You're outstanding because of who you are and how you work." With that validation, I pushed past my persistent lack of confidence and felt freed up and reenergized to dive into the work I was doing involving many departments and new initiatives. Then—kaboom! For the first time in the three years we had worked together, I disappointed her, not just once but three times in a row. Our disconnect, I wrote, "set me reeling in despair, distracted and distraught, in pain and hurt and deeply worried" (19; 73). Beyond the emotional pain, I was suffering physically—and noticeably so—from the all-consuming worry. In Journal 19, I wrote an entry about this which ended up giving the journal its title: "Perfect vs. Kaboom: Giving myself the approval I seek and risk disappointing others." The first disappointment was minor, but we were able to move through the third only because of the intensive work we did on the middle "huge kaboom."

The issue was that when working with a new partner, I followed *her* lead rather than trust my instincts. This led to the nurse director of the department where we were planning an intervention growing concerned and calling my boss, who was also the chief nursing officer. In trying to please the new partner, I wasn't using boundaries with the nurse director, and I was desperately afraid of losing the approval of my boss—which turned out to be a self-fulfilling prophecy. In the classic codependent pattern, I was concerned about protecting the offending person (the partner who was giving me bad advice) over honoring my own needs and emotions. I prepared in detail for the crucial conversation with my boss, ready for the worst, hoping for the best, and ready to acknowledge and apologize for my contribution to the problem. To my surprise, my boss also apologized (for overreacting), acknowledged our "covenant," said she treasured me, and owned that my part was a small piece of a much larger problem she couldn't yet solve. After this open exchange, we never had another miscommunication during the remaining four years we worked together. I know these types of work conflicts are common, and I know many, if not most, people move through them without my level of emotional and physical pain. But I also know I am not the only one. Had I known then what I know now, pursuing support from Co-Dependents Anonymous meetings and a sponsor would have been helpful. As one of their brochures indicates, codependent people often exhibit:

> **Denial**: difficulty identifying feelings, denying how they truly feel, and perceiving themselves as completely dedicated to the well-being of others

Low self-esteem: difficulty making decisions, judging themselves as never good enough, and valuing other people's approval over their own

Compliance: compromising their values and integrity to avoid rejection and other people's anger, being very sensitive to other people's feelings, being extremely loyal, and remaining in harmful situations too long

Control: offering advice and direction without being asked, becoming resentful when others decline their help, and having to feel needed in relationships

Avoidance: using indirect or evasive communication to avoid conflict, avoiding intimacy to avoid feeling vulnerable, and acting in ways that invite others to reject, shame, or project their anger onto them

My newly informed awareness led me to reluctantly own these traits, as if challenged in a courtroom and responding, "Yes, your honor." I saw the unconscious benefits to clinging to my suffering. In fact, reading about the origins of not feeling enough, I learned that "many of us suffer in a strange obligation to stay connected with our parents. Remaining in rapport with their pain is one of the surprising ways children convey their 'love.' Breaking that rapport can feel like a betrayal of the family system" (28; 84). I didn't want to be an outcast, but what price did staying in the family system cost me? These descriptions were clear and comprehensive, but like my criticism of most books on anger and conflict, their logic didn't match the emotions inside when I was experiencing these patterns. I couldn't think my way out of this, but only feel my way through it. Finally, I was ready to accept that only I could use all my insights and tools to give myself the love and understanding I was ever seeking. Isn't that what I needed most of all, to have compassion for my wounded self?

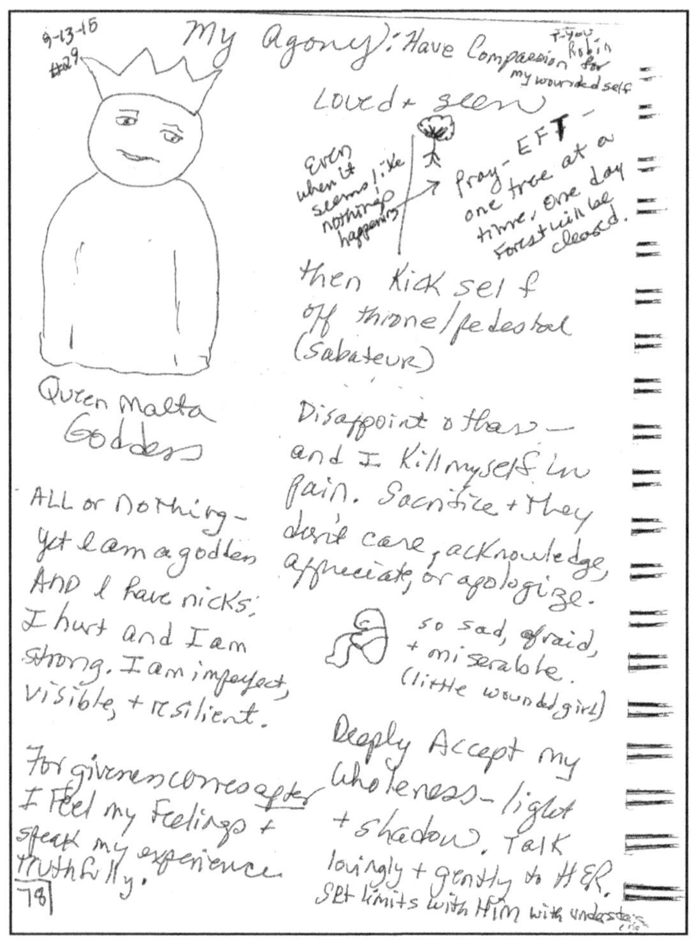

Image 74: Having compassion for my wounded self.

Addictive Searching

Who looks outside, dreams. Who looks inside, awakens.

—Carl Jung

Why was I addicted to searching? Was it because I was, in Eckhart Tolle's words, "addicted to unhappiness" (19; 146)? To seeking perfection?

To understanding my past and making sense of my pain? Was it psychological? Was I addicted because I was caught in a trap? I was driven to excel, but I knew the danger of being happier or more successful than my narcissistic parents and feared invoking their resentment and subtle, never-acknowledged punishments. Maintaining their approval meant maintaining my place beneath them and was a matter of emotional survival. Or, was I addicted to self-sabotage, as the frightened, guilty, punitive voice of my inner saboteur sought the love I couldn't give myself in the destructive parts of my parents' personalities (31; 106)? I think the answer for me was: all of the above. At the heart of my quest was a confused and lonely little girl left to figure everything out on her own. No wonder, then, that I sought answers wherever I could find them.

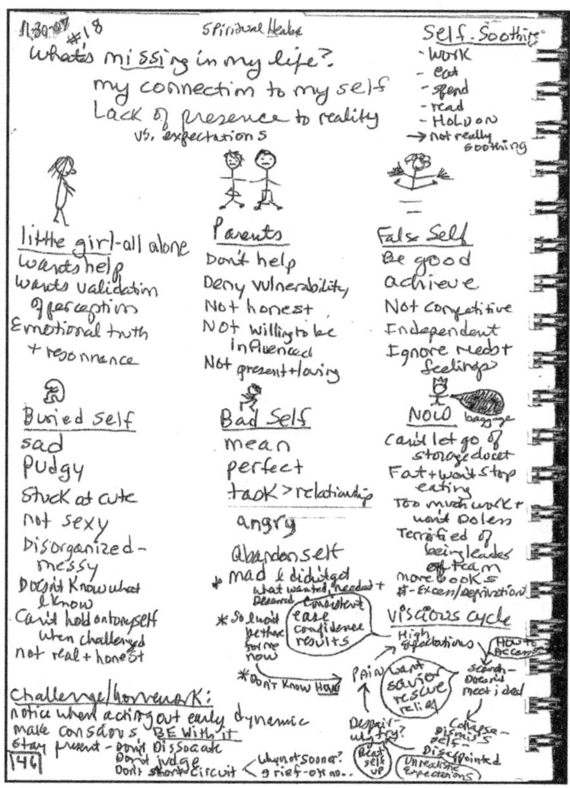

Image 75: "What's missing in my life?"

It was a comfort when I learned, after we had all left home and began to talk, that my sisters were searchers, too. We often spoke about our suffering and exchanged emails that showed our similar process and struggles (19; 15). To myself, I referred to our behavior patterns as the Kaplan Syndrome. Our outer lives and inner styles were different, both in childhood and adulthood, yet we were similar in forgetting what we learned from our searches and not remembering to use tools that had proven effective. It was my perception that early on Mom and Dad made the rules: I followed them, Karen broke them, and Lisa ignored them. Ultimately, we were each trying to write our own rules and live more authentic lives, free from imposed restrictions that didn't work. As an adult, Karen said, "We sisters are here to recognize who we are." She always wanted more of Mom's love and less of Dad's anger. Born three years apart, we were like two sides of the same coin; when she was thin, I was heavy, when I was achieving, she was struggling. But both of us wanted to do a better job at mothering Lisa when she was born. We didn't like how perfunctorily Mom was changing her diapers, so we gently took over until Mom yelled, "Enough! I'm her mother." Lisa, eleven years younger than I, was raised basically as an only child after Karen and I left the house. She said she always wanted our parents to make more sense. I always wanted to be known and valued (2; 27). We all searched to find what we were wanting and never found. Each would agree our parents shaped our dynamics and difficulties. All three of us now share our various resources, process our emotions, and encourage each other's journeys. As we acknowledge what we individually bring to the mix, we are proof of the damaging consequences of what appear to be the subtle hurts of narcissism.

My addiction to reading books and working with therapists was a compulsive attempt to heal my private hell (17; 72). One of the first books from which I took extensive notes was *There Is Nothing Wrong with You: Going Beyond Self-Hate* by Cheri Huber and June Shiver (1; 93–101). The authors' premise is that we are searching for a spiritual path, and that path is found inside ourselves. But when our needs are not met in childhood, we conclude those needs were bad, making us bad people. Since our survival depended on being taken care of, we couldn't risk inducing our parents' anger and causing them to withdraw the care and support we needed. Since it couldn't be our parents' fault our needs weren't being met, we must be the problem. Therefore, we tried to fix what was wrong, convinced of our own inadequacy. As the authors said, "Self-hate is the ultimate addiction." If something wasn't wrong with us, then people wouldn't have treated us in punishing ways. This logic was twisted of course, but it made perfect sense. We learned these behaviors to survive, but survival kept us separate and searching for answers outside of ourselves. The trap was believing we must be this way to survive, but we hated ourselves for being this way. Then, we sought ways to cope. The authors said the ego, with its illusion of separateness, was not capable of experiencing the wholeness it seeks. Eventually, the seeker, with practices like meditation, could move from the one hoping to be saved to the one who could save. When we realize what we are seeking is our true nature, we became the love, acceptance, and compassion we have always sought.

While the path outlined by Huber and Shiver offered me a broader view of what was possible, rereading my journal entries helped me see why their advice did not immediately take root. I identified with the problem—hating myself—but not the solution: loving myself. I didn´t know what I was searching for was a spiritual undertaking. I also didn't acknowledge that the spiritual path is not a quick fix. I was searching for my true nature, but I didn't frame it that way. I consistently said, "I want to discover my vision and hear my voice, to live fully from my true self" (3; 44). But I didn't really know what that meant, only that if I did it, I would feel better. My friends at the time were going to ashrams and meditation classes, but I didn't feel better when I went with them, so I didn't continue. Much later a spiritual therapist I was seeing said if there was one thing she wanted me to know, it was that the present moment is all there is. "While I'm searching for what I'm missing, I'm missing my life." How simple. How profound. Simple, but not easy (21; 66).

While I do integrate the spiritual as an aspect of my healing, it often feels too ethereal and not real. The vision and voice I seek are located in my senses and grounded in my body. Living fully from my true self is led by my heart and soul. I finally understand that struggles and suffering are unavoidable. My problem was collapsing into my pain, unable to hold my various parts without an adult self to negotiate and listen. Now, rather than freeze when in conflict with two or more opposing views, I find freedom when I connect my emotions with my body (24; 16). Instead of activities that make me feel light and airy, I prefer practices like yoga, where I feel my muscles stretch and connect my mind to my breath. Staying present helps me not miss the reality of my life.

And one reality of my life is that I now see how I have overused my strengths of being conceptual and resourceful. My exhaustive searching has been exhausting. It's like I have gone around the whole world only to take one step. Certain steps have definitely helped, such as studying the dynamics of narcissism in families and finally grieving the loss of my childhood. Significantly, rereading all my journals has helped me see myself, providing the mirroring I didn't have or couldn't take in. Rather than having arrived, I am in an ongoing process of awakening, with gratitude and surrender.

My opening to the spiritual aspect of healing took time and patience. Spirit has to do with respiration, the breath. With narcissists, they suck all the oxygen out of the room. It's no wonder I couldn't find my voice or my breath, or that I felt emotionally suffocated. Learning late in life about codependence, and how it fits like a matching puzzle piece with narcissism, I know I always felt if I didn't please, placate, agree, or give in, I couldn't breathe. So my spiritual journey has been to acknowledge more than the psychological, the concrete experience, and the memories, while not be suffocated by the damaging dynamics. My awakening with my parents and finding answers to all I had been seeking has led to finding air and breathing in the ineffable, the blessed peace, and the connection to an ever-present source of guidance and love.

I wished I had found, years earlier, this beautiful practice by yoga instructor Colleen Saidman Yee. It has helped me to accept all my feelings, letting them shift and be released, and coming to the present moment with more self-love and tenderness (29; 27):

> Just sit. Notice where you feel hard and sit with that. In the middle of the hardness, you will find anger. Sit with that. Go to the center of the anger and you will probably come to sadness. Stay with the sadness until it turns to vulnerability. Keep sitting with what comes up. The deeper you dig, the more tender you become. Raw fear can open into wide expanses of genuineness, compassion, gratitude, and acceptance in the present moment. A tender heart appears naturally when you are able to stay present. From your heart you can see the true pigment of the sky. You can see the vibrant yellow of the sunflower and the deep blue of your daughter's eye. A tender heart does not block out rainclouds or tears of dying sunflowers. Allow beauty and sadness to touch you. This is love, not fear.

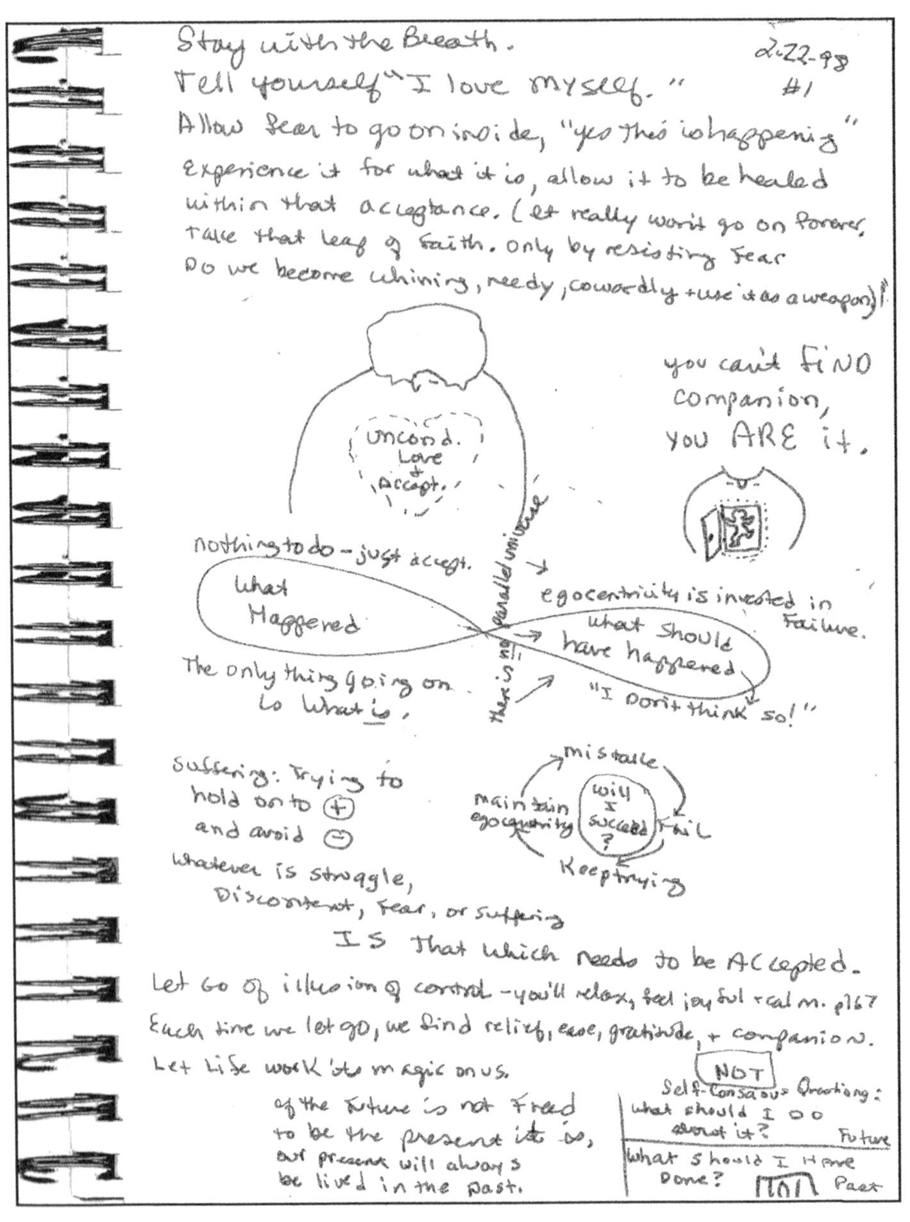

Image 76: Unconditional love and acceptance.

CHAPTER EIGHT

Living Fully

The real voyage of discovery consists not in seeking new landscapes but in having new eyes.
—Marcel Proust

My Life with Me in It

By examining the core themes that run through my journal series, I have found subtle shifts in insight, enhanced by time, change, and reflection, that have led me to a previously elusive sense of inner knowing. For example, I always thought I wanted a static, completed self that could handle every situation perfectly. What I discovered instead was that I needed to tolerate and even enjoy the colorful, messy, unpredictable life that was mine.

Once a therapist asked me point blank, "What would be enough for you?" She saw that I was thin, promoted, helping my aging parents, and in a growing intimate partnership; why wasn't all that enough? What was I still seeking (24; 16)?

In some ways, my truth at that time was, "enough was never enough." I could never have enough therapists, books, strategies, or new attempts to undo the past. I answered her that in addition to growing in confidence and intimacy, I wanted to create a business website and write a book from my soul—more expectations for achievement. I initiated the website four years later and this book three years after that, not because I needed more, but because these things were important to me. I always thought I was incapable of visualizing a future. But now I see I am just impatient; when the time is right for my visions to manifest, they get completed or, more accurately, arrive without distraction or resistance. It's the same with the house in the woods I always wanted. I never could have predicted when and how my dream would come true, but at last it did. Perhaps it's more of a house in the jungle, with a large banana tree in the middle of the backyard. The two stories allow Patrick to have his man cave downstairs and my office space upstairs. There is a lot of light here. In contrast to our tiny New York apartment, where Patrick would say, "Get out of my kitchen," because there was no room for two to maneuver, we have space not only to cook together but also to dance around the kitchen while listening to music and waiting for dinner to be ready.

Image 77: My photo of our "house in the woods."

What has given me brief respite from my "struggle to end the struggle" is consistently disconnecting from IT and THERE, connecting with HER, and entering Heartfelt Spaces. While I noted it in my first journal, it has taken years of permission to replicate the joy I felt when I took myself to the Mohonk Mountain House resort in the woods (1; 2–12). Recommended by a colleague, my soul loved walking in nature, being alone, reading, writing, drawing, and just following the flow of my inner guidance. Feeling safe and well cared for, I returned to work with more optimism and generosity. Once home, I made time to cook healthy meals, and to drift and daydream. Creating morning and evening rituals with meditation and prayer was grounding. Listening to music, sleeping, and taking bubble baths all brought me closer to my undamaged core. Yes, it's unrealistic to think every day could be like this, but making time for relaxation and renewal was something I didn't do enough. When you finally give yourself the things you need, suddenly "enough" doesn't seem so hard to achieve anymore (1; 1–12). Practicing self-care and honoring my creativity are the great rewards of retirement, like being on a permanent vacation!

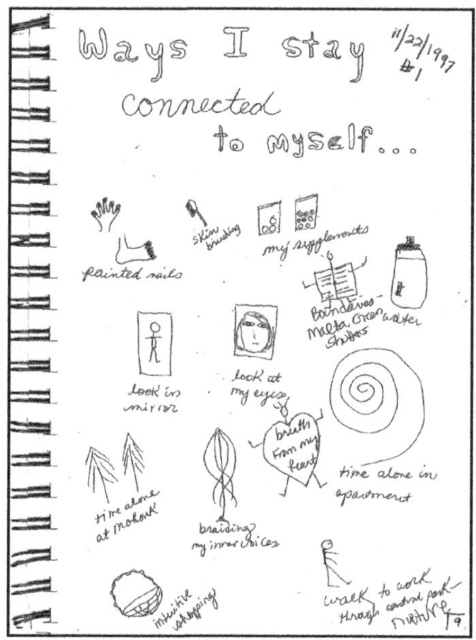

Image 78: "Ways I stay connected to myself."

During the time before Patrick and I left for our travel adventure, I had started reading books on aging and retirement. My observation was that people generally followed one of three paths. First, the ones who loved their work continued it; second were those who reinvented themselves with a new focus; and third were the ones who explored their often long-delayed passions. For example, one of my friends in finance now volunteers at an agency to help the incarcerated make a transition back to society and work. Another friend is learning violin and writing poetry. I, of course, was frustrated, because I didn't know what I wanted to do to reinvent myself. So I gave myself permission to follow my nose toward activities that seemed of interest. When we work full time, there is hardly a moment for this type of moseying. What I didn't realize is that in trusting my instincts, the reinvention would find me.

Like my collages and journals, stepping into my new self was a receptive, organic process. Who knew I'd be fascinated with language acquisition and be passionate about teaching English and learning Spanish? Or that I would finally dive into my journals, with the discipline and curiosity to discover what they meant? These were truly unexpected endeavors. Time in nature and reflecting on my journals helped me put my struggles, my accomplishments, and the stages of my life in perspective. It was as if I could watch hours and hours of footage of my life and suddenly see the patterns that weren't detectable while I was living it. I saw that while being the "story gardener" at work, too often my own plant was wilting (17; 41). Rather than approach taking care of my health as being selfish and self-absorbed, I needed to see it as a gift to honor life itself. I certainly did not want Patrick to have to take care of me because I let myself go or became ill or disabled. As I read in my journals about what kind of old lady I wanted to be, I wrote, "dying isn't hard, not living fully is" (1; 66).

Gratefully, I must have done something right, because from my 1998 list until now, June of 2020, I actually have become who I wanted to be: self-reliant and interdependent, interested in people and current events, loving and loved, respected and appreciated, in connection with spirit and my soul, and healthy. How I got here is the key, and I think my commitment to inner work and making a difference in the world mattered. Examining your life can be truly life changing. I always wanted to have a "little birdie" who could watch my interactions and tell me what they meant so I'd know what to say and do (2; 30). Now I'm able to be that little birdie, to be a witness to my inner life and the outer actions that flow from my no longer depressive but expressive core.

My awareness of how to cultivate and transform relationships has also changed over the years. I have come to learn that as much as I love creating collages, relationships are not collages. I don't get to pick and choose best qualities, matching interests, and satisfying attunement and expect to find all of them in one person. The secret, I believe, is to acknowledge my desires, grieve my losses when they're not met, accept what is, make decisions, take action, move on, and grow: a simple formula born out of the complexity of living, and echoing Katherine Woodward Thomas's insight that not all relationships are about growth. Sometimes they are just about loving people for who they are and adjusting expectations and investment accordingly (32; 108).

My current acupuncturist asked me if the issues in my journals are the same now as they were when I started. Upon reflection, I can say that certain patterns related to my body are the same, like when I overeat, don't exercise, or feel shut down. But I have actually changed a lot, and I want to keep that perspective. I am not tortured or miserable. I am fortunate to have the ease and calm I always longed for. I am grateful for the beauty of nature around me. Patrick and I are closer than ever. We live a simple and enjoyable life. Who knew that in three years here, I could feel this way? As my mother used to say, "If you live long enough, anything can happen."

How do I account for this change that, until not long ago, I thought would never and could never come to pass? I can relate it in large part to a quote from a Buddhist who studied the limbic system. He said,

"The only change was my relationship to my own failings" (28; 6). By reviewing my journals and asking my own questions, I identified clues for moving through the passage to change. Imagine making your way blindly through a series of tunnels, then suddenly discovering you have a strong flashlight to light your way. The pattern that kept me wandering was not integrating my negative with the positive. Instead, I held up my imperfections and mistakes as public humiliation. I refused to keep myself safe or love myself through my pain, and I kept searching for approval and recognition outside of myself rather than authorizing myself to live a life that made sense and was satisfying to me. In the repetitiveness of my journal entries, I finally realized there was nothing new. In fact, I knew myself and could drop the limiting belief that I was *a mystery to myself.* I had accomplished what I longed for, exemplified in the words of Florida Scott-Maxwell: "You need only claim the events of your life to make yourself yours. When you truly possess all you have been and done, which may take some time, you are fierce with reality" (4; 122).

Another frame through which to view my change is expressed by motivational speaker Les Brown: "You can't see the picture when you're in the frame." For years, I felt boxed into my life and had to get out of the box to create something new. But climbing out of a box bigger than you are isn't just hard—it's impossible. You have to break down the walls, not by demolishing them but by realizing they only exist in your imagination, or more accurately your lack thereof. Of course, there's always a new box we put ourselves in, and just as change isn't a once and for all event, I don't know how long this new normal will last. I do know, however, that the life I'm living now is more sustainable and satisfying than I ever felt possible. I may not have—or ever have—everything I want, but I am in constant contact with my soul's longing and my heart's desire, and that, yes that, is enough. As I always wanted, *I am living before I die.*

In addition to the box image, burying myself alive was the metaphor I used as shorthand for hating myself and my life. I so often felt overwhelmed by all my projects and obligations at work. My office collected too many books, piles, and files. I can tolerate creative chaos as well as any artist, even enjoying making a mess when cooking and cleaning it up at the end. But while I could effectively ignore the clutter around me, it lent a perception to others that I lacked the habits of a skilled executive or the ability to provide the peace and respect my husband wanted. The big "Aha!" didn't come until I was finally clearing out the apartment for our move. Feeling overwhelmed and so aware of my endless tendency to collect and save things, I went down the inner well of my pattern and decided to make a list, as I sorted and scanned, of what I observed about how I buried myself alive (31; 97):

> As I began to lower the imaginary rope down the well, I noticed that I valued how meticulous I was in documenting my whole process of a given activity. Yet, I realized this was an overuse of the research process, and it was not necessary for most work tasks.
>
> Next, I saw that I often didn't feel done (once again, how much is enough?) because the end result didn't match my expectations. But those expectations were unrealistic. I saved everything to improve on it one day—which, predictably, never happened.
>
> Then I acknowledged I had a great memory for certain passages in books and enjoyed finding just what I was looking for if I thought someone could benefit from it. Essentially, I was saving books and papers because it would be easier to find a reference on my shelf—if and when I might need it for some undefined future. This was probably a form of anxiety, preparing for eventualities that might never happen.
>
> I realized I felt secure having weighted energy in my environment—a false sense of security that actually limited my freedom to fly.
>
> Going deeper, I liked seeing around me all I had read and written. I enjoyed the memories of what, when, and how they played a

part in my life. Perhaps I feared losing all this because I didn't realize it was already integrated into myself, a fact that was hard to see because I wasn't in touch with myself. Or maybe I didn't believe I could create new memories that would be as enjoyable and meaningful.

Then I would beat myself up because I never seemed to find the purpose and passion that I was searching for in life, so I kept every clue, not realizing the degree to which the endless searching itself was holding me back.

Instead of digesting what I *did* get and discarding the rest, I saved it all, essentially constipating myself. What an important metaphor for my connection to my body and uncomfortable emotions.

New insight: I consistently felt regret at the thought of throwing things away, rather than grieving the loss and growing as a result.

I realized, at the bottom of the well, that I didn't go back often enough to any of it to warrant keeping all the stuff. Instead, keeping it was making me feel burdened and buried alive, the feeling I hated.

Imagining the bucket was now filled, I began the process of reintegrating my pattern with new awareness: I needed to explore creating future visions without unrealistic expectations. I needed to honor my needs for security and certainty in ways other than clinging obsessively to the past.

As I pulled the rope up, I felt an inner shift to move forward, being open to the universe and synchronicity.

Hand over hand, I decided to promise to give myself love and moments of joy every day, which would be more satisfying then being stuck in a past life that was largely unhappy.

> Further, I wanted to be more present with others to share my inner joy, not my overwhelm.
>
> At the same time, I would need to practice having boundaries and saying no when something didn't feel right.
>
> Placing the imaginary bucket filled with new insights on the top of the well, I was clear the answer was not to lie to myself about my true needs.
>
> The answer was to be honest *and* kind with myself and others.
>
> This is how I wanted to live until I died.
>
> This is what I meant by having *my life with me in it.*

Finishing this reality check, I finally had taken stock of my needs and habits. I didn't realize until then how little room a scan takes up on the computer in comparison to storing papers. Or how little room a book on Kindle takes up on my iPad. Giving up the pleasures I received from holding books and touching paper was made up for by the freeing up of tons of dead energy. Plus, with my eye condition, having a well-lit screen made it possible to read in a low-light environment, which would not have been possible with a paperback. I began to dig myself out, give things away, and let go.

Now that I am in my new location, I honestly don't miss any of it. I enjoy not having clutter and only keeping what I really need. It never seemed like an attainable goal, but I have done it, and Marie Kondo would be proud of me. More than that, I again found the "THERE" I had from my dissertation when interviewing the thirty-two women, and I can now see the synchronicity of my thirty-two journals also being my "labor of love and work of art." By reviewing and writing about "My Wise and Wonderful Black Book Series," I inadvertently discovered my legacy project, my new "IT" (5; 101).

At last I can give myself credit for my intense search for integration, done with my trademark impeccability and devotion (5; 60). As a "recovering perfectionist," I have awareness when I am trying to reach unrealistic goals, and I try to do better when I'm not being neat and tidy enough. I've stopped searching for the perfect teacher, healer, book, or magic to make me whole. I own that I was wounded as a child, but that doesn't have to define me still. I wished never to have been wounded in the first place, and it took me forever to take in the insights written so clearly by Swiss psychologist Alice Miller: children have needs that deserve to be met, or at least acknowledged (20; 112). Because of how much I loved my parents, and because I was an all-or-nothing thinker, I thought facing reality would mean I was betraying them. The prohibition on knowing what I know, which I always experienced as "not having access to myself," instead came from not knowing I could *both* feel my truth *and* then also extend compassion to my parents and myself. Now that I have written my truth, I feel a sense of peace and wholeness. My relationship with myself is stronger and more accepting. I have forgiven my parents, and finally, am forgiving myself for not growing up faster, not grieving my unmet needs sooner, and not having connected my suffering to the suffering in the world more actively.

I recently had an insight about the role achievement has played in my life. I knew it was a way to get attention from my parents as a child and adolescent. Excelling in my first career provided a path to being independent. I started writing to find my voice and publishing to help other clinicians and consultants create effective programs. My doctoral program was a step away from my family of origin and first marriage and a commitment toward taking myself, my intellect, and my soul seriously. How I listened to the women in my study made me see I could also listen to myself as a woman researcher. But when I couldn't turn my dissertation into a book, I felt such regret—as if I were a failure. But now I get it. The structure of the doctoral program expected achievement—even more so, an original contribution to the field. We were to build on the foundation of other professionals. I thrived in that environment. How different this was from the norms of narcissism in my family. In that structure, anything I contributed was to make my parents look good, even as I sacrificed myself in the process. I felt isolated, not encouraged to be part of a network of opportunities where I could find myself and give back to others. When I did my twenty-year follow-up research, I felt I had partially redeemed myself. But my new "Aha!" is that I didn't have the internal structure necessary to fulfill my potential until now. Reviewing my journals has given me the integration necessary to find my purpose, be resilient when facing challenges, and place achievement in perspective in my life.

I wrote in my journals about an article from a Harvard Business School professor who was asked how to help students measure their life. After being diagnosed with cancer, the author reexamined the impact of his career and concluded what was most important were the individual people whose lives he touched. In a similar reevaluation, I have decided being stellar is not the only way to be valuable. What has been most important to me are the people I have helped work through their pain and see themselves more clearly. These words from Zen Master Thich Nhat Hanh seem to validate the exploration of the joys and pain in my life, as my journals reveal. He says by bearing witness to our own suffering first, we can help others: "Understanding someone's suffering is the best gift you can give another person. Understanding is love's other name. If you don't understand, you can't love."

Three years into my retirement, I feel I have caught up with myself. "THERE" is here, the house in the woods I've always longed for, gardening and cooking with my husband, our creative writing and art projects, the ability to still use my central vision, and building community through teaching, volunteering, and seeing new friends. To our surprise, we have two little white kitties, a brother and sister, who bring us immense joy. I have no reason to beat myself up; setting boundaries is coming more naturally. Facing challenges is met with awareness of cycles and the ongoing nature of learning, taking action, and reflecting. It is such a relief not to be working and to get up and go to sleep when my body wants to. I'm not striving for perfection because I'm enjoying the present. I'm not trying to be anywhere (or anyone) else.

Image 79: Cover of Journal 32. From this point forward, I was finally living fully.

And still, I have the wisdom to know that life will inevitably change. What I hope is that I can rely on myself to face illness, loss, other moves, and death with my many tools and inner resources. All the work I did to connect with and take care of my inner children will serve me well at the end. My soul is the only thing I brought with me into this life, and it will be the only thing I take with me at the end. I am grateful for all the attention I gave to hearing my soul's longing throughout my struggles and journey. Even though I know we all will die, I often act as if we will live forever. At the end, it will be even more important to accept all my feelings no matter what is happening. This honors my commitment to live fully until I die. Because the one real "THERE" I can count on is dying.

After all the searching for and then forgetting who I was, I am finally settling into the comfort of who I've discovered I am. I now see how often I *have* understood others and given love to them. I also see how oblivious I have been to the appreciation from people's lives I have touched, even though I was hungry for it. I never took in, or even remembered receiving, the following poem, written for me by participants in a workshop I designed in 1997, "Creating Poem Portraits." They surprised me with this gift on the last day, writing it together in gratitude. I am so moved that they captured my essence and expressed it in this loving way (31; 13). I must have sent dear Robyn the poem years ago to process hearing something so precious. Then, in 2017, while sorting through her therapy files, she found it and sent it back to me—an example of Grace. I glued it in my journal, still forgetting about it until my journal review. It seems a fitting way to "end well" this unexpected memoir:

Ode to a Beautiful Woman

Ode to a Beautiful Woman
Without benefit of interviews
Or collective moments of in-depth talks
We strive to capture the essence
Of our teacher, our friend.

Yet her teachings seep through us.
And even though all we can paint
Is a nibble of a portrait,
We sense the feast within.

The devotion, the love,
The intense sense of wonder,
As she guides our baby steps
On to the endless road to uncovering
New systems and relationships.

Through her we see connections
Longed for in the past and desired for in the future
Between us, among us
As we become a close family of women.

How profound a difference she makes
By sharing what's hers alone.
We see it, we feel it
By her forever presence in our hearts.

Epilogue

And Then What Happened?

Just as I was completing this manuscript in June of 2020, writing about how I knew life would change, it did. I had hoped I would use all I learned about myself through this journal review to deal with whatever came, and I am. Still, unbelievably, what changed was my dear Patrick became seriously ill. He was well when, because of COVID-19 restrictions, we enjoyed a low-key dinner out for my seventieth birthday in July. Despite the lack of fanfare, he was emotionally present and it was meaningful to me. We discussed that perhaps by the end of 2020 we'd get to properly celebrate both of our big birthdays—his belated sixty-fifth and my seventieth—and our thirty years of being together with a vacation to a beach in Mexico.

Then two weeks later, in August, he didn't feel well. He woke up in the middle of the night throwing up for five hours straight. He was so weak he was lying on the floor in the bathroom in between bouts. He had been sick like this in the past while working in New York and always treated it on his own with time. But as the week went on, I grew concerned and insisted we see a local doctor. She said it was parasites and prescribed strong antibiotics. As he didn't feel better, and continued to have extreme pain in his abdomen, we returned for three total rounds of antibiotic treatments. During this time, he had no bowel movements and couldn't figure out why. He tried laxatives and different products that had always worked for me, but no response. Always strong and energetic, when he didn't feel well, he never complained. Finally, the morning of the day when the treatment was completed, he said in an uncharacteristically weak voice, "I can't do this anymore."

I knew this was serious. To stay strong and not give in to my emotions, I relied on my trusty motto: hope for the best and plan for the worst. I had contact information ready for us to see an internist in the next largest city, about forty-five minutes away. One of our young friends, who lived and attended university in Mexico City, had asked her aunt, who lives in the city nearest us, for a referral and the doctor came highly recommended. Fortunately, our dear friends, a daughter and her mother who have an Airbnb near us, were in town and offered to drive us to the doctor. It was providential, because I wouldn't have been able to identify the location with a taxi or speak sufficient Spanish at the medical office in what had quickly become an urgent situation.

The doctor couldn't have been kinder. At the end of his examination, he said to Patrick, through me in Spanish, "You know you can't go home." Patrick looked perplexed and scared. Then the doctor explained he seemed to have a blockage and needed to go to the emergency room for tests. After the X-rays and CT scans were reviewed, the doctor on call said Patrick indeed had a blockage between his small and large intestine. I handled the admitting information and we were taken right upstairs to a private room. Plan for the worst, hope for the best.

The hospital turned out to be a new, small surgical center that did not treat COVID-19 patients, so we were safe. Also, the room was lovely and had a couch with a pullout bed for me to sleep on for the entire three weeks we were there. The internist was part of a surgical team and the surgeon couldn't have been more skilled, caring, or positive. He explained to us what he was going to do and prepared Patrick for the surgery with IVs. There was some concern Patrick might need a temporary ileostomy (plan B), but Patrick begged the surgeon to do everything he could to stick with plan A. The surgeon promised he would stop the surgery momentarily to let me know as soon as he knew the plan, so I heard the good news about an hour before Patrick was in recovery. When he was wheeled back to the room, I was wearing a sign I made saying "Plan A!" But because he had a bag on his side to drain the incision, at first he didn't believe me.

The next significant event was when the surgery team, including the oncologist, came to discuss the results of the surgery. It revealed graphically that 85 percent of his colon had been removed and reattached to the small intestine, because—plan for the worst—the blockage was a malignant tumor. In addition, they found stage 4 tumors in his lungs and liver. To give him a chance of surviving the cancer, these would need to be shrunk and then later surgically removed. This was an "Oh My God" unbelievable moment for both of us. But being planners, we were at least somewhat prepared. I knew from previous discussions that Patrick had no interest in further surgeries, and how to move—or not move—forward with treatment would be his choice. The fact that we had talked about illness and death over the years enabled us to move past the initial shock and engage in productive conversation about options. However, it's one thing when the future is hypothetical and another when one of your worst and most feared outcomes is imminent. With surgery off the table, we asked about the pros and cons of chemo. The oncologist said it was necessary for prolonging Patrick's life. If he didn't do any treatment, he would have six to eight months to live, maybe a year. Patrick asked what to expect in that scenario. The oncologist said he would end up in a wheelchair, sleeping more and more, until he finally slipped away.

Before leaving the hospital, Patrick decided he had things he needed to take care of in New York. They gave approval and he and I traveled there, returning the day before starting chemo. While in New York, he fell twice and was extremely weak but determined to handle everything—and he did. But given his condition, he relied on me in a way he'd never had to before, and I was there for him.

I was scared to see what chemo was like, but the nurse giving the IV was quite capable, the facility calming, and the oncologist optimistic as he gave the oral doses to take over the next three weeks and then return. I also knew he was trying chemo for me, just to see how he responded.

Unfortunately, within two days Patrick was not only vomiting and nauseated, as predicted, but he could hardly move. The oncologist said not to take pills for a few days, then come back to the office. By this time, Patrick was bent over like a ninety-year-old man, drooling, and emaciated. The oncologist weighed him; he had lost sixty pounds since March. I know they say unexplained weight loss is a sign of cancer, but it never occurred to us during those months, prior to the parasites and surgery, that cancer was the cause.

Support, Support, Support

While in the hospital, Patrick dictated and I sent updates to his immediate family and close friends as well as mine. They were as shocked and scared as we were, but they sent love and stayed connected. Our next-door neighbors went above and beyond to provide rides and support between the hospital and our home. Local friends offered to get clothes or buy food, but I told them we would rely on them later. Although neither of us had been patients, as consultants to health care in our work we had comfort and familiarity with managing the system and building teams. At times the whole experience was surreal, but we fortunately never felt alone.

Thank goodness we had each other. The first night in the hospital, it was dark but we couldn't sleep. We each expressed our feelings and fears, crying together from our beds. It was tender, honest, and bonding.

When we traveled to New York, one of our dear friends was out of the country and let us stay in her apartment. It was amazing to receive frequent emails and texts from her and friends all over the United States as if they were next door. We didn't get messages that made us cringe, as people in similar circumstances often experience. Instead, each was able to convey love and care without giving in to the helplessness that was the underlying truth. My sisters offered support to me, and Patrick's siblings were there for him. My cousins also became a significant and emotionally honest source of assistance. The quality of our connections with people from work and life over the years made us stay connected to our reality, grateful for everyone's love and feedback.

Stepping Stones

I was also deeply appreciative to be able to stay with Patrick in the hospital. While my Spanish wasn't perfect, it was good enough to communicate with the doctors and staff and translate back and forth for him. Being a project person, I took this on as my new project and put my manuscript-in-progress aside. I literally cleaned off the shelf to gather all of the medical reports, hospital bills, and medicine regimes that were already growing. As has been true during other challenging episodes of my life, I didn't journal either. It was time to live what was happening and document whatever was in front of us. I made lists of what Patrick needed to eat when he came home, contact information for all the healthcare team members, and arranged follow-up appointments. I always wondered if I could be a good caregiver, because Patrick had naturally taken on that role for me. He was my "sighted guide" and made navigating around town safe and fun. In the face of such a stressful situation, I was so relieved I was better at this than either of us imagined. Friends and family all said they were amazed by how well I was handling everything. I didn't feel amazing or good about anything, just clear about how much Patrick meant to me, how well I knew him, and glad I could rise to the occasion to meet his needs. I also felt supported by all I had written and integrated in my manuscript: I wasn't afraid to grieve what appeared to be the loss of our continued future together. I had learned so much about ending well with my parents, I could tolerate and manage my emotional triggers, and I was connected to my heart and values.

Then the universe offered support spontaneously through conversations. One of our colleagues, a nurse and dear friend, called to see how Patrick was doing. She talked about quality of life and hoped Patrick would be as courageous about himself as he was to others as a coach and consultant in large medical centers. Her input led to him eventually ending chemo.

A childhood friend wrote to say that as bad as this was, at least we were going through this experience together, unlike when her husband had died suddenly. She went out to do an errand and came back to find him on the floor, dead from a massive heart attack. Her perspective on the time Patrick and I were being afforded (in the face of the time we would be losing) helped us feel both the heartbreak and the blessing of his situation. Every day we acknowledged that at least we had time to enjoy every moment and mourn together.

A local friend who was a lawyer and holistic practitioner urged Patrick to try alternative remedies. This shaman came to our home and explained the potions he made himself and gathered from other sources. He said his Indian and Peruvian products had helped other cancer patients. Worst case, it wouldn't help, so Patrick decided to try it, having nothing to lose. As time went on, it seemed everyone had a healer or supplement or diet to try. We were grateful for the care but knew if it was so successful for cancer, by now it would be in the mainstream. Also, most people didn't have as many rapidly growing tumors as he did in both his lungs and liver. Patrick ended up trusting himself and his own judgment even more.

Every morning I prepared all the medicines and supplements he wanted, and he dutifully took them until finished. In the meantime, Patrick really wanted to know the location and size of his tumors, so he could send the information to an oncologist he trusted and had worked with in New York. He also repeated his blood tests to see if there was any progress. He was less anemic, having had two transfusions in the hospital, and most of the lab results were in the normal range. The day we went for his X-rays and ultrasound, the technician had the oncologist give the news about what she found. She pointed to where the rapidly growing tumors were—now up to fifteen of them. Her parting words were, "Enjoy your life in Mexico." Her partner, Patrick's oncologist, wrote a note validating that Patrick's results seemed good, if it weren't for the tumors. We never saw him again and he never charged us for any treatment.

I then began research to find a palliative care doctor and hospice team that could be our support for end-of-life care. It astonished me how easily Patrick and I accepted that this was the end, that we were not going to fight it and sacrifice quality of life but meet our situation with equanimity and grace.

Having used hospice in California with both my parents, I knew what to look for. Unfortunately, hospice isn't common in Mexico with their strong Catholic beliefs and rituals. Still, I was adamant about ending well, for Patrick and for us. I knew if I found resources I trusted, I could get everything arranged ahead of time and free myself to be emotionally present through the end. This was critical to me. No one else could do that, and if I was worrying about what to do in a crisis, it wouldn't serve either of us.

I listened carefully to Patrick to know exactly what he wanted. He said he didn't want to die in New York or with other family in the States. He also didn't want to die in our house. He didn't want to be in assisted living in the nearby city where the hospital was. What did that leave? No one in our town knew of a facility nearby. I reached out to friends, my acupuncturist, Visiting Angels, and our listserv for expats. I followed up on every lead, explaining what we wanted and finding out what they offered. A website I found detailed the types of end-of-life documents needed in Mexico for expats and how different the system was from the US. I took notes and continued looking for professionals here who could help and also spoke English.

Progress

On December 8, 2020, our prayers were answered. My research led to finding a place in our town, half an hour away, that no one seemed to have heard of. It was a new retirement community, beautifully designed by the geriatric doctor and owner to care for the elderly. Fortunately, the doctor spoke English and was passionate about what he did, but best of all he told us he would let Patrick be the first person admitted for end-of-life care and to die there, although we didn't know when that would be, and that I could be there with him. We picked our room, and the doctor promised to do whatever it took to meet our needs. He located a notary and translator for the documents and a palliative care doctor he could work with. Patrick was sleeping a lot each day, and I was weeping with the reality of this and the blessing of a wonderful, well thought out end-of-life plan.

The next night when I couldn't sleep, I read a blog by a woman whose husband, partner, and best friend for forty-four years had just died of cancer. She wrote with the emotional rawness and honesty that was just what I needed. The insight I related to was how, during her husband's time in hospice, she stayed strong by viewing their journey as a birthing. Using that frame had not occurred to me. She was accompanying him as he was being born to what comes after death, and she was being born to a life without him. When Patrick and I first met, I felt we were on parallel paths: he was renovating a farmhouse in the country and I was writing a dissertation. Both projects were fully engrossing, from big picture design to the smallest details of implementation. He sanded molding while I edited footnotes for accuracy and finishing touches. Now we were on parallel paths again, being birthed into two different and equally unknown realms. He to dying and whatever is there after death and me to a life without him. This truth required boundaries, to be his caretaker, to love him and be present with him to the very end but not collapse into his reality. I reminded myself each day to stay strong *and* loving, not either-or. Because of my diminished eyesight, if I had an accident, it would only make things worse, and this situation we found ourselves in wasn't about me. I told myself to do what I could to stay healthy, but not act selfish like my mother who used to attend only to her schedule for running, writing, painting, or whatever she had in mind for herself, no matter what was going on with her family's needs.

My priority was always to observe Patrick and what he needed. His weight dropped to less than mine, literally skin and bones. Everyday something else hurt: his knees, his liver, his back, a headache, nausea, an upset stomach. He was anxious at night and found it difficult to sleep. As his slow decline became familiar, I realized I could make a little more space for myself. I saw him planning meals and cooking more. I observed him surrendering to his limitations, even though he still had the desire to make things happen and give to others, as was his nature. I paid attention when I felt his "eyes were bigger than his stomach" and gently offered alternatives to get what he wanted done, but not at the expense of his energy or dignity. In addition to our daily life, I finally took care of a problem of my own—severe ingrown toenails—with day surgery. Anticipating that one day I might not be able to live in our house alone, I drew pictures of plants in our garden, making a calendar to give away to friends here and to honor Patrick's and my joint project and our joy with the garden. Not knowing when the end would come, I didn't know or even speculate what I would do or if I would move after that time. Instead, I focused on the present and living, with Patrick, fully and lovingly.

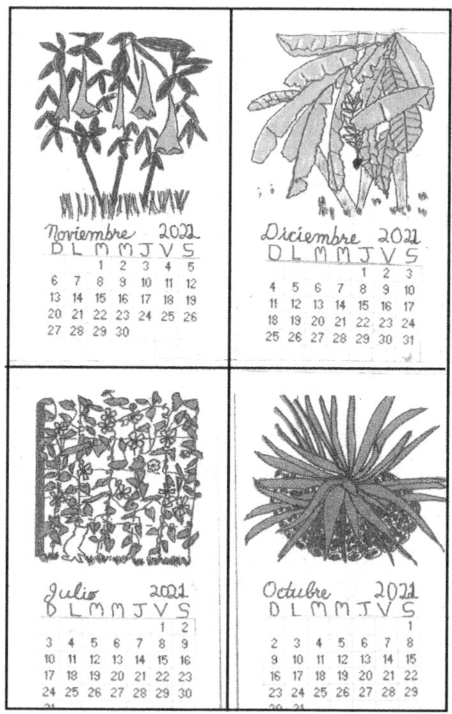

Image 80: My calendar of our garden.

Love

Life is not without conflicts and challenges. It took me a long time to become a couple. That meant learning how to honor both my needs and my husband's, and practicing communicating with honesty and kindness. Before, it was effective to divide up chores: he knew how to fix most things and I was good at contacting resources to keep things organized and in progress. But as we entered this new and uncharted phase, I found myself feeling anxious walking alone in the garden thinking, what do I do now? After thirty years of being a couple, I was grudgingly preparing for, but not looking forward to, being solo again. I didn't want it. I had thought we'd live to be old together. I was angry because we were clearly both being shortchanged. If the toilet needed replacing, in the past he would have handled that. Now it was up to me to do what my mother always did: "Call a man!" I found a good plumber and we were both pleased the problem was solved. Patrick and I had always balanced each other's styles and talents: extroversion versus introversion, logical versus flow, academic versus practical. We shared core values of giving generously and helping others, of being creative in our approach to projects and life, of loving to explore new places together. Now we were in new territory, stuck at home to deal with an inevitable fork in the road that would forever divide our future.

Early in our relationship, Patrick created a richly colored painting of two trees to symbolize his view of us. Both the roots and branches touched, with a view between the two trunks. The leaves of both trees were abundantly shared. I had left a twenty-year marriage and was not looking for another relationship. I would set boundaries with him, essentially saying "don't cross this line." It took me years before I let in his love and the many gifts he offered. He would say, "You never had an honest and real relationship, and we can have that." He offered peace, which I feared was hiding negative feelings, but he defined as, "feeling calm in the heart no matter what is going on, not denial or avoidance of conflict." Thirty years later, I know that to be true.

Image 81: Patrick's painting, symbolizing our relationship.

When we were in the middle phase of our early relationship, I was turning fifty and wanted to take stock so that I'd never have regrets in my older years. We decided to go to a four-day intensive Imago workshop for couples. We were not progressing with how to deal with tensions and wanted to see what could help. The facilitator reframed our frustrations as growth. When we left the workshop, we both knew we were each other's true love and intimate life partner. He bought a star in the sky for me called Kathryn's Jubilee. I wrote a poem tracking our growth called "Resolved? Dissolved!" We never looked back.

In 2005, after fifteen years together, we created our own commitment ceremony. It included Imago's "Commandments of a Conscious Marriage/Relationship" and Patrick's favorite Bible prayer, Wherever You Go. My image for our enduring commitment was an indestructible diamond. The two points that were apart represented our differences, as with politics, finances, or intimacy. The top and bottom points of the diamond symbolized the ways we were the same, as with our core values, ease and fun of being together, and loving to explore new adventures. Every year on our anniversary, we reread these entries in my journal and reaffirmed our commitment and love. In the year of Patrick's illness, life was harder for us and we lamented the loss of the future we thought we were creating together. Death and dying was a new adventure to share, but it seemed unfairly premature. It also created challenges for us professionally and personally.

Joyful Solutions

Having worked as an internal OD consultant in four major medical centers and having taught at five universities, when it was time to move on from this career, I knew I needed something different. With Patrick having worked as an external OD consultant in public service and healthcare organizations, he would invite me to join him in a partnership, creating our new firm, Kaplan Knowlton and Associates. We brought each other into our various contracts for strategic work, executive coaching, and training. We focused on leadership and team development, resolving intense conflicts, and innovative solutions for navigating complex organization dynamics. Together we optimized our skills and talents to make the greatest impact with clients. We loved working together and were our favorite partners.

When we moved to Mexico, Patrick continued to travel for work in New York and I supported the work from home. He would identify a need for a proposal, strategy, or resource and I would design, edit, or provide what was needed. However, his becoming ill changed our balance and our focus. His disappointment with his inability to consult affected our personal relationship, and we needed new tools to deal with our challenging situation. It wasn't surprising to have tension because one partner is dying, but it was hard to accept being "perfectly imperfect" at a time when our normal harmony would have felt much better.

I suggested we try SARK's four-step Joyful Solutions approach to solving problems in couples. The most important feature is to believe you can both get what you want without compromise or sacrifice. Our first problem to solve joyfully started with house cleaning. Patrick's memoir showed how important keeping control was as a child in his dysfunctional family. He took control by cleaning and keeping order—what I call "neat and tidy." When I didn't meet his standards, he felt disrespected. Since 1990, he had observed my penchant for creating chaos and clutter. Every time I/we moved locations, he was the one to thoroughly clean the apartment. I appreciated it and we both needed it.

Now that he was ill with cancer, cleaning became a huge priority. The problem was, he didn't have the energy, strength, or stamina to do what he was used to doing. I knew I couldn't maintain the house to his standards, although I did improve my dishwashing and organizing skills. Determined to find a joyful solution, I had to hold the tension between our desires for both of us and his disbelief that it could be done. But the friend who recommended our gardener told us his wife was a great housecleaner. I decided to hire her for his birthday. If he didn't like her, he could send her right home.

The person who came to the door was a petite, stylish young woman. Even behind her face mask for COVID, we could see she had smiling eyes and a pleasant disposition. Since I spoke Spanish, I explained what we wanted. Within minutes, she was moving furniture and rugs with energy and care. Patrick saw her dust the floorboards and clean the windows without being asked. While he figured she would last ten minutes, instead she stayed five hours and exceeded his expectations. He declared she cleaned even better than he did and agreed to have her come each week. That meant our house and garden were cleaned, neat, and tidy from the inside-out every week. It was the best present he could ever have at the time, and I was thrilled we finally had a Joyful Solution.

Then on New Year's Eve, we planned to stay home, as usual, and go to bed early. I was excited to cook my favorite recipes for us: Chicken Marbella with prunes, capers, and olives, from the *Silver Palate Cookbook*, and my famous chocolate souffle. But two issues emerged. During the afternoon he came down the stairs saying he had an idea, but I should give myself time to respond. He said he'd like to give some of our dinner to our next-door neighbors who were working late at their bakery and were probably tired. I loved the neighbors, but I was looking forward to our time alone together. Patrick had been using his dwindling energy to schedule social events, to get them off his list so he could rest and reflect on his condition. I had fun at all of them, but for me it was enough. My heart felt hurt and I felt raw and emotional. Rather than give myself time to respond without being triggered, I told him I felt hurt by his idea and that we weren't on the same page. He became furious that I was being weak and triggering him.

I went upstairs to journal and identify my needs and wants. I reflected on 2020 the way I usually do and focused on my intentions for 2021. Yet, I couldn't shake my feelings of disappointment and despair. Then, although I made the chicken dish, we literally (and metaphorically) ran out of gas for the oven. It had been relatively cold and the gas company was delayed in filling our tank. By the time we ate the dinner, it was too late to bake the souffle. My spirits had similarly fallen and we went to bed irritated with each other. Not a great way to start the new year.

The next day we avoided each other. I stayed upstairs and he downstairs. Finally, he asked me to come downstairs and talk with him. He apologized for his anger and said he didn't really want to process this, but knew I needed to. So, he started by telling me his truth. He said he felt set up by me. I apparently had an expectation I had not shared with him. I owned that and felt badly because I knew this was an old pattern and I didn't know if I could change it. He then said, rather than try to get rid of it, what if I just acknowledged when I had an expectation and tell him what it was. If I had said earlier that I had wanted us to be together to bring in the New Year and do a ritual for our reflections and intentions, he wouldn't have brought up the neighbor idea. I realized he had come up with the joyful solution this time for both of us. Thanks to his insight, I was blessedly off the hook about having to change my feelings or patterns. But I was also invited to take responsibility for my internal state and share it with him directly. He pointed out that I could have said what he realized on his own: he was planning a paella dinner with them in a few weeks and maybe that was enough. It turns out, when they came home, they dropped off a gift and said they were too tired to eat and were going to bed. So his idea wouldn't have worked out anyway, but that wasn't the point. I felt great that I had a way to now rise to the occasion and not set him up for disappointment or to disappoint myself with unexpressed expectations.

Anger

Oh, that again. I don't like feeling anger because it seems ungenerous. And if I had cancer, I sure wouldn't want my husband—or anyone—to be angry with me. Yet, my learnings about emotions included feeling them all, even amplifying the feelings so I could know how they showed up in my body and mind, and dialoguing with them to hear what they want from me. For instance, on the morning I'm describing, I awoke with a dream about my first husband. I knew these dreams were usually about my current relationship and/or my inner marriage—the dynamic between my feminine and masculine sides. At first, I was angry about the dream. Then, I went for a walk in the garden to process it, staying curious about its meaning. One part of the dream was him blaming me for his illness (a symbolic substitution for Patrick as my first husband wasn't sick) and walking away to give himself shots in his stomach. In the dream I felt angry he was superficial and then keeping his deeper feelings to himself and abandoning me.

How this pattern rang true for me and Patrick was that he had been feeling especially ill the past few days. I had a taxi wait for me while I bought him cough medicine. His fever and chills finally broke and the medicine seemed to help. He wanted me to sleep in the other room to stay safe. He asked me to make biscuits in the morning so he could have strawberry shortcake. In between being nauseous, he had been identifying essentially a bucket list of foods he wanted to taste one last time. He baked ham, but felt it was too salty. Eggs gave him diarrhea. I was fine with going with the flow of his choices, even though they put weight on me and had no impact on his emaciated frame.

I woke up and quietly baked and cleaned up, eager for him to join me. Three hours later, he finally came downstairs to the kitchen. His first words were a criticism of something I overlooked. Immediately this flipped my switch to anger and disappointment. I pointed out all I had done and asked if he was feeling badly again, suggesting that might be why he was focusing on whatever I hadn't done. He denied it. But that was it. The day was spent in our separate corners, never resolved or owned. I again slept in the other room to keep my space and feel safe. Then I woke up in the middle of the night with a cough and aches and pains. I wondered if my anger was making me sick. I took two medicines that usually work for me, and fortunately they did. I woke up feeling fine, but still angry from the dream and disappointment that Patrick wasn't willing to own and resolve what was going on between us. His memoir is titled *As If It Never Happened,* and that's what I felt was happening. He was hiding things under the rug and I was tripping on them. However, this dynamic wasn't new. What was really going on beneath the anger?

My part of the dynamic was wanting what I couldn't have. I couldn't have him be better and continue our future together. So I would focus on what he wasn't giving me—true connection—rather than what he was: criticism and distance. Then I reminded myself that I was not a novice at self-growth and needed to go deeper. I needed to let him go through his own process of dealing with terminal cancer. It was crucial not to take his emotions personally, and more important, not to abandon myself. Yes, I felt guilty he was sick, as if it were my fault. But the deeper issue was facing my lack of control over what was happening to him and also the extreme and painful vulnerability I felt around our ultimate separation. I felt so heartbroken, sad, and scared.

I read a novel recently in which a woman had terminal cancer and her husband, a surgeon, wanted her to try chemo and radiation because he couldn't accept his lack of control and face the grief of losing her. Unlike Patrick, she immediately achieved acceptance and did not go through the phases typical of grief, such as anger, bargaining, or depression. But I knew how emotional Patrick was, and often it had made me feel more normal because of his roller coaster of expressiveness, matching the emotions I feared and tried to contain. I was also aware of my tendency to want to romanticize this journey of ending well. Yet, as I had written to Robyn when I told her what was going on back in October, "Sometimes I am so irritated. In the past I would have hated myself for my reactions. Now I ask all of my parts to express themselves to me. I make sure I include my little ones and my connection to divine spirit. I forgive myself if I don't handle situations perfectly, because I no longer aspire to perfection, just the truth of who and how I am. Being so ill, he is more perfectionistic and angrier than I'd like. I aim to understand and also take the moments where we do connect and fill my soul with these memories as gifts to treasure. I will save them for my private grief process. I expect I will feel disappointment, resentment, and lack of closure at the end, because I already do. I accept it all as part of the real and messy life and love that is mine. I save for later my anxiety about what life will be like without him in it. Now I am as present to him, myself, and our relationship as much as possible."

Joining Him

Rather than distance myself from Patrick and blame him for abandoning me, I made a conscious choice to lean in and join him where he was. For instance, while he was recuperating from the deadly effects of chemo, his niece and her husband asked him if he would like their spiritual guidance. Given that they were born-again Christians, he had to think carefully about what they were offering and what he needed. After a month, he decided he did want them as his spiritual guides to help him learn what God wanted of him before he died. Being Jewish, when I heard this, a part of me recoiled inside. I felt he would go on his journey of ending this life without me or my spiritual input, and that made me very sad.

Always looking for my next novel, I decided to read one by one of my favorite authors that was about Jesus and the story of him having a wife. When I had previously downloaded a sample, the book was of no interest to me. But now it offered a way to think about what Patrick was drawn to from a feminist perspective to which I could relate. I also always prefer learning about history from novels, and this one did not disappoint. I knew little about Jesus, and this novel awakened my curiosity. As I asked Patrick questions, he asked me not to talk about what I had read because it was blasphemous to Christians he knew. Yet, he appreciated that I was opening to him and his journey.

In Patrick's memoir he wrote about the influence of religious instruction on his childhood. Coming back to the Bible made sense for him. I, on the other hand, had never read the Bible. I was observant as a Reform Jew up through the coming-of-age ritual at age thirteen, my bas mitzvah. After that, religion did not address my high school needs and I withdrew. Later, as an adult, I considered becoming a rabbi, but I felt that Judaism was too patriarchal. Whatever my past interest was, I decided to pick up that thread and read the Old Testament—the Five Books of Moses. Next, I asked Patrick what he would want me to do when we were at the hospice-type facility, and he answered to read him the Bible. I offered to begin now. Many nights before bed as I read from Matthew or Luke, we discussed the passages' relevance to current issues of politics, violence, and leadership. We wrote down the numbers of parables that we had questions about and then discussed them with his spiritual guides.

While this was a path I would never have taken on my own, by joining Patrick I was able to enlarge my knowledge and, more significantly, feel closer to him. This joint interest met my need to end well. It also met his need to feel closer to God—and me—during this sacred time.

Trusting Myself

When I feel mean, like my Evil Twin, I know I've abandoned myself and need to listen to the little ones inside. They are yelling for my attention and love. Even if what I have been doing is important, like taking care of Patrick, at some point they have things to tell me that I'm not aware of. They informed me I was unbalanced. I was being the Drill Sergeant part of myself, wanting to get all details and contingencies in place. I was also the Romantic, wanting Patrick and me to end well—for him to get his soul's wish to see his family one more time. But if they didn't feel safe to visit us, how could they expect someone dying to visit them? What if we couldn't make it back to Mexico for his end-of-life care?

I comforted myself by remembering times during this unexpected journey where I trusted myself and it worked out for the best. The first example was when Patrick was getting ready to leave the hospital and go home to recuperate. I was obsessed with the idea that he needed slippers. He never wore slippers, but I was picturing our stairs at home and wondering how he could possibly go up and down without them. I told him I was taking a day to shop in preparation for his discharge. I hired a taxi and went to a nearby mall where there were shoe stores. I finally found what I was looking for, hoping I had the right fit in Mexican sizes. Feeling triumphant, I showed Patrick my prize. He was less than interested. But when we were leaving, he realized his feet were so swollen, the shoes he wore to the hospital no longer fit. This continued for weeks and he ended up wearing the slippers not only at home but even to follow-up doctor appointments.

During the time he was in the hospital, friends would pick me up and take me home to do laundry and get whatever else we needed. I noticed my tolerance for organizing clothes diminished. I would throw all the undies in one drawer, T-shirts in another, arranged haphazardly. I imagined if friends had to pick up things for me, they would be horrified and I'd be embarrassed. But my priority was life and death, not neat and tidy.

Finally, after recuperating four months, Patrick had down time and I found myself thinking about buying boxes for my drawers. When we moved from New York, Marie Kondo's approach was a savior, but I never got to the stage of rolling clothes and putting them in boxes so they were beautifully arranged. Now I was intrigued. I'd looked at videos online to learn the method. Then I looked on Amazon for boxes. There were none available where we lived, but there was a DHL office where I could have them delivered. I carefully measured the drawers and what size boxes would fit. When they arrived, I had such joy figuring out what went where and getting the rolling technique down. A month later, I was easily maintaining the approach. I had great satisfaction every time I did the laundry, and I'm so glad I trusted myself.

Another example of trusting myself involved finding the right palliative care doctor for Patrick. Before I found the facility where he'd go for end-of-life care, I followed up with a lead about a palliative care doctor in the neighboring city. We had a video chat, with her English and my Spanish sufficient to understand each other. She explained that if Patrick wanted to see her, she would do a thorough history and physical exam. She would also explore what his illness and death meant to him. After we spoke, I had great confidence in her and thought Patrick would, too. However, he didn't want to go to that city to die, so I let it go.

Once finding the facility in our town, the wonderful doctor in charge said he had a palliative care doctor who we could meet in January, at the same time we scheduled the notary appointment for end-of-life documents. Unfortunately, the holidays were delaying progress. He said we could meet with the palliative care doctor earlier, but he was busy. Curious, I asked how he worked, describing what the doctor I had found had explained. He didn't know, so I suggested he contact the palliative care doctor I had met.

Because of COVID-19, our doctor invited the palliative care doctor to meet at his facility. The meeting was magical. Patrick felt totally listened to and supported by her. The doctor in charge was impressed with how she connected and foresaw more opportunities to work together. I was thrilled our team was taking shape and again so thankful I trusted myself.

My final example relates to this book. After the expansion of our palliative care meeting, I crashed inside, feeling irritated and fussy. I was well aware of my tendency to contract after energetically expanding and realized this pattern had reemerged. Beneath those feelings were the tender sadness of watching Patrick sleep most of the day, getting confused about appointments, and both of us knowing he was declining. I didn't want to leave him in case he needed me, but what could I do with the lonely hours stretching out for me?

For some reason, I felt called to take the manuscript out and off the shelf where it had been since Patrick got sick. A little voice told me it was time to determine if the book wanted to be published. Though I was consumed with Patrick's illness, I appreciated the distraction of a project and worked through my grief to complete this book. But more honestly, was I thinking if I kept looking at the horizon the *Titanic* wouldn't sink? In writing this epilogue, I validated my sense that I was no longer a mystery to myself. I could see my patterns and was able to accept myself, warts and all. I could also feel confident that my journaling and journal review were necessary for my healing and dealing with these new challenges and changes. I was fully in reality and seeking peace, growth, and love with my dear Patrick.

Yet, everything was so horribly uncomfortable. On some days I wished it was all over already. But then, I knew that as bad as his losing his life was, what I would be left with would be worse for me. To be a single person, with the imprint of an "us" but lacking Patrick's daily companionship. I accepted that I wouldn't be as good alone as I was with him. He had so many ideas, was always trying to make things better for people, and brought so much fun. I could try to bring those qualities forward in my relationships, but what was really me? What would my purpose be? I thought about becoming an end-of-life specialist once I worked through my grief. But what about now? I had a sense of what grieving would require of me, so I took my manuscript to be spiral bound and put it away for at least a year. The *Titanic* was sinking and I knew it.

The End

When Patrick could no longer sit up without assistance, the geriatric doctor came to drive us to his facility. I packed for Patrick, and even in his weakened state, he chastised me for bringing too much. "What am I going to need a belt and jeans for?" I guess I was in denial, not ready for this new part of our death adventure, and laughed as I put back most of his clothes.

I had a false sense of security that he would be well taken care of with nurses around the clock, as was promised. But it soon became clear to both of us that I was doing everything and the end-of-life experiment there wasn't working for Patrick. Always being attuned to the present moment, he changed his mind a few times but ultimately said he wanted to go home. I talked to the palliative care doctor to be sure about what this meant and what to do. She said, "Listen to him." So I hired round-the-clock nurses and adapted our "infirmary" and adjoining bathroom for all his needs. Four days later, Patrick died at home with me by his side as he took his final breath on April 21, 2021.

A Year Later

It's a good thing I learned how to grieve, because losing Patrick was the most painful experience in my life. The palliative care doctor continued to be a support to me as did my sisters, cousins, and close friends, both in the States and Mexico. I knew I needed meaningful activities to keep from falling into a well of despair. No longer acting from black-or-white thinking, I started Spanish lessons with a new teacher and individual art lessons. I had a desire to metabolize my grief by learning to draw realistically in black and white—to match my internal state, no color. With poignant photos of Patrick that I took with his permission throughout his cancer journey, because he knew how I processed grief with my parents, I gradually learned to capture his likeness. Trusting myself, this nonverbal approach greatly augmented my tears, walks in the garden, writing about him, and feeling all my feelings. Image 82 shows my final drawing, *Sorrow*, which signaled not the end of grieving, but the end of needing to have him as my artistic subject.

Image 82: Sorrow, my final drawing of Patrick.

When I finally picked up my manuscript one day, planning to send a chapter to the palliative care doctor, I reflected to myself, "Maybe this isn't so bad. Maybe I'm not the only audience." That's when I called an old friend who is a prolific author and had sent me a condolence note, even though he had never met Patrick. He referred me to a publisher who was interested in my manuscript. Through our work together, I finally understood on a deeper level what my unexpected memoir is about.

My journey through journaling has shown me that my story is about becoming whole. I finally can admit this is a process and not a destination. I leave you here to trust yourself—your feelings, your needs, and how to best meet them. My wish is, as you resonate with my insights and experience, that they accompany you on your unique journey toward wholeness.

PART TWO

Practical Application

CHAPTER NINE

How to Begin Journaling

My hope is that after reading my story you might be inspired to begin your own journal, or deepen your reflective practice, and this section will show you how I do it. I used my journals to learn about and empower myself, and you can do the same. Here you'll learn how to begin a journal and then, how to decide what to put into it. While my approach has helped me, I offer my guidelines not as a recipe or model for you to follow but rather as a loose framework with concrete samples of possibilities and ideas for journal entries. The important thing is to trust yourself and experiment with what resonates.

How to Get Started

Selecting your journal: First, you'll start by purchasing a journal. There are so many to choose from. Go to a gift shop, bookstore, or art store that sells journals, blank books, and sketchbooks. For your first one, don't order online. You need to see how you feel when you look at and hold your book. One at a time, notice the size, the cover material, the surface of the pages, colors, binding, weight, and whether there are inspirational quotes. As I learned when buying crystals years ago during the hippie days, *let it select you*. Let your journal's qualities reveal their potential for supporting you on this journey. Let it be an intuitive process rather than overthinking the choice. Rather than passive, see the process as receptive.

You want your journal to be inviting, a space that calls to you, welcomes you in, and accepts everything you have to offer. If, as I did, you are writing and collecting images and ideas help you in your outer life, your journal becomes a sacred space that supports your inner life.

The wonderful thing is, you can't really get it wrong. If you don't like your journal after a while, try a new one. My very first journal for my storytelling group was eight-by-ten inches with a swirling pastel color cover and 160 blank cream-colored pages. I loved it, and it is still my favorite due to the content. It was my partner for over a year, all through my research study. Yet, my fellow storytellers felt I played myself too small. After that journal was filled up, they urged me to take up more space, symbolically, by buying a larger book. However, the larger journal never was comfortable for me. I tried it for a while and then quit using it for two years. After returning once to complete the "too big" art journal, I have happily bought the same spiral-bound, seven-by-ten-inch, 160-page sketch book each time I need a new volume. I am currently on my thirty-fourth, and have another one for my drawing lessons.

Protecting your journal: The second part of getting started is your sense of privacy with your journal. I know this is a huge concern for most people because you often write to get to know yourself better. That means you expose thoughts and feelings you do not wish to share with others. And for good reason—you may be sorting through leaving a marriage or making a job change. In cases like this, you need to keep control of your timing and not have someone see your private thoughts until you are ready to reveal them. If you live alone, you have it easy. Just put the journal by your bed or wherever you like to write. But if you live with a roommate, partner, or family, you'll need to be more discreet. If you are committed to your self-growth, as evidenced by your journal keeping, you will find a way to keep yourself and your journal safe and secure.

How Journals Can Empower You

In reviewing all my journals, I discovered eight ways they have empowered me. James Joyce said: "In the particular is contained the universal." I have seen that to be true in some of the best writing, such as that of Oliver Sacks. It means to me that a specific personal experience has meaning beyond yourself. Further, you can learn about yourself by resonating with and reflecting on the stories of others. As my particular details will be different from yours, they may still guide you in the right direction for your journal process, and it is my hope that my examples will offer insight into what you may find when you review your own first journal.

I began this process well before social media and ubiquitous access to the internet. My goal in keeping a journal was not to share my private life with an anonymous public but *to become visible to myself.* However, as high-school student Bianca Vivion Brooks explained in her 2019 *New York Times* op-ed, "My only fear is being a nobody." Tapping into a widespread fear of obscurity, Brooks's admission (which began as a tweet), resonated with a millennial audience who felt that life without a social media presence was no life at all. A decade later, Brooks is not tweeting but writing, discovering her deeper "fear of forgoing the sacred moments of life, of never learning to be completely alone, of not bearing witness to the incredible lives of those who surround her." She was able to get to the bottom of things, to find her center through writing. And you can, too, through keeping your journal and reviewing what you have written so you learn, grow, and empower yourself.

Getting to the bottom of things: This means getting below the surface, like peeling the layers of an onion. When reviewing my journals, I saw I was often trying to discern my true calling. I was frequently asking myself why I wasn't satisfied, why I stayed too long at jobs and sometimes relationships. I finally learned, through my journal entries, that what worked for me was when I identified the most relevant value in the situation. For example, I had to dig deep to discover why I had never written the book about my original research on the women in OD. After giving myself permission to write about this regret again and again, I reviewed all my entries. And then I got to the bottom of it: I didn't know how to write for a broader audience and I didn't have support to do it. Then I had to forgive myself, and go deeper again, asking how I could make myself feel better. I realized I could do a twenty-year follow-up study instead. Then, I did it. I knew I had gotten to the bottom because my research made a contribution and I felt satisfied.

Remembering meaningful experiences from your past: When I was working on a painting of an octopus's garden for our backyard water tank, I discovered on the first page of my very first journal a drawing I had done of a coral reef in the Caribbean. I never would have remembered drawing that picture twenty-five years ago if I hadn't been showing that journal to my friend, Ana. Pure serendipity. Seeing it was surprising, and it was meaningful to me because it brought back a time when I was working hard and also taking good care of myself. The drawing gave me confidence to design and paint the coral reef on our outside water tank. As in, if I did it before, I could do it again.

Image 83: My drawing of the Caribbean in my very first journal.

Image 84: My photo of the octopus's garden that Patrick and I painted on our water tank.

Identifying themes in your life: I discovered patterns I realized later were repetitive themes that ran through all my journals. "I can't" was one of them. For example, every time I had to do a work presentation, I had doubts about my capacity to do it. It didn't matter how many times I had proven I could do it; I always believed my fears first, then had to overcome them. By telling myself I couldn't do something, I saw it was part of the theme of "not fulfilling my potential."

In the same way, while reviewing my journals, I saw many examples of when I had "authorized myself" to speak up to people in power at work. I hadn't realized how my voice was getting stronger until I saw the situations I had documented over the thirty-two journals. This theme was crucial to me and my growth.

Documenting feelings to review at a later time: Another benefit of journaling is capturing details about how you are thinking and feeling during intense or uncomfortable interactions that you can't process in the moment. For example, when I visited my parents, who lived across the country from me, I would enter into my journal all of the family dynamics I observed during our time together. Once I returned home, I would look at what I had written and see what additional insights came to mind in retrospect.

I also discovered I was keeping track of what pushed my buttons at work. I noticed what triggered me to shut down. As I read the journals, I discovered I was learning how to set boundaries with people and certain situations.

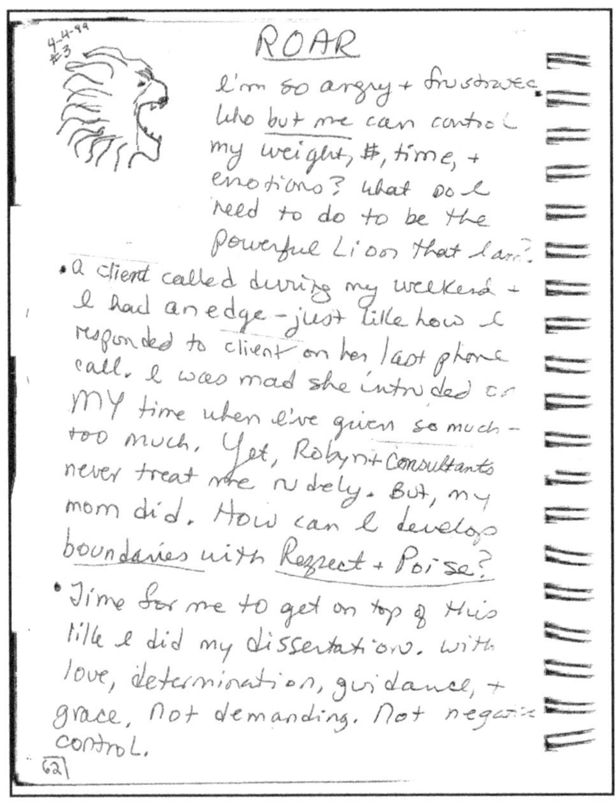

4-4-99
#3

ROAR

I'm so angry + frustrated.
Who but me can control
my weight, #, time, +
emotions? What do I
need to do to be the
Powerful Lion that I am?

• A client called during my weekend +
I had an edge - just like how I
responded to client on her last phone
call. I was mad she intruded on
MY time when I've given so much -
too much. Yet, Robyn + Consultants
never treat me rudely. But, my
mom did. How can I develop
boundaries with Respect + Poise?

• Time for me to get on top of this
like I did my dissertation. With
love, determination, guidance, +
grace, not demanding. Not negative
control.

62

Image 85: "ROAR": Feelings to review at a later time.

Capturing joyful moments: I loved remembering how I began my first journal of the Black Book Series. During the time when I started my first job in my second career, I was working long hours and knew I needed some renewal, but I didn't know where to go. A colleague told me of a retreat center a few hours away that he thought would connect me to my soul. Surprisingly, I started this new journal with a drawing I had made of a potato masher from an art session there. It was amazing to see that for the first time I was I experimenting with adding shading and shadows to that piece of art. This was followed by pages of little figure drawings of all the things that made me feel connected to myself at the place: hiking paths, gourmet food, and the view from the rocking chair on the porch. I found through reviewing subsequent journals, that I was learning to take breaks for renewal and participate in these types of activities closer to home. The journal review brought me such joy by reflecting on moments of bliss I had forgotten. It also helped me make more choices based on noticing what brought me satisfaction.

Trusting yourself: Keeping a journal provides a safe place to experiment and take risks. Just by pasting images and writing entries, I was taking initiative. I discovered more and more that I could trust my instincts without overanalyzing what went in the journals. By reviewing the journals, I was learning what was of value to me. I saw, for example, that making time to be creative and to take long walks, exploring different neighborhoods and resting in the parks, were essential for my well-being.

Similarly, when I would review a journal, I often saw I had more insights than I realized at the time. As I experimented with different approaches to getting organized, I realized that even though I might never be consistently neat and tidy, I was learning to clean up messes and decrease unnecessary chaos. I began to give myself more credit than I was used to, building self-confidence and trust.

Capturing vivid memories: Vacations especially provide lots of images to bring back the joy of exploring a new place. I like to make color prints of prized photographs: the colorful markets, curvy streets, and intriguing doors on houses I discover. I add notes about what I did and felt and appreciated about the time away.

I always include pages of special birthday celebrations. I often cut and paste portions of the cards I received, writing what they meant to me. I also wrote about other special occasions, for example the birth of Patrick's granddaughters, which allowed me to feel love and excitement as an honorary grandmother.

Image 86: Vivid memory of a work trip with the VPs.

Making decisions: Throughout my series of journals, I used various approaches to making decisions. Sometimes I just wrote freely to discover all my thoughts and feelings. A circle chart model I frequently used would help me think through a choice, for instance, what I wanted to do for a vacation or work intervention. I also used a two-by-two table to help me think through consequences of each decision. Although I sometimes made lists of pros and cons, they didn't usually work for me unless I let my heart weigh in on each option. During periodic reviews of my journals, I was able to make better decisions because I knew how previous decisions turned out. In reviewing all the journals, I could see the progress I had made in decision-making by using these tools.

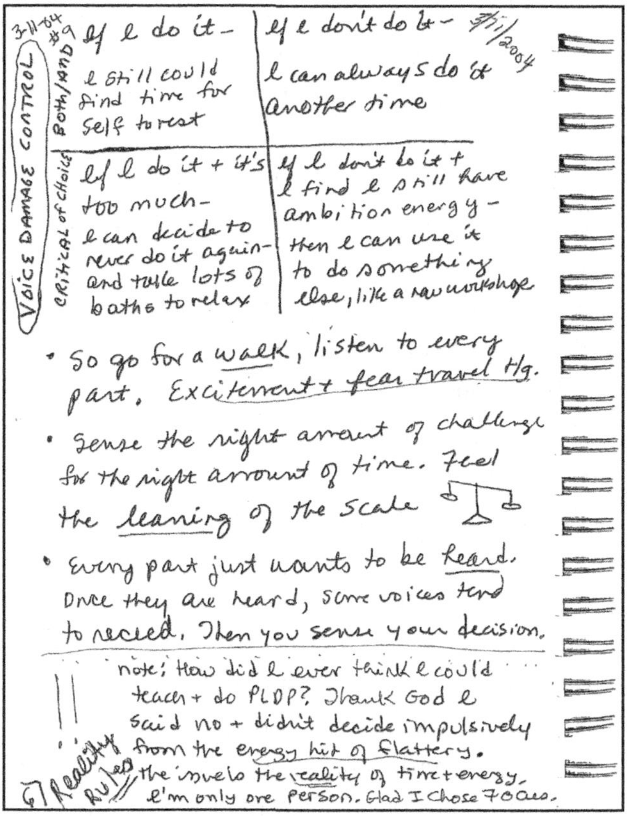

Image 87: Example of how I made a decision to focus.

How Do You Know What to Put in Your Journal?

Some journal experts have studied the type of things to put in a journal. For instance, Kathleen Adams is a psychotherapist who teaches and studies journal therapy and theory. She found early in her career that disclosing psychological issues through freewriting or stream of consciousness actually wasn't helpful to many of her clients. They would tend to spiral down into a dark hole and have no way to get out. Instead, there were myriad other more fruitful ways to use a journal for self-growth, which she called the "Journal Ladder." She used this approach to teach her clients a continuum of more structured techniques. If you are interested, she has written many books, such as *Journal to the Self: Twenty-Two Paths to Personal Growth* and has a website full of resources and programs at the Center for Journal Therapy.

My cousin, a psychotherapist who knew of my long-standing journal practice, recommended I attend one of Adams's workshops, thinking I might eventually want to conduct my own journal workshops and would benefit from meeting someone who does this for her career. The workshop, "Your Brain on Ink," linked lessons on neuroplasticity with the Journal Ladder. During a break, I showed Adams and her cofacilitator, Deborah Ross, a couple of my journals. I received validation from them that my process was well-developed and impressive. Further, they affirmed that my process was all about integration: I had writing and images (utilizing my left and right brain) and used that content to gain insights. This was consistent with their definition of integration as "the psychological process of maturing and creating new neural pathways through changes in behavior." Needless to say, I was thrilled about the feedback because integration had been a key goal and value for me. Seeing that aspect in my journals gave me confidence to continue and realize that one day I could share my approach with others.

Since journal writing has never been my career, I didn't feel the need to attend more workshops, peruse the literature, or defend my frame of reference. You don't either, unless you feel called to do so. You can use your journal as I do—*as a safe haven to trust your intuitive self and integrate your life experiences*. The main takeaway I got from Kathleen Adams was to deepen my appreciation of each of my entries, or a series of them, by reflecting on my observations after reviewing them. To ask myself with curiosity how I felt about what I wrote, if there were any surprises or new insights that emerged. You can start the practice of "curious reflection" at any time.

What I Put in My Journals

By reviewing my first and most recent journals, I found fourteen categories of entries that I most often used. Again, I am including examples from my journals to give you concrete ideas to stimulate your own creativity and variety of entries. If a category resonates with you, explore it. If not, skip to the next one. This is *your* journey.

Collected images: I mentioned before that selecting your journal is about how it *resonates* with you. Well, resonating is equally the path to filling the pages. For all the ways I can be analytic and methodical in my work, I am freed up when it comes to the journal. I just *know* what wants to be included. It might come from an email attachment, a brochure, magazine, or online newspaper.

For example, here are some of the things I glued on the pages and was drawn to in my most recent journal: I pasted a brief description of "Sight Versus Vision" that I received in an email from an eye doctor. Why? Because I am losing my sight and thought these distinctions would be helpful, inspiring, and worth keeping. I included pictures of Linda Ronstadt because I wanted to see her documentary when it came out. I am inspired by her amazing voice and also how she is dealing with Parkinson's disease now. Knowing I was a *Downton Abbey* fan, my husband gave me photos from a magazine he was reading because he knew I couldn't wait to see the movie. I watched every episode of the television series. I guess if I wasn't such a workaholic, I would have been addicted to soap operas!

My youngest sister, Robin, sent me a link to images of Mayan and Aztec calendars. She said my art, with its wavy lines, is more Mayan than Aztec. Once I saw what she meant, I glued these images into my journal for future reference. Then, since I was still working on the painting of the octopus's garden on our old water tank, I put the lyrics to the Beatles' song "Octopus's Garden" in the journal, along with an image of a coral reef I could adapt for my painting.

Reflections on a special day or trip: Often after a birthday celebration, high school reunion, niece's wedding, or a trip to see the grandchildren, I will make notes on what made it so special. For instance, on the page "My Happiest Birthday" I made headings for a recent trip to New York: Friends, Doctors, Restaurants, Shopping, Birthday Wishes, and Schedule. Under each heading I listed the friends I saw, the doctor appointments I had, the restaurants I ate at. I like to remember all the details once I get home. Why? Because I know that soon other daily activities will take precedence and I don't want to forget the joy of that time. I created a similar page for when my cousins came to visit. This one is less structured, and it has little figure drawings of taxi driver conversations, the mango margaritas we made, and visiting the local market with its fresh fruits and vegetables. This page brings back the memories and details of our time together, and it also is something to refer to for ideas when others come to visit.

Certificates of accomplishment: This category notes things I am proud of achieving. I put in a copy of my recent Teaching English as a Foreign Language (TEFL) Certification. In an earlier journal I included a copy of the award for my follow-up research article. These are the milestones that represent hard work and focus. When I forget and lose confidence when faced with challenges, these remind me to have faith in myself.

I also scanned a copy of a drawing my best friend, Nancy, asked me to make for her seventieth birthday. She said it was exactly what she wanted and imagined. I entered it because I felt gratified that my love for her was received and appreciated. I also included the cover of my husband's recently published memoir. I have notes about his stepping stones to completing such a huge endeavor. I entered this because remembering and writing about his early life was such an accomplishment for him, especially given the emotional memories it evoked.

Quotes or articles that resonate: Every once in a while, I'll see something that either validates my perspective or sheds light on long-standing issues or concerns. For example, I read a novel that had a great paragraph on motherhood. It said that no matter how you do it, someone is going to criticize you. Then, there was a poem that talked about how parents may not mean to, but they are going to screw you up. I included these because they resonated with my decision long ago not to have children. It wasn't an easy decision, and these items shed light on why I decided not to be a mother. Plus, I never know when I may share the quote and poem, so here I know right where to find them.

In the past I took a lot of notes on self-help books and my responses to the exercises I completed. Now I tend to print parts of novels that speak to me. Because I can sense when something is relevant to me, when it is said in words I wouldn't think to say, I'm reassured and inspired. I want to remember the quotes to reflect on them and refer to them later. In fact, all the quotes in my memoir I found from my journal review.

Things I find inspiring: Inspiration may be a photo or blog posting, poems, quotes, songs, or anything else that lifts my spirit and makes me want to do better and keep going. For example, I find the photos from Dewitt Jones's weekly "Celebrate What's Right With the World" emails beautiful and uplifting. So are cards with messages I've saved: "Being an Artist is like being yourself for a living." "If I had one wish for this day, I would wish for you to know all the joy and kindness and laughter that you bring to the world." "You're braver than you believe, stronger than you seem, and smarter than you think."

I love the photos of my granddaughters' birth and those of my best friend's grandchildren. I find trees are a dominant symbol for me. I saved a photo of a bare tree in winter that is still fully alive. It reminds me that one day spring will come; the winter seasons in my life are temporary—a time to rest and nourish myself.

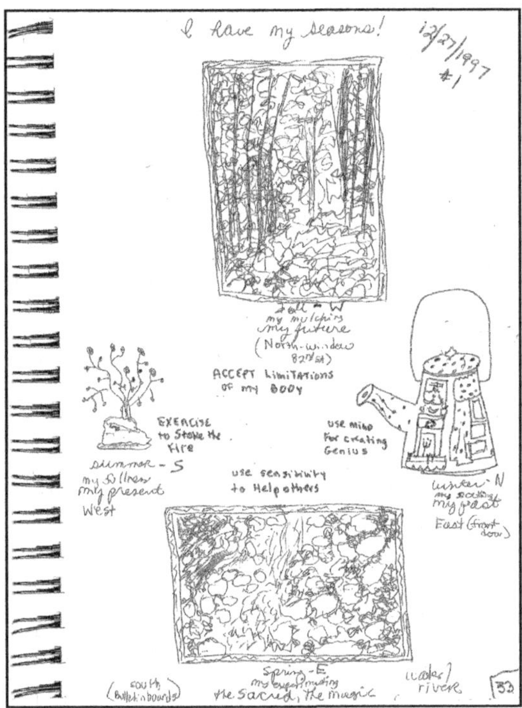

Image 88: Drawing symbols of the seasons.

Notes on how I did something I valued that turned out well: Here I want to capture a process that worked or a pattern that was revealed to me that I wasn't aware of when initiating it. For example, when I was teaching English last year, my Spanish-speaking class asked me if I would do a special session on how people in the United States celebrate Christmas. My page in the journal has little pictures and words that bring it all back to me: singing songs, making decorations, eating homemade holiday cookies, and identifying common rituals. They were so grateful they made me dinner and bought me a Mexican blouse. Now I can repeat the session next year, or at least take in the satisfaction of a job well done.

Until I reflected on it, I didn't realize all the ways I'm still doing Heartfelt Spaces, even though they aren't like the pieces of art I used to do. My page of current Heartfelt Spaces has little drawings and words showing the apple pie I baked, the Renaissance music I went to hear, the dream I had of our dream house in the woods, and the unexpected call from an old friend. I want to cherish these moments that don't often exist in daily life. These images keep me aware and grateful every time I look at them.

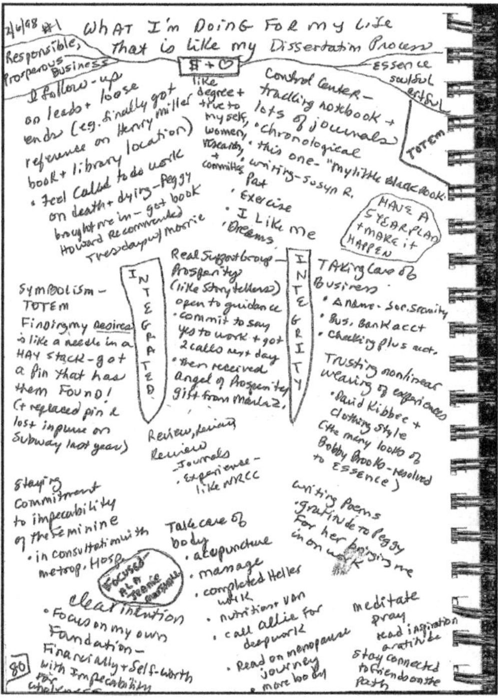

Image 89: Applying the success of my dissertation process to my current life.

Tributes to those who have died or are struggling: This category makes a space for grief, making explicit what I've learned from others. For example, I have a page titled, "Mom would have been 90 today." I have bullet points reflecting on what our relationship brings up for me—ways I was hurt, ways I healed, who she was to me in all the complexity and ambivalence. I included the notes I said about her at our celebration ceremony of her life, a photo of us together, and the lessons I've learned. Creating these pages helps me feel deeply and remember what is true for me, then and now. It's a growing edge to compare each year.

When I finished my follow-up research, I reflected on the women I interviewed and what they meant to me. I wrote about them in the categories that occurred to me, for instance, those who were inspiring role models, those who were challenging for me, and those who were notable in their presence and positive attitude—no matter what they were dealing with. These reflections tell me what I perceive in people I know well and how to generalize my insights to new relationships. The lessons I captured help me know my emotional landscape better and to have growing compassion toward myself and others.

Working through unfinished business: Sometimes situations arise that don't end the way I wished. I know these are important because I get easily triggered when I think of them. For example, I included the unsent letter I wrote that I wished I had received from a colleague who ghosted me. There was no way to contact him, but I felt anguish and knew it was for me to admit and transform. Getting it off my chest and into the journal was healing for me.

Another big one for me was being let go at work. Even though I handled it with dignity, and appreciated the respect they showed me, my departure was raw for a long time. I have pages where I reflected on certain people: those I still felt hurt by, anger at, and sad about. I wrote about what I wished I would have said, questions I wish I had asked, and things I wish I had done. Taking the time to own my dis-ease and work through it shows me how to take care of myself now and in the future. Over time, I realized I am no longer triggered by this event. I own that it happened *and* that it is no longer part of my daily reality. These pages remind me of how I am learning to take exceptional care of myself.

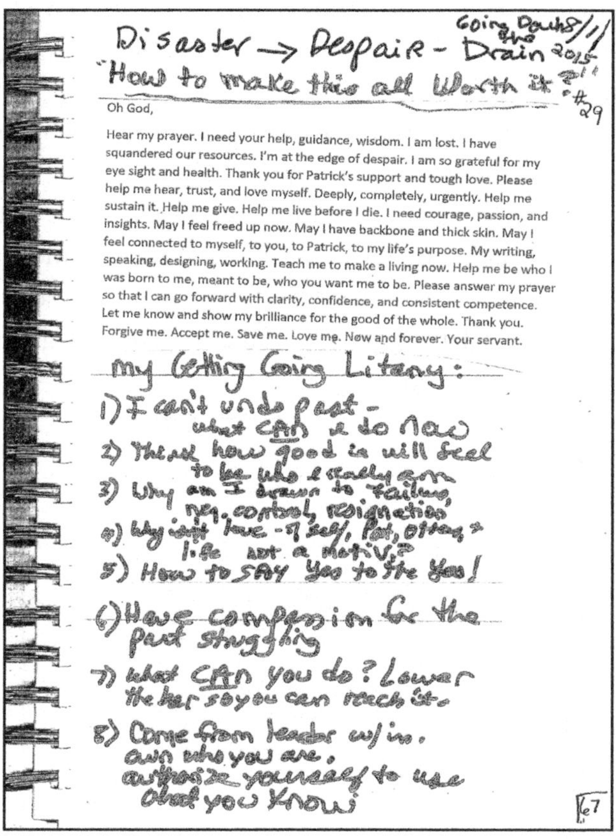

Disaster → Despair - Going Down the Drain 8/11 2015

"How to make this all Worth it?"

#29

Oh God,

Hear my prayer. I need your help, guidance, wisdom. I am lost. I have squandered our resources. I'm at the edge of despair. I am so grateful for my eye sight and health. Thank you for Patrick's support and tough love. Please help me hear, trust, and love myself. Deeply, completely, urgently. Help me sustain it. Help me give. Help me live before I die. I need courage, passion, and insights. May I feel freed up now. May I have backbone and thick skin. May I feel connected to myself, to you, to Patrick, to my life's purpose. My writing, speaking, designing, working. Teach me to make a living now. Help me be who I was born to me, meant to be, who you want me to be. Please answer my prayer so that I can go forward with clarity, confidence, and consistent competence. Let me know and show my brilliance for the good of the whole. Thank you. Forgive me. Accept me. Save me. Love me. Now and forever. Your servant.

My Getting Going Litany:

1) I can't undo past - what CAN I do now
2) Think how good it will feel to be who I really am
3) Why am I drawn to failing, neg., control, resignation
4) Why can't love - of self, Pat, others & life act a motive?
5) How to SAY Yes to the Yes!
6) Have compassion for the past struggling
7) What CAN you do? Lower the bar so you can reach it.
8) Come from leader w/in. own who you are. authorize yourself to use what you know

67

Image 90: A prayer and list to work through unfinished business.

Gatherings: A frequent category is when I just note all over a page some of the key things that occurred during the month or other period of time. I may draw a pumpkin with little pictures inside, or whatever symbolizes the season of gatherings. For example, in September last year I noted the following: I was in transition from a three-week Spanish immersion program; we served hot dogs and hamburgers for a local Labor Day party;

I was experimenting with structured mornings through yoga and exercise classes; I made plans to go to my fiftieth high school reunion in Chicago; and our neighbors who were moving begged us to keep their two little kitties. A page like this helps ground me in all the thoughts, activities, and plans circling around in my days and mind. When I look back at them, I'm often surprised at how much I was doing that was good for me, even if it didn't feel like it at the time.

In June I had pictures and words of my "trifecta": Spanish lessons, classical guitar lessons, and salsa lessons. I later dropped the guitar and salsa to put more time and energy into learning Spanish. When I reflect on the year and on the journal, these types of pages help me remember the activities I did and decisions I made, what inspired me, and what didn't last over time. When I track how I make decisions, I gain confidence about my process and instincts.

Image 91: Example of gatherings from 1998 in Journal 1.

Unexpected happenings: Things can happen that aren't planned or expected. For example, I have an image of my old laptop that got fried when it was hit by lightning late at night. I was sitting right there next to my desk, so lucky that it didn't hit me. I just watched the columns of electricity on the screen, helpless and scared. I eventually replaced it, and all is well, for now. These pages remind me of the situation and how I dealt with it. They are part of my history and reality.

I also have pictures and bulleted notes from when we survived two major earthquakes four months after entering a new country. These pages remind me what we don't have control over, and that I need to plan for emergencies better. I also included the letter from the editor in chief of our professional journal, who chose my article as the "Outstanding Article for 2015." A few pages later I kept the criteria from one of the professors involved in the selection process, which made me really internalize the accomplishment. Sometimes unexpected things are good news, and this was thrilling. I didn't have in mind an award when I wrote the article; the effort was intrinsically rewarding to me. This was a bonus.

Making collages from magazines: I have frequent pages drawn from magazines I read on a plane or receive in the mail. Whatever words and images I resonate with, I cut out and paste on the page. For example, one collage is titled "Live-Laugh-Learn" with a photo of older women in a dance class, big letters of JOY, and quotes about taking leaps and living boldly. These images from my health insurance magazine tell me what I am drawn to without any conscious thought. Doing them is a tiny art project. They are easy, fast, and fun.

Another collage is from local brochures for salsa dancing and art materials. These predate my salsa lessons and art projects for my best friend and our water tank. Mini-collages tell me what I might be interested in doing that I'm not aware of yet. One more collage is from an article in *O, The Oprah Magazine* on getting unstuck. I cut and pasted the types of strategies that most related to me in collage format. Now I don't have to reread the article; I have the most relevant features right there.

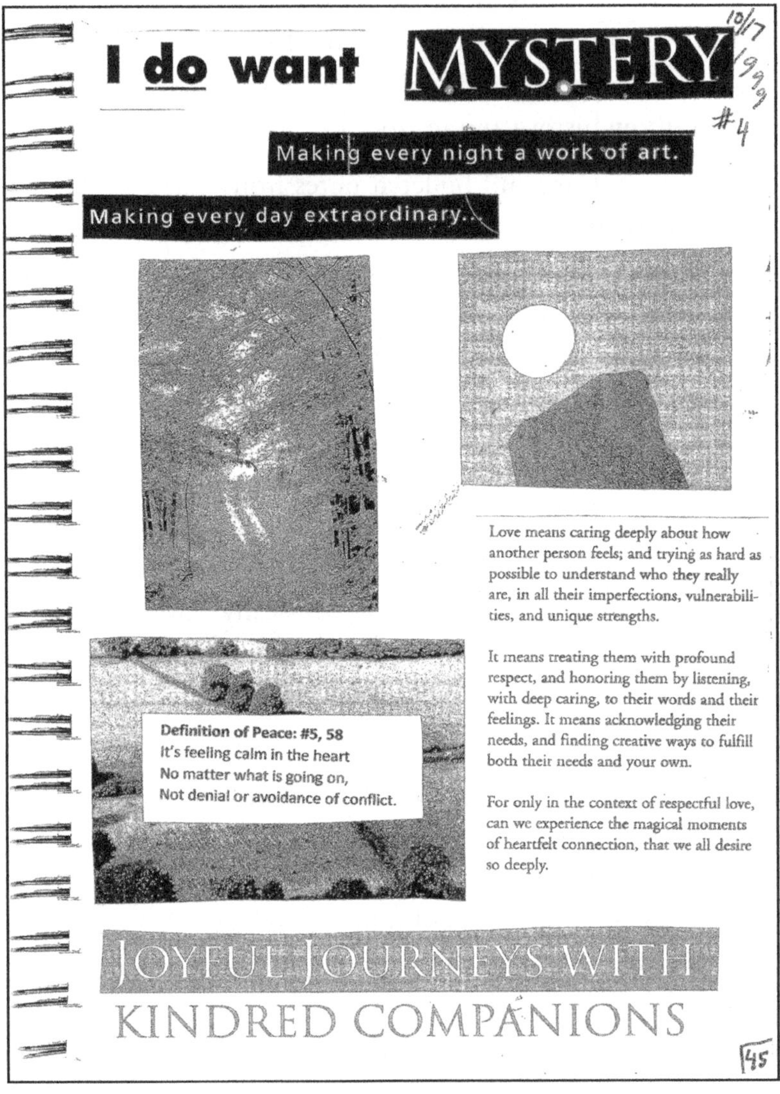

Image 92: Magazine collage with definitions of peace and love.

Pieces of things that come into my life that relate to a new interest: It is fascinating and fun to gather evidence of a new interest with items that reflect that topic. For example, I have a card a friend sent me in Spanish, which I then translated. Similarly, I have the words to a song a guitar player serenaded me with at an outdoor restaurant, and then wrote in Spanish and English on a napkin. When I reread them, I can measure what I understand now in the new idiom I didn't at the time. I also have the Spanish and English words to common Christian prayers I want to learn in both languages. It feels good to see how I am joining the community and culture here, even though I am not Christian.

Insights and personal themes: Often when starting a new journal or new year, I give expression to what I most desire. For example, I titled the entry at the beginning of Journal 32, "The Bridge from Here to There." I drew an image of a rainbow-shaped bridge with "My Current Life" on one end and "My Future Life" on the other. On the bridge was the word LOVE. I included a quote I found that echoed my belief that no one can build you the bridge that crosses the river of your life, only you can. This type of entry is a powerful statement of intention that shapes the priority I give to my choices and actions.

I have another page about my desire for aliveness in contrast with the broken record list of why I'll never have what I want. Facing my resistance and beliefs is an important way to integrate more of who I am with what prevents me from getting what I want. Toward the end of the journal, I note progress about how I finally learned what a mentor taught me years ago on "Chairing My Agenda." I used to think advocating for myself was selfish. Now I see it as finding my voice and honoring my needs.

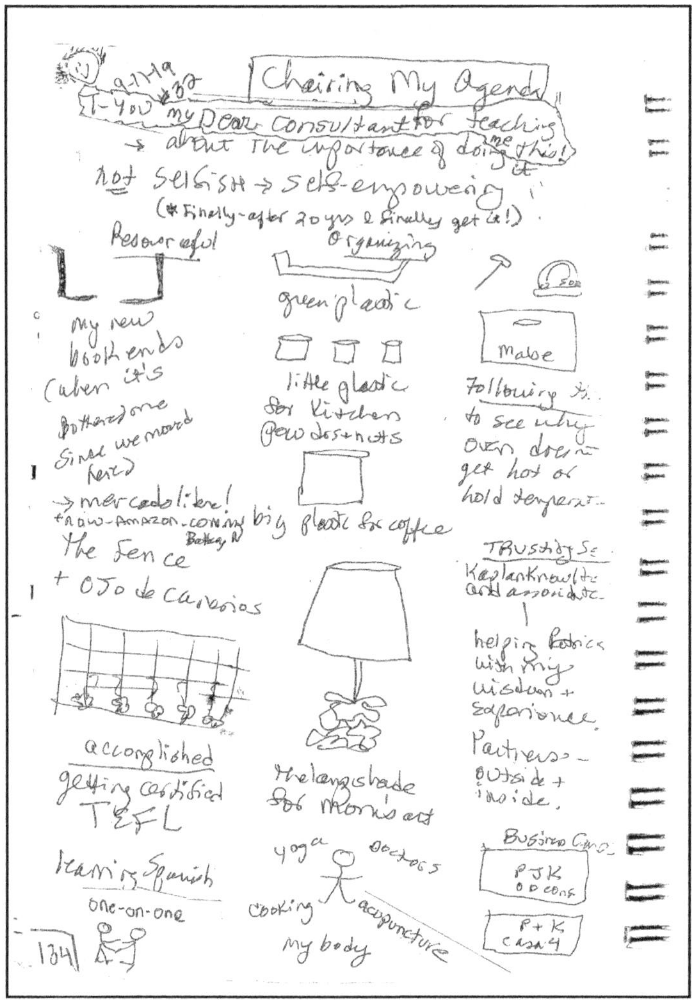

Image 93: Finally "Chairing My Agenda" in daily life.

Write about your dreams: What I love to do is write about my dreams. I happen to have vivid dreams every night and remember them on awakening. If I describe them right away, they are there for me to reflect on and analyze, either then or later. If I don't write them down, they evaporate. Sometimes the feeling remains and intrudes on my consciousness, even though I can't place why. For me, writing my dreams down makes me feel more grounded. Since I'm always trying to better understand myself, I believe dreams tell me something my conscious mind doesn't already know.

Over the years I've read a lot of books on dream analysis. I don't look up symbols in dream dictionaries or try to influence what I dream, as with "lucid dreaming." Instead, I start with writing down the dream as I remember it. I look for associations and make interpretations. Viewing each person in the dream as part of myself is enlightening. So is looking at it from various perspectives, such as what it means in my current life and what it means from my original family constellation. I know I am on the right track in my life when I dream of the dog I had for eighteen years during my first marriage. Barley was "my favorite teacher" and when he died, so began my spiritual awakening. When you track your dreams, you will discover your own symbolic code and guidance.

Image 94: Surfacing dream themes in my awake life.

Additional types of entries: All the above categories and their examples show you how to trust your instincts about filling your journal. It may feel risky to try new things, but really, what do you have to lose? The whole goal is *to build a relationship with yourself.* Discovering more about your thoughts and feelings, and doing things that bring insight and joy, is what your journal is all about. I found additional types of entries in the remaining journals I reviewed. Especially when anxious, I tend to do a lot more writing, tracking, and analyzing. Sometimes it's excruciating to reread them; my writing gets really small and detailed, and I can see how hard I was working to figure out my feelings or what to do about a conflict.

Other options: These include making lists of priorities and valued qualities of activities, writing timelines labeled with milestones, and analyzing days, weeks, and situations in detail in order to stay more cognitive and less emotional. I often have reflections on specific topics or events, efforts to define my feelings in depth, and explorations of options and choices made. I have periodic reviews of my recent journals with specific insights gained. Sometimes I create prayers for protection and guidance, expressions of gratitude and forgiveness, and writings about my relationship to my body, husband, finances, and organizing. When overwhelmed or lost, I create a dialogue, asking each of my parts to speak their point of view and address their concerns and questions. The idea is to come to some mutual understanding and integration.

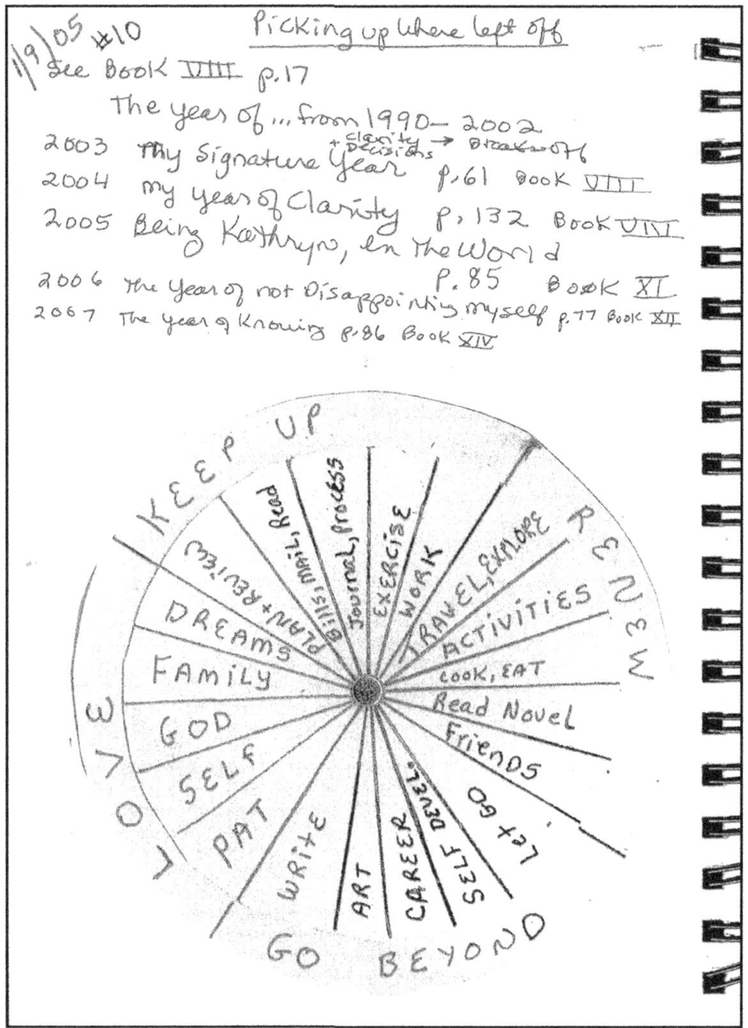

Image 95: Keeping track of personal progress and priorities.

The options are limitless. I recommend you try things from this list that wouldn't have occurred to you. At the same time, you may no doubt discover your own topics that I haven't included. The point is for you to trust your intuition and let the instrument that is *you* guide your choices. Your journal will become a mirror of who you are, what you are dealing with, what you regret, what you are learning, what gives you joy, and what your hopes and dreams are. Again, these will change as you change. In my review, I found my recent journals are more joyful, less intense, and take longer to fill up. Instead of two or more journals per year, they now take two or more years to complete. They are less about figuring things out and more about being present in my life.

CHAPTER TEN

Advanced Journal Review

When I was trying to capture the essence of the women in my study in preparation for writing their Poem Portraits, I created a series of "fill in the blanks" to help identify each woman's key characteristics. One was, "This woman is nothing if not _____." Asking myself this now, I'd have to admit, I'm nothing if not thorough! This trait can be an asset if used appropriately and a liability if taken to an extreme, so I've tried not to go overboard. I'm well aware that not everyone has the time, interest, or background to use qualitative research to analyze their journals. To that end, I have tried to make my process accessible, logical, and step-by-step for the prolific journal keeper or those merely curious about how I got from here to there.

What has worked for me in reviewing my journals may work for you wholly, partially, or not at all. You may have fewer categories or more, and your categories will likely look different from mine. What I am stressing here is the value of using your journals to know and grow yourself.

The templates I offer depend on your objective. If you want to identify your themes, I give suggestions and a form I used for each journal's review. If you want to gain perspective and not get lost in the details, stand back and create a title for each journal. If you want to think about your turning points and milestones, try organizing your life into phases and describe them. If you want to remember what is in each journal, write a brief summary including the title and dates covered for each one.

If your objective is to collate your own self-help book of Keepers, I show the categories and definitions that I created for sorting them. I also include a template for how I easily find each Keeper by category, journal and page number. Finally, if you want to look for overarching themes across your journal collection, start with writing each topic on notecards. If you prefer, you can transfer them to an electronic document. Not everything I collected made its way into the memoir. For instance, I had lots of specific examples of dealing with anger, but these were too detailed for the memoir. The purpose of the overarching themes template is to establish a foundation for you to synthesize your insights into writing, collage, or other forms. Making something concrete is a way to honor what you have learned about yourself from your own review process.

My Step-by-Step Process

I find there is "freedom in structure." I learned that phrase from a spiritual therapist, and I discovered its truth mostly through my writing—and trying new diets! The structure I use forms a container that allows the creative mind and nonlinear emotions to run free. I ended up writing my unexpected memoir by creating and following seven steps.

Step One: Create an index for each entry and a title for each journal.

I am blessed that my mentor Peter Vaill also kept journals. Early in my doctoral program he encouraged me to structure my journals the way he prepared his—with page numbers and an index in the back for the title and date of each entry. After writing page numbers on the bottom of each page, I create a title that sums up each individual entry. I save the last four pages of the journal for the index, which makes it easy to find and refer to something at a later date, enabling you to engage in an ongoing dialogue with your journal. I often star certain entry titles when I do a random review of a journal. Remember, a journal is not like a book with sequential chapters; it covers diverse topics in no special order. The entry titles and page numbers in your index help keep you organized amidst the randomness of your creations, allowing your whole journal collection to remain alive and accessible.

While writing this book, I realized I needed a typed index of each journal. Rather than sitting on the floor and taking out each journal to search for a particular entry, I have the indexes printed and in order in a folder to review at my desk. Image 96 shows my typed index for Journal 10.

Journal #10

**Title: Being Kathryn in the World:
Going for It While Keeping Her Little Ones Safe**

Dates: 1/9/05-6/16/05

PAGE	INDEX Title	Date
i	Picking Up Where I Left Off	1/9/2005
ii	Ithaca poem	1/21/2005
iii	Finally, Time to Reflect	
1	Two-Week Review	
8	Presentation Feedback	
9	Why Do I Wake Up Like This?	1/23
13	Turning Up the Heat	1/28
16	A New Day	1/29
17	Month in Review	
18	Tracking the Truth	2/5
21	Dreams and Waking Nightmares	2/11
23	Still in Agony	2/19
24	More of the Same	2/26
26	Dear God and Goddess	2/27
29	The Artist's Way	3/2
32	Robyn, Robyn	3/5
33	My Perfect Day	3/6
36	"I Must Have a Practice"	
38	The First Collage Came	3/13
39	What a Week	3/18
42	Hard on the Outside...	
45	How Do I become the Rainbow?	3/20**
48	Dear God	4/2
54	Dear God	
57	Going for It	***
60	Dear God	4/13
66	Wanting to Be So Proud of Myself	4/16
72	The Unlived Life Is Not Worth Examining!!!	4/18
74	I'm So Scared	4/19**

Image 96: The first page of my index for Journal 10.

You'll notice that I've given Journal 10 a title, "Being Kathryn in the World: Going For It While Keeping Her Little Ones Safe." You'll want to do the same with your own collection. The purpose of doing this is to synthesize your life experience during a particular time period. The best time to create a title is right after completing your journal, because the content is fresh in your mind. You may look at your index and the entries you starred as most important. Maybe you have sticky notes coming out of significant pages. Perhaps you wrote a summary of the year, providing you with clues, as I did in Journal 5, "My Jubilee! Discovering True Freedom and Living My Heart's Desire." (See Image 97.)

Image 97: Sample of a year in review.

Once I've indexed and titled a journal, I glue a large sparkling number on the outside front cover, indicating its placement in the series. This makes it is easy to keep all your journals in sequential order without having to look inside.

Step Two: Organize the journal collection into phases.

When I reflected on the factors influencing my journey as a whole, I realized that external events could account for phases in my life. Image 98 shows how I separated my collection into five phases, covering all thirty-two journals. Once I had determined these phases, I created an overview document that listed each journal by number and title under its designated phase. I referred to this document constantly when writing the memoir and keeping track of what happened when. Image 99 provides an example of this overview.

MY FIVE PHASES

Phase 1: "If I Can Make It Here, I Can Make It Anywhere, NYNY!" (Embracing new career and city.)

1997-2004 Covers my first job in my second career. (Journals 1-8)

Phase 2: Stepping Up to Leading for Culture Change: "The Life-giving Queen on Sacred Ground"

2004-2010 Includes the blessings and challenges of working at a different medical center with a more visible leadership role. Journals 9-22)

Phase 3: The Reluctant Vice President: The Beginning of the End

2010-2013 These three journals trace the accomplishments of losing weight (from size 12-2!) and getting promoted. (Journals 23-25)

Phase 4: Desperately Seeking My Purpose and Passion

2013-2017 I had to face my shadow and not expect my next step to be handed to me. (Journals 26-31)

Phase 5: Finally: Living Fully!

2017-2019 The two years of the new adventure are revealed in Journal 32.

Image 98: Journals 1–32 broken down into five phases.

Phases and Titles

1996 - 2004

Phase 1:" If I Can Make It Here, I Can Make It Anywhere" (NYNY! Embracing New Career and City)

#1 The Struggle to End the Struggle

#2 On Coming Home to Myself

#3 Life as a Test: Pass/Fail, Progress/Regress

#4 Everyday Creativity: The Art of Work and Relationships

#5 My Jubilee! Discovering True Freedom and Living My Heart's Desire

#6 Wisdom of the Body, Tending My Inner Garden

#7 Losing Weight and Gaining Myself

#8 The Year of Taking My Brakes Off: My Signature Presence

2004 – 2010

Phase 2: Stepping Up to Leading for Culture Change: "The Life-Giving Queen on Sacred Ground"

#9 Full Court Press: Making Changes in Sync with My Soul's Longing

#10 Being Kathryn in the World: Going for It While Keeping Her Little Ones Safe

#11 I Have So Much Going for Me, But I Worry: What About Tomorrow?

#12 Making Thrilling Commitments: My Personal Life and Professional Growth

#13 The Accident: Flipping the Switch for My Breakthrough (healing my shoulder and my life)

#14 Committed to My Integration: Accepting Only I Can Change How I Feel about Myself

#15 Up and Down the Roller Coaster: Realizing My True Needs and Remarkable Contributions

#16 Eye of the Needle: The Nub of the Problem and Core Insights

#17 My 1000-Piece Jig-Saw Puzzle Life: Finding the Missing Pieces, Filling in the Gaps

#18 A Banner Year: Visible, Publishing, Getting Recognition, and Having More Balance

#19 Perfect vs. Kaboom: Giving Myself the Approval I Seek and Risk Disappointing Others

#20 Weaving the Fabric of My Life with Gratitude, Honesty, and Joy

#21 My Dreams, Therapy, and Journal: Bringing More Integration and Deep Satisfaction

#22 Bereft: Hating My Despair Yet Determined to Transform "IT"

Image 99a: An overview of my journals, broken down into phases and journal titles.

2010 - 2013

Phase 3: The Reluctant Vice President: The Beginning of the End

#23 Skinny! Promoted! But Still Dreading

#24 "Life Begins at the End of Your Comfort Zone," But Not for Me

#25 Public Humiliation: What Is It Going to Take to Turn This Ship Around?

2013 - 2017

Phase 4: Desperately Seeking My Purpose and Passion

#26 Stuck: Wanting Success and Satisfaction Handed to Me

#27 Progress: Weaving My Life with Me in It!

#28 Committed: To Feel and Write My Truth Powerfully

#29 Vision to Fruition: Research, Publication, and Presentation

#30 Desperate to Get from Here (Downtrodden) to There (Taking Risks for New Possibilities)

#31 We Did It: Jumped Ship, Let Go and Moved On!

2017 - 2019

Phase 5: Finally: Living Fully!

#32 Creating Community, Art, and Aliveness

Image 99b: An overview of my journals, broken down into phases and journal titles.

Step Three: Write a brief summary of each journal in the collection.

If you're like me and you keep producing journals endlessly, you may want a summary of each journal to remember what was happening in your life during the time period it covers. In order to do this, I created a two-column table with a separate row for each journal. On the left is the journal number and dates it covers. On the right is a brief summary of key points in the journal. Image 100 shows an example of this from Journal 20.

Journal 20 6/20/2008 to 1/15/2009 ***Weaving the Fabric of My Life***	NO! Eckhart Tolle; HBR; Mourning; Cultivate Alive Girl; Why I write journal; Palm Springs; birthday; our loving staycation—the universal experience; Omega, Boston, Utah, Spring Lake NJ; developing the developers; our indestructible diamond; wanting more; Alice Miller/Norman Fischer; Aqua Caliente; Margarite and RP; move to apt. 6D

Image 100: My shorthand summary for Journal 20.

For many of you, this may be enough, though writing a longer narrative summary of each journal is one way of telling your story chronologically. When doing the journal review, I rewrote the shorthand summary of Journal 20 to explain more fully what was included in the journal and what led to its title. Obviously, it's easy to change a title and/or your shorthand summary when what you have learned about yourself becomes clearer. Image 101 shows three narrative summaries in chronological order from Phase Two of my journal collection. I combined all my narrative summaries into a single document that includes each of the thirty-two journals.

Journal 20 6/20/2008 to 1/15/2009 ***Weaving the Fabric of My Life with Gratitude, Honesty, and Joy***	Journal 20 starts with a big black NO filling the first page and ends with images of gratitude, inspiration, and joy. The NO is a rant on hating my life and myself, "distraught, disappointed, despairing, dissatisfied." Attending the four-day retreat on death and dying with my husband, I saw that my preparatory "NO" was part of the process; connecting to my body, heart, and soul because vacations end and ultimately, we don't live forever. At the end of the year, I wrote about the past year and cultivating my aliveness for the coming year. I saw I was really weaving the fabric of my life with gratitude, honesty, and joy (the title).
Journal 21 1/16/2009 to 6/30/2009 ***My Dreams, Therapy, and Journal: Bringing More Integration and Deeper Satisfaction***	My affirmation for the year was to enjoy both the journey and the destination through my books, body, and bounty. The journal contains dreams, therapy, reviews, and tracking, but reveals more integration and satisfaction than usual. (Reason for title). My therapist said I dissociate from parts of myself I don't like. Rather than get to know them with inquiry, curiosity, and compassion, I send them to the corner with a dunce cap and expect they'll change while I yell, "stupid, bad, I hate you." My husband gave me the most loving gift: a set of backyard furniture for our terrace for my birthday. My work partner and I won an award for our outstanding efforts in raising the caliber of physician leadership throughout the institution.
Journal 22 7/1/2009 to 5/9/2010 ***Bereft: Hating My Despair Yet Determined to Transform "IT"***	What stands out in the beginning of journal 22 is the New Yorker cover symbolizing my summer sanctuary (relaxing while reading on the terrace). Then I re-read my whole dissertation, and felt such regret that I never wrote the book for publication. I decided to write an article on the enduring wisdom from the senior leaders in my study. My long-term mentor validated my courage. Then I created a collage of three views of mountains that is still hanging in our house. Even though I was being successful at work, I was in a pit of despair, bereft, determined to transform "IT" (title of journal). I counted my blessings and hoped spring would bring much needed freshness and renewal.

Image 101: My narrative summaries for Journals 20–22.

Step Four: Identify themes.

Your goal in identifying themes is to discover things about yourself you don't yet consciously know. You may be aware of them from the work you have done in therapy or from reading self-help books. Reviewing what you have written in your journals is another way to identify your unique and core themes. As you review a journal, certain images and entries will capture your attention more than others. You will feel it in your body as your stomach contracts or your heart speeds up. You will have a sense that there is something important here; you should trust that instinct.

To help you generate ideas for identifying and defining your core themes, here are some of mine:

> **Not fulfilling my potential**: Ever the seeker, looking to the past for answers, beating myself up.
>
> **Anger as a trigger**: Not denying my own or disintegrating in response to other people's.
>
> **Soul issues**: My default feeling that "My Sad, Sad Story" was true, and burying myself alive.
>
> **Heartfelt Spaces**: Creating time and space for joy, art, and special moments.
>
> **Authorizing myself**: Expressing my voice, sharing my wisdom, standing up to authority.
>
> **Strategies to end the struggle**: Tools and approaches to help deal with emotions, set boundaries, make decisions, and authorize myself.

My themes encompass three negative aspects (not fulfilling my potential; anger as a trigger; soul issues), two positive aspects (Heartfelt Spaces; authorizing myself), and one about getting from stuck to freed up (strategies to end the struggle). I notice my core themes are all tied to emotions: anxiety leads to endless searching for strategies to end my struggle; sadness is the dominant feeling of my unresolved soul issues;

frustration typifies realizing each time I am not fulfilling my expectations and potential; anger is an emotion of its own I explore because otherwise it leaks out or turns into depression; joy is what drives my creativity and heartfelt expression through various activities and art forms. Fear is what I transform to courage when I authorize myself to express my voice, confidently create new programs at work, and build honest relationships. Not liking surprises, I try to anticipate and stay vigilant for things that will be upsetting and negative for me. When I can, I take a deep breath and take risks to move through my issues.

Image 102 shows a template I developed to review each journal for themes. I often include notes about my journal content, organized by page number. You can expand the space following each theme to accommodate your observations and reflections. In addition to this digital version, I keep a completed hard copy of my template folded inside each journal.

THEMES TEMPLATE

Journal # ______________

Outer events: (see phase summaries)

Year of: (review of journal and intentions for new year and journal)

Ongoing themes: (note core themes consistent in each journal, add examples by journal and page number)

Additional themes: (identify significant themes unique to a specific journal)

Examples for copying: (entries to remember and use in future journals, Keepers!)

My reaction to journal as a whole: (surprises, feelings)

Observations: (significant changes; what problems am I trying to solve?)

Essence of journal: (give it a title)

What did I learn from this review that I didn't previously know or remember?

Image 102: The template I use to review each journal for themes.

Step Five: Organize Keepers.

Because my journals cover such a long period of time, my journal review includes looking for entries that will serve me in the present. I select the individual entries that resonate with me, print them out, and sort them by categories, such as "What to do when I feel anxious" or "How I got more organized." This practice can help you learn from your own wisdom and experience. Image 103 shows the categories I used to organize and sort Keepers from my entire series of journals, and the definitions I wrote for each category.

KEEPERS DEFINITIONS

ANXIETY: pain and complaints, self-analysis, what could help

AUTHENTICITY: insights hat I discovered from myself ("I think")

AUTHORIZING MYSELF: to listen and act ("I want", "I can") YES!!

CLAIRTY/ SEEING SELF: mirrors through movies, tools and other forms outside myself

DEALING WITH "IT": knowing it, not making it worse, grieving

DISORGANIZATION: revisit insights for order, strategies for being neat and tidy

ENDING WELL: how to recognize it

FORGETTING: Things that have worked and I've achieved

HEARFELT SPACES: drawings, pictures, memories, joy

INSPIRATION: songs, quotes, pictures, ideas

INVISABLITY: ways to be more comfortable with visibility

LOVE: for intimate sharing

MY BODY: issues and suggestions

PARENTS: understanding dynamics, parenting myself

PATRIARCHY: Intimidation, authority figures, sexism

PERFECTIONISM: performance anxiety, fear of failure

PURPOSE AND PASSION: hints and clues

RELATIONSHIPS: skills and insights, boundaries

SPIRAL OF CHANGE: wisdom about different models and strategies

STUCKNESS: the source, Bell Jar feeling

TAKING MY PULSE: repetitious awareness, reviewing accomplishments again and again

VULNERABILITY IS A STRENGTH: reframe from outside eyes to inside knowing

WHEN LOST: ways to ground myself

WHO I AM: declarations and validation

WORK: dynamics, behaviors

YEAR OF: intentions, images and words from journals

Image 103: Keeper categories and definitions for my entire journal series.

Based on these definitions, I printed the entries out and put them in a spiral-bound notebook organized by category, journal number, and page. See Image 104 for a list of Keepers in the "Anxiety" category sorted in this manner. Images 105 and 106 show examples of actual Keepers from this list. You can see my entire notebook in Image 107.

KEEPERS BY NEEDS

ANXIETY: pain and complaints, self-analysis, what could help

Present in the darkness #1, 76

What is this agony? #1, 114

Back to O.P.U. #1, 139

Need a thinner filter, #7, 44

Performance anxiety, #7, 45

Fear #9, 39

My pattern of overdrive, brakes on, collapse #10, 61

Anxiety Closet, #11, 8

Anxiety and addiction for recognition and approval #19, 91

The steps for facing Kaboom #19, 92-96

Addicted to unhappiness, loss is worse than blindness #19, 146

When shut-down #30, 26-27

On pain #30, 55

Image 104: Keepers in the "Anxiety" category, organized by journal number and page.

Image 105: "Need a thinner filter," a Keeper from the "Anxiety" category (7; 44).

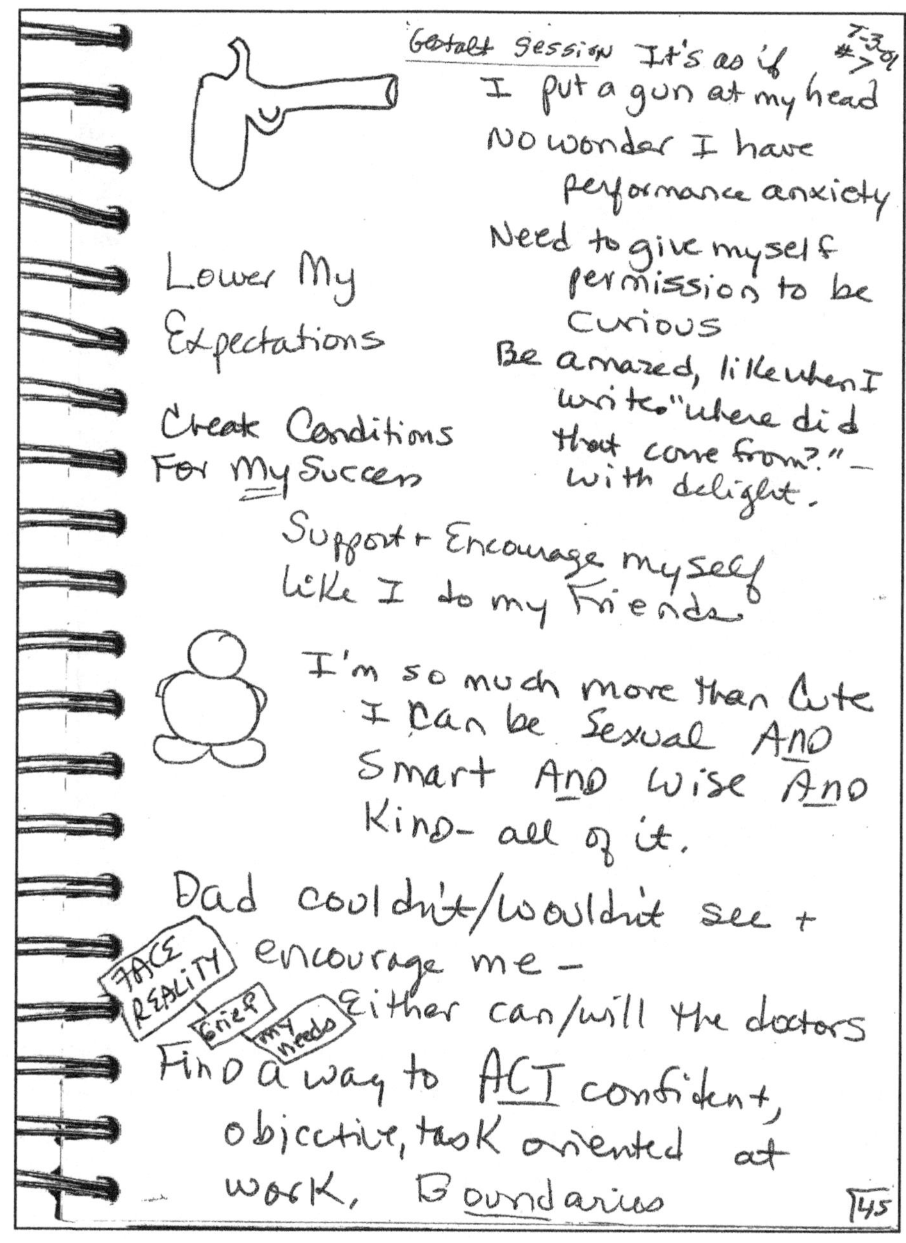
Gestalt session It's as if I put a gun at my head
7-3-01 #7
No wonder I have performance anxiety
Need to give myself permission to be curious
Be amazed, like when I write "where did that come from?" — with delight.
Lower My Expectations
Creat Conditions For My Success
Support + Encourage myself like I do my Friends.
I'm so much more than Cute
I can be Sexual AND Smart AND Wise AND Kind - all of it.
Dad couldn't/wouldn't see + encourage me -
FACE REALITY
Grief
my needs
Either can/will the doctors
Find a way to ACT confident, objective, task oriented at work, Boundaries
45

Image 106: "Performance anxiety," a Keeper from the "Anxiety" category (7; 45).

Image 107: My spiral-bound notebook for Keepers, organized alphabetically by category.

This system offered an easy way to find strategies that really work for me. When I'm feeling a certain way or needing to access my process and wisdom, Keepers can help me quickly remember who I am and what is true for me. Then I can decide what to do. For example, if I know I need to set a boundary and I feel a bit triggered in anticipation, I will go to the "Relationships" category to see what has worked for me in the past. There I have notes from self-help books on setting boundaries and examples of situations to ground and prepare me.

Step Six: Identify overarching themes across the collection.

With the Keepers now out of the way, it is time to look for themes that are evident across the journal collection. Image 108 shows the twenty-five themes that evolved when I was reviewing each journal and looking for those that showed up in the collection as a whole. They are different from many of the Keepers categories; this is not a problem, since they serve two different purposes. Keepers are for my self-help; overarching themes are for understanding my life and sharing it with others. I didn't feel obligated to write about each theme or limit myself to these themes once I started to write my story. I let my intuition and growing confidence in my process guide me.

CATEGORIES OF OVERARCHING THEMES

Addictive Search	**Narcissism**
Anger	**OD**
Authority	**Patriarchy**
Book	**Procrastination**
Change/grief	**PTSD**
Death and dying	**Sisters**
Decisions	**Taking pulse**
Ending well	**"There"**
Insights	**Tools**
"IT"	**Triggers**
Journals	**Visibility**
Me/strengths	
Mission	
Mom	

Image 108: The overarching themes of my journal series.

Step Seven: Write your story.

This step is about claiming, owning, and perhaps even publishing your story. Everyone has one, and yours is waiting to be told. Because I was experienced with the qualitative research process and relied on my four-phase writing process (Get it ready, Get it down, Get it good, and Get it out), I completed a first draft of this entire book by working daily over nine months. That said, give yourself permission to take as long as needed, and let yourself be surprised by what you are moved to express. Convey in some creative form what you learned from your journal review. In other words, demonstrate how you have become visible to yourself.

In order to start writing my memoir, I transferred each relevant entry, with journal and page numbers, to a separate notecard by category. Image 109 shows two sample notecards: the category titled "Ending Well" and a comprehensive list of card categories. You can see how I numbered them one at a time, not needing to use them all.

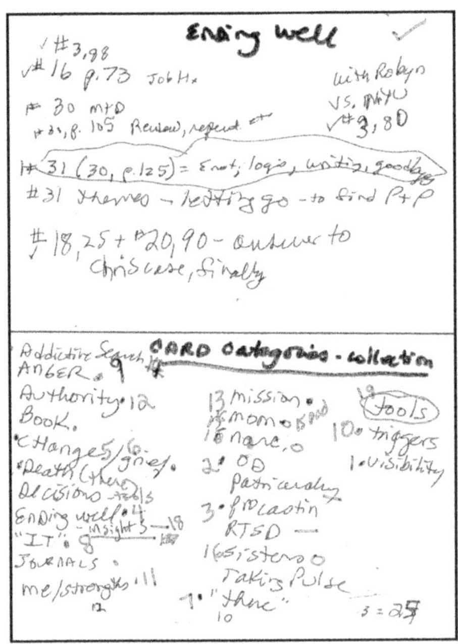

Image 109: Example of note cards for categories across the series of journals.

Using the notecards allowed me to focus on one topic at a time. However, I didn't write in alphabetical order, starting with "Addictive Search." Instead, I let the categories tell me where to start and how to keep going. I started with "Visibility." Once I completed a draft of a section, the next category would tell me, "I'm next." Trusting this process, I could organize the sections into chapters, ending up with a completed manuscript.

Not only have I now become visible to myself, but I have made my process transparent to you. It is my hope that you find your way to becoming visible to yourself using my steps and templates as a guide while also discovering your own. I wish you all the best on your journey.

Author's Note

This week as we were editing the last chapter of this book, the publisher asked me for some final thoughts. Did it accomplish what I was aiming for? Equally important, what did I learn? The word that comes to mind is "validation." Both my story with its themes and my process of keeping and learning from my journals feel validated upon reflection. Let me explain how I have come to that sense.

It's been two years since I wrote the manuscript and a little over one year since Patrick died so unexpectedly. I'm still in the same house, with his presence and memories in every room, which is such a comfort to me. I am also two-thirds of the way through a thirteen-month thanatology program studying grief and how to help others through it—taking painful experience and turning it outward, just as I've done with this book. I am still taking private drawing lessons and Spanish lessons every other week. I weave in seeing my sister and close friends here, and staying connected to my other sister, family, and friends who are abroad. In this sense, I am gratefully continuing to have "my life with me in it," which was my goal all along.

Then there are the challenges. My thanatology program is in Spanish and I struggle to understand it all. The readings and conversations remind me there is no "THERE" of perfect understanding. Then, recently, "IT" reared its ugly head. We were given an assignment to put together our end-of-life documents—something no one wants to do. It was one thing to assemble them for Patrick when we knew his death was imminent. But facing my own death, when I have been feeling so well and happy, put me in a foul mood. In fact, I reverted to procrastination, putting it off until the final two weeks. Sure, I got it done, but at a substantial cost emotionally. I got triggered and asked myself when I had felt like this before. Were there any clues that could soothe my soul?

Interestingly, I wasn't seeking outside of myself, as I used to, but returning to my journals for insight and solace. First, I looked at the "My Shadow" Keeper. All fourteen of my observations of "what gets me through" were still apt, from determination to forgiveness. Then I went to Journal 13, from 2006, remembering the vacation I took right before "The Accident: Flipping the Switch for My Breakthrough." What was the reason I went alone to an island for a long weekend? "The deep and unrelenting sadness, anger, frustration, hopelessness, discouragement, and 'bereftness' I feel . . . knowing I can't go home like this." Working through questions I explored while there, and open to the synchronicities that occurred in the new environment, I wrote: "I want to start writing my life in chapters. I think it would help me enjoy, integrate, and make meaning of my past while going forward in the present. I could be an example, one particular case study, not to emulate in content, but to reassure others who search and search." As I point out in the beginning of this memoir, it takes as long as it takes—this dream of "capturing my essence" wasn't begun until fourteen years later.

I also discovered I had written about how I fluctuated between being mean to myself (a behavior attributed to my Evil Twin) and the childish fear and deer-in-the-headlights reactions of my Poor Little Girl. Occasionally surfacing was my Wise Woman who, in the receptive organic mode, could love the flow of my internal experience while in my own world. What ensued was a dialogue I had with my inner jailor, asking "What would it take to pry the fingers off the gatekeeper who has my wholeness locked away and keeps me fragmented in prison cells?" The answer that emerged was metaphoric: exploring a new role, where this part could relinquish its keys and instead symbolically hold on to the hose that waters my inner garden. All that followed reminded me of who I am and who I have been.

It provided a way for me to accept and relax into my current angst, gaining perspective and remembering to love myself, warts and all.

Yes, I still struggle at times, wondering, "Am I allowed to be happy?" and "Do I have to keep on being miserable?" But what I now have is my own self-help manual, based on years of exploration and experiences, of "Becoming Visible to Myself." And my experience is validated by my understanding of Brené Brown's latest book, *Atlas of the Heart*, in which she asserts, "Feeling invisible is painful." Some of the reasons she cites may be from losses others can't see, discrimination and prejudice, and creating disconnection by being judged. My memoir focuses on the painful invisibility that results from growing up in a family dominated by narcissism. Once I finally understood those dynamics and worked through their implications in my life, I was able to start seeing myself, my true self, in the mirror. I could begin to love my true self and take in the love that was and had been available to me. That is when and how I began "Authorizing Myself" to believe in, build on, and embody my lived experience.

Dear readers, this is what I offer you: a reliable and repeatable process that is yours and yours alone. My way will not be your way, but by example, I demonstrate it can be done. When you fall into the well of that not-knowing place, you will realize you are the only one who can get yourself out. You will find the rope to climb out or build the metaphorical stairs to emerge once again. Each time you feel lost or miserable and back in the well of despair, you will remember that place and eventually find your way. Asking the purpose or meaning of the fall will help you grope out of the darkness. Not being able to see in the dark, I never saw the colors of the northern lights, but that doesn't mean you won't. Then again, even reaching your highest heights, you will still have moments when you touch your wounds and feel their pain. Frustrated and angry, you may shout out, "Why this again?"

Having your own recollections to revisit in your journals is exactly what you can create for yourself. As a fellow seeker, you can not only examine the self-help literature for how it informs your circumstances, but you can also rely on your memories and perceptions. Your journal is your greatest resource. You can mine it for your emotional truths and validation of your lived experiences. I have taken the risk to expose my vulnerable self and reveal my entire process. My intention was to both heal myself and to partner with you on your own journey of self-discovery and wisdom. I wish you strength as you courageously face what has been invisible. It was not an easy or fast process in my experience, but I encourage you to stay with it. You know from this book that you are not alone in spirit. When you are ready, please seek support from trusted people and resources, and let go of them when they are not right for you. The reward is seeing yourself in your mirror of truth and beauty, finally (but not once and for all) becoming visible to yourself.

With love,
Kathryn
June 25, 2022

Appendix: Tools and Resources

The longest journey you'll make on this earth is the one from your head to your heart.
—Lissa Rankin

The next step on your journey of joy, self-discovery, and integration is to look for what you need to help you get from here to there, especially when dealing with emotions. As you are now well aware, I have always been searching for strategies to end the struggle with "IT." While not exhaustive, my list provides a fairly comprehensive road map for deepening your own journey. Some of the techniques I have developed were just-in-time for a certain situation, others became my go-to method for repetitive patterns. Most of my searching was stimulated by being in the "dead zone," the void, when I'm lost because I finished something big but don't know what my next step will be. I looked to the past for what worked before, but those approaches almost never generated any aliveness in the present. Perhaps I have created, after all, a version of *The Last Self-Help Book*, which my dear Patrick envisioned for me years ago!

Here then are my most useful tools and resources that will serve you well in your ever-expanding toolkit, organized by the function they served for me. Some of my personal recommendations are enduring classics, while others are recent additions. I have repeated here some I mentioned in previous chapters for ease of reference. I've also included strategies learned from my litany of therapists and healers. As they did for me, each will likely lead you to discover other gems. Note: I have not provided full references for book titles, because you can easily find these books and authors, as well as their blogs, online courses, later books, and other offerings on the internet. The first three topics, Making Decisions, Dealing with Emotions, and On Changing offer the greatest variety of specific tools and resources. The remaining twelve categories center on books.

Making Decisions

Circle chart from *Getting to Yes* by Roger Fisher and William Ury. One of the first tools that made a difference in my life, the circle chart helped me make decisions about situations, such as how to handle conflicting styles when cooking with a partner and how to design an intervention for a department in the hospital. The tool walks you through a four-part process: understanding the problem in the real word; understanding it in theory; conceptualizing what might be done; and choosing options for action. Since most of us don't use all four aspects equally or naturally, going around the circle and answering the questions posed helps to balance your inner and outer life with the conceptual and practical aspects.

Validation of decisions. Sometimes you have to wait a long time to find out if a decision was the right one. I made the decision not to have children because I didn't want my children to suffer as I had, and I had no confidence I'd do a better job than my mother. Instead, I took on a nurturing role with my half dozen "Goddess Daughters," young women I've loved and mentored, which was mutually beneficial and satisfying. I have also worked hard to be a good mother to my little ones inside. Then last year I read a passage in Celeste Ng's *Little Fires Everywhere* that captured what I remember feeling when I was making the "baby-maybe" decision in my twenties (32; 107):

> Motherhood seems to be a no-win battle: however you decide to do (or not do) it, someone's going to be criticizing you. You went to too great lengths to conceive. You didn't go to great enough lengths. You had the baby too young. You should have kept the baby even though you were young. You shouldn't have waited so long to try and have a baby. You're a too involved mother.

You're not involved enough because you let your child play on the playground alone. It never ends.

Decision-making models. One of my colleagues offered a decision-making model that encouraged me to analyze how I would feel if each option came true: A = better than I think, B = same as usual, C = worse than usual. By assigning a percentage to each option, you can evaluate which outcome seems worth the risk. This tool helped me many times to decide when to say yes or no to opportunities (21; 48).

"She Let Go." A poem by David Deida, sent by my sister Robin, reveals how organic and easy some decisions can be. Here is a quote from the last stanza: "There was no effort. There was no struggle. It wasn't good and it wasn't bad. It was what it was, and it is just that" (29; 108).

Reflecting on experience. Conducting my extensive reading to decide about my leadership journey, I wrote conflicting things in my journal. First, I told myself I'd learn more by staying at work and getting promoted. Then, when offered another position, I told myself I'd learn more by leaving. Both reflections were partly true, but both were made hastily, disconnected from my heart and feelings. In both cases, I saw in hindsight that I didn't listen to my inner voices, which wanted to make a major change but needed time to think it through. Rushing is a clue that I am not making an integrated decision. Impulsivity to act on my initial reaction is a red flag for me because it is just that, a reaction and not a measured response (24; 132).

Paradoxical intention. I learned this psychological technique long ago, as an occupational therapist, to help psychiatric patients gain control over their anxiety by engaging directly with what they fear most. Later, as an OD consultant, my two bosses used this technique unknowingly with me when they gave me feedback on my "remarkable" performance evaluation. One of them had discussed the benefits of knowing who I am and how good I was. She said I could let go of the part of my identity always asking, "Am I OK?" When I asked the other boss about it, he cracked me up. He said, "If you let go and you miss that unhappy part, you can always go back to it again!" His perspective freed me up to take on changing as a pilot experiment and ultimately, to choose to keep excelling by evolving (15; 139).

Damage control. At one point, facing the decision of whether to continue teaching at the university while working at the medical center, I learned to set up a two-by-two table. On the top is "If I do it" and "If I don't do it." The bottom two boxes are "If I do it and it's too much," and "If I don't do it and I still have ambition and energy." The top two boxes allow your brain to process "both/and" options. The bottom two address negative consequences and voices critical of the choice. In my case, filling in the four boxes made it clear I didn't have time or energy for the teaching opportunity and helped me not regret the choice to let it go (Image 87).

Totems. When I'm metaphorically painting the canvas of the next stage of my life, a visual image provides inspiration and embodies the qualities I want the completed work to project. This wholeness enables making decisions in line with the imagined finished product. The first time I used this technique, Renoir's *Luncheon of the Boating Party* suggested to me the depth, richness, and celebratory aspect I wanted my research to have, and helped me to achieve that. In another instance, Patrick found a round glass copy of the "Creation" Rose Window at the Washington National Cathedral that perfectly embodied my fiftieth Jubilee birthday vision. As a leader of culture change, a tile painting of a whole field of sunflowers hung on my wall, symbolizing the alignment and positive collaboration I sought throughout my career.

These totems worked best when they found me, through Grace, rather than when I searched for or invented them. I once decided a pointillist painting would evoke the detail I needed to find purpose and passion for my life after I left the medical center. I selected a painting by Georges Seurat showing a community of energetic and joyful people creating music and entertainment on a stage. It seemed to fit because it captured a symbolic way to overcome my youthful regret that "I should have been a dancer." Unfortunately, this totem didn't work its magic for my future in the manner and time frame I expected. It taught me that you can't force something that isn't or was never meant to be (8; 127 and 27; 47).

Marie Kondo. "Miss Tidy," as I call her, has a simple, practical approach to making decisions. She addresses what to keep and what to let go of based on what "sparks joy." Hers is the only system that helped me get out from under being "buried alive" by my stuff. Having read many books on organizing—by styles, for the creative person, the highly distracted, the procrastinator—I appreciated her comprehensive, methodical, spirit-driven, and accessible volumes. Now she even has a series on Netflix showing her working with different people and solving their various problems. Clearly my journals spark joy for me, while serving as records of personal history and acting as sources of wisdom and inspiration. Discovering what sparks joy for you will align your surroundings with your heartfelt values, enabling you to preserve your treasures and toss the rest.

Dealing with Emotions

Welcome all your emotions. For me, the best advice on emotions is to welcome them all. Yes, it's uncomfortable and our impulse is to get rid of them. That is why Rumi's poem, "The Guest House" is so popular, showing up countless times in my journals and inspiring my deepest knowing (14; 85 and 31; 108). It also helps to learn to identify your feelings and get to know your internal saboteur. Booklets by Martha Baldwin Beveridge on these topics are basic and practical.

Myths and stories. I thought I was destined to live the myth of Sisyphus, constantly pushing the rock of achievement up the mountain only to have it roll back down and start over, again and again. This began to shift when I read Clarissa Pinkola Estés's *Women Who Run with the Wolves,* one of the deepest books about understanding emotions through stories. Estés has an extraordinary ability to infuse myths with timeless wisdom. During graduate school, I learned that "the solution for malaise is always the opposite; so new action is the cure for boredom, closeness the cure for loneliness, solitude the cure for feeling cramped." Because everything in nature has what Estés calls a "life/death/life cycle," she advises us to dance with it and live as we breathe, taking in experiences and knowing when to let go and grieve. In terms of integration, I was always surprised and humbled when after each story Estés reminded readers that every character represents a part of our own psyche. Certainly, it is an ageless book for many people and purposes, worth rereading over time.

Childhood wounds. Two authors who have helped me understand my early trauma and what to do about it are Alice Miller in *Drama of the Gifted Child* and *The Truth Will Set You Free* and Norman Fischer in *Taking Our Places: The Buddhist Path to Truly Growing Up*. Further help with growing up and dealing with anger came from John Lee in *Growing Yourself Back Up: Understanding Emotional Regression* and *Facing the Fire: Experiencing and Expressing Anger Appropriately*. Years ago, I read in the works of Melanie Klein about how splitting (defined as the failure to integrate good and bad in one person) and the depressive position are created in childhood. My experience of feeling disconnected is echoed in *The Bell Jar* by Sylvia Plath. Another meaningful and special book for me was the sensitive and vivid memoir of a child growing up in a dysfunctional family, *As If It Never Happened: Stories of a Young Boy's Secrets, Fears, Love, and Loss* by my dear Patrick J. Knowlton. A great storyteller, Patrick created a book that helps the reader experience buried emotions.

"Disidentify." This is a practice I learned from a therapist, Helene Brenner, who wrote the book *I Know I'm in There Somewhere*. To "have your feelings without them having you," Brenner explains that you need to relate to them as parts of yourself. Rather than get engulfed with sadness, you can be empathic to that feeling and say, "There is a lot of sadness there. Can you tell me about it?" You learn to listen for what each part needs. In *Focusing* by Eugene Gendlin, he suggests that when the sad part feels listened to, you will feel a "felt shift" in your body. I often "collapsed" into my feelings, and this practice helped me stay on dry land rather than drowning.

Keep perspective. Instead of catastrophizing and making things worse, I finally learned to ask myself, "What *can* you do?" and not focus on what I can't do. It's the same with relationships—we need to let people be all they *can* be, instead of focusing on what they can't be (9; 4).

Play with emotions. I identified a series of actions for dealing with emotions that I displayed in my journal. They reminded me to "play" with them and not take them so seriously. I told myself that emotions are temporary and want my attention, but I don't have to get so scared of them. Instead, I imagined lots of options. I could make "IT" shrink, capture and suffocate it, mock it, beat it up, dance with it, just say *no*, make it sit in the corner, escort it out of the audience, shout at it, or set it on fire and watch it burn (Image 54).

Nonviolent communication. Books and workshops developed by Marshall Rosenberg helped me get to the bottom of emotions by revealing our underlying basic needs. I learned that when needs aren't fulfilled, negative feelings such as anger and hopelessness will dominate. When our needs are fulfilled, we more easily feel and express confidence and joy. Knowing my needs helped me express them more sensitively to others with whom I was in conflict (31; 106).

Endure polarities. As Ellen Burstyn has said, *"Bring forth what's in you, or it will destroy you."* In this vein, my acupuncturist used to say that integration is about living in both places at once: the deep knowing of the treasure inside you and the vigilance to guard that treasure. He advised telling myself with absolute certainty, "I can heal" (16; 96). Then, he suggested I notice my success when I trusted my step-by-step, one day at a time methodical approach (22; 99).

Prepare for triggers. When triggered, how do I start? I made a list in my journal: realize I was safe right here and now; breathe and connect to the feeling of freedom; and talk nicely to myself, "You can do this, honey. You're doing a beautiful job." I could also go to a movie, get a manicure, and relax away from work. It also helped to review old journals I knew contained wisdom and enduring truths about my patterns. I would listen to my soul's calling: cry, light candles, pick angel cards, listen to music that evokes my emotions, write letters for guidance, meditate, and pray (10; 25).

Release grudges. In her *New York Times* article from January 2, 2019, Sophie Hannah offers great insights about holding a grudge and advice for releasing one. I kept the questions posed in my journal and wrote down the steps for reference (32; 100).

Set a boundary. When we're challenged, distracted, and potentially hijacked by emotions, it's usually time to set a boundary. In *Senses of the Soul,* GuruMeher Khalsa offers six steps for setting boundaries with increasing intensity:

1) Inform: Share what you see and what's bothering you.

2) Request: Ask to do or not do something.

3) Demand: Say directly what you want or don't want.

4) Warn: Let others know the consequences if they don't listen.

5) Attack: Say, "That's it!"

6) Leave: Because that's all you can control (29; 89).

Write an unsent letter. When upset because I didn't hear from someone or dissatisfied with their communication, I would write a letter laying out what I wished they had said. Of course, I never sent these. Just hearing and honoring my feelings and identifying my needs was intensely healing and a marvelous way to let go of resentments and behavior I can't control (32; 74).

Julia Cameron. Having read most of Julia Cameron's numerous books, I frequently returned to her first, *The Artist's Way: A Spiritual Path to Higher Creativity*. Her nine-step process for working through blocks never fails. Visualizing true north and naming creative U-turns is honest and nonshaming. Her "Morning Pages" help immeasurably with managing emotions by giving us a place, as she says, to fall apart. It was much better for me to vent there instead of leaking my emotions at work (10; 30, 16; 106, and 22; 50).

Acceptance. Cheri Huber's excellent books on depression, self-hate, and the motivation for seeking are both insightful and accessible. I once ordered her CD on unconditional self-acceptance and listened to it over a three-day weekend. It was so on target for me that I wrote that it was right where I lived emotionally and consistent with my work with my therapists (10; 119). Also helpful is *Radical Acceptance* by Tara Brach. I find some new insight every time I reread it (27; 107). To remember about love, loss, and acceptance from a child's perspective, try rereading Margery Williams's classic, *The Velveteen Rabbit*.

Inner children. What also helped me manage my emotions was working with a book on inner children and collecting images of each of the seven developmental stages. It was fun to look for photos online and to consult my albums for inspiration and resonance (14; 77, 84–85, 95–97, 138 and 15; 114–122). The author of *The Inner Child Workbook*, Catherine Taylor, had the best advice for me on healing: "You cannot heal unless you are willing to experience the pain left over from childhood. If you do not separate from the pain, then you will collapse into it. When this happens, you are as vulnerable as you were when you were young and act in childlike ways that limit yourself to the same coping mechanisms you had as a child" (14; 125). My core battle was between my inner adolescent, who wants to be accepted as she is, and my inner critic, who always thinks I can do better. This power struggle affected every area of my life: weight, career, intimacy, appearance, and experience of joy. Taylor says the adult has to mediate and negotiate without rigidity, so the adolescent doesn't rebel, yet not so flexibly that the critic gets alarmed. Otherwise, when the inner adolescent feels unsafe, unfair, or that her individuality is threatened, she would rather sabotage herself than disappoint, fail, or look bad. Without practice, patience, and persistence, the inner adult will often treat these parts the way she was treated by her parents: walking on eggshells and acting intimidated, uninvolved, or intrusive (15; 95 and 16; 109).

Relationships. Dealing with emotions in intimate relationships is even more complicated than the individual journey. I was most helped by Harville Hendrix's *Getting the Love You Want: A Guide for Couples.* When my intimate partner and I went to an Imago workshop, it helped us understand our feelings and resolve our issues so we could make a wholehearted and lasting commitment to each other. We followed up by reading the book by our facilitator, Rick Brown: *Imago Relationship Therapy: Introduction to Theory and Practice.* He normalized and reframed conflicts as having their origin in unconscious images from early childhood. With awareness, the current partnership can be cleaned up and helped to heal. Later, I found helpful Christian Pankhurst's *Insights to Intimacy: Why Relationships Fail and How to Make them Work.* Just knowing others have felt distraught and found ways to healthy relating is inspiring and applicable.

Forgiveness. My favorite book with application to personal and professional negotiation is Kenneth Cloke's *Mediating Dangerously: The Frontiers of Conflict Resolution*. The chapter on forgiveness is the deepest and most helpful writing I have found and was made even more emotionally relevant at his weeklong conference I attended. My takeaway is when you really get to the root of conflict, both parties fit together like puzzle pieces. Also insightful is *12 Steps of Forgiveness* by Paul Ferrini. He offers a process for shifting from perfectionistic expectations to discovering those heart and soul-based qualities that already exist.

Robyn Posin. Robyn probably knows me the best of anyone and has helped me integrate my various emotions and voices. One technique she shared that I always use when overwhelmed is focusing on "the smallest slice of now." Another great reminder I learned from her when I got anxious and felt miserable was, "Don't put a spin on your wobble." In other words, everyone makes mistakes. Don't make it worse by calling attention to them, adding a spin with negative self-talk and shame (3; 46). A three-step approach she customized for authorizing myself was not to beat myself up but instead find ease; appreciate my gifts and not compare myself to others as if I'm inadequate; and accept who I am at every moment and have faith I am divinely protected (11; 63). Through Robyn I learned I have little ones inside that need a "good mommy voice." When I treated HER, my undamaged core, with love and patience, then I had an invincible partnership. When I treated HER as I was treated as a child, with disdain, disgust, and impatience, then she didn't feel safe, and I sabotaged through accidents, illness, mess, and excess weight. Robyn has since written her wisdom, perspective, and stories in several books that I highly recommend, in particular, *Choosing Gentleness: Opening Our Hearts to All the Ways We Feel and Are in Every Moment* and *Go Only as*

Fast as Your Slowest Part Feels Safe to Go: Tales to Kindle Gentleness and Compassion for Our Exhausted Selves.

On Changing

Cycles of change. What has been helpful to me is to think of producing creative work as akin to the cycle of a plant (14; 87). The germination stage is for the seeds to absorb moisture and the warmth of the sun through the earth until they organically develop roots. Once sprouts are visible, leaves and buds appear. Then they flower and eventually wilt and die. Even before germination, the soil has to be prepared. These steps are analogous to the creative process. Again, before the incubation stage of an idea, preparation needs to occur with feeding the brain lots of material. Then, the individual lets their unconscious work on the problem, perhaps taking a walk and daydreaming. The "Aha!" moment of the light bulb going on is akin to the gold. But unless that gold is mined, the creative insight won't see the light of day. The ideas need to be evaluated, packaged for the intended audience and purpose, and then implemented. In other words, remember that the garden relies on the seasons (16; 41).

Upward arrow or spiral. There are so many ways to think about change. It's common to imagine achieving goals as an upward arrow directly aimed at the target. However, psychological issues generally resurface at different times and stages, more like a spiral. It helps to be aware of the diagram that best describes your process of change and matches your intentions.

U-shaped model. While some models of change are logical and step by step, I have been drawn to those that make room for disorganization before reorganization can occur. For example, Lee Hecht Harrison has a U-shaped diagram with five phases (25; 136). Starting at one side is the anticipation that something is going to happen, leading to letting go of the past, and then hitting the bottom because of the disorientation from when things are not what they were and still not how they are going to be. Going back up the other side of the U is the reappraisal of the situation and looking at options followed by recommitment to a new sense of purpose. A simpler version is the initial optimism on one side of the U, the valley of despair at the bottom, and acceptance on the other side (28; 54). As my dentist would say about pain, "All you need is a tincture of time."

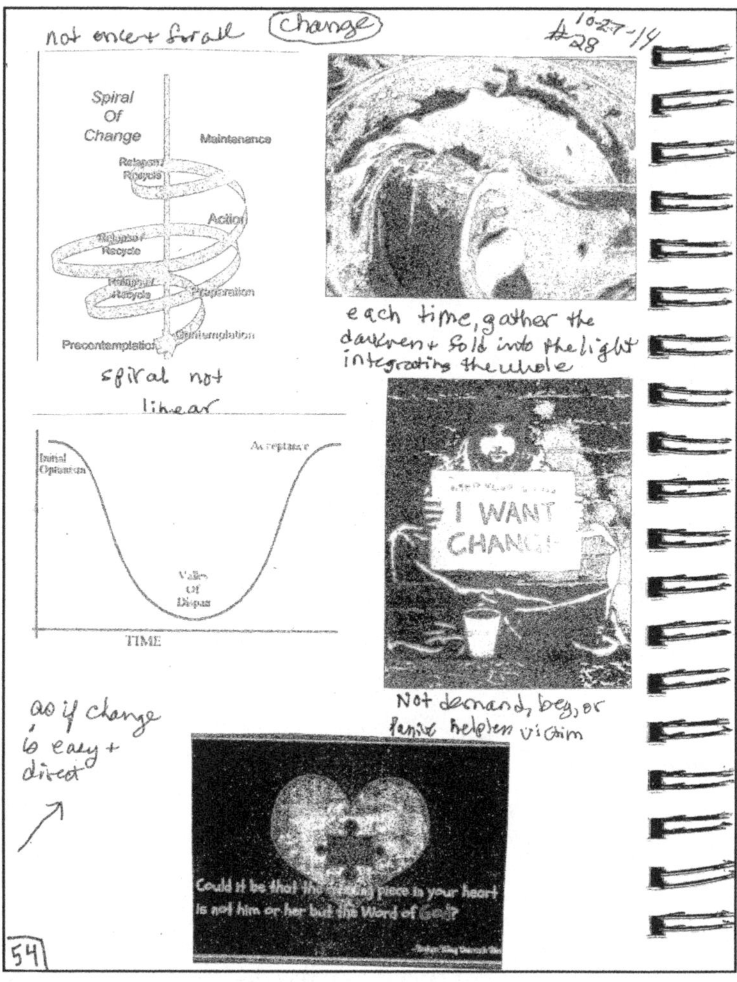

Image 110: Various models of change.

Contraction follows expansion. After completing a project, I often want the fullness of the expanded space I've entered to continue. It could be after having a great time with friends and coming home to an empty house, the end of a vacation and needing to go back to work, or handing in an in-depth report and feeling lost about refocusing on other priorities. There is a natural and necessary drop in energy between the end of one activity and the start of the other. I had to learn to expect contraction and find ways to tolerate the void. Meditating helps because as the breath goes in and out, we realize that good times don't last, but neither do bad ones. It's like the seasons, winter comes before spring.

Reacting to not changing. When I feel frustrated because I think I should be changing faster, I get demanding and have a private rage attack. It often feels like I'm covered in flypaper and can't get it off. When I become afraid that I can't and won't change, I resign myself to staying stuck and acting cranky and self-oriented. What helps is realizing I will always have two parts of myself competing for my attention—one creative, the other critical. The creative part likes possibilities, but the critical part is plagued by what I didn't do and need to do and often takes the form of internalized voices or actual put-downs and bullying outside of myself. When that part is activated, the trick is to settle down, feel all your feelings, hear all the voices, and ultimately trust your instincts and enjoy the ride. A spiritual therapist I had always tried to point out that life is fluid, so seeing myself as solid and stuck is a misperception.

Review your journals. Reviewing, reviewing, and more reviewing reminds me of my process and what works for me and helps me focus on past successes to unleash actionable next steps.

Ask yourself questions. Robyn posed two questions to help me analyze my patterns and motives: "If I succeed, what do I fear I will lose and what danger will be drawn closer to me? And if I fail, what benefit do I get from revealing weaknesses?" These are important questions to consider when not sure what you truly want to change.

Cheat sheets. Since I lose perspective when emotional, I keep handy numerous step-by-step processes to apply when facing change. Here are a few:

> **Head, heart, and feet**. When something happens and I'm triggered, first name it, to become more rational (head). Then, ask myself how big or bad it is, to connect with my values and feelings (heart). Finally, decide what to do about it and actually take action (feet) (5; 83).
>
> **Total Biology**. Similarly, a simple process from the Total Biology mind-body approach to understanding disease is to name it, own it, and dump it. It's that last step that was hardest for me; rather than keep berating yourself, let it go and move on (17; 114).
>
> ***The Inner Child Workbook***. This book offers a more in-depth process for asking yourself: What do I want that I don't have? What specifically has to change to achieve my goal? It helps with visualizing an outcome exactly the way you want it, with emotions; managing your resistance and negative self-talk, saying instead, "Isn't that interesting?"; and taking action and creating support: "Do this twice, to internalize and work it through" (17; 72).
>
> **My own cheat sheet**. To counteract my tendency to either over-listen to others or be impulsive and reactive, here are my four steps: Tolerate my anxiety, lower my expectations, take baby steps in the now, and don't leak my emotions (17; 61).
>
> **Stop, look, and listen**. A simple, accessible practice: when I am not thriving, I need to stop, look, and listen. If I am overwhelmed, angry, afraid, or shut down, I only need to accept where I am, love myself no matter what, and see what tiny movement I can make to shift things in the short or long term (15; 61).

"Autobiography in Five Short Chapters." Since forgetting my good advice is a continual pattern, I have loved and appreciated this poem by Portia Nelson. She helps me remember to practice seeing the hole in the sidewalk and eventually taking another path (3; 54):

I.

I walk down the street.
There is a deep hole in the sidewalk.
I fall in. I am lost. I am helpless.
It isn't my fault.
It takes forever to find a way out.

II.

I walk down the same street.
There is a deep hole in the sidewalk.
I still don't see it. I fall in again.
I can't believe I am in the same place.
It isn't my fault.
It still takes a long time to get out.

III.

I walk down the same street.
There is a deep hole in the sidewalk.
I see it there. I still fall in.
It's habit. It's my fault. I know where I am.
I get out immediately.

IV.

I walk down the same street.
There is a deep hole in the sidewalk.
I walk around it.

V.

I walk down a different street.

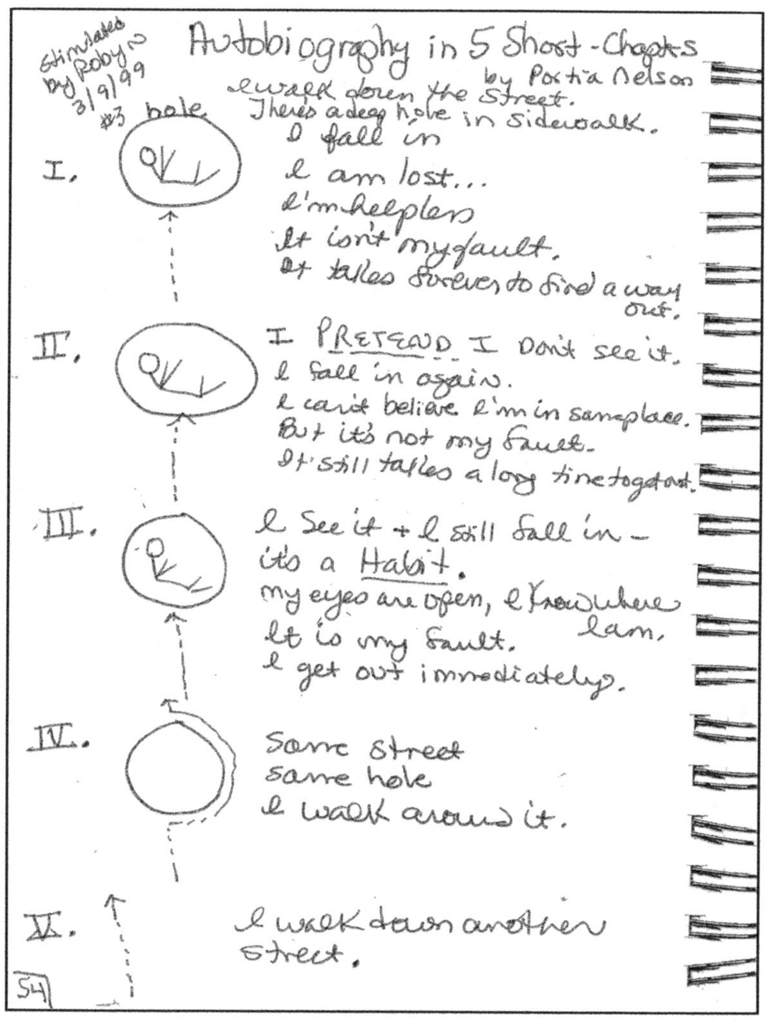

Image 111: My journal version of Portia Nelson's "Autobiography in Five Short Chapters."

Metaphors. Depending on your learning styles, metaphors may help you know instinctively what to do. For instance, when making a change from being a victim to finding my voice, Robyn helped me visualize two ice flows (10; 6). In order to avoid falling into the freezing water, I could picture leaping from one (the old behavior) to the other (the new desired behavior). When I was really at the bottom of my U after my department was dissolved, she suggested the metaphor of a large cruise ship in the process of making a 180-degree turn to help me understand how slow the process would be and how many tiny, hard-to-see micromovements would be required (25; 136). But I could not turn this ship around. I had to ask myself, "How do I get from sad, stuck, fearful, and downtrodden (shown vividly in a photograph of me at this time) to living a life of love, presence, confidence, and courage?" I wanted to believe what Rumi said: "Love is the bridge between you and everything" (30; 36-37). However, I went even lower than before, hitting a bottom so painful that the only metaphor that helped was "jumping ship." I didn't do this consciously, but something had to change, and it required a whole different location and life. This is when my sister Karen mentioned that Robin might be leaving her wonderful house in Mexico. Patrick and I had been wanting to see where she lived, and that information gave us the impetus to make plans and not wait. Robin decided not to move, so we didn't have the option of renting her house, but we loved staying with her. Six months later we had packed and moved to the next town, in a house she found for us to rent. Jumping ship gave me the energy to start fresh and be stimulated by everything new.

Be aware of all-or-nothing thinking. Bouncing from one extreme to another makes sense to me in the context of Newton's third law of motion, "For every action there is an equal and opposite reaction." When I am wildly successful, such as when I received a perfect performance evaluation at work, I scare myself thinking I won't be able to sustain it. Then, I put the brakes on and hang out in despair and indecision. This is similar to a pattern I noticed about my weight. Often, I would only give myself permission to lose weight after I had shown everyone how miserable I was being fat. In my logic, their desire not to have me struggle and complain would overshadow any envy they might feel at my being thin. Similarly, I trained hard for and completed a marathon successfully, only to then stop running altogether, as if I had gone past my usual self-imposed restrictions and needed to revert to my baseline behavior. As Robyn put it, I moved from trusting my own experience using my "inside eyes," to judging myself with imagined or real "outside eyes." I should have learned to expect sooner that the seesaw inevitably swings the other way.

BOOKS, BOOKS, BOOKS

As Thomas Jefferson once said, and I agree, "I cannot live without books." What follows are mostly book recommendations tied to a dozen categories in no order I can explain logically. The reason I haven't given you a reference list or even more comprehensive bibliography is this: I want you to have a personal feel for why I recommend these books. Imagine you are in my office for mentoring or counseling, and you want to know what's most relevant to your project. I would then offer you some options and explain what they are about. Or picture yourself at a cozy bookstore asking for guidance on just the topic you are exploring, be it a novel, self-help book, or memoir. You'd get a customized tour to the right section with a lively exchange about your potential choices. Better yet, we're at a small cafe talking about our lives and books. If you asked, I could tell you how I found each one, what was going on in my life at that time, and even where I was sitting when reading it. And I bet you could do the same. In other words, books are treasures. I have carefully selected these to guide and inspire you on your journey.

Understanding Dreams

My first book to understand dreams was *How to Understand Your Own Dreams* by Louis Gottschalk, which offered a structure for analyzing and interpreting dreams. I also used *The Way of the Dream* by Marie-Louise von Franz, *The Interpretation of Dreams* by Sigmund Freud, and *Inner*

Work: Using Dreams and Active Imagination for Personal Growth by Robert A. Johnson. For reference I relied on *Ego and the Mechanisms of Defense* by Anna Freud, *The Hidden Meaning of Dreams* by Craig Hamilton-Parker, and *Dreams and Nightmares* by J. A. Hadfield.

Perfectionism

SARK. I am a great fan of all of SARK's books. I have read her unique and personal perspectives on change, prosperity, creativity, and relationships. Her tools for dealing with the "marvelous messy middle" and "micro-steps" are a great antidote to all-or-nothing thinking (27; 4).

***Cathy* cartoons**. Did you ever read them? I have hilarious ones in my journals about perfectionism and what cartoonist Guisewite called the "four basic guilt groups: eating, work, relationships, and having a mother." After thirty-four years, she no longer publishes her comic strip, but Guisewite has written books about her personal, human, and funny takes on life, such as *Fifty Things That Aren't My Fault: Essays from the Grown-up Years.*

I Love You Even Though . . . Patrick and I wrote an illustrated booklet about dealing with imperfections in ourselves and relationships in couples. It identifies common patterns in a funny and relatable manner, building trust and acceptance. We finally saw we each had different patterns of perfectionism. He focused on form (neat and tidy), while I concentrated on content (always raising the bar). From OD I learned to shift my attention to progress and continuous improvement. Patrick's way of making everything look good made him the more perfect perfectionist, if you will, and I now see how our two modes instigated power struggles for control. This dialectic also inspired our creative, collaborative, and humorous approach to writing the booklet. He'd say, "If you weren't such a perfectionist, you'd be perfect!"

Image 112: Our booklet, I Love You Even Though . . .

Inner Mean Girls. One way to counteract messages about perfectionism and other internalized voices is to explore the process by Amy Ahlers and Christine Arylo in *Reforming Your Inner Mean Girl: 7 Steps to Stop Bullying Yourself and Start Loving Yourself.* By drawing pictures, naming names, and making commitments, I discovered my inner saboteur and named her "Pressure Makes Perfect, Prudence." It was a fun and funny way to turn down the inner critic and turn up the volume on my inner wisdom (29; 8).

Shadow. *Taming Your Gremlin*, by Rick Carson, has a humorous way of helping deal with self-defeating behaviors and emotional upheaval. As he points out, "I change not by trying to be other than I am. I change by being fully aware of how I am." A deeper dive into the disowned shadow parts of the personality is available in a book by Debbie Ford, *The Dark Side of the Light Chasers.* Yet another approach for exposing the unconscious is found in Robert A. Johnson's *Inner Work: Using Dreams* *and Active Imagination for Personal Growth*. And of course, Jung's *Man and His Symbols* and his autobiography, *Memories, Dreams, Reflections*, are both classics in the field.

Self-acknowledgment. When I began my expanded and visible role, a leadership mentor helped me stop acting as if work was a test and I was failing. Rather than be self-effacing (my default to point out all my imperfections) or self-promoting (as others did and I found intimidating), she advised me to be self-acknowledging. I should focus on helping others, not on my defects or gifts. She told me to neither be too nice and accommodating nor overprepared and not present.

Pema Chödrön. The American Tibetan Buddhist is a source of wisdom and perspective on perfectionism and just about every other part of life. Her books include *Start Where You Are*; *Living Beautifully with Uncertainty and Change*; *Taking the Leap*; *The Places That Scare You*; and *When Things Fall Apart: Heart Advice for Difficult Times*. I wrote quotes in my journal (26; 96) from three chapters of *The Wisdom of No Escape*. Most relevant is an example of her humanness:

> When you find yourself with this old familiar anxiety because your world is falling apart and you're not measuring up to your image of yourself and everybody is irritating you beyond words because no one is doing what you want and everyone is wrecking everything and you feel terrible about yourself and you don't like anybody else and your whole life is fraught with emotional misery and confusion and conflict . . .

Need I say more?!

Feminism. During my dissertation I read excellent books on perfectionism from a feminist perspective: Ann Wilson Schaef's *Women's Reality: An Emerging Female System* and *When Society Becomes an Addict*;

Marion Woodman's *Addiction to Perfection* and *Leaving My Father's House: A Journey to Conscious Femininity*; *Toward a New Psychology of Women* by Jean Baker Miller; and *The Mother-Daughter Revolution* by Elizabeth Debold, Marie Wilson, and Idelisee Malavé. In Schaef's book I learned about "stoppers," which are designed to shut down someone whose speaking up challenges patriarchal norms. In Debold's book I was shocked at the eye-opening reframe of perfectionism, again from the perspective of patriarchal norms.

Brené Brown. Later I was helped by Brené Brown's book, *The Gifts of Imperfection*, as well as each of her other works. She has brilliant and accessible guidance and insight on owning your story and reflecting on the role shame, empathy, vulnerability, and courage play in leadership and life. Similarly, I have found Rachel Naomi Remen's *Kitchen Table Wisdom* and *My Grandfather's Blessings* great sources of wisdom and inspiration through exquisite storytelling.

Losing Weight

Geneen Roth. I have read most of Geneen Roth's books on her honest relationship with overeating and losing weight. The best is *Women Food and God: An Unexpected Path to Almost Everything*. Once, when I awoke in the middle of the night with a spasm in my upper back shoulder area, her writing on "The Voice" helped me deeply get in touch with my body and the critical messages that were not serving me. If you are ready to trust yourself, she is a skilled guide.

Emotional eating. At the same time that I read Geneen's book, I found *Shrink Yourself: Break free from emotional eating forever!* The psychiatrist (shrink) Roger Gould provides vivid self-reflection exercises and examples. I was able to get to the bottom of my feelings and patterns related to my body. This is highly recommended reading if you are ready for a deep dive into the psychology of eating and weight.

Dieting. I have not written a lot about my issues with food because they are an ongoing process, and I now have major self-acceptance in this area. Having lost weight three times with three different approaches (fifteen, twenty, then thirty pounds), I believe *any diet works if you follow it*. Every diet author thinks they are right, yet there are endless possibilities, each mostly in conflict with the others. I've written articles about all the food regimes I have used, but I also believe the philosophy behind the first feminist book I read on why diets don't work, *Fat is a Feminist Issue* by Susie Orbach. She showed how fat was about protection, sex, mothering, strength, assertion, anger, and love—not food. My skinny mom used to sneak ice cream at night, which I knew because I would see the empty bowl next to her bed in the morning. I ate to connect with her, comfort myself, as creative expression, to stuff or soothe emotions, and to protect myself and take up space. Because of the continued tendency toward emotional eating and my love of trying creative recipes, I resist any plan right now that advocates deprivation, eating only what seems healthy and satisfying to me at this age and stage of my life.

Dealing with Money

Stay involved. Just reading about money helped me decrease denial and avoidance. The main books that helped me over the years were: *Your Money or Your Life* by Joe Dominguez and Vicki Robin; *Prince Charming Isn't Coming*, by Barbara Stanny; *How to Get Out of Debt, Stay Out of Debt, and Live Prosperously* by Jerrold Mundis; *Women and Money: Owning the Power to Control Your Destiny* by Suze Orman; and *The Seven Stages of Money Maturity* by George Kinder. *Tapping into Wealth*, by Margaret Lynch, has a great section on perfectionism, along with other insights.

Dealing with Going Blind

Personal Stories. Two authors who were each afflicted with retinitis pigmentosa, my eye disease, revealed in inspiring and honest ways their experience of being blind: *Cockeyed* by Ryan Knighton and *Touching the Rock* by John M. Hull.

Looking for Inspiration

Memoirs. *Find a Way* by Diana Nyad, *My Beloved World* by Sonia Sotomayor, *Becoming* by Michelle Obama, *Educated* by Tara Westover, *Born a Crime* by Trevor Noah, and *Becoming Myself* by Irwin Yalom have all inspired me.

Wise souls. Writers who inspire by their humanity, wisdom, and experience include Oliver Sacks in *The Man Who Mistook His Wife for a Hat* and his other books; Audre Lorde in *Sister Outsider*; Victor Wooten in *The Music Lesson: A Spiritual Search for Growth Through Music*; and Jon Kabat-Zinn in *Wherever You Go, There You Are*. Of course, *O, The Oprah Magazine* has a plethora of monthly advice, images for collages, recommended readings, and featured columnists.

Artists. Poetry from *The Essential Rumi* by Coleman Barks; *The Prophet* by Kahlil Gibran; *Devotions* by Mary Oliver; and *Love Poems* by Pablo Neruda are worth owning. Roz Chast, cartoonist for the *New Yorker*, has a hilarious book about taking care of parents: *Can't we talk about something more PLEASANT?* The illustrated little book that I used for many of my dissertation collages is *If You're Afraid of the Dark, Remember the Night Rainbow* by Cooper Edens. I also love Yo-Yo Ma's baroque music, art by Vermeer, ballet and modern dance concerts, and one-woman plays by Anna Deavere Smith.

Novels. My favorites from Elizabeth Gilbert are *Eat, Pray, Love*; *Signature of All Things*; and *City of Girls*. Any Toni Morrison book will serve you well, especially *Beloved*. I could go on for pages on other treasured novels. My only anxiety when finishing a great read is finding the next one.

Books to help with creativity. Besides anything by Julia Cameron, see: *Turning Pro: Tap Your Inner Power and Create Your Life's Work* by Steven Pressfield; *The Nine Modern Day Muses (and a Bodyguard)* by Jill Badonsky; and *The Creative Entrepreneur* by Lisa Sonoro Beam.

Greeting cards. I adore the original paintings and quotes on Marylou Falstreau's set of cards called "Women and the Hourglass." They begin with the prompt, "One day she woke up and . . . ," and delight with endings such as: "decided to write her story," "decided to love herself more than she ever thought possible," or "decided to simplify everything."

Understanding Your Story

Approaches. *The Hero with a Thousand Faces* by Joseph Campbell; *The Heroine's Journey* by Maureen Murdock; *The Virgin's Promise* by Kim Hudson; *Men and the Goddess: Feminine Archetypes in Western Literature* by Tom Absher; and Brené Brown's *Rising Strong* are all very helpful.

Authorizing Yourself

For some, being the author of your life might be obvious and straightforward. But of course, not for me. This is probably the area in which I devoured the most books. I have greatly shortened my list to highlight titles I found most helpful. While some could easily fit with my other categories of self-exploration and inquiry, the titles below were my go-tos when trying to find my voice and enlarge my perspective on what was holding me back.

The authors of *Crucial Conversations*, by Kerry Patterson, et al., developed their approach by observing and analyzing what effective leaders actually did. At Maimonides Medical Center my physician partner and I trained numerous departments to learn these skills to create a culture of mutual respect. Most useful to me personally was how to first establish emotional safety so you can speak your truth and make it heard and received without defensiveness.

Carol Gilligan's *In a Different Voice* was not only a landmark book for reframing moral reasoning by gender, but it also inspired me to begin to listen to and value my voice. Similarly, *Women's Ways of Knowing* by Mary Field Belenky, et al., made me realize I am a "connected knower." That awareness encouraged me to contact the women in my study and learn from them through conversation. Two books written by women in my study gave unique perspectives at work: a feminist reframing of behavior in *New Rules for Women* by Anne Litwin and an organizational rationale and accessible approach to bringing your full self to make contributions with others in *Be Big* by Judith Katz and Frederick Miller. *Leadership on the Line* by Ronald Heifetz and Marty Linsky, among other perspectives, made "going to the balcony" an important metaphor for detaching from conflict and asking, "What is really going on here?"

Emotional Intelligence by Daniel Goleman made emotions a legitimate arena at work and *Resonant Leadership* by Richard Boyatzis and Annie McKee furthered its application to developing leaders. *Immunity to Change* by Lisa Laskow and Robert Kegan; *The Confidence Gap* by Katty Kay and Claire Shipman; *How to Stop Acting* by Harold Guski; and *Voice Dialogue* by Hal Stone and Sidra Winkelman show how finding your voice can be inspired by different approaches depending on your style of learning. For those intuitive and often misunderstood people at work, *The Highly Sensitive Person* by Elaine Aron gives a more positive spin on such challenges. Likewise, the *Book of Qualities*, by Ruth Gendler, offers short, creative definitions of ninety-nine valuable ways people show up. Peter Vaill bought this for me as a graduation gift, writing, "You are all these things, but I like you in 12 [courage] the best." Besides being freed up and inspired by *The Invitation* by Oriah Mountain Dreamer, I was challenged to find the word that most defined my life's work: integration.

The Scapegoat Complex: Shadow and Guilt by Sylvia Brinton Perera was important for me to understand my tendency toward being Velcro and not Teflon, as was *Romancing the Shadow* by Connie Zweig and Steve Wolf. *The Measure of My Days* by Florida Scott-Maxwell gave me permission to take as long as it takes to "be fierce with reality." *Will I Ever Be Good Enough?* by Karyl McBride was life-changing in helping me understand my core wounds.

For crucial understanding of my issues with separation and attachment, I relied on *Between Generations: The Stages of Parenthood* by Ellen Galinsky. To deal with boundaries, I had to be able to identify people who were the most difficult to understand, as in *The Sociopath Next Door* by Martha Stout. *Care of the Soul* by Thomas Moore made me realize it was legitimate to feed my soul what it wants, which is often different than what the mind thinks it should want.

Inventories

I have taken a slew of inventories for self-knowledge about my personality type, decision-making style, resilience, you name it. What I've learned is, while they are one way to hold a mirror to an aspect of yourself, I don't usually fit neatly into the boxes or models they describe. Most important to me is to build on the models and then learn from experience. For example, a typical guideline for staying organized is to handle each paper only once. But because of my nonlinear brain, and my necessary work-around to review, review, review, that approach is not meant for someone like me.

Healing

Spiritual and body-centered approaches. Many self-help books have profound and practical guidance, such as: *The Power of Now* and *A New Earth* by Eckhart Tolle; *The Nature of Bliss* by Maureen Moss; *Mind Over Medicine: Scientific Proof That You Can Heal Yourself* by Lissa Rankin; *You Can Heal Your Life* by Louise Hayes; *My Stroke of Insight* by Jill Bolte Taylor; *Your Body Believes Every Word You Say* by Barbara Hoberman Levine; *Getting Past Your Past* by Francine Shapiro; *Seeker's Guide* and *Broken Open* by Elizabeth Lesser; *Breakdown, Breakthrough* by Kathy Caprino; and Bethany Webster's blog on the "Mother Wound." What I most remember from *Courage to Heal* by Ellen Bass and Laura Davis, is their advice that if you don't know if you were sexually abused, or some other violation, imagine that your house was broken into and robbed while you were away. Are you going to waste precious time trying to figure out who did it, or would it be better to just clean up the mess and move on?

Dealing with Aging

What's the alternative? These books made me smile, cry, learn, and accept: *Getting Over Getting Older* by Letty Cottin Pogrebin; *Prime Time: Making the Most of All Your Life* by Jane Fonda; *The Gift of Years* by Joan Chittister; *This Chair Rocks: A Manifesto Against Ageism* by Ashton Applewhite; *Wise Aging: Living with Joy, Resilience, and Spirit* by Dr. Rabbi Rachel Cowan and Dr. Linda Thal; *Smart Woman Don't Retire—They Break Free* by Gail Rentsch; *Second Act Careers* by Nancy Collamer; *Your Life Calling: Reimagining the Rest of Your Life* by Jane Pauley; *The Last Gift of Time: Life Beyond Sixty* by Carolyn Heilbrun; and *It's Never Too Late to Begin Again* by Julia Cameron.

Dealing with Grief, Death, and Dying

Insights. My first influential book on this topic was *The Denial of Death* by Earnest Becker. Also helpful are *Tuesdays with Morrie* by Mitch Albom; *When Breath Becomes Air* by Paul Kalanithi; *Being Mortal: Medicine and What Matters in the End* by Atul Gawande; *Final Exit* by Derek Humphrey; *Transitions* by William Bridges; and *On Death and Dying* by Elisabeth Kubler-Ross.

Practical. When grieving after my father's death, I read *Healing Your Grieving Soul* and *Understanding Your Grief* by Alan Wolfleet; *A Grief Observed* by C.S. Lewis; and *Grief's Courageous Journey* by Sandi Caplan and Gordon Lang.

Resources. When designing bereavement circles, I referred to *Great Occasions* by Carl Seaburg; *In Memoriam* by Edward Searl; *Grief Counseling and Grief Therapy* by William Worden; and *The Grief Recovery Handbook* by John W. James and Russell Friedman.

Writing

Encouragement. These books have helped me with the writing process and my development as a writer: *Bird by Bird* by Anne Lamont; *Writing Down the Bones* by Natalie Goldberg; *Becoming a Writer* by Dorothea Brande; *The Artist's Way* and *The Right to Write* by Julia Cameron; *Your Brain on Ink* by Deborah Ross and Kathleen Adams; *Writing Without Teachers* by Peter Elbow; *Overcoming Writing Blocks* by Karin Mack and Eric Skjei; *Writing the Natural Way* by Gabriele Rico; *On Writing Well* by William Zinsser; *Your Life As Story* by Tristine Rainer; *Writing as a Way of Healing* by Louise DeSalvo; *Journal to the Self* by Kathleen Adams; *The Journal Workbook* by Ira Progoff; and *Between You and Me: Confessions of a Comma Queen* by Mary Norris.

Phases in writing. As an avid reader of books on writing well, I developed a framework for helping others gain confidence in their writing process. I then designed and led workshops based on my four steps: Get it ready, Get it down, Get it good, and Get it out. Getting it ready involves preparation and gathering materials. Getting it down is giving yourself permission to write a bad first draft because you know you will revise it. Getting it good is when rewriting occurs. Getting it out is when you check the format, footnotes, and send it out. Through all my reading about how well-known authors discuss their writing process, I have learned to distinguish the brainstorming and freewriting phase (Get it down) from the censor and critical analysis (Get it good). All the phases are necessary, but in the proper order and separated so each can flourish.

Qualitative Research

For the academics among you, these books were very useful: *Heuristic Research* by Clark Moustakas; *Writing Up Qualitative Resear*ch by Harry Wolcott; and *From Dissertation to Book* by William Germano.

Women in OD. Publications I've written pertaining to my qualitative research, available for free as a PDF by emailing me at kaplan.kathryn@gmail.com, include: "Women's voices in organizational development: questions, stories, and implications," 1995; "Women Weaving Wonders in the Workplace," 1998; "Enduring Wisdom from Women in OD," 2010; and "Women's Voices: Follow-up Study on the Second Generation of Women in OD," 2015.

Made in the USA
Middletown, DE
24 July 2023

35682734R00216